# BLUE-COLLAR HOLLYWOOD

PUBLISHING FOR THE WORLD
*125 Years*

THE JOHNS HOPKINS UNIVERSITY PRESS

# BLUE-COLLAR HOLLYWOOD
## Liberalism, Democracy, and Working People in American Film

JOHN BODNAR

THE JOHNS HOPKINS UNIVERSITY PRESS
BALTIMORE AND LONDON

© 2003 The Johns Hopkins University Press
All rights reserved. Published 2003
Printed in the United States of America on acid-free paper
9 8 7 6 5 4 3 2 1

The Johns Hopkins University Press
2715 North Charles Street
Baltimore, Maryland 21218-4363
www.press.jhu.edu

Library of Congress Cataloging-in-Publication Data

Bodnar, John E., 1944–
    Blue-collar Hollywood : liberalism, democracy, and working people in
American film / by John Bodnar.
        p. cm.
Includes bibliographical references and index.
    ISBN 0-8018-7149-2 (alk. paper)
    1. Working class in motion pictures.  2. Motion pictures—United States—
History.  I. Title.
    PN1995.9.L28 B63 2003
    791.43′6520623—dc21

                                                                2002006481

A catalog record for this book is available from the British Library.

*For Brenna, Donna, Eric, and Kipp*

Liberalism needed democracy. It had to have a
politics to complement its antipolitics.

*Benjamin Barber*

All culture is mass culture under capitalism.
There is no working-class culture that is
not saturated with mass culture.

*Michael Denning*

# CONTENTS

# ILLUSTRATIONS

# ACKNOWLEDGMENTS

About ten years ago I concluded that the teaching and reading I did on twentieth-century America involved two important topics that were seldom joined. Political history and cultural history—especially the impact of mass culture—were key ways of discussing modern America, but they did not appear to take substantial note of each other. One thought that kept recurring in my mind was that serious political historians almost never took mass culture seriously. Consequently, I set out to look more closely not only at how these two fields of inquiry could be more effectively linked, but also at how such a conjuncture could illuminate aspects of political life that were less apparent in standard treatments that focused on political movements, class tensions, and racial and gender discord. The result of my inquiry was this book in which I focus on the way Hollywood films have represented the individuals and concerns of working-class America since the introduction of sound pictures.

The process of completing the study involved not only the normal trials and tribulations of scholarly research and publication but also the joy of unexpected discoveries in the vast trove of social dramas of ordinary people that appeared in the American cinema over the course of more than a half-century. It was a discovery that not only stimulated my scholarship but changed my teaching as well, resulting in the introduction of several new courses. Thus, when I express my thanks to individuals and institutions that helped me, I want them to know that they not only contributed to the completion of a book but to the education of hundreds of students as well. My best scholarly advisers and critics turned out to be James Naremore, a colleague at Indiana University; Steve Ross, who had much to offer on the treatment of the working class by Hollywood; Judith Smith; Eric Smoodin; and Daniel Walkowtiz. Graduate students from

Indiana University's history department also served me well at many junctures. I especially want to thank Lisa Orr, who is now a professor herself; Jane Armstrong; Beth Marsh; Justin Nordstrom; and Steve Sheehan. Jo Ellen Fitzgerald of the department's staff filled endless orders for books and films with good cheer and patience. Becky Bryant and Barb Truesdell helped me to keep track of a good number of administrative responsibilities while I attempted to pursue scholarship as well.

I received expert assistance from the dedicated professionals at the Academy of Motion Pictures Arts and Sciences and at the American Film Institute, both in Los Angeles; the Warner Brothers Archives at the University of Southern California; and the film archives at the University of Wisconsin. I want to pay particular attention to the valuable help I received from Leith Johnson at the Cinema Archives of Wesleyan University and from the staff of the Motion Picture, Broadcasting, and Sound Division of the Library of Congress. The library's collections on American film are superb. I also want to thank Indiana University for granting me a sabbatical during the course of writing this book. The final revisions on the manuscript were completed while I was a fellow at the Center for Advanced Study in the Behavioral Sciences at Stanford University. I am grateful for the support rendered by staff at the center and the financial support provided by The Andrew W. Mellon Foundation Grant #29800639, and the editorial assistance of Elizabeth Yoder was invaluable.

# INTRODUCTION
## Mass Culture and American
## Political Traditions

The images are familiar to millions of Americans: Tom Powers chasing power and money at all costs in *Public Enemy;* Stella Dallas suffering for her ambition; Tom Joad going off to fight for social justice in *The Grapes of Wrath;* the "fighting Sullivans" eagerly defending their nation in World War II; Stanley Kowalski beating his wife; Norma Rae rallying downtrodden mill workers; Tre Stiles dodging bullets in South Central Los Angeles in *Boyz N the Hood.* These are among the hundreds of proletarian protagonists deployed by Hollywood since the Great Depression to tell the story of working people and the lives they have lived. Such characters have appeared in thousands of movies that have collectively reproduced a tale of plebeian experience in America both fixated on the issue of human desire and complicated by it. Like many in the audience who watched these feature films, these characters and others who shared the screen with them invariably met a number of different destinies. Powers was killed for his crimes; Norma Rae gained justice and more self-confidence; Kowalski's future was anyone's guess.

This book probes the way ordinary men and women have been depicted in feature films since the 1930s and argues that these images and the narratives in which they were portrayed resulted from a broad political discussion that was endemic to American mass culture. Specifically, it seeks to explore the relationship between one of the central forms of mass culture in twentieth-century America—the movies—and the tensions that emanated from powerful political traditions like liberalism and democracy that continually shaped American life over a long period. Preoccupied with the lot of the liberal individual, mass culture opened up for public discussion the rich and varied world of human emotions and private desires, and in so doing, it posed definite challenges to mainstream political movements and their ideological arsenals, which assumed that politics could be carried out in an orderly manner. Neither the left nor the right was comfortable with endorsing the full expression and pursuit of personal longings; both instead always favored some ideals and wants over others. Moral reformers continually sought to constrain the passions of individuals; social reformers under the New Deal, for instance, favored the collective goals of working men over the individual wants of women. Mass culture could often lend support to the methodical processes of mainstream politics, but it constantly undermined them as well. Its purposes were ultimately not about regulating or prioritizing human cravings but about imaging them or exploring where they might lead.

The unpredictable relationship between mass culture and organized politics had particular relevancy for the history of the working class in twentieth-century America. Standard scholarly discussions about the fate of working people in America have been grounded in political tensions between the left and the right or between forces mobilized around labor and those around capital. Recently, students of culture and of workers have argued convincingly that older paradigms of a class struggle can no longer explain how political interests are articulated in a capitalist world and pursued "through individual and collective action, within and beyond orientations of class." For instance, it is now well known that calculations based on race and gender can explain political mobilizations as much as class-based movements. And modern scholarship in many fields contains abundant references to the rise of a politics of individual rights in our time that is not sufficiently explained within the context of class-based paradigms.[1]

The move away from class-based perspectives constitutes both a shift from a structural view of politics and a greater recognition of the way power is contested on a cultural level. Discussion inevitably becomes more concerned with images and representations than with parties and organizations. To move away from the politics of class, in fact, is to embrace to a more significant extent the importance and power of cultural forms like narratives and symbols. Margaret Sommers, for instance, has pointed to the need to recognize the capacity of "narrativity" as a means by which individuals come to know their social worlds and determine who they might be within those worlds. Sommers calls upon scholars to look beyond the idea that common people act only from interests they may derive from their position within the class structure of society and to recognize that they live in a culture in which their identities emerge from encounters with "culturally constructed stories" that offer a "repertoire" of identities from which one can choose as well as a guide to how relations between individuals can take place. It makes some sense, therefore, to explore at least one aspect of this process of narrating both the larger cultural world in which proletarians lived and the stock of identities that populated it over a long period of time.[2]

Stories of gangsters, brutes, union organizers, housewives, boxers, victims, and ambitious women appear on the surface to constitute a muddled repertoire of cultural images, but I believe it is one that we can ultimately understand. I have tried to get at this understanding by choosing to study film narratives produced by Hollywood in the half-century after 1930. Although my selection process was not scientific, I looked for dramas or depictions of real life in which working people were protagonists of consequence. The total possibilities, of course, would be in the thousands and could not all be included. What I attempted to do was to identify a range of plebeian types—such as miners, gangsters, or fallen women—in each decade from a reading of published collections of film summaries in *Variety Film Reviews* and the *New York Times Film Reviews*. My goal was to pinpoint a dozen or so lower-class models for each decade and to include workingwomen as well as men. Over time, I also began to include films that dealt with lower-class people of color as such films became more available. I did not consider box office appeal as a key criterion for selection. Thus, the films discussed in this book include top-grossing features for particular years such as *The Grapes of Wrath* in 1940 or *Rocky* in 1976. However, attention is also devoted to movies like *Black Fury* (1935), *Human Desire* (1954), and *The Molly Maguires* (1970), which attracted considerably smaller audiences. The objective was to look for images and stories that would offer clues to the complex ways in which Americans imagined working people. Some of the plebeian models I chose, such as gangsters, are well known. Others, I believe, have not been analyzed all that much. In this category, I would mention the postwar brute or the angry patriot of the 1970s.

If the stories in which these types were portrayed were simply the product of a battle between militant laborers and their supporters on the left, and conservative capitalists on the right, we might have expected to see a less confusing parade of such figures marching across the screen. Theoretically, left-leaning films would valorize workers and sympathize with their problems, while more conservative movies would discredit them or minimize their exploitation by capitalists. This sort of tension certainly existed. *Body and Soul* (1947) evoked compassion for ordinary people struggling to get ahead in America and suggested that the quest for gain and upward mobility in capitalist America was destructive. *Rocky* (1976), on the other hand, said the same struggle was worth the price. Yet the labor-capitalist matrix for explaining the representation of working people could not account for much of what I watched. For example, the plebeian couple in *A Streetcar Named Desire* (1951) appeared preoccupied by their emotional rather than their economic life; and in *Taxi Driver* (1976), a common man was driven by the task of morally cleansing society and was disconnected from the older questions about labor and capital.

From their inception in the working-class neighborhoods of the modern city, films certainly reflected some of the battles between labor and capital that pervaded American society. Steve Ross has demonstrated that before the 1930s silent films could endorse the rise of powerful labor movements, portray proletarians as dangerous radicals, or glorify consumption to such an extent as to suggest that class politics of any kind was simply unnecessary. But ultimately the movies were—and still are—what Michel Foucault might call "heterotopias," or sites where many of the most powerful ideas in a culture could be represented at the same time. They merged attitudes that were rational and emotional, moral and immoral, angry and sentimental. A typical film story generally contained contrasting images of common people and tended to integrate numerous points of view—what Michael Roth would call "existing mental schemes"—into one feature that often rendered any one view or image "less potent." Thus, by looking at a collection of working-class archetypes and the complicated narratives that framed them, we can begin to see a wider political process at work.[3]

Common people have certainly been represented in media other than film over time. Tony Bennett has studied the emergence of museums in nineteenth-century Europe and found that many were able to present the experience and daily life of ordinary people in ways that suggested they were devoid of politics—and of human desire, for that matter. Shaped by the money and influence of a rising bourgeoisie, numerous displays depicted working people as good natured, industrious, and prospering under the rule of middle-class entrepreneurs. Seldom was any mention made of their trade union activities or their degradation. Another study of the depiction of the British working class in film following World War II found their representation to be marked by decency, common sense, and strong ties to family and community. A recent analysis of the image of workingmen in American monuments found evidence that early in the twentieth century their presentation emphasized a sense of pride in work, powerful masculinity, and support for the capitalist work ethic.[4]

In stark contrast to some of the museums Bennett looked at, moreover, American literature frequently presented a view of working people that was more attentive to both political and personal longings. Consider for a moment the explosion of "proletarian novels" in the 1930s. These books, such as Ruth McKenney's *Industrial Valley* (1939), offered totally coherent narratives that endorsed the view of capitalists as evil and the need for workers to mobilize. In McKenney's story, powerful workingmen were driven more by political ideals than by personal desires; they carried clubs, marched in the streets, surrounded industrial plants, and demanded their rights as Americans.[5]

Working people were neither compliant nor militant, however, on the pages of pulp-magazine fiction that filled American newsstands during the 1920s and 1930s. Erin Smith, who has examined these stories, has discovered how well they expressed the utopian longings of proletarian readers who were mostly men. But the plots of these books were not about a democratic utopia where strong unions took their place at the national table alongside capitalists, but a darker story where men who were "moody" and "hostile" carved out lives free of the control of industrial managers and family obligations in saloons, back streets, or at boxing matches. The cover of a "hard-boiled" text was more likely to be adorned by scantily clad women or violent men than working people who were dutiful or militant. These examples do not exhaust the range of possibilities, but they point to a tension in the way the desires and attributes of common people were represented culturally and to the possibility that the prevalence of some images of common people—especially those that made them appear moody and hostile—had very little to do with the political interests of the left or the right.[6]

The American cinema certainly did not grant a broad endorsement to the sentiments found in proletarian novels, but neither did it deny that the people had a politics. It devoted considerable attention, in fact, to the various passions and feelings of ordinary individuals. Film, in other words, moved extensively into a world that was both more intricate and more emotional than the one represented by proletarian fiction—or, for that matter, by conventional political organizations of the time. This is a point seldom found in recent interpretations of the relationship between mass culture and progressive politics, which have been grounded largely in a matrix of class conflict. Lary May, for instance, in his study of Hollywood film and American politics, demonstrated that during the thirties Hollywood films, especially those starring the immensely popular Will Rogers, brought stories to the screen that expressed a "republican creed." At its heart was a vision rooted in the nineteenth century of a producer's democracy that hated monopoly capitalism and welcomed diverse racial and social groups into a community of free citizens who were tolerant, "engaged in self-governing," and free of oppression from both an aristocracy and elites. May located the source for this vision in activists like Rogers who brought populist sympathies from their life experiences into the world of cultural production. He added that studios like Warner Brothers and directors like Frank Capra embellished this concept with movies that incorporated the "vernacular tastes of the lower classes" and the idealizations of inclusiveness. Following logically from this democratic upsurge, May discovered that films featuring a theme of "wealthy decadence as a danger to individuals in society" peaked in number in 1936.[7]

The work of Michael Denning paints a more aggressive and militant picture of democratic upsurges in the thirties but still stresses the force of the decade's egalitarian expressions. Denning identified artists and intellectuals from working-class backgrounds who were energized by the rise of the Congress of Industrial Organizations (CIO). He calls this loose aggregation of culture workers the Popular Front and claims that it took up the same goals as the new industrial unions: "a social democratic laborism based on a militant industrial unionism, an anti-racist ethnic pluralism . . . and an anti-fascist politics of international solidarity." Denning reveals how extensively these ideas appeared in plays, novels, songs like Paul Robeson's recording of "Ballad for Americans" and films such as *Native Land*.[8]

May, Denning, and other scholars argue that this onslaught of democratic images and figures was ultimately destroyed by the political events of the 1940s. May astutely observed that many of the films released during World War II adopted less militant outlooks and tended to revere authority. In the war's aftermath, Hollywood became—as he tells it—a bastion of conservative, pro-capitalist thinking, whose leaders generally stigmatized class conflict, saw labor as "unpatriotic," and drove suspected Communists from the film industry completely. He notes how the Screen Actors Guild, which had been staunchly pro-labor in the thirties, was taken over by Cold Warriors like Ronald Reagan and John Wayne, who saw it as their mission to defend capitalism and blunt any criticism of American traditions. The result, for May, was an expansion in film content that affirmed business and consumer values and the classlessness of

American society; the "republican creed" of the thirties was seldom found. Denning was in essential agreement with this view, suggesting that the Popular Front was "defeated by the shakedown of 1947 and 1948," when Communists were repressed and social democrats were forced to pledge allegiance to the anti-communist crusade.[9]

The work of May and Denning and many others posits a direct correlation between class, politics, and culture. For them the democratic content of film depended largely on the ability of lower-class perspectives and progressive politics to shape the content of mass cultural products. While much of this argument cannot be denied, it fails to explain why so much of film content did not speak directly to debates between labor and capital in American life or simply validate the ideals of the conservative political formations at a given time. For instance, films continually expressed dissatisfaction with the consequences of capitalism and the competitive nature of American society even during the early years of the Cold War. And they incessantly deployed images of plebeian desire in every decade that could not be fitted neatly into any sense of a left/right or labor/capital political discussion. Consider a figure like Stanley Kowalski in postwar America. Neither a militant blue-collar guy nor a dutiful patriot intent on fighting communism, he was mostly an individual ruled by powerful emotional drives who appeared unconcerned about progressive or conservative politics. Moreover, these recent treatments do not allow for a full explanation of why women were always so central to cinematic representations. In fact, the discussion of women in film and of the impact of class politics on Hollywood have been disconnected for a long time. I suggest that a move away from class-based paradigms and toward a more comprehensive understanding of the cultural representation of common people can begin by looking more broadly at powerful American political traditions that have played pivotal roles in American life and at the way those traditional ideas were deployed and remade in American culture. This book hopes to position itself exactly at the point where traditions like liberalism, illiberalism, and democracy met the regime of mass culture.

Consider for a moment the arguments of Robert B. Ray. Despite the fact that the Hollywood cinema was dominated by powerful studios and moguls who controlled much of film production more before the 1950s than it was afterwards, Ray suggests that there was a persistent "tendency" in film that transcended the changing political climates engendered by the Great Depression, World War II, the Cold War, and Vietnam. In all decades, Hollywood continued to represent a larger social reality always through an ideology of individualism and the representational mode of the narrative. Ray argues convincingly that these strategies were employed because they helped to accomplish the industry's goal of attracting a diverse and enthusiastic audience. This meant, of course, that some things were included in depictions of reality and others left out. Thus, Ray notes a certain "indirectness" in the way films captured and reformulated historic events like war and depression, because these occurrences were usually reworked through the prism of personal struggles and achievements. Films were not normally sites of a full engagement with the complexity of social reality. Thus, Americans could come to understand World War II in film, not so much from a full-blown discussion of democracy and fascism (although there was some of that), but from observing the actions of characters in films about females maintaining the home front or eager men volunteering to fight the Japanese after hearing the news of Pearl Harbor. In the modern era, the political effort of the silent majority to restore law and order could be filmed best by presenting a character like Travis Bickle in *Taxi Driver* or Harry Callahan in *Dirty Harry*.[10]

The other component of Ray's "tendency" was the reliance on the narrative form. He argues that the industry succeeded by shifting from "presentational modes" of representation like vaudeville, the circus, and magic shows that often dominated plebeian culture prior to the onset of the Hollywood system, to "representational modes of the bourgeoisie" like the realistic theater and the novel. This, I suspect, would ensure that when the democratic impulses described by May and Denning invaded the culture in the thirties, they were already co-opted a bit because they had to conform to middle-class forms of representation and reasoning, not to mention the bourgeoisie preoccupation with individualism. Thus, when mass culture introduced social realism into its stories, it was inevitably blunted by the need to include as well extensive discussions of private desires and other devices necessary to construct a complete story narrative. In other words, the narrative form ruled rather than any one politicized version of reality. This would mean that you could have films in all decades that could take up or rearrange various political viewpoints; however, seldom did they stray from the plight of the individual protagonist. This is not to say that they constituted a simple veneration or defense of individualism. They never did. They were more intent on considering its promises and pitfalls. Thus, one could watch stories of failed individualism in the thirties—like those of gangsters or fallen women. Yet the same was true for the sixties and seventies—even after the political transformations of the late forties and early fifties. This is clear after  watching the struggle of a solitary man like Jake LaMotta in *Raging Bull*.[11]

It is also clear that film stories promoted a range of desires and interests at all times. It was certainly a "democratic art," as Garth Jowett has explained, because it could bypass existing channels of communication and authority in politics, religion, economics, and education and establish "direct contact" with millions of individuals. Throughout its history, for instance, it was able to articulate the views and desires of women in ways that both reinforced and countered the prevailing norms of gender relations at any given time. Jeanine Basinger's study of films about women's concerns has clarified nicely how such features were filled with contradictions, simultaneously ratifying marriage and domesticity on the one hand, and lingering on the delights of female "potency and freedom" on the other. And slowly but eventually, film brought African Americans into a more visible and mature role as individuals in the cultural marketplace. And yet it was never a truly "democratic art" in the way it paid more attention to individual issues than to communal ones. Hollywood often portrayed common people as individuals beset with emotional frustrations and antisocial tendencies that they could not control—individuals who could not be imagined as worthy partners in a democratic community. It certainly demonstrated this in a character like Jake LaMotta, but it also did this during more democratic and progressive times when it put the image of the gangster on the screen in the 1930s.[12]

Part of the problem was the penchant of mass cultural narratives to be complex and contradictory. What else could be expected from a cultural form that brought a vast change by breaking the constraints on the public expression of human appetites and elaborating on their mixed-up nature. By insisting that most lives were determined by the enigmatic explosions of human feelings, mass culture upset the historic project of the Enlightenment linking human progress to the exercise of individual freedom and to the use of reason. Like modern advertising, it emerged out of a new culture of consumption that sought to attract audiences across class, regional, racial, gender, and even party lines by playing with the intricate puzzle of human desires. Despite its attachment to the narrative form, it constantly subverted any attempt to organize the restatement of social reality in coherent terms—and this was as much of a problem for labor as for capital. Conservatives have attacked mass cultural forms for decades and viewed them as threats to moral stability, especially to the formative minds of children. But even an ardent Marxist such as John Howard Lawson argued in 1953—in the midst of the highly charged atmosphere of the Hollywood blacklist—that films that stress violence, murder, and sex were detrimental to labor's goals because they emphasized human "depravity" and rejected the possibility of "rational social cooperation." In fact, intellectuals on both the left and the right frequently expressed reservations about mass culture throughout the twentieth century.[13]

Norman Cantor has described the transformation in the cultural representation of human desire in the twentieth century as a shift from Victorian regimentation to modernism. For Cantor the first half of the century was marked by an increase in the advocacy of "self-referentiality," moral relativism, and the "microscopic" rather than the "macroscopic" dimension of life. Thus, he notes the tendency of the modernist novel to move away from presenting "an epiphany" and toward the project of exploring the "disappointments of modern life." Eschewing the effort of Victorianism (and Marxism and nationalism, for that matter) to locate the individual within the grand narrative of history, Cantor sees modern stories as more intent on probing the dilemmas and delights of self-realization. In films this has meant the production and consumption of countless narratives that not only widened considerations of the plight of the singular person but also diminished concerns over the fortunes of associations based upon class, party, or nation. [14]

The ability of mass culture to serve as a site for the expression of private emotions and wants certainly predated 1900. In the previous century, working-class audiences vented racist sentiments by laughing at blackface minstrelsy shows in which working-class performers fashioned humor and entertainment at the expense of African Americans. Eric Lott detected elements of sympathy for blacks in such performances, but mostly they allowed lowborn whites to temper anger over their inferior status by casting derision on those below them. Mass culture catered to both conservative and democratic views, however, and nineteenth-century Americans were also able to buy copies of *Uncle Tom's Cabin* or "dime novels" that gave voice to calls for a more tolerant and equal society.[15]

In the twentieth century, however, the industries of mass culture simply became more powerful. By the late 1920s large studios could produce filmic tales for millions to see each week. With technological improvements that blended sight and sound, the industry proved to be as effective a place to exchange or articulate political ideas as parties or civic rituals themselves. Mass culture broke down the barriers between elites and the lowborn and between regions and cultural groups. Already in the nineteenth century political rhetoric began to abandon the high tone of moral instruction and formal speech of elites and to incorporate more democratic images and words. This, in part, is why Abraham Lincoln interpreted the struggle in the Civil War as one for a government "of the people, by the people, and for the people." He wanted to appeal to the widest possible audience. City newspapers also began at this time to identify themselves less overtly with party politics and sought to generate more circulation by using "popular accents" and entertaining readers with human interest stories. Historian Michael McGerr has adroitly demonstrated that by 1900 political campaigns were finding it more difficult to challenge theater owners for their audiences.[16]

As cities expanded at the beginning of the twentieth century, public amusements like dance halls and amusement parks attracted a highly diverse audience with a promise of personal pleasure and the potential to escape the surveillance of parents or moral authorities. Goals of religious, educational, and reform organizations to organize or limit the display of human desires were clearly subverted by these new forms of leisure. If one were to study the "emotionology" of the Progressive Era, it would be evident that the public expression of desire still tended to reinforce the ideals of dutiful citizens or sexual purity. But the era's hope to restrain alternative assertions of human longings was simply more difficult to manage. Mass cultural forms like the cinema stimulated this emerging chaos and disorder in the depiction of human desire by offering a continuous stream of representations—moving pictures—that came to stand for what the world and its people really were and could become.[17]

From the perspective of our times, we know that the tension between what Jackson Lears calls the "sorting and categorizing institutions," such as schools, unions, parties, and churches, and the new organizations of mass culture was resolved in favor of the latter. As a consequence, the cultural display of society and all of its inhabitants became more elaborate, less willing to endorse any system of order or class position, and more focused on inner emotional lives. The performance of "psychoanalytic styles" came to play a greater role in defining class standing, for instance, than simply where one stood in the division of labor or goods. Often people of the lower orders were seen as less able to manage their primitive impulses than their middle-class counterparts, who were thought to practice greater self-control. But even the bourgeoisie were not insulated from the harsh scrutiny of personalized narratives, as a film like *King's Row* (1942) makes clear.[18]

Thus, in our lifetime we have witnessed what Homi K. Bhabha described as a move away from the "singularities" or essential categories that had organized cultural and political understandings like nation, class, religion, and family. In fact, these categories do not even complement each other as they did in the 1944 films *Going My Way* or *Since You Went Away*, where different social ranks and genders interacted harmoniously. We now encounter what Bhabha would call "disorientation," or a vast multiplicity of cultural images and messages that have wreaked havoc with collective identities or the "totalizing" ideologies grounded in older identities like right wing, left wing, class, religion, and nation.[19]

The Hollywood narrative films led the charge to "disorientation" by blending the epistemologies of melodrama and social realism. Both were means of looking at the world that emerged in the nineteenth century along with industrial society and the middle class. They were ways in which people living in a society that was becoming highly secularized and individualized attempted to see the world in opposition to the images and messages from traditional religious and regal authorities that were rapidly losing power. Melodramas talked more about the difficulties and emotions people (especially women) faced as they struggled in a world torn between good and evil. Social realism—in science, literature, and in the arts—promised to show society in more detail by closely observing people and imitating the conditions of real life. Regardless of its reliance on narrative structure itself or on generic conventions such as the woman's film or the social problem film, Hollywood brought new mindsets to both culture and politics that infused the overall depiction of people and society with stories and images that accentuated the difficulties of individual moral and emotional life.

Consequently, the representation of the social and the political world became inherently unstable. Walter Benjamin suggests as much when he argues that "filmed behavior" was subjected to more (camera) angles of analysis than depictions found in traditional forms of art. These cultural formations took a less didactic and confident approach to the interpretation of the past, present, and future and to the reproduction of a sacred symbolic order. Consequently, films had the capacity to locate virtue in the victim as well as the hero, to depict common people as both vulgar and honorable, to long for justice as well as venerate the desire for retribution, to highlight the utopic as well as the dystopic, to problematize family life as well as support patriarchy, to articulate ideals of racial superiority and cooperation, and most of all, to recognize the complicatedness of individual desire and emotion. Some have argued that melodramatic impulses were ultimately grounded in the subjective view of women and longed to undermine male hegemony. This argument is cast too narrowly, however, in one set of contradictions. And some have argued that social realism existed apart from melodrama. The ultimate rise of both these views, however, resided in a broader political world that was rapidly reworking tradition, older forms of hierarchy, and coherent ways of seeing the world and was merging all kinds of outlooks that formerly stood apart.[20]

The debate about the relationship between mass culture and politics has been a long one and has involved a discussion about more than simply the politics of Hollywood. On a larger theoretical level, many have attributed antidemocratic elements to mass culture, calling it a "narcotic" that distracted people from a full and serious engagement with real-world struggles for power and privilege. Some of this view is inferred in Ray's ideas and Peter Stead's study of film and working-class issues in America and Britain. On the other hand, a few observers have been struck by what they feel are populist and radical elements in mass culture. Bennett called this perspective a "romantic" explanation that saw mass culture as grounded in the authentic views and values of the lower orders. But clearly mass culture was more than this and was more frequently a site where all kinds of views could be expressed at the same time; views that could affirm, debunk, or even proclaim indifference to the dreams of democrats, conservatives, individuals, or parties.[21]

This study does not see mass cultural forms as simply a resource for the top or bottom of society but as a site where various positions or subjective viewpoints are exchanged. Taking intellectual cues from Antonio Gramsci, I see political relations determined less by an older form of left/right politics or a struggle between social groups and more by a contest over signification and narrative construction. Instead of pitched battles in the streets or public parades, negotiations take place over symbols and lifestyles in television narratives, movie features, or various forms of popular music. Skilled specialists manipulate images or conduct radio talk shows that encourage what Todd Gitlin has labeled "apolitical passions," or emotions that fall short of what he would consider a standard for a coherent political discussion or that fail to encourage significant participation in public life. At the same time, powerful messages and ideas regarding the fairer treatment of women and minorities have infused mass culture regularly in modern times.[22]

Certainly mass cultural products like the Hollywood narrative film were driven by capitalist desires. And to the extent that its producers convinced people to take their products like films seriously, they reinforced what Fredric Jameson calls "capitalist logic." That is to say, people saw the products of mass culture as important enough to consume—to see how the stories end. They accepted the idea that anything that can lead to a profit is important. Jameson also suggests that many of these products contained utopian elements that attracted audiences, although this study will make it clear that films were pervaded by dystopian components as well. This triumph of capitalist enterprise, in other words, should not prevent us from seeing the transformations that took place in the overall cultural construction of social reality and identity. It was this change—despite the uniformity of consumptive practices—that caused Stuart Hall to conclude that the struggles of mass culture were endless. With precise meanings always in doubt, Hall felt there were "no once and for all victories" in this poststructuralist world, but only "strategic positions to be won or lost." Decades ago, for instance, mass culture tended to restrict the depiction of sex and violence; today it presents these practices almost at will.[23]

To leave the story of mass culture at a point where positions are simply won or lost, however, infers that the world of traditional politics has been left behind. In some instances, this is true. Labor unions and political parties no longer exert the power they once did; capitalism has regained much of the luster it lost during the Depression. Yet an enhanced discourse about racial and gender equality and the quest for personal rights in our times suggests that strains of democracy and liberalism have not disappeared. This study attempts to recognize the endurance of traditional politics in mass culture even as it documents the demise of customary ways of acting in and seeing the political and social world. It does this by noting the persistence in filmic representations of working people of longstanding political ideas that transcended simple class-based political formulations. In fact, when it came to the story of working people, traditional American political creeds—especially democracy, liberalism, and illiberalism—never left the movie stage. They persisted in providing both political movements and filmmakers with another repertoire of ideas from which they could draw selectively from time to time, and they explain in part what made these films American. No matter if one looked at the era of the classic studio system or at the post-sixties years of greater directorial independence, this invocation of political traditions intermingled with narrative form and the presentation of personal lives.

Film did not so much "shatter" tradition as rework it.[24] It certainly contributed to the expansion of "self-referentiality" in the culture and helped to efface the power of traditional institutions in society. But it also provided a framework in which traditional political ideas could be invoked and discussed. It was this conjunction—the flow between the unstable trove of personal desires in a massive audience and the persistent power of an American political culture—dominated especially by liberalism—that undercut efforts to make film serve organized politics in a dutiful way, regardless of whether those politics served the left, the right, women, or minorities. And when it came to deploying images of working people on the screen, a vast multiplicity emerged that was far greater than any card-carrying radical or conservative would have preferred.

At the core of American political tradition was an effort to blend liberalism and democracy. Liberalism erupted in North America during the American Revolution as a struggle for individual freedom against the tyranny of political and religious absolutism. Its basic appeal was to be found in the idea of individual rights and the belief that a society could advance collectively if free men were allowed to pursue their economic interests in an unencumbered fashion. It was quickly joined in the early nineteenth century, however, by the idea of democracy and the call for greater popular sovereignty than imagined by the Founding Fathers. If you were going to replace the hierarchical regimes of Europe, something more than a collection of autonomous white men pursuing their own interests was needed to prevent either chaos or the return of absolutism. The answer for Americans was participatory democracy and the creation of public institutions like public schools and political parties that are necessary to promote broad participation in public life and regulate the expression of individual desire. An astute observer of early-nineteenth-century America realized that men suddenly "intoxicated" with new ideas of egalitarianism and freedom often concluded that they did not need other people. Alexis de Tocqueville explained that it was from a fear of such attitudes that American citizens created "free institutions" at the local, state, and federal level that could foster a common political life and allow men to act in concert.[25]

Scholars like Robert Wiebe have demonstrated how democracy merged effectively with liberalism in the early nineteenth century. Many Americans defended the right of free men to acquire property and determine

their own economic futures. Yet a conception of popular political participation was also spreading at the time and was manifested in the act of
free (white) men coming together to cast their votes. This was a practice
that would not only ensure the end of absolutism but would underscore
the need for citizens to remain attached to a collective political community and not simply to individual or group interests. Indeed, we can draw
from the work of Andrew Bunstein the notion that Americans of the early
republic held a "sentimental" self-image of their nation. That is to say,
many believed it could be "moral community" of citizens who aspired to
be benevolent by moderating their "base instincts" for self-indulgence as
well as to be free and independent."[26]

The union of liberalism, with its ethic of individual rights, and democracy, with its vision of broad participation in political life and communal
obligations, was enshrined by Abraham Lincoln during the era of the
Civil War. Lincoln affirmed the collective dimension of democracy—
government of the people, by the people, and for the people—in an effort
to save liberalism. He realized that government had a role to play in
ensuring that some individuals would not deny to others the right to
shape an economic and political life. He opposed, in other words, both
unrestrained liberalism and illiberalism. He saw the need for government to take an active role in protecting the rights of all individuals so
that a political community could be preserved.[27]

The alliance encountered significant problems, however, the closer
one moved to the twentieth century. Industrialization produced a powerful capitalist class that began to wield enormous political and economic power. Capitalists were not the only issue, however. Their pursuit
of unrestrained liberalism was matched by the illiberal tendencies of all
kinds of people to deny personal liberties and opportunities for political
participation to racial minorities, women, and immigrants. Illiberals
worked against democracy in an expanding urban and industrial economy not so much by exercising their freedom but by denying it to others
whom they considered second-class citizens. Indeed, I would suggest
that, absent any overpowering democratic ethos, it was impossible in a
culture that was strongly liberal to avoid the extensive expressions of
illiberalism. They went together. In the Progressive Era, a rising group of
experts also emerged who sought to regulate liberal and illiberal drives in
people at the top and bottom of society. Reformers like Walter Lippmann
were less than enthusiastic about "the romantic idea that all men should
actively engage in governing" and felt society needed the "reason" of
experts to better control the prejudices and aspirations of both the capi-

talists and the lowborn. In the 1930s the New Deal expanded the idea of government by experts and incorporated many democratic activists into a broad political agenda that supported strong industrial unions, consumerism, and social welfare ideas. The New Deal certainly represented a significant step toward the creation of a democratic community with elements of a social contract between citizens of different classes and between citizens and their government, even if some observers felt the emergence of big unions and big government actually tamed democratic impulses from below. And for the next three decades, American politics and culture would contain strong expressions of New Deal democracy.[28]

During the era after World War II, however, the democratic surges of the thirties and forties met strong opposition. It is true that civil rights for African Americans were expanded dramatically and that women asserted various claims to equality. Yet conservative attacks on labor unions and the government itself—a key agent of sustaining democracy—were widespread after the war. In the 1960s Roosevelt's party fell apart over its war policies in Vietnam and its plans to promote racial justice. This was a particularly devastating blow to working-class organizations but less so for those pursuing rights for minorities and women. Vietnam also undermined faith in the capacity of government to take up all kinds of initiatives. American politics in the sixties and seventies was marked more by visions of personal rights and group entitlements than by dreams of a cooperative society marked by social contracts or ideals of reciprocity. It was not surprising, therefore, that a modern study of an American democratic thinker like John Dewey concluded that Dewey's dream of furthering participatory democracy in America had been essentially rejected by the "dominant strain of liberal-democratic ideology in this century." Dewey was optimistic about human nature and had faith in the ability of democratic institutions and schools to bring larger numbers of people into fuller roles within a political community.[29]

Benjamin Barber explains that for a proper balance to be struck between liberalism and democracy, rights must be based on the idea of citizenship or membership in a political community of equals. "We the People are all the rights there are, " he argues. If the demand for rights becomes privatized and grounded primarily in arguments that they are possessions of individuals who acquire them by membership in a special subgroup or some biological category, then we not only move away from the ideal of a community of equal citizens with obligations to each other but also from the idea of citizen participation in political life. Citizens in this political scenario need not contribute to the common good or work for political equality; they need simply to demand what is theirs by birth or membership in a special subgroup. That is why Barber refers to America today as a "thin democracy," or a society that is marked by a high degree of liberal individualism. He notes that liberalism—"with its focus on the hypothetical rights-bearing individual"—was far more suited to starting a revolution in America than to sustaining democracy, for it places private interests above mutual ones.[30]

In our times, the call for personal and special rights claims a substantial amount of political space. No longer are rights invoked primarily as a way to participate in a democratic community of equals; they have become, to use Barber's term, "privatized" and are seen as the possessions of individuals who acquire them by birth or membership in a special subgroup. Political organizations by which these rights were once secured—such as government or labor unions—are often seen as "alien adversaries" that have nothing to do with us. Most scholars locate the origins of this "rights revolution" in the aftermath of World War II and see it emanating from the massive movement for African American justice. Mary Ann Glendon has argued that the "civil rights generation" shifted legal attention to the courts as a way of pursuing their claims, in part because other institutions were seen to be riddled with racism. During the 1950s, the Supreme Court began to systematically exercise the power of judicial review as a means of protecting individual rights, although the cause of civil rights also benefited from governmental initiatives after the war like Harry Truman's order to integrate the armed forces. Today 70 percent of the decisions of the Supreme Court involve individual rights; in the thirties, the figure was 10 percent. It also now clear that the position the United States held on the world stage as a champion of fairness and justice opposed to totalitarianism brought its racial traditions under severe scrutiny from other nations. Eventually the pursuit of rights through the courts shaped the politics of female activists and others and resulted, for all their democratic gains, in a culture of "hyperindividualism," to use Glendon's term, that inhibited dialogue about what we owed to each other as citizens and about the search for any common ground between individuals themselves.[31]

Today democracy no longer appears to play the central role it once did. Downward trends in voter participation, the deterioration of popular faith in government, and the demise of institutions of representative democracy like labor unions and public schools all offer evidence of this change. To some extent, however, this should not be surprising. The effort to create a liberal democracy was haunted from the beginning by the emphasis Americans placed on the idea of the free individual. As Benjamin Barber suggested, liberalism was always the priority. When liberalism and its inevitable counterpart, illiberalism, were recast in the vast repertory of cinematic narratives, the resulting mix was sure to be anything but coherent. That this fusion would pose a problem for democracy—and for liberalism itself—is one of the points made in this book. But democracy did not go away. In fact, nothing was resolved for sure, although over time the hopes and drawbacks of liberalism stood at the center of most films. To a considerable degree, the working-class models that populate this study—figures like Tom Powers and Stanley Kowalski—were liberals and illiberals. And yet, men and women just like them kept returning to the screen with messages that carried aspirations for greater justice and for more equitable racial and gender relations.[32]

This book will look chronologically at the relationship between Hollywood's treatment of working people and mainstream political ideals. Chapter 1 will examine depictions of the lower classes in films from the era of the Great Depression. It will attempt to explore figures who reminded Americans that hard times had severely undermined faith in the ideals of liberal individualism. More importantly, it will look at the degree to which the cinema refrained from any outright endorsement of the political crusades of the decade. When it came to working-class politics in the thirties, on the one hand, films kept much discussion focused on the promises and pitfalls of liberalism rather than on the rhetoric of union mobilizations. It did not ignore completely, however, calls for working-class democracy that reverberated throughout America at the time. In fact, in the way that it addressed the needs and position of women in society, it actually surpassed the democratic chants of the New Deal and the CIO.

Chapter 2 will take up the matter of representing the people during the crisis of World War II. The war induced a massive amount of "totalizing" language in American culture and, in a substantial way, blunted the diverse politics and social and cultural realism of the thirties. A more extensive treatment of the real world of the ordinary Americans returned in the films of the late forties, and the ultimate portrait, presented in chapter 3, was difficult to understand. The plight of unions received scant attention to be sure, but anticapitalist messages were revived and antiracist messages became more evident. More strikingly, the inner world of common people came up for extensive review, a direction that threatened to undermine hope in political ideals like democracy and liberalism even with the return of prosperity.

Chapter 4 attempts to make clear that the newly discovered world of the common people—the one marked by tangled passions as well as by economic problems and possibilities—would continue to be filmed regardless of the considerations of conservative and reactionary interests who had hoped to contain unflattering portrayals of America and its people during the high tide of the Cold War. Blacklist or no blacklist, the repertoire of lower-class characters continued to serve a broad range of political inclinations. Chapter 5 suggests that after the 1960s the imagined lives of plebeians became even more elaborate. Stories focusing on women and racial minorities multiplied, and common people embarked on a number of familiar and fresh political journeys in the aftermath of the demise of patriarchy and Vietnam. A concluding essay makes an effort to connect the tortured road traveled by America's ordinary men and women envisioned by Hollywood to political ideals that coursed through the real world in which citizens lived during much of the century just passed.

# BLUE-COLLAR HOLLYWOOD

# ONE

# POLITICAL CROSS-DRESSING
# IN THE THIRTIES

In the face of the massive economic disruptions of the 1930s, both Hollywood and political organizations scrambled to articulate versions of American liberal and democratic creeds that would win adherents, but they did
not do so in the same way. Hollywood never mounted a strong defense of
union power in the decade; the working people on the screen were seldom the committed labor activists or the determined strikers found on
the pages of proletarian novels, who knew exactly that it was strong industrial unions that were the answer to the problems of capitalism in the
thirties. But neither did Hollywood offer an uncritical view of liberal capitalism. Rather, it took a middle ground by offering features that affirmed
both the need for individuals to explore their personal dreams and the
reality of economic and political exploitation in the nation as well as the
requirement that greater measures of fairness and cooperation be imple-
mented. Thus, it explored issues pertaining to liberalism and personal
longings when it presented movies about gangsters, boxers, and female
factory workers and related tales of how unregulated capitalists had
caused the Depression in the first place. When it offered images of striking miners, displaced farmers, and women who were exploited by men,
it strongly suggested that ordinary people were often victimized and in
need of greater measures of justice in their lives.[1]

Under the emblems of the New Deal and the Congress of Industrial
Organizations (CIO), union leaders and political officials sought to pull
workers away from identities grounded in ethnicity, race, skill, and region and to mold them into a collective force for working-class democracy. Thus, they were more committed to social democracy than was
Hollywood, but they invested less of an effort in pushing for the realization of personal goals. They supported a democratic vision of a nation

where working people could not only hope to participate in the exercise of political power more than they did in the twenties but could expect some form of reward for their years of toil and sacrifice. In other words, they had a right to share in the wealth of a democratic and capitalistic society more than they had in the past. But CIO politics was not without its prejudices. In this political culture workingmen stood above women, and family heads stood above all others. And while a democratic sense of sharing power and a respect for the rights of individual citizens were notions that could be found both in the movies and in politics, the balance between democracy and liberalism was not quite the same in each realm. In film, more attention was devoted to the problem of the individual and the extent to which he (and especially she) could be free of economic distress and moral obligations—even as moral standards were often defended at the end of many stories. In the political world, the expectations were more about the need to restrain individualism—whether it was in the hands of working men, free-wheeling capitalists, or women, who were of secondary importance to unionists and New Dealers.

Hollywood also sought to wean people away from older identities, but it was more likely to do so under the sign of the individual than of the union or the state. Some democratic-minded films were more likely to explore the fate of individuals within the context of their social worlds and the idea that just futures were desirable if not always possible. Feature films that were more liberal, however, narrowed the frame of reference considerably and pictured the individual as living in a world that was severely more circumscribed. Movies expended some effort at reaffirming the legitimacy of democratic claims, not so much by endorsing the CIO and the New Deal—although a feature like *Gabriel Over the White House* (1933) suggested the need for powerful government intervention into the economy—but by acknowledging the wide range of personal turmoil and wants in the minds of males and females and the possibility that they might be realized in some way. In other words, Hollywood could not discuss democracy without pondering the fate of liberalism—its central question. Thus, Hollywood did a better job than the CIO or the New Deal of envisioning life outside the orbit of large-scale organizations and of picturing private desires, especially the longing to escape rather than solve the problems of working-class life. It realized what Raymond Williams has asserted—that since the Renaissance, dramatic stories have tended to be more about the fate of individuals than about the fate of societies—or, for that matter, of social groups.[2]

The predominant character of thirties culture, in any case, was not its proletarian or conservative dimension as much as it was its composite nature. This is not to suggest that every possible point of view was evident. There was no large-scale attack on white supremacy or heterosexuality during the decade. But cultural narratives were marked by the merger of all kinds of "grim antagonisms": worker versus capital; collective versus individual; male versus female. A debate between moral conservatives and liberal individuals was often at the center of film production itself.[3] This cross-dressing was driven by the need to reconcile and embrace polarities that existed in the mass audience itself as well as in the range of desires within individual audience members. The wide use of the term "the people" in the era suggested aspirations for crossing traditional social and emotional borders. No single political doctrine—conservative or radical—could generate mass support at either the ballot box or the ticket booth. Hollywood would have folded if it had simply made films that entirely pleased radical militants, moral conservatives, or even studio heads. The most successful form of politics and entertainment, therefore, moved beyond narrow appeals to partisan sensibilities. Thus, the CIO blended unskilled and skilled workers, and Communists and Catholics. Hollywood studios crafted narratives that spoke of dreams of sexual and material desires, and condemned acts of adultery and violence. Indeed, in this climate, movie scripts were negotiated between conservative studio heads, anti-Fascist émigrés, supporters of the CIO, Catholic priests, and audience tastes. Thirties literature not only embraced the proletarian style but also eschewed protest and asked only for compassion for the struggling poor in works like *Let Us Now Praise Famous Men*—or even managed to ridicule them in stories like *Tobacco Road*, which created humor at the expense of poor southern whites. There was extremism to be sure, and New Deal politics moved more in the direction of the proletarian novel than did Hollywood, but to be a pure partisan in the thirties—insensitive to the assorted emotions, ideologies, and attachments of the people—was to run the risk of not being heard.[4]

Millions of working people and leaders abandoned traditions that had separated them in earlier times and pragmatically formed alliances to press their demands for economic justice during hard times. Previously kept apart by corporate resistance to unionization and the cleavages of ethnicity, race, religion, and gender, people forged new forms of labor solidarity in the thirties throughout the United States. In New York City, transit workers forged a powerful union of Catholics and Marxists. In New England, secular radicals and deeply religious French Canadians joined to form the powerful Independent Textile Union. Over time some of these alliances could not be kept together, but the initial response of workers was to mediate long-standing differences, to entertain associations with others that had been excluded from their political lives, and to abandon the idea that justice and improvement were attainable only through personal struggle.[5]

Leaders of this mobilization of working people were astute in recognizing that symbols and ideas with broad appeal would be needed to rally disparate groups and people to the cause of industrial democracy and the New Deal. Michael Kazin saw much of this when he argued that labor leaders in the period realized that they had to stress conceptions of "the common good that transcended the world of docks, mines and factories." In a similar vein, Gary Gerstle discovered that in Rhode Island, labor leaders employed traditional patriotic language and symbols like Washington and Lincoln to attract the loyalty of textile workers with different political, ethnic, and religious backgrounds. Gerstle called this new formation "working-class Americanism," a notion that encapsulated the essence of a society based on reciprocity by arguing that American workers not only owed allegiance to the nation but also that the nation owed them an improved standard of living. His work countered an older argument by Warren Sussman that the widespread use of patriotic language and symbols during the Depression was inherently conservative and encouraged adjustment rather than rebellion.[6]

Workers came together not only over dreams of democracy but over a growing personal desire to act as consumers. The findings of Lizabeth Cohen reveal that already in the 1920s working people were acquiring a taste both for consumer goods and for a more rewarding economy through associations with corporate welfare programs. In fact, labor activists within the New Deal like Sidney Hillman consciously sought programs that would stimulate greater "material well-being" for all of the laboring classes—not just more power in the workplace—through the creation of a cooperative commonwealth that rested on visions of harmony between labor and business and between public and private concerns. Consumer desires were not simply relegated to Hollywood productions.[7]

Although the attachment people felt toward the ideals of corporate and state paternalism as a reward for their devotion and toil had radical implications for the politics of capitalism as it was practiced in the twenties, its impact on gender relations was less challenging. New Deal political movements generally reaffirmed conventional notions of gender roles that were centered in the valorization of a father-headed, mother-centered household. This left the economic sphere primarily in the hands of a male breadwinner, although households headed by low-paid workers always found it difficult to survive on one income. And although women did play vital roles in local unionization drives, they were continually relegated to subordinate positions both in unions and in political affairs, and they received a very small percentage of jobs from New Deal relief agencies.[8]

The crisis of the Great Depression, in reality, reinforced patriarchal ideals in society by raising concerns about the employability of male breadwinners. Social surveys of the period documented the erosion of paternal authority within the household and the humiliation many men now felt. Although hard times caused many families to rely more on female earnings, union and government officials strove to achieve a family wage level for men that would allow them to keep their wives tied to domestic chores and thus to regain their self-respect. This concern for the male worker and the veneration of the traditional family resulted in criticisms of women who worked. The secondary status of women was affirmed in essential pieces of New Deal legislation. Men were not only the chief recipients of government job and assistance programs, but ideals of female domesticity were literally inscribed into key pieces of welfare law. Linda Gordon has proven that provisions for Old Age Insurance and Aid to Families with Dependent Children (AFDC) were not only a response to working-class needs for economic stability but represented efforts by middle-class reformers to ensure the viability of traditional household arrangements. AFDC, for instance, was granted only to women who did not have access to the support of a breadwinner. Put simply, men earned Social Security because they worked; women earned AFDC only when they were "dependent." Gordon's work also shows that many of the female reformers who helped design such legislation were imbued with a traditional view of the separation of male and female spheres in economic life and viewed poverty as essentially a lapse in male breadwinning.[9]

This anxiety over traditional forms of manhood in the decade manifested itself not only in the politics of the era but in the culture as well. Sometimes this response was intended not to reaffirm the value of the breadwinner but to assert the attractiveness of powerful men. In the first issue of *Superman* comic books in 1938, an ideal of a strong male who could help others but was independent of women and families proved to be popular. These books even contained advertisements by Charles Atlas explaining how through bodybuilding ordinary men could transform themselves into powerful and dominant individuals. Similar images were also found in federally sponsored art of the decade; one scholar who has examined murals and monuments created in the era concluded that they "bolstered an image of manhood battered by a discredited war and a demoralizing depression."[10] These versions of strong men actually moved away from some of the democratic impulses of the CIO and the New Deal, for they encouraged a more liberal belief that individuals could actually stand alone and resist exploitation and human degradation. In some moments, strong men could even veer away from conventional behavior completely and pursue wealth and power though a life of crime as they did in *Scarface* (1932). But in the hands of mass culture, ideas always threatened to become more liberal than democratic. Faced with such an array of cultural images, it is no wonder that Sherwood Anderson saw Americans as "puzzled" by their overall condition in the 1930s.[11]

Mediation and contradiction reigned in the political culture of the thirties, and this meant that democracy and liberalism survived together and alone. Ultimately, the politics was more democratic and mass culture more liberal and illiberal, but all of this circulated in a wide and confusing fashion. Thus, one can understand the point made by Lawrence Levine that a singular idea like "the people" could be understood during the decade both as a source of hope and as a sign of how the masses were "confused sheep" susceptible to manipulation.[12]

Regardless of the conflicted nature of the culture, it is difficult to accept any longer the notion that the mass culture of the decade was essentially a flight from reality. The legacy of state control of film in totalitarian regimes in Europe supported such a view, especially in the forties and fifties. And the idea has enjoyed something of a career ever since. Robert Warshow even suggested that because films tended to focus more on personal experience, they screened the full reality of partisan conflict and divisive political and economic issues of the period from public view.[13] The fact is, however, that personal experience and individual emotions were partisan issues that were often hidden from sight in collectivist politics. The reality of human nature was a political realm that presented visions of a democratic community or any community with its greatest challenge: how to reconcile personal and public needs. This was a problem the CIO and the New Deal addressed to some extent. Hollywood did as well and in a way that was less friendly to some political interests than to others.

•

## MAKING FILMS IN THE THIRTIES

All cultural statements must both screen and mediate reality. The Great Depression, its causes, solutions, and impact, was of such enormity that no one person, studio, or party could hope to interpret it fully. Filmmakers, politicians, and labor leaders were all forced to select words and symbols that would best serve their ends or their constituents, whether they were male auto workers or female moviegoers. Thus, an observer like Andrew Bergman concluded that movie audiences during the Depression "did not escape into a void each week" because "people do not escape into something they cannot relate to." Bergman saw that the movies of the time represented much more than the views of studio heads. Rather, by offering explanations for hard times, preserving and demolishing traditional values, and acknowledging the extent of individual wishes, they performed all kinds of cultural and political work important to the audiences. Bergman thought that ultimately films sustained a faith in the nation and its traditional institutions. Thus, in the "gritty realism" of the gangster film, a criminal could fulfill his desire for escape from the ethnic ghetto or for power and wealth but would finally be punished for his moral transgressions. But one cannot deny that the camera lingered for a great while in such stories on the pleasures afforded by such transgressions: violence, greed, and sex.[14]

Certainly the entertainment (or political) industry could not move too far from the tastes and concerns of its audiences. Roosevelt knew this; he used the radio to gain direct access to private homes and hired men as speech writers who had also written plays and scripts. Movie producers realized that films that were overly didactic or too far removed from the anxieties and desires of everyday life ran the risk of economic failure. That is why, as Bergman noted, a film like the Marx Brothers' *Duck Soup* (1933) did not attract large crowds. It attacked the sanctity of the state at a time when people wanted to have some faith in that institution. Similarly, Charlie Chaplin's *Modern Times* (1936), a feature that tended to cast the plight of the workingman in somewhat hopeless terms, did not win much popular approval at all. And it is important to note that, despite some decline in the early thirties, the movie audience grew steadily through the thirties and forties as moviegoers shared experiences of hard times and war.[15]

The quest for popularity forced the film industry not only to challenge the dominant political verities of the twenties and employ a variety of narrative strategies but to enter into political alliances of its own. Hollywood was an industry that not only resisted organized labor in its own ranks but was wary of conservative religious leaders and charges that its products were eroding the moral standards of Americans. In 1930 the Motion Picture Producers and Distributors of America (MPPDA) created a Production Code to govern the moral and political content of feature films. Pressured by bankers who wanted to minimize the risk to their investments in films by avoiding controversy and by officials of the Catholic Church who expressed fears that films eroded internal checks of conscience that were needed to restrain passion and sustain the traditional family, Hollywood moved to censor itself.

At first their efforts were timid. For this reason many of the films of the early thirties, like *Heroes for Sale* (1933), cast a more critical eye on established authorities and carried more sexually explicit messages than were to be found later in the decade. The publication of studies by social scientists in 1933 accusing the industry of encouraging immoral behavior, and the formation in 1934 of the Catholic Legion of Decency, which sought to regulate movie attendance by Catholics, however, forced studios to enhance the power of their own censorship office under the direction of Joseph Breen, a Catholic layman. For the next thirty years, movie production would include a significant set of negotiations over film content and over what a mass audience could see.[16]

Beyond simply responding to these external pressures, many in Hollywood also felt that most moviegoers—that abstract body that existed beyond the realm of region, class, or ethnicity—were genuinely interested in entertainment that was largely wholesome and supportive of existing institutions. Will Hays, the president of the MPPDA, claimed that the "vast majority of Americans" were devoted to "things that are wholesome and healthy and . . . live lives similar to those of their forefathers." The accuracy of such statements were not so much the point as was the perception by some officials in the industry that they had to avoid moral and political squabbles and, to a considerable extent, excessive partisanship. Hollywood's code acknowledged that film had the potential to reach "every class in society." This sort of audience penetration meant for these moral guardians that films needed to be placed under more restraint than, say, a novel or a work of art that would reach only a highly discreet group. Thus, in addition to calling for films that upheld values such as conventional marriage and sexual restraint, the code affirmed the need to reinforce the power of legal and religious authority and not to make heroes out of criminals.[17]

The search for universally acceptable film narratives had particular consequences for the status of working women. Early thirties films often depicted lowborn women longing to flee from both class and moral restraints. In a sense, one narrative strand dealt with a social democratic issue and another with a liberal or individual one. Females of modest means were often shown pursuing wealth and status through sex, although censors and moral critics felt such stories only promoted "sexual delinquency among women." *Baby Face* (1933) actually allowed millions of people to contemplate the possibility of a woman rejecting the traditional boundaries of family life and pursuing sexual freedom and social mobility. This tale questioned both moral censors, proletarian fiction—and, for that matter, the CIO—by inferring that women could want more than domesticity and partnerships with hardworking breadwinners.[18]

To the extent that they relied on the melodrama with its enigmatic excursions into daily life, Hollywood films were actually incapable of being censored. Any effort to sanction the status quo was almost always accompanied by the acknowledgment of alternative desires. Melodrama itself was a way of seeing the world that invoked both the real and the imagined, the sacred and the profane, regardless of whether it took the form of a gangster film, a western, or a women's story. It was dependent on the representation of antagonism, not the reassertion of dogma. It is no wonder that religious leaders and publications like the *Daily Worker* were usually troubled by these shows.[19]

Many scholars have argued that after 1934 Hollywood produced fewer melodramas that were critical of established authorities or flouted sexual conventions. But disturbing views of society and human nature would never leave the Hollywood screen. In fact, some of the most popular Hollywood films of the thirties suggested that people were not only interested in circumventing moral standards but also in escaping the influence of both big government and big business, two pillars of modern life. Some of this was due to nostalgia for a premodern America devoid of large-scale government and corporations where people knew each other on more intimate terms. But thirties films did more than retreat from the present, they also endorsed versions of democratic politics in order to solve contemporary social problems. Michael Denning's account of the Popular Front described a group of writers, artists, and intellectuals who had grown up in working-class neighborhoods and who promoted proletarian goals in mass culture. Sympathetic to radical politics and to the CIO, these individuals contributed to what Denning called the "laboring of American culture" in their work by calling for more social democracy, racial equality, and opposition to fascism. In thirties films, they would all come together—moral conservatives, the anti-labor studios, nostalgia buffs, and assertive CIO loyalists. The results would be a cinema marked by a breathtaking array of political positions that might veer onto highways that were democratic or liberal at any moment.[20]

## FIGHTING ALONE: GANGSTERS AND BOXERS

The discussion over liberalism in the thirties was vibrant but unsettling. The Depression had discredited both the idea of liberal capitalism and the standing of capitalists themselves. For the lower orders, this meant that a dream of uplift and improvement remained but was fraught with uncertainty and difficulty. Men from humble backgrounds could still take up the quest for gain on their own, but the movies were quick to remind them that dangers lurked in the competitive streets of America. Stories of gangsters in the early thirties attested to the fact that money and power could still be grabbed by men with the will to surmount all obstacles and ignore any sense of responsibility to those who shared their social world. Tales of boxers imagined similar dreams but rendered the quest and hope to escape the depths of society and accountability to others even more arduous and uncertain.

The popular image of the gangster dominated early thirties films about plebeians and portrayed a social world in which much confusion existed regarding the potential both for individual opportunity and for cooperation. The point of these features was that American society was threatened by the failure of capitalism to distribute its rewards more justly. Consequently, some common men, like the gangster, simply took what they wanted. Gangsters were not only men from the working classes but unscrupulous businessmen operating without constraints to get whatever they wanted and bandits who turned their backs on conventional standards and morals. These stories were appealing to many in the audience because they combined a harsh critique of unfettered capitalism with the glorification of hard-driving men who refused to accept a fate of routinized toil and moral regimentation in the blue-collar neighborhoods of America. The turn to this form of banditry itself underscored the fact that many now believed that traditional practices and standards had failed. The gangster was a "self-made man." However, he was much more. He was a sign that radical liberalism was out of control. For it was self-made men that had brought about the Depression in the first place.

Despite its ambiguous portrayal of liberalism, however, the image of the gangster did not comfort those who hoped America might now see a greater expression of democracy. He was not like the "forgotten man" of some early-thirties films that evoked the need for a more cooperative society that was sensitive to the needs of the poor and to the rights of veterans that had served their nation. In movies like *I Am a Fugitive from a Chain Gang* (1932), *Gold Diggers of 1933*, and *Heroes for Sale*, audiences viewed stories that told of respectable working-class men who had fought for America in World War I but were now denied basic economic needs and rights. The protagonist in *Heroes*, despite his victimization, ended up donating his money to help feed the poor; a factory worker and vet in *Chain Gang* found only abuse from law enforcement officials in the South. In fact, specific references to Roosevelt's inaugural speech were inserted near the end to offer people some optimism that the Depression could be overcome. To be sure, the gangster resisted forces in society that had restricted his desire for money and power in ways that the "forgotten man" did not, and this probably accounted for some of his popularity. Ultimately, however, in order to please moral censors he was destroyed for his lust and ambition, but not before he spent considerable time enjoying the fruits of his violent quest for money and power, dressing in flashy clothes, and dating provocative women. He sent mixed messages, but ones that spoke mainly about the danger and disorder society faced if capitalist values were allowed to proceed unchecked and about the joy of getting anything you wanted. These films brought no comfort to either labor activists or right-wing ideologues.[21]

The subversive qualities of the genre—both to the veneration of capitalism and to the hope for constraining working-class desire—were evident in *Little Caesar* (1931). Evidence in the files of the Production Code indicated that audiences loved the film. Yet complaints were registered that the story glamorized crime, although some did argue that the movie "performed a service by exposing the criminal strata that underlies society." What audiences liked was the character of Rico Bandello, played by Edward G. Robinson, and the fact that he exemplified the doctrine of an independent man, free to pursue money, power, and sex without entangling alliances with morals, institutions, or women.[22]

There was a longing for independence in the public approval of the gangster, but it must be stressed that this desire was fueled by the perception that alternative paths to happiness and stability had failed. The origins of the gangster were both social and emotional. Rico's ambitions are boundless. Raised in a lower-class Italian-American neighborhood, he wants to control the rackets in his city and "be somebody." He tells his trusted friend, Joe Massara, that he hopes to "make people dance."

Rico is no simple glorification of the bandit: he is positioned as a threat to family and community stability—a reminder of what an uncontrolled capitalism could do. He and Massara debate the merits of family life and the need for aspiring businessmen like Rico to remain apart from domestic relationships. Massara is not prepared to let go of a home life with a woman. Rico, on the other hand, sees it as a true obstacle to his dreams and tells his partner: "You're still in my gang, you got that. I don't care how many fancy skirts you got hanging on to you. That Jane of yours can go hang. It's her that's made a softie out of you. . . . where she's got you, you ain't no good for anything."

At one point Rico's Italian mother pleads with him to remember the immigrant world of family and religion that was at the heart of his upbringing. "You used to be a good boy, " she recalls. "Remember you sing in the church choir?" However, when the young man, prompted by his mother's pleadings, goes to talk to a local priest about the crime in their neighborhood, he ends up shooting the cleric on the stairs of the church.

Rico was ruthless, but the source of his callousness was to be found in the vast disparity between the humble world of his immigrant mother and the profits and promises that awaited him in the larger society. His mother was the voice of the Production Code; Rico spoke for the audience that lived in a deteriorating world of inequality. Rico's end was tragic and predictable. Working-class ambition and male violence exercised outside the boundaries of conventional morals could not be tolerated even in the cinema, and he was gunned down by police. And yet, the impression that more men like Rico would continue to charge out of the lower orders was fresh in everyone's mind.

Industry censors were preoccupied with the moral behavior of individuals and usually did not address the way films dealt with the complex construction of the society and the press of social forces on the individual. In discussions between Warner Brothers and censors during the production of *Public Enemy* (1931), code officials were certainly worried that the film might promote violence in society, but they appeared uninterested in exploring the possible ties between such brutal behavior and the failure of American capitalism. Moral authorities were more interested in regulating personal behavior than in the vagaries of the world in which the audience lived. Thus, a censorship board in Wisconsin objected to the picture because "it taught criminals new tricks." And a similar body in Maryland, which at first rejected the film completely, approved *Public Enemy* only after requesting that scenes involving young boys drinking beer and unmarried adults clad only in pajamas in a hotel room be eliminated. They also requested that the star, James Cagney, not strike his girlfriend in the face and that the ending not depict Cagney's murdered body falling into a room. Although these scenes remained in the film, the concerns of local censors suggest that their sense of ethics was focused mostly on individual rather than social action.[23]

Gangster films ultimately did not share the dream of regulating the individual. They were more interested in exploring the fate of a person in a larger community that was under stress. As such, the final product exposed injustice even as it somewhat appeased moral censors. Industry censors complained in 1931 that the gangster was often made to look heroic in battles with police and that "crime pictures" evoked severe criticism from "chiefs of police, newspaper editors, exhibitors, and leaders among the citizenry." The production of gangster films, however, continued. Darryl Zanuck, an executive at Warner Brothers, argued that *Public Enemy* actually had several moral themes. To him the film demonstrated, on the one hand, that pleasure and profit in crime were only momentary and would ultimately lead to "disaster for the participants." He was also convinced, however, that the story illustrated that it was not Prohibition that caused the "present crime wave" of mobs and gangs but social disorder. Zanuck was no friend of organized labor, but he asserted that the repeal of the 18th Amendment could not possibly stop crime and gang warfare. The only thing that could temper the violence, he told the code office, was the "betterment of the environment and living conditions in the lower regions." Thus, the studio executive denied the power of moral endings to effect fundamental changes in attitudes and behavior and revealed some longing for a democratic community with more egalitarianism.[24]

*Public Enemy* centers on Tom Powers, a man who grew up in a lower-class Irish-American neighborhood like Cagney did in real life. On these urban streets, Powers learns about ambition and avarice, not patriotism and love; he realizes early in life that energetic men can acquire a good deal of money if they remain free of family responsibility and corporate regulation. *Public Enemy* explores the destructive impact of inequality in industrial America by exhibiting some of the issues of Powers' early life. His working-class father is authoritarian—a familiar trope of Hollywood representations of such men—rather than understanding; he often prefers to take a strap to his defiant son. It is a character named Paddy, the operator of a local pool hall, however, who introduces Powers to the rewards of petty crime by offering to share profits from local robberies with him. Tom's mother is devoted to him, but her tears are not enough to dissuade him from a life of crime. Neither is the example of his brother Mike, a model working-class man who conforms to public morals and corporate rules as an employee of a local streetcar company. Powers, of course, discovers quickly that adherence to duty does not bring substantial material rewards and, by inference, that the model workingman in a society of inequality is probably never going to be able to acquire a sizable collection of goods.

Powers sees Prohibition not as a restriction but as an opportunity. He quickly realizes that if he can market sufficient intoxicants to local bars, he can make a fortune by running his own business. And that was the point; America had been an unjust society; it had rewarded self-made entrepreneurs in the twenties but not its common men. Powers is now simply taking steps necessary to join the emerging consumerism of the decade when he buys tailored suits, new cars, and women. He pursues his dreams relentlessly. When his customers purchase beer from other gangsters, he destroys his competitor's supplies and warns his buyers that if they do not take his product "someone will kick their teeth out."

The moral dilemma of the lowborn male is probed (but not resolved) at the family dinner table. Tom proposes a drink to his brother's health. But his sibling, dressed in a Marine uniform and aware of Power's connections with local gangs, will have none of his brother's beer. In front of their mother, he defames the gangster's achievements and throws the beer on the floor. Powers retorts by accusing his brother of enjoying the act of killing in battle. A distraught mother can only plead for reconciliation in a family troubled by the crosscurrents of an unstable social and moral order.

The Hollywood code always sought to uphold the institution of marriage, and officials were troubled by the fact that Powers lives with a woman who is not his wife. Angered one morning because his girlfriend will not give him a drink, he stuffs a grapefruit in her face, an act designed to further address the secret longings of some in the audience as much as Power's pursuit of money and power. Powers, who is clearly "not the marrying kind," soon leaves his "moll" for another more appreciative of his rough demeanor. She admits, in fact, that she likes him because he is "so strong." "You don't give, you take," she exudes. "Oh! Tommy I could love you to death."

As expected, Powers suffers for his indulgence and his errant ways. A rival gang ultimately kidnaps and murders him, leaving his bound body at his mother's doorstep in a dramatic finish. Audiences were told, and moral critics reassured, that the end of Tom Powers was the end every hoodlum would face but that America must still solve "the problem" that created these figures in the first place. What better way to divulge the clash between liberalism and democracy in this feature. Even if the goals of the code office were achieved and the unregulated individual punished, the unfairness and marginality of the "lower regions" had to be addressed. By revealing that the dream of preserving classic liberalism by simply imposing moral virtue was an insufficient response to hard times, this film revealed its democratic sensibilities.[25]

By the later thirties, the gangster film had evolved from a simple cautionary tale of working-class men attempting to cross ethnic, class, and legal borders into a more considered debate over the alternatives that were available to young "toughs" raised on city streets. Some of those options had been suggested in films like *Public Enemy* and *Scarface* (1932), but in *Angels with Dirty Faces* (1938) they were explored in more detail. Thus, the film revolved around what *Variety* called "different paths to opposite poles of manhood." Rocky Sullivan, played by James Cagney, becomes a hoodlum who defies conventional behavior. His boyhood friend, Jerry Connolly, portrayed by Pat O'Brien, becomes a Catholic priest who runs a gym in the urban neighborhood that offers youths basketball and an ethical life—with no guarantee, of course, of economic improvement. In fact, it is striking that although the narrative took great pains to punish the hoodlum in the end and not to glamorize his lifestyle, it could not censor the idea that working-class life led mostly to hardship—a point that almost never left films about proletarians in any decade and that ensured that they would always present some basis for democratic claims. Thus, at one point, when the mobster Sullivan gives some cash to boys in a local gang, one of the youths exclaims, "My old man never made that much dough in his life working for the department of sanitation." And a young woman endorses the view that working-class jobs have distinct limitations by relating the story of a spouse who "tried to give me a lot more than he could by driving cab."[26]

Again the concerns of censors during production of the tale ran less to the politics of class and more to the desire to restrain what one of them called "primitive emotions" with the force of moral authority. Film producers were told to reduce the number of scenes in which kids were depicted as gambling in a local pool room and law enforcement officers being shot. And a great deal of effort went into ensuring that at the end of the film Sullivan would die in the electric chair and not be transformed into a popular figure. Nevertheless, a women's club in Los Angeles still complained that the final film glorified crime and that the electrocution would still not deter "five or ten million boys and girls who see this gangster as a glorious hero, even in death."[27]

In adult life Sullivan becomes a hero to adolescents in his neighborhood. His cultural opposite, Connolly, devotes his life to running a recreational center for the juveniles and keeping them from following in Sullivan's footsteps, an effort that brings him no adulation whatsoever. For these kids, playing basketball in the gym is for "creampuffs." They prefer to explore the logic of capitalism—or in this case to listen to Sullivan explain how to work the rackets and amass vast sums of money. When Sullivan demonstrates confidence in the boys by hiding $100,000 he has stolen with them, there is nothing they will not do for their champion.

The more notorious Sullivan becomes, the more the boys worship him. In one scene the priest enters the pool hall and warns the juveniles that they will end up in jail if they do not change their ways and come to the gym to play basketball. One boy counters, in a display of disrespect that troubled censors, "Father, there ain't no future in playing basketball." Sullivan even attempts to help the priest in his efforts at moral reclamation and makes a large contribution to the center. But Connolly returns the money and tells him that it is "tainted" and that he does not want to build a center on a "rotten foundation."

Finally, the priest launches an all-out effort to end mob operations. Some critics have noted that producers felt the priest-hero, who was classless, worked very well as a promoter of moral values. With the backing of the city press, the cleric declares war on the underworld and exposes corruption wherever he finds it. "We must wipe out criminals and officials who are allied with them," he declares. When the mob plans to kill the priest—a move that ran completely against all the rules of censorship to protect the integrity of traditional authorities—his old friend Sullivan intervenes by shooting a mob leader. Ironically, this act leads to his arrest and to his execution in the electric chair.[28]

In the film's climax, Sullivan becomes a subject of much debate. The adolescents at the pool hall are convinced that their hero will be exonerated at a trial. They still admire him for telling police he would spit in their eye. Connolly worries that his act of defiance will sustain antisocial attitudes in the youths for the rest of their lives and persuades Sullivan to die as a coward rather than as a brave person. Initially, the gangster objects. He claims that one has to have "heart" to express fear, and "I had the heart cut out of me a long time ago." This rebellious attitude, he asserts, is all he has left. At the end the mobster relents and pleads for mercy, fearful that the next generation of working-class kids will follow him into a life of crime. Newspaper headlines screamed: "Rocky Dies Yellow. Killer Coward at End."

The solutions to the turmoil and danger in this imagined proletarian world were not nearly as obvious as those offered by the CIO and the New Deal. In *Dead End* (1937) the coming of age of young, working-class men was again raised as an issue for the culture to review. The dream of the CIO to establish a world of male wage earners and breadwinners was challenged in this feature. The aspirations of proletarian toughs living in New York in this story dealt mostly with plans to escape the blue collar world and its meager resources entirely. They are again presented with two models of behavior: one an architect and the other a hood. The professional has a hard time finding work; the gangster, played by Humphrey Bogart, walks through the neighborhood with money in his pockets. In the end, the mobster is killed while planning a kidnapping, but the story still left viewers with no hint as to how these kids might find a way out of their social and economic predicament. They are truly at a dead end, with no hope offered that either democracy or liberalism can work.

The boxer, on the other hand, was not at a dead end. He had an idea of how he might attack his marginal status in society, although it often involved some moral dilemmas. In *Kid Galahad* (1937) a fighter and his sister pursue a better life through boxing but also mount an attempt at moral reform by convincing a domineering fight promoter to treat people around him in a kinder fashion. In *Golden Boy* (1939) the dream of upward mobility through the boxing ring is articulated by the boxer's girlfriend. Standing on a rooftop overlooking the city, the woman, played by actress Barbara Stanwyck, tells boxer Joe Bonaparte (played by William Holden) to abandon his dream of becoming a violinist, a goal encouraged by his father. Locating the liberal drive in a woman, Stanwyck makes her point in unmistakable terms: "Listen, Joe, be a fighter. If you made your fame and fortune, you could be anything you want. Do it. Bang your way to the middleweight crown. Buy that car. Give some girl the things she wants. . . . I like men who reach for a slice of fame."

Bonaparte accedes to her wishes but angers those who care for him by signing with a disreputable promoter (read businessman). The bittersweet nature of capitalism and of liberalism is reinforced when the boxer wins a brutal contest against an African American named "The Chocolate Drop," who eventually dies from injuries received in the match. Revolted by such destructiveness, Bonaparte cannot bring himself to accept his cash prize. Even the ambitious woman loses interest in the rewards of such a struggle and tells him she now only cares that they have each other. If the quest for material advancement and a higher standing involved such a high cost, these common people now said it was not worth the price.

The promise of boxing to reward the sweat of the common man was also offered and withdrawn in films like *The Champ* (1931) and *City of Conquest* (1940). In the latter, Danny Kenney, played by James Cagney, finds that an ordinary truck driver cannot muster sufficient resources to hold the affections of a woman who wants more fame and fortune than he can ever offer. The woman he loves tells him that she cannot stay with him and repeat the lives of their parents who struggle continuously "always trying to make a dime." Like other stories of gangsters and boxers, this film failed to venerate either liberalism or democracy. There was certainly no account of the value of a collective struggle on the part of ordinary people or a defense of the ideal of obligation. The woman leaves Kenney to find fame and fortune as a professional dancer when Kenney loses most of his vision trying to become a boxing champion. However, the woman feels sorrow for the man now reduced to selling newspapers on the street. She tells her roommate that she regrets having thrown away her relationship with a "grease monkey in a junkyard garage" who made twenty dollars a week because she was a "dizzy dope" who was going to "burn up the world."

## LEADERS FROM THE RANK AND FILE

Not all common men sought to escape their working-class worlds. Some were willing to stay home and lead struggles for the benefit of the class from which they came. They were actually able to perceive futures and a degree of happiness within proletarian communities by meeting responsibilities to both men and women within their social group. Characters like Marvin Blake (*Cabin in the Cotton*), John Sims (*Our Daily Bread*), Joe Radek (*Black Fury*), and Dutch Miller (*Riff Raff*) allowed audiences to explore the joys and pitfalls of seeking social justice for fellow workers and the difficulties of establishing a working-class democracy. The end of their stories brought no guarantees that America would be a more egalitarian society, but the films that centered on them did remind viewers that the fate of the individual was not in his hands alone.

In *Cabin in the Cotton* (1932), a Warner Brothers production that came at a time when the studio struggled for economic solvency early in the Depression, the issue of growing class conflict in America was confronted head on. The setting was not the urban neighborhood, however, but the rural South and its system of sharecropping. Although Holly-wood usually tried to avoid offending the economic and racist outlooks of the region, this film did portray the exploitation of white tenant farm-ers. A wealthy landowner and his daughter, played by Bette Davis, live in a state of high luxury in stark contrast to the meager conditions of fami-lies who pick cotton for them. Marvin Blake, a lower-class male, gets the opportunity to join their elite lifestyle. He becomes a bookkeeper for the owner and wins the affection of his attractive daughter.

Blake, however, is plagued by guilt over the fact that he has abandoned the needs of poor farmers like his father who are desperate to improve their way of life. In fact, a group of tenants organize to protect their inter-ests by stealing cotton, and they try to convince him to become an agent for them and sell their stolen goods in Memphis. This is a rare instance in film when working people are not only highly organized but quite rational (and businesslike) in contemplating how they can challenge pow-ers that oppress them. When Blake sees wealthy owners lynch a white man who has stolen from them, and when he learns that his employer cheated his father years before, he can no longer ignore the pleas from his comrades for justice. In a resolution that calls explicitly for a more democratic community, Blake presides over a town meeting between the planters and the tenants. The wealthy claim that they have earned their privileges by taking economic risks; the tenants assert that they are mis-treated and underfed. Blake is the one who calls for more cooperation and a fairer distribution of the available resources. Audiences get a hint at the end that his conversion from liberalism to democracy may even drive him into the arms of a lower-class girl.[29]

Another workingman, John Sims, proves to be an effective leader in response to hard times in *Our Daily Bread* (1934). This feature has often been called the "most radical film of the thirties" because of the way it acknowledged the devastation of the Depression and because of its mes-sage of collective action as a means to economic uplift. But those mes-sages were only some of the many that pervaded this social text. Numer-ous scholars like Stuart Hall have shown how generic boundaries are seldom fixed even within the same narrative. In *Our Daily Bread*, this admixture was evident in the employment of tales that were both roman-tic and radical and that were directed toward issues of class and gender. Audiences could readily identify with the working-class couple at the center of the film, John and Mary Sims, who faced economic adversity to-gether. Indeed, the stability of John's male identity is crucial to this fea-ture. He frequently exhibits an ideal of strong male leadership that is not only a reminder that men from the lower orders can take control but also a sign of hope that the working classes can take their future into their own hands. Critics have felt that the film's portrayal of a collectivist agricultural enterprise made it a radical political statement. But collective farming was not really a plausible alternative for the millions of people who walked city streets. The theme of a future on the land reflected genuine anxiety about contemporary civilization and capitalist production, but it drifted far from the modern politics of the CIO and the New Deal. It was the strong characterization of Sims that really made the picture insurgent.[30]

The film was directed by King Vidor, who actually mortgaged his home to help finance the production. An opening preamble reminded audiences that the Depression was the central political fact in their lives and that they need not be overwhelmed by discouragement or failure. Unlike the gangster films, which encouraged a discourse over the merits of unrestrained ambition, *Our Daily Bread* gave up the attempt to find justice in the modern world—which made it in some ways more conservative than the gangster films—and offered the ideal of creating a cooperative commonwealth in the rural hinterlands. The central protagonist, John Sims, sought not the destruction of capitalism or even its reform, as Marvin Blake did, but the opportunity to retain his status as a breadwinner by investing his sweat in the land. "I don't want any favors," he asserts. "All I want is a chance to work."

John and Mary Sims are not powerful signifiers of extremism because they actually reaffirm traditions like marriage and patriarchy. They are neither contemptuous of authority nor cynical about capitalism. Anxious, above all, to be an economically stable couple, they threw themselves into farming with little knowledge of what they were doing. An itinerant farmer from Minnesota suggests to them the possibility of forming a "sort of cooperative community where money is not so important." Soon John erects a sign along a nearby road calling for men with skills to share the work.

*Our Daily Bread* not only affirmed conservative sexual behavior but confirmed conventional history lessons as well. Joining the public discussion over the American past that pervaded the decade, Sims tells his fellow toilers that John Smith and the early settlers in North America did not stand around when they arrived and "beef about the unemployment situation," but they started to "make their own employment" by building their houses and growing their food. Someone in the group responds by suggesting that they throw all they own into a "common pot," a direct attack upon liberal capitalism if there ever was one. But Hollywood was more interested in circulating various images and ideas for mass consumption than about articulating coherent ideologies, and none were offered here. In the discussion of ideas, concepts like "immortal democracy" and "socialism" are also dismissed. A Swedish-American farmer claims that he does not even know what the terms mean. He is certain, however, that they all have to get to work rather than debate the merits of any political philosophy and select a "big boss," whom everyone knows is John Sims. Perhaps Sims represented Roosevelt, but this film was far from being an endorsement for working-class protest or New Deal programs that accepted modern society and tried to make it work.[31]

Difficulties in farming cooperatively are often acknowledged. Creditors attempt to take over the enterprise, but the group pools their resources to keep them away. And when John is attracted for a time to another woman who suggests that he leave Mary, he makes the decision to curb his desires and remain faithful to his loyal spouse, a reminder that stable gender relations are crucial to a sound social order, regardless of one's political predilections. In the film's climax the group is threatened by a drought, but Sims, the enlightened leader and faithful spouse, formulates a solution. The collective will dig a long irrigation ditch; women will support the hardworking men by holding torches at night so that they can swing their picks in unison. Solidarity (and sexual restraint) will build the ditch and save both the crop and the community. There was democracy in this solution and the image of a society where citizens met obligations to other citizens. Liberalism—and, for that matter, militant protest—were held in check.

The anti-union outlook of most studios was manifested quite clearly when this feature was completed. Fearing that the film's message of cooperative action would translate into greater public support for Upton Sinclair in the 1934 California gubernatorial race, executives at United Artists delayed the film's release in the state until after the election. And Metro-Goldwyn-Mayer studios actually produced phony newsreels pretending to show ordinary working people in the state who were suspicious of Sinclair's "socialism" and fearful that he would drive "all the capital out of the country." Yet such corporate attitudes did not mean that the products of these studios masked the anger millions had with the failures of capitalism itself.[32]

*Black Fury* (1935) represented a more frank confrontation with worker exploitation in industrial society and the culpability of industrialists for engendering working-class discontent. Joe Radek, its central character, was a Slovak-American coal miner in Pennsylvania who had a notion of someday returning to live on the land, an idea that was quite real in industrial communities where immigrants raised in rural Europe often longed to restore their homeland lifestyles. The original story was authored by a Pennsylvania legislator, Michael Musmanno, who had worked in the mines and who had forced the state to launch an investigation into the actual beating death of a miner by company police near Pittsburgh in 1929, an incident that was presented in the movie itself. In Musmanno's narrative and in the film, Radek, a militant miner, is angered by the brutality of the owners and leads a strike for improved conditions and treatment.

A significant effort was made by the Production Code office and the mining industry to tone down the harsh treatment of miners and the violent potential of workers in the movie. An early working version of the script was entitled "Black Hell" and offered an even more critical perspective on working conditions in the mining industry. It was Joseph Breen who constantly admonished Warner Brothers to temper the portrayal of employer abuse and miner radicalism. In fact, he told Jack Warner to exercise care so that "excessive brutality" was not shown between the Coal and Iron Police, who were employed by the company, and the striking miners. Breen had some personal knowledge of affairs in the coal fields and believed that over time miners had actually caused more damage than was depicted in the movie itself. He was now concerned that audiences not see these men initiating widespread unrest and damage against company property, and Warner Brothers did rework some of the script in order to soften the indictment of labor conditions. Breen also insisted that the story suggest that despite problems in the mines, circumstances were improving. He did not want to make a hero of a workingman who won a strike by dynamiting a mine, although such a conclusion did remain a possibility in the final version.[33]

Despite the movie industry's sensibilities toward mine owners, the film offered audiences a number of glimpses into the serious issues that roamed the subconscious of real miners. The existence of unsafe conditions was duly noted as well as complaints that workers were forced to spend time on tasks for which they were not paid, like separating slate from coal. During a lunch conversation underground, one man explains that he has "been working around coal mines for years" and has never seen "conditions as bad as this." He criticizes company officials for not fairly weighing the cars when loaded, a complaint articulated in the real coal fields. The man claims that the company just assumes they are a bunch of "dumb hunkies," and he tells his colleagues that they will never get their "rights" unless they put up a fight. In giving cultural life to the idea of worker rights, this film actually eclipsed the "radical" implications of *Our Daily Bread*.

Like John Sims, however, Radek needs a woman. Early in the story he is clearly more interested in marrying his girlfriend, Anna, and eventually buying a farm than in fighting for worker rights. The woman is not enthusiastic, however, about his heavy drinking and the prospect of farm life. Unknown to the miner, she has started a relationship with a member of the dreaded Coal and Iron Police, a group hired by companies to protect their property and break strikes. She has even convinced the object of her affections to take her from the coal town so that she will not become "another worn out miner's wife pinching and starving, trying to raise a bunch of kids." When she leaves Radek and flees to Pittsburgh, the jilted miner resumes his heavy drinking. Ironically, because he now has more time on his hands and is not completely sober, he finds himself in a union meeting one night calling on the men to challenge a union leader who has told them that conditions are not as bad as they believe.

Ultimately, the film tries to locate the impetus for insurgent action on the part of the men in the activities of outside agitators or labor racketeers who want to foment a strike only to create a pretext for the owners to bring in security forces to suppress an authentic union movement. This narrative ploy offered some consolation to people like Breen who did not want to blame conditions for fomenting unrest. But it is still clear that the men are upset over workplace issues and their treatment; when strikebreakers are brought into the town, the entire working-class community erupts in a riot. Police push back protestors, and the owners, declaring that a no-strike pledge had been broken and the existing labor contract nullified, start to evict families from company houses and close the mines. A brief but effective scene of families being evicted from company houses only serves to reinforce the idea that capitalists too—not just the racketeers—have contributed to the emergence of class conflict.

Now radicalized by the killing of a friend by the security police and the return of Anna, Radek takes matters into his own hands to help his class and win the approval of the woman he loves. Interestingly, promotional materials sent by Warner Brothers to theater owners tied Radek's actions mostly to the influence of Anna. "Her kiss unchained a Hell of Horrors 1000 feet below the earth," one studio poster proclaimed. Sud-

Joe Radek—third from right, front row—leads angry miners in protest in *Black Fury* (1935). Radek, played by Paul Muni, was a flawed individual but still managed to gain concessions for his fellow toilers. Credit: Film Still Archives, Museum of Modern Art, New York

denly the genial immigrant with a drinking problem has become a union leader capable of inducing others to fight for improved conditions and a more democratic way of life.

Some historians have interpreted this film as an effort to "strip the labor issue of its socioeconomic rationale and complexity and personalize it." The *Daily Worker* even complained that Radek seemed "slow-witted" and that labor's potential for "organized action" was hidden behind all the attention paid to one man. Certainly there were instances in the story when Radek appeared to be less than heroic. Yet at the moment he becomes a union militant, it is also clear that this angry man feels strongly about others in his community and the way they are treated by powerful capitalists—so strongly that he takes the law into his own hands. Conservative censors could not prevail in this negotiated social text of the thirties. [34]

Eschewing collective bargaining and deference to the laws of private property, the emotional Radek devises a bizarre plot to end the conflict by entering the mine with explosives and threatening to blow it up if the

dispute is not resolved. Some call him a "crazy hunkey," especially because his plan promises to end the men's source of income, but Anna
expresses pride in him, and the owners capitulate to the demands of the
men. Radek embraces her at the end and—since the cause of a workingmen's democracy has been furthered—now thinks of moving the two of
them to a farm.

In *Riff Raff* (1935) Dutch Miller, a tuna fisherman in California, seems
to be as content with his ordinary life as Joe Radek had once been. Miller
shows no attachment to the entrepreneurial spirit as a means to move
upward as did gangsters, boxers, or even truck drivers in the movie *They
Drive by Night* (1940). He also appears disinterested in unions or reform.
When a "red" attempts to push local fishermen into a wildcat strike in
order to get higher pay for their catch, the reactionary head of a local
union urges Miller to warn the men against such action for fear of rup-
turing an existing contract with a cannery. An illegal strike action would
also allow the owner to bring "scabs" who work for lower wages into the
town. Miller, who is portrayed as a natural-born leader of men, asks the
agitator if he thinks he is in Russia and then pushes him off the dock. He
then turns to a group of his peers and reminds them that "when we was
kids we used to fight like wildcats, but if an outside gang came in, we
stuck together and threw them out," a point that resists the growing idea
of industrial unions in society at the time.

Like Blake, Radek, and Sims, in his natural state Miller has little interest in militant action or even radical ideology. Blake was moved to action
by the realization that his father had suffered injustice; Radek was angered by the violence of the company police. Miller comes to militancy
when the owner of the cannery attempts to intrude on his dancing with
the woman he loves. Driven by a sense of personal outrage, he mobilizes
a strike for higher pay. The men grow anxious about what they are doing,
however, and vote Miller out of his leadership role. Dejected, he leaves
the woman who cares for him and his fellow fishermen, and wanders off
to a hobo camp, telling another tramp, "You and me are not going to pull
off no revolution."

At the end, Miller does return to his village, but mostly to help his
wife, who has stolen money to help him and has ended up destitute and
in jail. When he takes up his role as breadwinner and union member again,
stability is restored in both his life and that of his spouse. There are elements of the New Deal and CIO democracy in this ending, but clearly it
tempered labor militancy by allowing worker stability and happiness to
turn on the restoration of the patriarchal household without aggressive

labor action. In fact, the reconciliation of husband and wife—something that was also important to *Our Daily Bread*—was an important part of "reel politics" in the thirties. Women often served as symbolic forces who could regulate men and coerce them into following conventional roles. Miller's wife, played by Jean Harlow, is certainly upset with men who do not meet the standard of the breadwinner ideal. Thus, when she marries Miller, she is elated by the union and the opportunity to acquire consumer goods like a small house and electric ice box on the installment plan. In fact, she has feared his leading role in a strike action mostly because she thought it would undermine their domestic stability. At the film's end their future as man and wife is certainly restored, and, to an extent, it met the conservative desires of censors interested in containing male and female sexuality.

But this film was more than a simplistic effort to read labor protest as an obstacle to domestic stability. It was clear from both *Riff Raff* and *Black Fury* that unstable conditions in the work lives of common men were also a threat to the stability of society itself. This was very much a critique of capitalists who remained indifferent to the desires for some measure of working-class democracy.

## FEMALE MOBILITY

Hollywood did a better job than the New Deal or the CIO in acknowledging the outlook of women in American society during hard times. It was not unusual to see female characters placed in supportive roles and charged with ensuring that the goals of the New Deal and the CIO for traditional families with strong mothers and breadwinning fathers were met. That is why countless films portrayed female love and support as a necessary ingredient in a man's quest for success or stability. Sometimes, as in *Three on a Match* (1932), women were severely punished for their failure to meet conventional expectations to be supportive wives and good mothers. Yet in films where the protagonist was a common woman, instead of a gangster, boxer, or coal miner, female agency was cast in a decidedly individualistic or liberal direction. In some instances, such as the "fallen women" films of the early thirties, females ignored moral conventions to gain love and security. In other cases, they simply found a man to marry who could offer them a better life. Whether they adhered to moral standards or not, however, they almost always reminded audiences of two fundamental points: there was no future worth living in the working class, and the path to upward mobility invariably depended on a man.

This female frame on social reality, so central to the rising popularity of mass culture, was somewhat indifferent to the political outlooks of both the left and the right. Films featuring female proletarians had little to say about labor militancy or were at odds with the more conservative dream of morally reforming the lower orders. The political problem for women usually had something to do with men and with their own desires. Thus, both labor radicalism and conservative morals as approaches to the problems of proletarian life are explicitly discredited in a film like *Street Scene* (1931). In this melodrama a mean and insensitive man forces his wife to find love in the arms of another man and then murders the adulterous couple. Life in this city neighborhood is framed entirely by the passions and dreams of the individual; a larger political and economic world is merely background. For women this meant that they were often reduced to using the only resources they had—their bodies—to escape poverty and deprivation. Bergman considered the "fallen women" movies of the 1930s the obverse of the gangster film. Women tried to get ahead through sex rather than violence. He also noticed, however, that such women were not always punished, and he detected some softening in moral judgment by seeing instances where they were forgiven by the men in their lives, although such a convention would reinforce the idea that women were dependent on men for their happiness and, for that matter, for their absolution.[35]

Not all proletarian women could demonstrate their power as forcefully as Mae West did in *I'm No Angel* (1933) when, as a girl working in a carnival, she conquers men and tells a friend to "take all you can get and give as little as possible." Yet female agency was extensively delineated in a story like *Baby Face* (1933), which delved into the plight of a working-class girl. Barbara Stanwyck played Lilly Powers, a young woman living in a wretched family in the industrial town of Erie, Pennsylvania. Powers begins and ends this story in a proletarian world that is depicted as mean, violent, and utterly lacking in a satisfying future. Warner Brothers, in fact, consciously attempted to make scenes of Erie and its mills seem "oppressive." This world was not only a place from which any reasonable person would want to flee, but it was populated by blue-collar men who were beyond redemption and the appeal of liberalism or democracy. These were cruel individuals who had no concern for the welfare of women at all. This story offered audiences not only the image of the "fallen woman" but also one of the blue collar brute that would serve as an influential image in the representations of workingmen in the post-war era.[36]

As a young girl, Powers has to work for her father, who runs a speakeasy. This man not only expects his daughter to put in long hours waiting on tables, but he forces her to have sex with local politicians who allow him to run an illicit tavern business in return. Eventually she rebels against her father, her condition, and her place in society. "Yeah, I'm the tramp and who's to blame. My father. A swell start you gave me," she tells him. "Nothing but men, dirty rotten men. I'll hate you for as long as I live."

The character of the corrupt and abusive father, of course, exonerates the woman's subsequent descent into immoral sexual behavior. In this story the female does not really fall but is literally pushed into a life of sexual indiscretion. Production decisions at Warner Brothers led to a story logic in which female immorality was prompted by "low-down characters of the mining town."[37] This victimized woman of the lower classes is forced to strike out on her own and abandon a man and a class that is

Barbara Stanwyck as Lilly Powers in *Baby Face* (1933) represented many women who dreamed of fleeing their lives in the working-class. Credit: Film Still Archives, Museum of Modern Art, New York

indifferent to her well-being. Accompanied by an African-American girl-friend, she heads for New York City where she discovers that she can earn money and status by sleeping with men who run a large bank. Using her body like a lowborn boxer, she fights her way to the top of the corporate hierarchy and eventually finds a life of luxury in Paris as the wife of the debonair head of a large financial institution. When his bank suffers from mismanagement and reaches the brink of bankruptcy, Powers' spouse asked her to give back much of the wealth she has amassed in order to bail out the bank. At first she sees his request as frightening, an act that would send her back to the deprivation she had known in Erie. In the end, however, she decides to secure the love of a man rather than the riches of the world. It would be hard to say she was actually punished for her moral transgressions—certainly not in the way the gangster or boxer often was. She enjoyed a rich lifestyle for a time. And at the film's end, living in an industrial town again, she might regret her loss of wealth, but she still has the love of her spouse and is free of the cruelty of her father. In *Baby Face*, liberalism had its rewards.

Censors were greatly concerned over many aspects of this story during its production, but ultimately they were unable to eliminate the powerful implications that individual desire and illicit sexual activity actually resulted in some advantages. Some in the code office were placated by the fact that many of the men in the film that had affairs with Lilly Powers came to destructive ends. One lost his job and another shot himself. The code office was also able to temper but not eradicate the portrayal of illicit sex, an indication that these narratives were products of a complex set of negotiations and not simply what one studio or segment of society wanted. In fact, in the story Powers is cautioned at one point by an old man that there is a right way and a wrong way to get what you want in life and that "the price of the wrong way is too great." To enforce this point, the censors argued for (and received) some sign that Powers could not retain the wealth she had accumulated from her sexual undertakings. Even with this ending, censors continued to worry that Powers had not been punished sufficiently for her "brazen" method of using men for financial gain. Darryl Zanuck of Warner Brothers, the studio which produced the feature, told industry officials he only made films like *Baby Face* because he had to meet the competition by other studios; he also indicated that his sales manager argued that at least 20 percent of Warner movies had to be "women's pictures, which inevitably means sex pictures." Zanuck's point suggested that such films were not only the result of negotiations with moral authorities but with audience desires as well.[38]

*Marked Woman* (1937) presented another story of working-class women trying to find a place in society that offered greater rewards and opportunities outside customary gender roles. Violent men and limited economic opportunities plague Mary Dwight, a character played by Bette Davis, as she tries to make a living as a dancer for hire in a nightclub. The club owner, Johnny Vanning, often resorts to violence to keep women like Dwight from leaving. The story makes it clear, however, that the women have concluded that life in the club under the dominance of man like Vanning, who is involved in a number of shady operations, is still better than anything they could find in local factories or in proletarian marriages.

Like Lilly Powers, women in this film appear to be victims rather than simply moral transgressors. This sense of oppression is intensified when Dwight's sister is killed by Vanning for rejecting the sexual advances of one of his men and Dwight herself is hurt by one of the mobsters. Movie censors actually worried more about the portrayal of brutality toward women than about any other aspect of this film, an indication that they were not simply intent on constraining the behavior of females. Warner Brothers worked against the attempt to soften the presentation of violence by telling theater owners in its press books to place radio advertisements for the movie directly following reports on crime "in order to exploit its realism." One studio suggestion even encouraged operators to promote the film to local women's clubs and let them know they could see "a side of life you've never known."[39]

In the end, the women in the club prove strong enough to resist their abuse. They take Vanning and his cronies to court and offer testimony that sends them to prison. Legal officials praise them for doing what people in even higher social stations had failed to do: contest the power of the mob. In a sense, the females reclaim at the end some of the moral ground they lost whey they abandoned motherhood for the seedier side of life. Yet this alone does not ensure them a rewarding future. As they walk off into a foggy city in the final scene, audiences cannot tell if they will ever find domestic happiness, wealth, family, or freedom from hurtful males. Their future is as uncertain as that of everyone who watched them.[40]

A woman faced with the necessity of adopting accepted roles such as mother or wife was still faced with the need to display individual resourcefulness in a world where her future was contingent on the decisions of men rather than on the realizations of political visions in society. Three film characters who faced this challenge were Alice Adams, Jessie Cassidy, and Stella Dallas.

Actress Katharine Hepburn played the title role in *Alice Adams* (1935), a story of a young woman growing up in a modest home in a small town in Indiana. RKO, the studio that produced the feature, made every effort to promote the tale as representative of all females who shared the same social position. Previews claimed that Adams was an "ambitious small town girl who longs for the attention of men and the luxuries enjoyed by the more fortunate girls of her acquaintance but is thwarted by a shabby home and lack of money." Publicity for the film stressed how Adams lived in "social obscurity" and became a "young social climber" who "battled poverty and social obscurity." Censors saw nothing wrong with depictions of working-class life as "shabby" and as a site people would want to flee rather than reform. But they did insist that Hepburn's body be "fully covered" as she sought to move up.[41]

Alice's mother wants much more in life for her daughter than her spouse, Virgil, can provide. This common man is not "forgotten" but is ridiculed for his failure to be a better provider. His wife holds him directly responsible, in fact, for failing to give Alice the type of wardrobe she needs to attract more affluent suitors. At one point she screams that others in his company have managed to move "right up the ladder of success" while he has remained an ordinary clerk. His daughter reaffirms this critique by expressing shame at having to go to a party at the home of the town's leading citizen in the family's old car.

In a desperate attempt to move up through marriage, Alice finally invites one of the town's wealthiest bachelors to her home for dinner. The Adams family is unpracticed in the ways of sophisticated society, however, and the entire dinner scene manages to evoke not only humor but pathos for common people and the shame they come to feel for who they are and where they stand in the class structure of America. Alice's mother goes so far as to hire an African-American maid for the evening, and the entire affair is bungled by these unrefined folks who see no other way of helping their daughter get ahead. In Booth Tarkington's 1921 novel, Alice Adams fails to win the love of the man she wants and is forced to go to business school and become a mere secretary. But Depression-era audiences were treated more kindly. In the film, Hepburn's character succeeds at love and upward mobility. In addition, her father is able to strike a business deal that suggests he will net a handsome profit. *Variety* claimed that the movie would allow "Mr. and Mrs. Joe Audience" to "hold up the mirror of reality." But surely there were numerous facts of existence in the lives of working-class women and families that did not find their way into this one story.

In the 1937 feature *Mannequin*, Jessie Cassidy's proletarian world seems bleaker than that of Alice Adams, but her desire to escape it is no less real. Cassidy, played by Joan Crawford, punches a time clock in a garment shop on the lower east side of Manhattan. The film reproduces the sounds of factory whistles and the crying of babies in the hallways of crowded tenements that were familiar to many who watched it. And life for women is oppressive. At work the young woman endures the heat of the shop floor with dreams of green fields and flowers. At her crowded family apartment, her mother toils away, cooking and cleaning, and the place is plagued by leaky faucets, dirt, and foul smells. "Maybe I should want to spend the rest of my days in beautiful Hester Street," Cassidy told her mother, "[but] I hate it. I'm gonna get out."

With her father and brother not working much, Cassidy decides to flee by marrying a small-time fight promoter named Eddie, who insists she stay home and allow him to earn the "cakes." When Eddie experiences financial setbacks due to his penchant for gambling, Crawford's character ignores moral conventions and leaves him, becoming involved with a wealthy businessman and planning to become more self-sufficient. In fact, she abandons Eddie with her mother's blessing. The old woman tells her that Eddie reminds her of Cassidy's father and tells her to "live your life for yourself" and to remember how much she hated being poor. Eventually Cassidy is able to get work as a fashion model and leave audiences with the impression that she will be able to take care of herself.

*Stella Dallas* (1937) continued the cultural assault on the idea of a future for women in the working class. This melodramatic tale evoked familiar pictures of authoritarian fathers and downcast mothers beaten down by years of household drudgery in a New England town. Like other women of her age and class, Dallas dreams, not of political reform or moral growth, but of breaking away any way she can. She takes a business course in the hope of getting a decent job but is unable to make financial headway until she meets a prosperous man named Steven Dallas. During a brief romance that leads to marriage, she tells him that she detests who she is and wants to be "like all the people you have been around."

Enamored with her new life—a fine home, membership at a country club, and a daughter—Dallas can not bring herself to move to New York with her spouse for the sake of his career. The price she pays for failing to sacrifice her own interests, however, is steep. Apart from her husband, she no longer gains acceptance from town elites, and eventually her marriage falls apart when Steven marries a woman from the upper classes. In an act of maternal love, she decides to relinquish her role as a mother and send her daughter to live with her father, where she can gain advantages only he can provide.

Over time Dallas—due to her own actions—has lost the benefits of being a supportive wife and mother. When her daughter marries, she is reduced to the role of a spectator, no longer an integral part of the young girl's life. Many observers have seen this story as one in which a woman is punished for her inability to meet roles traditionally expected of women. But the entire story can also be read as an unsympathetic attack on working people who were incapable of making the transition to a middle-class lifestyle where professional needs and social respect depended on one's ability to manage emotional drives and meet obligations.

In the real world of the New Deal and the CIO, women were basically denied active participation in political and economic reform movements. In the Hollywood film, they were allowed to explore a wider range of options beyond simply those as mothers or supportive spouses. In *Gold Diggers of 1933*, lowborn women attempt to find financial stability on their own during hard times by becoming performers on Broadway. One of the girls is the daughter of a mailman, and another is the offspring of a saloon keeper and "a woman who took in washing." When the show in which they are working is threatened with closure, the women realize that they have almost no means of support. Their situation becomes desperate enough at one point that they are reduced to stealing just to buy milk to drink.

Salvation in this story comes in the form of a wealthy man, hardly an endorsement for female independence. Brad, the son of a rich Boston family, agrees to finance a new stage production of the Depression itself. The girls are overjoyed at the prospect of work, and Polly, the mailman's daughter, is smitten with feelings of affection for him. Brad's parents are outraged over the possibility of a union between their blue-blooded son and a lower-class girl whom some referred to as a "little gold digger." Dismissing threats of disinheritance, the young man proclaims his intention to surmount class barriers and marry Polly. Family lawyers sent to induce her to sever the relationship quickly succumb to the charms of other working-class girls in the show and conclude that they can not fault Brad in any way.

Audiences were left with ideas that class tensions were not inevitable and that women had to take advantage of any opportunity they found, including winning the affections of men who could support them. Democracy claimed some space near the feature's end when a big production number reminded moviegoers of the rights of American veterans, who still held claims on society in the early Depression. Beyond the individual striving of the women, there was the idea that obligations existed in society that had to be met. In some ways the wealthy helped those in need in the story, and in the song "The Forgotten Man," audiences saw that unemployment was unacceptable for the warriors of World War I. It was also detrimental to the interests of women, who depended on male support. With depictions of men standing in bread lines and somber women without male companions, the Depression was clearly represented as a threat to a larger community of citizens with obligations and responsibilities to each other. No doubt the tone of this presentation constituted an affirmation of patriarchy as the standard form of gender relations, but it also exposed a broader and more democratic version of society than was normally displayed in features like *Street Scene*, *Baby Face*, or, for that matter, *Public Enemy*.

## CAPRA AND THE PEOPLE

The need to build a democratic community of equal citizens in America was a point seldom stated in unambiguous terms in the films of the thirties. In part, this issue could command little attention in features fixated on liberalism and on the promises and pitfalls of the individual's fate. The image of the "forgotten man" did call to mind some idea of a national community with a reciprocal set of obligations, and the continuing criticism of liberal capitalism supported a social logic from which democratic visions could be fashioned. To be sure, all of this was usually embedded in narratives filled with a complex array of objectives that included the moral reform of the individual and the portrayal of the delights of self-gratification. But democracy was still asserted in various forms through the features of the decade. In a 1934 film like *Judge Priest*, starring Will Rogers, pleas were sometimes made for racial tolerance and understanding. More frequently, democracy was represented metaphorically in stories that stressed the necessity for gender and class cooperation as preferable to relationships in which one side held inordinate power over the other. This was certainly the point of John Ford's 1939 movie, *Stagecoach*, although explicit demands that females or workingmen assume positions of leadership in public life were hard to find. And the closer American society moved toward World War II, the more the definition of democracy came to resemble anything American that opposed the totalitarian images emanating from Europe.

Despite the fact that elites were frequently ridiculed in films and elements of democracy endorsed, much ambiguity existed in the culture over the capacity of common people to lead any political movement. Some of this is evident in films like *Stella Dallas* or *Public Enemy* in which lowborn women and men have a difficult time regulating their passions. Where leaders do emerge from the ranks, as in *Black Fury*, they appear to be disinterested in sustaining any sort of political action, and they are happy to return to everyday life as quickly as they can. Some films made warnings against putting too much control into the hands of the masses, who were seen as easily misled by unruly emotions or anti-democratic inclinations. For instance, in *Fury* (1936), a mob in a small American town throw out the tenets of the law and burn a jail housing an alleged kidnapper. Originally titled *Mob Rule*, this story offers images of common men and women in the American heartland willing to abandon democratic procedures in an instant. Censors had cautioned the film's producers not to portray law enforcement officials "unfairly" for their unwillingness to stave off the mob. They made no mention of the producer's effort to portray ordinary folks as individuals with evil in their hearts. Similarly, in *Black Legion* (1937), a worker upset over the loss of a promotion in a factory in Michigan joins a hate group of native-born Americans to murder the individual (from a foreign-born family) who got the job he wanted. Warner Brothers claimed that it was the "duty" of every American to see this drama drawn from real contemporary news accounts as a way of protecting "Liberty and the Pursuit of Happiness." Yet it was also evident in both of these films that there were limits to how much liberty the mass of common Americans could handle.[42]

Director Frank Capra took up the challenge of reviewing the need for a democratic society in the thirties even as he articulated some doubt about the merits of popular rule. He offered almost no support for working-class political mobilizations or the New Deal, but he did manage to present solutions to the problems of inequality and hard times in thirties America that reinforced democratic longings in his audience. His suggestions generally included virtuous leaders who often came from the middle classes and the affirmation of an ideal of neighborliness that pulled all sorts of people together into cooperative efforts to resist greed and injustice. His politics was rooted more in a premodern vision of a small town or community and less in the large bureaucratic organizations like labor unions or government. His critics have claimed that his populist visions and dreams of peaceful mobilizations merely served to blunt a true understanding of the complexities of modern life and the idea of class conflict. Certainly his veneration of individual leaders like Jefferson Smith (*Mr. Smith Goes to Washington*) and Longfellow Deeds (*Mr. Deeds Goes to Town*) appeared to be devoid of specific class sensibilities or coherent political agendas. And yet his films were among the most "socially aware films" of the thirties and forties for their refusal to abandon the question of the fate of the larger political community or to enshrine liberalism over democracy at all costs. He never succumbed completely to the temptation to meditate simply on the fate of individuals (although this was something that interested him a great deal), and he seldom failed to point out the faults of capitalism and the need to make it just and fair. Moreover, his plea for class reconciliation—or "getting together and working things out"—appeared to reflect a very strong desire on the part of many people in the audience itself.[43]

Capra's film politics were the quintessential politics of American mass culture. That is to say, they were imprecise speculations that seeped over and around conventional boundaries like class and gender rather than explicit polemics designed to serve either the upper or lower classes. Like most other films studied here, they occupied a common ground that raised as many questions as they answered. They vacillated constantly between extremes of liberalism and democracy, and considered the fate of the individual in the context of both ideals. For a long time they supported the hope that the future could still be better than the past or the present—that social problems could be solved. To say this is not to ignore their bias against the concept of labor radicalism or their preference for strong male leaders from the middle class. None of Capra's heroes and heroines ever wanted to actually end up in the lower classes, although a wealthy woman in *It Happened One Night* (1934) thought for a time that common people had more contentment in their lives. Avoiding powerful displays of factionalism, he blended various viewpoints as effectively as the CIO or Roosevelt himself.

Because Capra's narratives contained a mix of political positions, they have elicited contrasting interpretations. Lee Lourdeaux saw Capra's subjective position influenced by his Italian immigrant heritage and his desire to merge ethnic cooperativeness and American individualism. Unlike a number of émigré directors in Hollywood at the time, Capra's formative years were not spent in an environment of social disorder and growing despair. Rather, he lived within the confines of a warm Italian-American family in Los Angeles. For Lourdeaux, this meant that Capra wanted both to assimilate and become a successful person and still to affirm "communal values and family scenes" he had experienced during his childhood. Lourdeaux disagreed with critics who saw Capra's films as simple retreats into a sentimental version of the American past. He reasoned, instead, that his movies attempted to hold together ideals of individual uplift and social cooperation; various classes and religions would find common ground here. In a sense, we might add that there was hope in these features that liberalism and democracy could remain allied.[44]

Raymond Carney saw Capra differently. Instead of an effort at harmonizing ideals of personal striving and communalism, he thought that ultimately Capra films mounted a strident defense of individualism. In many of these stories, characters become embedded in highly articulated societies and never completely escaped their attachments to them. The issue for Carney is that they frequently expressed a desire to be free of their place in social arrangements and often criticized or questioned them. Carney saw in Capra an impulse to create new forms of individualism or at least new relationships between the self and society; it was a form of "romanticism" that was "truly democratic" because it imagined that ordinary people could break free of conventional roles and identities and express themselves "anew in the world." Carney does acknowledge, however, that this demonstration of individualism was usually made through social action directed toward the national or common good, an indication that Capra may have thought that there should be some limits to being a singular person.[45]

Capra's own project at self-realization stood behind much of his creative endeavors. He frequently expressed appreciation for the support his family had given him but was seldom inclined to seek redress for those who shared his lowly origins. "I hated being poor," he said at the beginning of his autobiography. "I hated being a scrounging news kid trapped in the sleazy Sicilian ghetto of Los Angeles." His desires were similar to views articulated in hundreds of films: the best response to life in the working class was escape, not reform. If some of his biographers are to be believed, he may have developed a feeling of contempt over time both for his ethnic heritage and for those among the lowborn who had failed to pull themselves out of poverty as he had. When he had amassed a considerable amount of wealth, he even harbored a deep suspicion of Democratic reformers who wanted to increase taxes on the income he had earned. He was realistic enough to see, however, that audiences could be attracted by the defense of ideas he may have found personally disagreeable.[46]

Capra's political blend of individualism and cooperation were evident enough, as long as one understands that the central protagonists in most of his stories were middle-class men who worked assiduously for a more just community even as they undertook their own projects of self-realization. The sort of heroic individual who stood at the heart of his political vision, however, did not appear to exist within the working classes. In Capra films, "the people" remained a mass of reasonably good citizens who could be led in a number of political directions. For him the path to a more democratic community was ultimately not in the hands of common people themselves but in the hands of the right kind of leader. Thus, in the film *American Madness* (1932), it is a banker with democratic leanings, Tom Dickson, who contests selfish and greedy capitalists who sit on the bank board. Dickson seeks to restore customer confidence and limit the insensitive views of elites by fighting for loans that could put more money into the hands of average people who would use them to buy homes and spend the nation out of the Depression.

Longfellow Deeds (*Mr. Deeds Goes to Town*) was another of Capra's middle-class luminaries able to challenge economic elites who threatened to destroy the American social fabric. The director situated Deeds in the small town of Mandrake Falls, "where no hardship ever befalls." The mere invocation of the small community—and not the city—signaled audiences that the stories and images they were watching were tied to the larger discussion of a just and fair nation and the fear that the fate of a democratic community could no longer be taken for granted.

Deeds is a fortunate man who has inherited millions of dollars. Unlike his selfish lawyers, who try to gain access to his funds, he wants only to redistribute his wealth and pursue whatever interests him in his hometown. In a very real way, his vision of a more democratic and less competitive America comes closer to what historian Gary Gerstle might call "working-class Americanism." When Deeds visits New York and nationally significant sites like Grant's Tomb and the Statue of Liberty, Capra's text tends to reject completely the association between hyper-individualism and true Americanism that had dominated the twenties.[47]

Deeds exhibits unlimited faith in America. He tells a female reporter who is intent upon getting a good story from him how impressed he is with Grant's rise from an Ohio farm to the presidency and Lincoln's achievement in creating a "new nation" by winning the Civil War. Deeds' interest in Grant, in this case, causes the woman to reflect on her own life and her childhood in a "beautiful small town with a row of popular trees along Main Street that always smell as if they had a bath." As FDR did, Capra persistently linked personal memory and national history in a way that was designed to sustain the belief that a democratic republic

could be saved during the thirties. Eventually Deeds returns to his hometown, where he launches his plan to help fellow citizens. His approach
rests, however, not on unionism or government programs, but on individualism. Instead of rights to collective bargaining or social security, he
gives people land they can work themselves and transform into a source
of economic stability. Both Deeds and Capra realized that a simple retreat
to a preindustrial past would not solve the problems of modern times. Yet
the story also demonstrated that personal striving alone would not pull
people out of the Depression; dramatic acts of kindness by those with
political or economic power were also needed. If this was not the New
Deal or the CIO, it was also not some blind yearning for a Jeffersonian
vision of America.

Capra continued to probe the fate of individuals and society in his immensely popular films. In *Mr. Smith Goes to Washington*, democracy
was saved again by a middle-class male from outside the city. Smith,
played by Jimmy Stewart, lives in a western state and is inherently compassionate, devoting much of his time to the welfare of young people. His
concern for others is matched by his love for his country. When he arrives
in Washington as a new senator, he climbs the steps of the Lincoln
Memorial and reads (along with the audience) an inscription on the monument that says the sixteenth president is "enshrined forever" in our
memories because he saved the nation from destruction. The message
that the nation had survived hardship before was loud and clear and was
found in countless other cultural expressions of the decade.

Smith's attachment to democratic institutions and ideals is severely
tested by special interests that dominated the Senate. Like Deeds, Dickson, and even Roosevelt, he takes up the cause to contest powerful elites.
The Lincoln-like Smith attempts to stop developers in his state who
want to use federal funds to build a dam that would increase the value of
their property holdings. Smith wants to save the acreage for public purposes, specifically as a camp where young boys would learn about American democratic principles. The senior senator from Smith's home state
cautions the young politician that Congress is a "man's world" where
"you have to check your ideas at the door." But the newly arrived crusader for fair practices, with the support of a woman who loves him and
eager youth from throughout the nation, defies partisan interests that
threaten democracy. His girlfriend tells him that he should not submit to
the greedy developers and that the nation needs his "sense of common
rightness." As Smith ponders again the words on the Lincoln Memorial
about government of the people, by the people, and for the people, he

decides to mount a filibuster to prevent the "dam" bill from coming up for a vote. Newspapers back home, allied with political bosses, suppress news of what he is doing in Congress. But a youthful cadre of supporters circumvents the censorship of the press and spreads the word themselves of his heroic quest. As one might expect, Capra expressed the belief that elites could be contained and that democracy and goodness could prevail over the illiberal tendencies of men in power.

In *Meet John Doe* (1941) Capra again took up the issue of a democratic society, although by this time many Americans saw the dangers to representative government to be external rather than internal. Again the best insurance "the people" had for a democratic future resided not in union or partisan politics but in the leadership of a fair-minded hero. Ironically, although Capra thought the economic problems of the nation were largely in the past by 1941, he made a film with a hero more distinctly working class in background and with language that was more explicitly critical of capitalism than was normally his pattern. Warner Brothers extended this celebration of the common man—now that the Depression was subsiding—by encouraging theater owners to offer a number of promotions intended to honor the average American. In San Francisco, operators invited residents with the last name of Doe to attend a party at a local hotel. In Los Angeles, a man named John Aye won a contest as the "average John Doe sports fan." The rationale for the contest was that the average fans usually got the poorest seats at sporting events but were the most loyal to their team. Aye was invited to a banquet where he was able to meet a number of sports celebrities.[48]

The film suggested, as did *The Cabin in the Cotton* and *Our Daily Bread*, that an undistinguished man could lead a movement for a democracy. First, however, he needed the imagination and support of a female. In this case, an enterprising news reporter, fighting hard to hold onto a job during hard times, hatches the idea of writing articles about a fictitious man who is contemplating suicide over his own unemployment and over the level of unfairness and greed in the world. When the newspaper is forced to offer a public version of John Doe, they select a former baseball player named John Willoughby—a typical American—who quickly becomes emblematic of all people in need. In a series of radio addresses, Doe gains a wide following by playing on public fears of war in Europe and inequality at home. He tells Americans that "free people can beat the world at anything from war to tiddlywinks if we all pull together in the same direction." But Doe realizes that the people are more likely to defend a nation they perceive to be just and caring. Consequently, he reminds them that the "guy next door" is their teammate. "If he's hungry feed him. If he's out of a job find him one . . . tear down the fence that separates you and you'll tear down a lot of hates and prejudices." The CIO, the Popular Front, and most of Hollywood never made a more explicit appeal for a moral community.

In this narrative, Doe's message of social harmony and collective responsibility are subverted, not by greedy capitalists or radical workers, but by unsavory men who long to establish a fascist dictatorship in America. Democracy is now threatened not by liberalism but by illiberalism. D. B. Norton is the disagreeable and aspiring right-wing dictator who dreams of an ordered society and surrounds himself with his own paramilitary forces. But Doe, the natural-born democrat and liberal, is the one to confront such treachery. Again, Capra's hero, like most movie heroes, needs the encouragement of a woman. With the love of Ann Mitchell and her argument that democracy is worth the fight ringing in his ears, Doe leads a grassroots movement of citizens that eventually destroys Norton and saves the day for government by the people.

## FINALLY THE FAMILY

The Depression created considerable anxiety about the survival of the American family, especially in its traditional form. This is why, in part, the New Deal and the CIO exerted so much effort to restore the status of the male wage earner. Certainly there were elements of this dream in many films, especially the notion of female support as a key to male confidence and success. And both Hollywood and the New Deal did not hesitate to debunk the glories of unfettered capitalism. By now it should be clear, however, that few of the features paying attention to plebeian life explored family life extensively. The interest of lower-class family members in seeking personal desires was made plain, but full explorations of the impact of hard times on family life were the exception rather than the rule.

A family frame on social reality stood somewhere between the extreme liberal meditations of the gangster film and the broad architecture offered by Capra. In *The Grapes of Wrath* (1940) we finally see Hollywood coming to terms with the crisis of the American family and its place within a larger society of democratic and antidemocratic forces. When *Variety* reviewed the film, it claimed that John Steinbeck's novel "has lost none of its impact, none of its documentary frankness or biting irony and makes no concessions to possible censorious protest." The journal even thought the frankness of the film's portrayal of labor problems was unprecedented and that the tale of a family in trouble, "like the novel," offered no utopian or "cheap dramatic" solution.[49]

Actually the film, while essentially faithful to much of what Steinbeck wrote, did moderate in important ways some of his calls for sustaining the ideals of democracy and social justice. At the end of the novel, Tom Joad leaves his family and goes off to fight for a good society. "Wherever they's a fight so hungry people can eat," he tells his mother, "I'll be there." And his younger sister, Rose of Sharon, is left poignantly to breast-feed a starving man she does not know as the book closes. Her act left readers with the impression that the need to render kindness to strangers, to fulfill our obligations to other citizens, would be continuous.[50]

In the movie version, Joad does leave his family at some point before the finale to join a vaguely defined struggle against oppression. But movie producer Darryl Zanuck accepted the ending of screenwriter Nunnally Johnson that left out the more pronounced images of rendering kindness and fighting for justice. Film audiences watched as the mother-head of the Joad family, Ma Joad, tells her husband, now emasculated from years of deprivation and the loss of his breadwinner status, "Nobody wipes us out. Can't nobody lick us. We'll go on forever, Pa. We're the people." In this version an American family, under the leadership of its mother-head, promises to endure, to continue to look for low-paying farm work. No indication is given, however, that they will ever mobilize for any sort of concerted political action or even try to escape their lowly existence. Clearly, however, the somber mood of the film's ending served as powerful reminder that the Depression (and mass culture) had already significantly undercut political and cultural projects that had sought to deploy coherent narratives of progress and hope.[51]

In projecting the vast reality of the Depression onto the plight of one family, *The Grapes of Wrath* diluted the politics of the CIO without entirely denying some of its essential arguments. Concerns over the emasculation of breadwinners were repeated and incorporated into the portrait of "Pa" Joad. To identify a strong mother as a source of hope and strength, however, moved closer to the aspirations of females in the audience than of labor leaders. Unlike the characters in proletarian novels, moreover, the Joads are disoriented: they are unsure of what forces are responsible for hard times and what their future holds. The fact, as Charles Shindo has suggested, that they are a white, Protestant, American-born family allows them to attract considerable popular attention. If these emblems of common and sturdy American people could be destroyed in the land of opportunity, no one could feel safe or secure. Movie producers like Zanuck knew that a family story, rather than a tale of radical protestors, would generate more appeal. Yet there was no escaping another point that was quite revolutionary itself: America had betrayed some of its most loyal citizens—forgotten men and forgotten families—and had driven them into poverty and despair. This point, and the one that said that American capitalism was invariably unfair, reminded audiences that the films they watched during the Depression were far from being fanciful flights from the lives that they lived.[52]

Despite the uncertainty of the ending and the instincts of moviemakers to stay away from radical politics, this picture still offered a broad and sweeping indictment of capitalism and human nature in the United States. At every turn the dispossessed sharecroppers are defrauded and persecuted in the land of freedom and democracy. The point is repeatedly endlessly. They are pushed off the land in the "dust bowl" by their landlord; neighboring landowners want them gone. A bulldozer, representing large and impersonal economic institutions, tears down their home and helps to drive them to California. On their departure to the West, the traditional site of opportunity in American culture, Ma Joad engages in her own act of protest by burning a postcard image of the Statue of Liberty, a souvenir she has kept from the 1904 St. Louis World's Fair, which had commemorated dreams of national progress.

Instead of work and opportunity, the Joads find only hardship and maltreatment in California. Fellow migrants, who see them not as victims but only as competitors for the few jobs that are available, threaten to hurt them. The police side with capitalists and property owners. Some kindness for strangers is found at government-sponsored camps that take in migrants and offer a democratic experience by allowing them to share resources and cooperate in the running of the camps, but clearly the idea of participatory democracy is confined to these federal enclaves and excluded from vast stretches of the American terrain. Steinbeck had lived for at time in such facilities in order to see what they were like, and Zanuck even hired private detectives to investigate their conditions in order to learn if they were as inadequate as the novel said they were. Regardless of the level of comfort in the camps, both the book and the film admit that the larger world in which this American family moved was harsh and vicious. Old ideologies and institutions no longer served them well. The Joads could find little relief from American institutions and the neighborliness Capra had promised.

When Tom Joad is eventually driven to militancy, the movie's words come essentially from Steinbeck. He tells his mother, "I've been thinkin' about us too, about our people livin' like pigs, an' the good rich lan' layn' fallow. . . . And I've been wondering if all our folks got together and yelled." Ma Joad pleads for him not to fight back for fear he will be hurt. But the young man has now become a partisan, a defender of his class, and realizes that he must wage a battle on behalf of the dispossessed and not simply defend his family, despite his mother's appeal that he is needed at home to help the family from "cracking up."

In reality there are two endings to the story. One is articulated through the language of class conflict; the other addresses directly the private psychological realm of anxiety and doubt that pervaded varied components (and genders) of the mass audience. It transcended the coherent proletarianism of the times and is possibly why this film and many others were so popular. Films were attractive because they crossed the boundaries between organizational and personal outlooks, between dogmatism and disbelief. Michael Denning has described the existence of a radical, proletarian literary effort in California in the 1930s to foster massive strike efforts by farm workers, something from which both Steinbeck's novel and the Warner Brothers film departed. Denning also acknowledged that proletarian novels did not capture the attention of the nation the way a tale like *The Grapes of Wrath* did. Denning thought the appeal of this narrative was grounded partially in the fact that it spoke to very large questions like what caused the Depression, and partially to the fact that it "fused" many ideas or "populist rhetorics." It did all of this, but it did more. Like most blends of melodrama and realism, this film moved directly into the unsettled domain of the private as well as the public. Despite its discussion of democracy, its engagement with personal quandaries—like Ma Joad's reservations over her son's desire to fight for social justice—actually made it liberal, cognizant of individual and personal dilemmas. It also raised the question of the fate of the nation—something that concerned all citizens. In sixteenth-century England, the term "the people" usually referred to the rabble, or the lower orders. In the modern nation, it came to mean a broad mass of individuals invested with sovereignty. If "the people" were in trouble or, as some suggested, could not be trusted, the life of a democratic nation was in peril. When Americans went to the movies in the thirties and ruminated about the Depression, they worried not only about themselves but about their collective future in a national experiment that involved both democratic and liberal aspirations.[53]

# REACTIONS

Responses to films that explored the condition of common people in Depression-era America can be gauged to some extent from published reviews. Although critics seldom used the formal language of democracy or liberalism in their discussions, they still displayed democratic or liberal sensibilities. A survey of these appraisals in mainstream journals and newspapers cannot tell us the entire story of viewer reception, of course, but it does suggest something of how the tension between liberalism and democracy was perceived and received during the era of the Great Depression, and it suggests that film producers and members of the audience all participated in the same political discussion that had attracted the attention of the New Deal and the CIO. In other words, the strain between these two ideals was exposed in products of a mass culture that employed the aesthetics of realism and melodrama to simulate the social and emotional experience of the thirties. At times commentary leaned toward the aspirations of democracy; some movies were valued for the extent to which they explored the social or political context in which the individual struggled. More frequently critics found themselves evaluating the depictions of individual problems and feelings that were uppermost on people's minds. This more liberal perspective relegated traditional social and political frameworks to a background status. In films that thought out loud about the prospects for fulfilling personal desires, the plight of women figured prominently. Since the films studied here never really separated the conventions of social realism and melodrama, however, the contemporary analysis of them invariably merged political streams of consciousness and furthered the modern project of "disorientation" at a time when traditional politics was fixed more intently on the "realism" of the Depression.

Realism—like melodrama—was never a literal recreation of experience. It was selective in what it portrayed and was always historically specific. In the late nineteenth and early twentieth centuries, according to Amy Kaplan, it was often used in literature as a progressive force that exposed the harsh conditions of industrial society and offered some sympathy for the lower orders. In the early 1930s a radical organization like the short-lived Worker's Film and Photo League of America aspired to produce documentaries about human suffering and exploitation as a way of fighting what they felt to be "capitalist censorship" of feature films. It also was a notion by which many intellectuals criticized what they thought was an inclination by Hollywood and its customers to ignore democratic political issues and drift into the more feminine and emotional realm of melodrama. Thus, reviews of the film *Street Scene* often complained that the movie was focused so much on the "self-contained" worlds of its many individual characters that it failed to give a unified story of New York tenement life.[54]

Yet reviewers were never consistent. They were as capable of lauding democratic realism as they were liberal melodramas. This might be explained by Kaplan's point that the realist writers she studied were not simply driven by goals of social justice but were involved in a more intricate project of trying to figure out just how to represent reality in a period that was increasingly dominated not by class conflict but by mass culture and its assorted versions of society and culture. She declared that realists were often less concerned with the accuracy of portraying "the other half" and more with depicting an "interdependent society composed of competing and seemingly mutually exclusive realities." In a sense they were struggling as well with the proliferation of images and representations that mass culture now offered.[55]

There are two aspects to Kaplan's analysis that can be linked to mainstream movie reviews. First, there is a discussion about realism that can be found in a number of commentaries and that warrants our attention. Second, reviewers definitely appeared to be approving, on the whole, of a variety of political messages and images that were embedded in film narratives. That is to say, they were as likely to accept liberal as democratic versions of experience. Seldom, moreover, does one find in reviewer's reactions any sense of real moral outrage like the kind that could be found in censorship debates during production or in reform or religious groups who often reacted to films with hostility. Perhaps in the overall culture of the audience—fans and reviewers who reported to them—there was an implicit understanding that the political crossbreeding and moral ambiguity of these films' narratives was perfectly acceptable. To put it another way, both political and moral dogmas were in trouble in the narratives of mass culture not only because of the complexity of their meaning but also because of the willingness of the audience itself to accept such uncertainty.

Social realism in thirties culture was a movement that not only took up the discussion of the problems of the lower classes but often, by portraying their strength and dignity, sought to offer hope that these people could endure hard times. The documentary photographs of Dorothea Lange did this as did John Steinbeck's novel, *The Grapes of Wrath*.[56] Movie critics assumed that Hollywood veered from the realist path more often than not because of its desire to entertain and thus were encouraged when they saw what they felt were substantive treatments of social conditions. *The Nation* liked *Cabin in the Cotton* because it contrasted the vast gulf between the "ceaseless toil and squalor" of the tenants and the "ease and luxury" of the owners. The journal felt it was "a relief from the juvenile trivialities of the average Hollywood film." In another review, the same magazine affirmed the belief that Hollywood tended to avoid disturbing social scenes and explicit politics because it felt extreme forms of partisanship would hurt its box office and because it felt (and this revealed some disdain for critics who wanted realism toward the lower orders) that it had to appeal to the "least intelligent" level of its audience.[57]

Social realism was certainly a key way in which critics judged films that concentrated on a solitary workingman. Thus, in writing about *I Am a Fugitive* in the *New York Times*, Mordaunt Hall praised the film for its "vehement attack on convict camps" and for the fact that the "producers do not mince matters in this melodrama." This reviewer repeated the customary assumption that the mass audience did not really want such "vehement" depictions of social reality when he said that Hollywood did not bow to "popular appeal." To put it mildly, it was not (and is still not) possible to say with certainty that the mass audience generally desired only an escape from reality when they went to the theater. In the same newspaper, a reviewer criticized *Black Fury* for essentially taking a middle ground between those who would see labor walkouts as a powerful device that could improve conditions and those who were more critical of the viciousness of labor's police forces. Others noticed that "left wing" thinking was muted a bit too much by making villains out of outside agitators rather than the coal companies. Still, the review expressed a high degree of satisfaction that Hollywood had moved beyond its "commercial inhibitions" and made a "trenchant contribution to the sociological drama." Given the fact that the production had outraged several state censor boards, Andre Sennwald, the critic, felt Warner Brothers had "exhibited almost a reckless air of courage" in exhibiting the film at all. And a commentator in *Variety* liked the fact that the story was "provocative and attuned to a day and age when the administrative New Deal lends added significance to the story."[58]

It was left to a highly partisan publication like the *Daily Worker* to keep the focus of "realism" more directly on the question of the relations between labor and capital. The newspaper continually decried portrayals of radicals as misguided or "vile," demanded that capitalist exploitation of labor be revealed in its full scope, and expressed much regret when it was not. Nothing was guaranteed to evoke complaints about films from this newspaper more than images of workingmen who were meek, compliant, or disinterested in collective action. Thus, the journal praised pickets from union locals who protested showings of *Riff Raff* as a film that discredited the "ability, integrity, and intelligence" of "union labor." According to the *Daily Worker,* such protests reduced box office receipts considerably. Similarly, the news journal claimed "malignant purposes" were behind the production of *Black Fury.* It disliked the fact that Joe Radek was portrayed as "slow-witted" and that he was inclined to take individual rather than "organized action" to solve the miner's problem. It also said the film failed to recognize that there were legitimate grounds for militant protest in the coal fields, preferring to locate the source of the miner's problems in the action of a strike-breaking agency. Insightfully, the militant paper recognized that radicals in the film—and, for that matter, in *Heroes for Sale*—were now portrayed as rather meek "stool pigeons" and not the more threatening "bewhiskered Bolshevik agitators" that were seen a decade before.[59]

Commentary on social problem films had very little to say about transgressions of conventional moral standards, a hint that the quest for social realism was in part a challenge to the power and perspectives of moral authorities of the time. Their authors granted cultural preference to discourses over social problems rather than to ones over personal behavior. Thus, there was no decrying the possibility that Paul Muni in *Black Fury* would destroy private property by planning to blow up a mine or that he drank too much. In a review of *Dead End,* there was brief mention that the "salty street jargon" of the young characters had been had purged from a stage version of the story. But that point was unimportant. What mattered was that the film forced audiences to consider "the slum problem" and that it made "a prima facie case for a revision of the social system." Similarly, some reviewers saw *Our Daily Bread* as a "brilliant declaration of faith in the importance of the cinema as a social instrument" for its portrayal of "hungry and desperate men" struggling to find subsistence on a farm. The moral dimension of the story concerning the temptation of the male hero, John Sims, for another women was given only passing mention when the review noted the point about a "blond-headed siren" almost wrecking the "collectivist farm." But the story was praised for its ability to "bring the cinema squarely into the modern stream of socially-minded art" in the same way proletarian novelists of the decade had done. The radical *New Masses* was more cautious, claiming that the theme of the return to the land was merely an improbable idea and thus "escapist."[60]

It must be stressed that social realism, as Fredric Jameson has pointed out, is ultimately not possible in a pure sense, for it is ultimately only a form of representation itself; silences and distortions are both inevitable and pervasive. Thus, we could say that the gangster films of the early thirties depicted the life of the gangster with some degree of authenticity, but they also, to use Jameson's terminology, drained the working classes of their "subversive potential" by figuring them in the form of an assertive individual—the gangster—who eschewed the possibilities of class politics for the solitary pursuit of wealth. This silence or lack of "realism," however, was seldom mentioned in the assessments of critics who tended to treat these narratives of powerful and ambitious individuals approvingly. When it came to the gangster stories, critics generally embraced these displays of intense liberalism to an extent that made them forget the value of "social realism." One writer was enamored by the action and the "pugnaciousness" of the lead character in *Public Enemy* and unaffected by the moral issues raised by religious and social reformers. Another analysis of the film claimed that the story was "lowbrow material" with "highbrow workmanship" and rather liked the fact that "there was no lace" in the feature that was "raw and brutal with that brutality flying to the front in an uncouth boy's treatment of his women." Many reviews predicted moral outrage from some quarters but mostly a "flood of attendance" from moviegoers. A review of *Scarface* made similar points. Admitting there may be some moral concerns with the depiction of violent and criminal behavior, the writer claimed that the film represented "entertainment on an important scale" and that it would be as difficult to keep people away from theaters where it plays as it would be to keep them away from speakeasies.[61]

Among the most popular of the films discussed in this chapter, the gangster features devoted significant amounts of time to the greedy and killing instincts of individuals struggling to take all that they could. Seldom were they thought of as creatures of the streets, products of a harsh economic struggle. Rather, critics tended to focus their attention on the action and violence in the film—without censuring it—and on the gangster as an individual driven by emotions. Sometimes writers would ratify the hopes of the censors and indict the gangster for his criminal behavior and moral transgressions. One critic claimed that "terrible" crime movies were inevitable because they insured profits but hoped that if enough people saw them, they would become angry enough to do some-thing about the problem of crime. More often, however, the point of reviews was to evaluate the actions of the lead character. Thus, the *New York Times*, noting the large crowds attending *Little Caesar*, claimed that Caesar Bandello was a "disagreeable lad" who rose to "startling heights in his `profession' by reason of his belief in his high destiny." The review praised the acting of Edward G. Robinson, who presented Bandello as a "figure out of Greek epic tragedy, a cold, ignorant, merciless killer driven on and on by an insatiable lust for power, the plaything of a force that is greater than himself." The same newspaper saw the violence in *Public Enemy* as emanating not from social disorder but from the gangsters themselves, who simply pursue a "career of outlawry." Another observer seemed to delight in the fact that Cagney was "a bully behind his gun with men and the same with his fist toward his women."[62]

Women's films were also less likely to be framed within terms of so-cial realism and more often seen as stories of individuals struggling with their emotions. This meant that in a film like *Baby Face*, in which a woman fled the rough-and-tumble nature of male culture in a mill town, reviewers almost ignored the issue of deprivation as an explanation of female behavior and concentrated mostly on the fact that a female en-gaged in adulterous affairs. Reviewers tended to understand women's lives to be rooted more in a world of emotions than in the standard po-litical and economic sectors in which men such as miners, boxers, and fisherman roamed. Thus, they repeatedly inferred that a film like *Stella Dallas* would surely appeal more to females because it was a "tear-jerker" and had "emotional high spots" that would "bring out the hand-kerchief." Along these lines, one reviewer thought women actually might like *Baby Face* because of all the clothes the leading actress, Barbara Stanwyck, wore in the feature. A reviewer who enjoyed *Mannequin* a great deal also liked the fact that the story touched "capital-labor issues" only tangentially and concentrated on the "romantic angles" and the "'emotional reflexes of metropolitan men and women." In fact, the writer offered approval of the fact that the "girl of the tenements," played by Joan Crawford, "set a mark of decency" by struggling to get out of the "dwarfed viewpoints [and] the inequalities of the domestic and economic setup" of a proletarian life. In a similar way, a reviewer thought *Alice Adams* would do well with audiences because its star, Katharine Hep-burn, was able to capture the emotional quandary of a small-town girl looking for a way to better herself and the story would not be burdened by "too much drabness and prosaic realism." In other words, despite their link to emotional realism, women could also be praised when they offered strong portrayals of individualism and acted as liberals.[63]

The working class lost both a liberal and militant edge when filmed through the lens of Frank Capra, but most viewers of his films saw his basic point—as stated in a *Variety* review of *Meet John Doe*—that the "little man" in America was besieged by "the burden of life's inequalities" and must therefore "fight the dragons of destructions," or the mean-spirited and powerful forces allied against him. If the testimony from fan letters is any indication, Capra's films, perhaps more than those of any other filmmaker of the Depression era, forced audiences to think about large issues and common destinies. He acknowledged significant problems in American society, such as the illiberal sentiments of dangerous men like D. B. Norton or the indifference and greed of elites. Yet he offered the promise that these concerns could be alleviated and that economic stability was still attainable for all. Importantly, Capra's solutions—as diffuse as they may have been—did veer away from simple Production Code reaffirmations of the need to morally reform the individual.

In reacting to *Mr. Smith Goes to Washington,* viewers continually affirmed their support for the idea that unscrupulous practices of the powerful could be checked. Members of the audience praised the film for implying that democratic ideals were still attainable. One woman told him that he had helped "people who want to desperately cling to American ideals." A man in Texas thought the film reminded him of his grandfather who "fought battles for the people" as a lawyer; he felt the film showed that "idealistic principles still permeate society." Others were glad that the film acknowledged the existence of antidemocratic forces in the nation as a step in their eventual eradication. And some thanked him for keeping alive a "spirit of critical loyalty" to democratic ideals. One writer even suggested he make a sequel about Mr. Smith staying in Washington to continue the battle against political corruption.[64]

Press reaction to *Mr. Smith* indicated that reviewers appreciated Capra's democratic vistas. But many, especially in Washington, resented the "lampooning" to which the Senate was subjected and the insinuation that so many senators would involve themselves "in a pork-barrel deal." The *New York Times* called Capra a "believer in democracy," and the *Motion Picture Herald* referred to Capra's "simon pure Americanism." Censors had expressed concern that the film might tend to discredit the image "of our system of government" by making it appear that Congress was dominated by unethical men. But the Production Code office felt that this negative potential was more than balanced by the "social significance" of preaching in favor of "democracy, Americanism, and clean politics."[65]

If *Mr. Smith* tended to evoke support for the idea that democracy could only survive by contesting corrupt authority, *Meet John Doe* reminded filmgoers that democracy also needed an ethic of reciprocal concern between neighbors and strangers. Leftist critic Herbert Bieberman thought Capra's version of "neighborhoodness" tended to blunt ideas that "common people" could assume more militant roles. Doe was a common man who attracted the support of ordinary people in a campaign to spread the ideal of mutual assistance as a solution to social ills. Viewers wrote about their desires to pursue "the philosophy of neighborly love" in their own lives and how much everyone needed to "get back down to earth and be neighborly." Capra responded to one writer by saying that his intention in making the film was to show that the "golden rule is the only law or commandment that can make for happiness" and that people were happy in the film when they followed its admonition and ignored the commands of "greedy men after power," which they did not always do. Again a fan proposed a sequel. Allen Burkhart of Indiana wrote that Capra should make another movie showing "the results of further breaking up of the political machines and the rise to power of John Doe clubs." Certainly by the early forties when *John Doe* opened, many in the audience saw the defense of democratic ideals as an attack on fascism, a point made clear in the writings of Eric Smoodin. But these two films and others never let up in their insistence that there were real problems not only within American society but inside the souls of ordinary Americans as well.[66]

Reviewers tended to stress the degree to which *Grapes of Wrath* moved beyond the politics of the left and the right and became a great story of the survival of an American farm family. They noted the "almost newsreel authenticity" of the photography. There had been much public discussion over the novel, with some political leaders and agricultural interests claiming that Steinbeck had exaggerated the plight of the Okies, and others, more sympathetic to their suffering, indicating that the problem was even worse than the popular story revealed. Most reviewers noted the protest that accompanied the decision to turn Steinbeck's novel into a film in the first place. Communists originally charged that Twentieth Century Fox paid for the screen rights only to keep the account of the migrant workers off the screen. Large agricultural interests in California threatened a boycott because they thought it would portray their industry in an unflattering way. But the critics appreciated the fact that the film appeared to transcend partisan politics and offered a "great human story" of "an authentic U.S. farming family" enduring hardship. "They are never quite defeated, and their survival is a triumph." They were thrilled by the resolve and the strength of these plain people and saw them as representative of millions who toil and struggle on American farms. *Commonweal* proclaimed that the picture "pleads for justice for the downtrodden" by simply showing the miseries the homeless and the jobless undergo.[67]

## CONCLUSION

Among the films discussed in this chapter, the most popular at the box office were gangster films, Capra's features, and *The Grapes of Wrath*.[68] Liberalism and democracy could effectively draw audiences, although obviously people went to the movies for many reasons. The point to emphasize, however, was that among people who saw these features about proletarians and their world, strong support existed for both liberal individualism and a just community. If the content of these films and the reactions they provoked are any indication, political cross-dressing was central to the representations of mass culture even during the reality of the Great Depression. Doctrinaire radicals on the left who hoped for working-class insurgency and moral reformers on the right who hoped to create model citizens ignored this point at their own peril.

And yet the stories were ultimately about individuals and by implication grounded in the preoccupation of the culture with liberalism. Some of the plebeian types projected on the screen worked at times to create a more democratic society. Tom Joad did this, and so did Joe Radek and Marvin Blake. Women were seen challenging male dominance, but time and time again, key female characters like Lily Powers and Jessie Cassidy were bent on realizing personal desires. The gangsters and the boxers, who were mostly concerned to see if liberal capitalism could still work, found mixed results. When common people were thrown into group action, they could end up as a mob that could destroy democratic institutions, or they could actually achieve more justice if given the proper form of leadership. The upshot of all this was not perfectly clear. Hope and anxiety coexisted in these fictive people, who were grounded in the complexities of a political imagination riddled with realistic doses of democracy and liberalism.

# TWO

# THE PEOPLE'S WAR

The ideal of unity was articulated everywhere during World War II. The reasons were obvious: a massive military conflict on two fronts demanded that personal and group interests of any kind be minimized for the sake of a collective effort to win the war. The United States had to stand united if it was to remain standing at all. And the administration of Franklin Roosevelt wasted no time in making the management of public culture as important a goal as the calling of citizens to arms. In 1942 the government organized the Office of War Information to help mobilize the press, radio, and motion pictures for the task of winning support for America's war policies at home and abroad. Hollywood had demonstrated even before the war, however, that this was a conflict it was ready to support.

The growing convergence between the interests of the state and the film industry, something that was considerably less apparent in thirties, had distinct implications for the representation of American political ideals and the people who adhered to them. Put simply, the vast discourse about the promises and pitfalls of liberalism was suspended. Discontent on the part of the lowborn and divisions between men and women were minimized. The range of human emotions attributed to the people narrowed; there were fewer tales of gangsters and women on the make and more sentimental or democratic idealizations of proletarians who were willing to fight for a nation that was just and cooperative.

The softening of emotional realism, however, did not mean that depictions of the dangers of unrestrained individualism were eliminated. There continued to be stories in the early forties of ordinary people who were disinterested in democratic goals and conventional morals. More importantly, the discussion of democratic ideas during the war was based more in the circulation of ideal images than in the contradictions of an American social order. Thus, less was said about social inequality; audiences were more likely to look at representations of ideal types like ordinary men and women who naturally hated totalitarianism or families that were populated by members who loved each other. To put it another way, both emotional and social realism were tempered. Political culture during the war moved away from the ambiguity that was at the heart of mass cultural representations toward a world that was at times utopian.

At the heart of defining and selling the war was a reformulation of the idea of American democracy. The major political mobilizations of the thirties had achieved economic gains for workers and unions. Business was now forced to share power to a greater extent with organized labor, and workers established the idea that the nation-state owed them some degree of economic security in return for their sweat and toil. But in the politics of wartime, the discussion of democracy shifted away from a focus on the needs and the place of the working class or calls for a moral economy to calls for civil rights for all people, not just industrial workers or poor farmers. These ideals were defined not so much out of class politics but in response to totalitarian images sweeping Europe and Japan. Thus, there was more discussion about the need to tolerate diverse racial and religious groups and to protect the individual's right to think and speak as he pleased. Roosevelt made a dramatic beginning with the announcement of the "Four Freedoms" in his annual message to Congress in January 1941. Several months later the ideals of freedom of speech, freedom of worship, freedom from fear, and freedom from want were reaffirmed in the Atlantic Charter, a joint declaration of the Americans and the British.[1]

At no time did a new definition of democracy simply replace an old one. Rather, citizens appeared to rework various personal feelings and rhetorical strategies into a somewhat dreamlike view of what American democracy meant and what they were fighting for. Many studies from the forties indicated that the average American fighting man was persuaded to fight more by obligations he felt to fellow soldiers or loved ones than by calls to defend freedom in its various forms.[2] But other expressions in the culture suggest that people constructed their own formulas both from the memory of the thirties and from the political language of wartime. Some of this is evident in a series of articles written by men in the armed services that appeared in the *Saturday Evening Post* in 1943. Albert Gerber, a Jewish American, acknowledged that his ethnic and religious background certainly motivated him to fight against Hitler. But he insisted that he was willing to sacrifice for the war effort for a larger goal of the toleration of all religions and, interestingly, for "economic freedom for all." Showing that the thirties had not died, he said, "I am talking about unemployment compensation, old-age benefits, and . . . all other things that will give the individual economic security in this complex society." Another man demonstrated a similar synthesis: "I am fighting for the right to go home . . . to go to any church I like . . . to join a labor union of my own choice." A recent study has even suggested that war planners carefully blended ideas of individual rights into images of the American military to convince citizens that they could still retain their sense of uniqueness within the structure of military training and team-work.[3]

In the language of wartime democracy, no group of individuals had any more claims to the heart and sympathy of the nation than any other. Victims of the Depression, indignant laborers, and even industrial moguls no longer garnered exceptional amounts of public space as they did in previous decades. Rather, in the words of Dana Polan, "a mythology of the strength of the ordinary person" came to dominate war culture, especially the symbol of the common soldier or GI, who became a representative American, someone who hailed from all classes and religions. Resistant to totalitarianism by nature, this idealized (and homogenized) American democrat did not even like violence—and certainly not the idea of domination—and only went to war because somebody had to defend the American home and the entire world against evil. He was a team player, willing to do whatever it took to win the war and then get back to the business of marriage, community life, hard work, and sustaining a democratic nation. Norman Corwin's famous radio address in the wake of the announcement of victory in Europe on May 8, 1945, reflected how much this exemplar of America life had become a blend of the common and the heroic man. "Take a bow GI. Take a bow little guy," Corwin exclaimed, "The superman of tomorrow lies at the feet of you common men this afternoon."[4]

Images were central to uniting Americans behind the war effort. Thus, the government withheld negative illustrations like photographs of American dead during the first twenty-one months of the war. But after the politics of the thirties, the people could not simply be organized behind slogans. Real promises of rights and a better material future had to be made. And representations had to embrace the various segments of the population in order to ensure a collaborative effort. Everyone had to be made to understand that they had a role in winning the war. Women could enter industrial plants; entertainers could sell bonds or sing for the troops; even children could help by collecting scrap iron. Corporate advertising constantly found ways to extend the idea of collaboration. A hotel in New York found a way to proclaim their war contributions by stressing how it offered a place for soldiers to meet their families during leaves. In another advertisement an aircraft company called its skilled workers "production fighters," and other companies depicted women on assembly lines taking up "Hitler's challenge."[5]

The picture of a harmonious workplace was particularly ironic. Organized labor, for instance, certainly demonstrated a willingness to sacrifice their more specific goals for the sake of the war effort. Industrial unions like the United Auto Workers agreed to a no-strike pledge during the war, concessions on "premium pay" or extra pay for overtime, swing-shift scheduling, and an effort at "all-out production." But some union leaders were also angry that greater controls were not put on prices and on the earnings of companies. Even more displeasure was manifested over the infusion of women workers, who were often seen as a force that would lower overall wage rates. The mix of more women and more African Americans in industrial plants also led to heightened tensions over gender and racial issues. And workers continually protested the controls placed on them during the conflict by launching work stoppages and wildcat strikes. One local union leader in Toledo, Ohio, complained that he wanted to "lick Fascism," but he was unwilling to let his employer "kick the hell out of us all around the place behind the American flag."[6]

Gender collaboration was venerated as much as labor and management cooperation. That is why figures of GI's who were natural-born democrats, husbands, and fathers were so widespread. This point is demonstrated nicely by Robert Westbrook in his examination of the popularity of the "pinup" posters during the war. He shows that Betty Grable, for instance, was much more popular than women with sexier images because she reminded men more of a girl back home that they might marry. With couples apart for long periods of time, suspicions began to grow about fidelity. And apparently there was good reason for this. American soldiers fathered tens of thousands of illegitimate children while serving in the armed services. The army discovered that after a year abroad, men felt they had a right to seek out sexual favors and thought that their girlfriends back home were probably doing the same thing. But the culture had more to say about how much the men wanted to return home and not much of anything to say about their unfaithfulness. Thus, war reporters, at the urging of government censors, constantly wrote not only about the GI as patriotic but also as longing to return home to a woman. A representative advertisement in the *Saturday Evening Post* in 1943 depicted a serviceman and a woman making a wish: "Victory! Peace! Then a home of their own."[7]

## HOLLYWOOD AT WAR

Mass culture now softened its traditional method of attracting audiences by exposing various forms of longing and restlessness within individuals. Like government, the culture industry narrowed the focus of its stories and essentially reinforced the mainstream politics of the nation, something it did not do all that much before or after the war. Sentimental and patriotic images of American society and scenes of gender cooperation and moral conservatism dominated cultural expression; signs of domestic disorder and violence were rare. Immediately following Pearl Harbor, the music industry, for instance, threw itself behind the war campaign. Songs like "God Bless America," or "The House I Live In" celebrated the nation as a place blessed by Providence, one that tolerated "all races and religions" and was filled with happy homes. These were not songs like "Brother Can You Spare a Dime" that painted negative portraits of the nation's economic system. And some music even sanctioned violent behavior against outsiders if it would produce victory. "Remember Pearl Harbor" promised that we would "kill 100 rats" [Japanese] for every fallen American.[8]

Hollywood's patriotism was never more utopian than it was during World War II, although much of this was forced on filmmakers by economic calculations and government censors. As scholars of the film industry have demonstrated, the war ignited an economic boom that pushed box office receipts to record levels. People were working and had few alternative places for entertainment outside the motion picture theater. In some cities theaters ran around the clock. The foreign box office, of course, declined as war engulfed Europe, but it made little difference. In 1940 profits at the top eight film studios totaled some $20 million. By the last years of the war, they were running at about three times that rate.[9]

Roosevelt did not favor a government takeover of the movie industry as happened in England, since he felt the movies were an effective way to sustain morale. However, the government did begin to influence the content of Hollywood films in 1942 through its Office of War Information (OWI). Hollywood, of course, had already moved well along the road toward war even before Pearl Harbor, in part because of the influence of émigrés from Germany with strong anti-fascist feelings who now worked in the film industry. In constant negotiations, the OWI and industry censors worked continuously to create stories and images that helped sustain positive pictures of Americans and their nation. In its "Manual for the Motion Picture Industry" the government insisted that Hollywood create pictures that help "win the war" and show that the conflict was truly a "people's war," one that would give individuals more political rights and a better material life once the conflict was over. Realities of class conflict, ethnic intolerance, racism, and gender betrayal were minimized. Lary May, who analyzed wartime film plots, concluded that Hollywood produced narratives in which heroes and heroines willingly attached themselves to large organizations like the military or to patriotic ideals rather than hold onto narrower interests. We can add that this loyalty extended to the institution of marriage as well. May says that in instances where characters had reservations about supporting the larger cause, they would undergo a "conversion" experience that would make them realize the benefits of American ideals and values like democracy and capitalism.[10]

Some of the most powerful films of the period contributed to the dominant narrative of the cinema, which supported the American war effort and the view that the nation and most of its citizens were virtuous. Patriotism and democratic participation were venerated over narrower identities like class or self. And a traditional narrative of American history was invoked to show that citizens had willingly sacrificed for the defense of the nation in the past, although such images had already appeared in many films of the thirties. In *Casablanca* (1942), an American expatriate gives up the love of a woman to join the French resistance. In *Wake Island* (1942), audiences were reminded of historic "last stands" made by Americans at Valley Forge and the Alamo, when outcomes were still in doubt. And in *Bataan* (1943), an American fighting unit of diverse ethnicities came together to bravely hold off a superior enemy force in order to buy time for citizens back home to mobilize.[11]

Feature films were also quick to mute domestic tensions by extending the discussion of democracy and unity to relations between men and women. It stood to reason that if there was a role for each citizen in "a people's war" a respected place had to be found for women as well as men, a notion that did not earn much political space in the previous decade. Beyond the imperatives of mobilization, Thomas Doherty argued that you had to give women roles to get them into the theater, since they were "the audience most fervently courted" by film producers. Thus, wartime films frequently attempted to focus on the ways in which women contributed to the war effort at home, at work, and in even in battle zones. Doherty identified at least three versions of the way "American womanhood" was depicted in these films. In some instances, females served the nation by serving men and adhering to traditional domestic roles. This was evident in a film like *Since You Went Away* (1944). At other times females blended traditional devotion to men with images of female independence as they did in *Tender Comrade* (1943). And some women began to imagine entirely new roles in domains previously reserved for men. Thus, in *So Proudly We Hail* (1943) a female learns to be a rear seat gunner in an American bomber, and in *They Were Expendable* (1945) nurses bravely perform their task under enemy fire.[12]

The turn toward equality and unity, and the campaign to minimize differences within America was part of an imaginative preparation for war even before Pearl Harbor. The Hollywood cinema moved explicitly in this direction, leaving behind much of the politics of the thirties. National loyalty and teamwork were celebrated in *Knute Rockne, All American* (1940). Americans were now figures marked by selflessness and high moral standing, much as they were in *Our Town* (1940) and not as greedy, ambitious, violent, or angry as they often were in films of the previous decade. Although *Knute Rockne* is often remembered today for a speech given by Ronald Reagan to encourage the Notre Dame football team to win under adverse circumstances, the narrative was ultimately an overt call for citizen loyalty and unity and a warning that a cancer was spreading in the world that would have to be attacked by good American citizens. Working people in this film, especially the Norwegian immigrant family named the Rocknes, were admirable individuals who were disinterested in joining unions or in making additional demands on the nation for more justice. They asked only for a chance to make a success of their lives. Immigrant Lars Rockne and his son Knute were model citizens who believed in hard work and the idea of opportunity in a new land. They stood as reminders that liberal and democratic possibilities were still alive in the land of the free.

The story begins in the old world, a place that frustrates dreams for a better life. Amidst snow-capped mountains in Norway in 1892, Rockne's parents express their faith in an American future. While constructing a carriage for the Chicago World's Fair, the elder Rockne decides that he will take his creation to America and stay there. Strangers are welcome in this story because they share a common faith. "It's a new country filled with new life and opportunities for a workingman like me," he declares, "and I want that for my children." Young Knute innocently asks his father if America is big enough "to play in." "It's big enough, son, for anything and for everybody to play in," the older man replies.

A broader history of immigrant struggle, exploitation, and return migration is erased in the story that follows. The Rocknes pass the Statue of Liberty and a message on the screen notes how "millions of simple, hardworking people" follow "a new road of equality and opportunity" in the United States. Their working-class neighborhood fosters, not gangsters or fallen women, but industrious men, eager to move upward through sacrifice and toil. Young Rockne learns character and patriotism by shoveling coal into a furnace and playing football in the streets of Chicago. He dreams only of saving enough money to attend Notre Dame, where he becomes an outstanding student and football player.

In this narrative, Rockne uses the playing field to develop good American men like himself and teach teamwork and integrity. He responds to rumors that he might leave the university for places that could pay him more by indicating that his attachment to his players is stronger than his desire for money. This flawless citizen does not even take a vacation, and he allows his "boys" to practice on the front yard of his home. One of his players, George Gipp, the role performed by Reagan, tells the coach that he has given his players "something they don't teach in school . . . not just courage, but a right way of living that none of us will ever forget."

The film's call for high standards of character and loyalty reaches a high pitch when Rockne addresses a congressional committee investigating sports in America and possible corruption in college football. He argues that sports serve the national interest by channeling violent impulses in all men into more constructive directions. "Every red-blooded young man in any country is filled with what we might call the natural spirit of combat," he reasons, but "we have tried to make competitive sports serve as a safer outlet for the spirit of combat." For him football actually helped to build "character" by nurturing courage, initiative, and persistence, qualities that all Americans would need to face the threatening world ahead.

Secular and religious faith did not come nearly as easily to Alvin York. *Sergeant York* (1941), which premiered about four months before Pearl Harbor, continued the effort by Hollywood to prepare the ground for war and rehabilitate images of common people. A reviewer of the film in 1941 noted that "a great many people are thinking deep and sober thoughts about the possible involvement of our country in another deadly war" and that the film offered an opportunity to reflect on the motives of America's greatest hero from World War I. Attempts to recall the last world war as an event of "needless slaughter" were countered by the story of York's conversion from a poor backwoodsman from Tennessee interested mostly in drinking and fighting to a God-fearing war hero.

The fact that York had discovered religion before America entered World War I proves troublesome for him. He does not believe in killing other men, and he attempts to gain an exemption from military service. In the army, however, he learns the elements of a secular faith that includes the idea that in the past Americans created a government "of the people, by the people, and for the people" in which all men were pledged to defend the rights of other men. York is told that if he ever hopes to marry and to farm the fertile soil of the Tennessee bottomlands, he must do the same. After taking time to read an American history book, this common man suddenly realizes that there will be no family or rich land to farm if the democratic nation is not defended.

The qualities that made York a good backwoodsmen serve him well in war. His skills with a gun and his individualism allow him to capture a large enemy force single-handedly. He serves his country without losing his sense of being a strong individual or his ties to home and family, showing that liberalism and democracy are compatible. He even turns down opportunities to profit from his deeds and returns to Tennessee to become a farmer and a breadwinner. A grateful government provides him with a home and the land he has long sought. Forties patriotism called for the abandonment of narrow desires, but it did not completely erase the democratic idea that the nation still owed its citizens something in return for their sacrifices.

Warner Brothers worried somewhat that the film would be interpreted as pure propaganda for war and therefore emphasized elements of the story in which York tried to resolve many of his personal problems, such as his bouts of heavy drinking. But the reconstruction of the people into beings of high moral stature able to put their personal problems behind them was very much a part of the new culture of wartime itself. Even York knew this in a sense, because he had refused to grant permission to do a story of his life before, but he now acquiesced because of his own realization that another conflict was probably imminent. When Norman Vincent Peale saw the movie, he wrote to the head of Warner Brothers that the picture "may actually help to save this country."[13]

The studio actually altered its promotional strategy for the production once the war began. When *Sergeant York* initially premiered, some four months before Pearl Harbor, Warner Brothers told theater owners less about its patriotic aspects and called for greater attention to Gary Cooper's status as a major star and the fact that the female lead, played by Joan Leslie, was a newcomer who was excited but not overwhelmed by working with him. Operators were even told to invite a "backwoods family" to local showings as a way of generating interest. After the Japanese attack, the studio issued a second press book that began to put more stress on the film's connection to war and less on the attitudes and standing of the stars. In the later campaign, posters now featured a full-body photo of Cooper charging with a bayonet and displays for theater lobbies that showed Hitler or Tojo in miniature running from images of the star. Before December 1941, similar posters featured a large picture of Cooper's head but not the full-body image with the fixed bayonet.[14]

## REMNANTS OF THE THIRTIES

Film biographies of Rockne and York not only prepared the ground for wartime sacrifice and elevated the depiction of ordinary men but also attempted to redirect the discourse on democracy that permeated the thirties. Both films tended to frame the plight of the common man as the singular struggle of an individual to become a virtuous and patriotic citizen. There was a movement away from the social realism of the previous decade and no sense in these narratives that people in America were exploited in any way. Yet critical views of American life and the nature of lower-class life were never completely removed from the American cinema of the time. Two films in 1942, *Native Land* and *Talk of the Town*, avoided strong bias toward working people but still managed to take a frank look at America. They disclosed that more than private desires had to be curtailed if democracy was to be saved.

Presented in the style of a documentary, *Native Land* suggested that ordinary people went about the daily routine of school and work willingly but also added that they had to vigilantly defend their unions from capitalist attacks through blacklisting and unfair firings of union sympathizers. One scene actually recalled the shooting of strikers in Chicago in 1937 as an "act of fascism," and footage was presented of proud people marching in union parades and calling for a "new declaration of independence." Paul Robeson, the movie's narrator, even offered a working-class version of the four freedoms that included the right to a job, adequate medical care, collective bargaining, and the need to live in peace. The latter point reflected that fascism as well as unregulated capitalism was considered a threat to workers at this time, although the film took pains to show that fascism existed at home as well as abroad.

In *Talk of the Town*, a workingman is framed by the owner of a large mill in a New England town. The "talk" of this town is whether Leopold Dilg, played by Cary Grant, actually set fire to the mill in which a foreman was killed. In this story threats to the stability of a democratic society emanate, not from the bottom, but, as in *Native Land*, from the top of society in the desires of powerful people to deny others their rights. The mill owner in this case pays another man to burn down his factory and collect the insurance money, spreads rumors that Dilg is responsible, and hires a corrupt judge to ensure that he will not receive a fair trail. But democracy is saved here, not by victims defending themselves and asserting countervailing power, but by the workings of an American system of law in the hands of reasonable men. In this case a future Supreme Court justice, with the help of a woman who cares for Dilg, finds the man hired to set the fire in the first place and proves the accused worker is innocent. This information comes just in time, since the people of the town, fed by gossip, have turned into a angry mob ready to take the law into their own hands. Dilg's defender, however, tells the crowd that they must do battle to save the rule of law and not administer it themselves. The emotions of both the top and bottom layers of society must be restrained if reason, law, and America are to be saved.

*King's Row* (1942) also subverts the wartime image of a good nation of morally upright citizens, although the origins of this story predate the war. A sign outside this fictional place proclaims that it is "a good town to live in and a good place to raise your children." But inside the town limits, malevolent forces wreck private lives, and social classes are separated by a wide gulf. Censors lamented the fact that the film's suggestion of insanity precluded its release in Britain, but this theme marked this film as an important step in the cinematic discourse over the darker aspects of human nature that would expand considerably once the war over. Unlike the tale of *Our Town*, the local physician in this story is not essentially a caregiver but a disturbed man who dominates his wife and daughter. Interested in the study of psychiatry, the doctor encourages a young man to take up such a discipline himself since "the modern world is more stressful on mankind than ever before." But this physician does not handle stress well himself, and he actually poisons his daughter in order to keep her from running away with his young protege. Eventually this troubled middle-class man takes his own life as well.[15]

Class differences and middle-class hostility toward working people are made clear. The poor side of King's Row houses considerate individuals like Randy Monaghan, played by Ann Sheridan, with modest means but large capacities for helping others. When Drake McHugh, a middle-class male played by Ronald Reagan, demonstrates an interest in Monaghan, a friend from his side of the tracks refers to her as "trash." Even Monaghan feels that a relationship between them can not work because most people in the community "don't think I am good enough for you. . . . Your family is rich and high-toned. My pa is a railroad section boss." When her suitor explains his dream of developing local land to sell high-priced houses to the rich, she confronts him with the need to build low-cost housing near the railroad tracks where "people who work in clay pits, mills, and mines" want to be homeowners as well. And when McHugh faces financial ruin, Monaghan's modest family takes him in.

Indeed, throughout the war period, Americans could still watch tales that sabotaged the narrative aspirations of the OWI and the government for unity, social harmony, and heroism. The sentimental view of American goodness was dependent on the assumption that wickedness within the nation could be contained or repressed. For that reason American soldiers and women on the home front were usually depicted as dreaming of a future of happy homes and rewarding marriages. Gender harmony, like ethnic and religious tolerance, was considered a predominant American value. Such views were facilitated, moreover, by the ability of many cultural texts to position depravity and corruption abroad and mask their existence at home. King's Row had no such aspirations to do this, but neither did the 1944 classic Double Indemnity. In the same year that Americans watched Going My Way, a sentimental story of Catholic priests devoted to helping the lowborn, they could view this account of a "bored housewife" and a salesman who conspired to murder her spouse for insurance money. Often cited as an example of the tendency of postwar films to expose the shady recesses of American life, Double Indemnity appeared very much before the war's end. Indeed, its portrayal of female treachery spoke to a significant cultural issue of the war period with men and women usually separated for long periods of time.

As in King's Row, the origins of the story resided in a period before the war in the social experience of ordinary Americans. During the 1930s Hollywood censors had actually prevented the filming of Double Indemnity because the leading characters were murderers who were not punished by law officials but died at their own hands. When the story finally did appear during the war, however, it not only countered wartime sentiment but kept alive a narrative about the dark side of human nature. Emotional liberalism was tempered in the war years to be sure, but it was not eliminated.[16]

In 1942 stories of class relations in America still carried much of the cultural baggage of the decade just ended. This meant that, despite broad indictments of American society and its upper classes, working people were still vulnerable to pejorative images. Warner Brothers, which had certainly approached the plight of common people from a variety of different perspectives by this time, employed a number of familiar tropes in representing common people in *Tortilla Flat* (1942) and *Juke Girl* (1942). In the former story, Mexican Americans living in the hills above Monterey, California, were portrayed, not as proud toilers, but as shiftless and lazy vagrants who preferred wine to work. There was humor in this story by John Steinbeck, and the author had some affection for the characters he created, but clearly they ran the risk of perpetuating negative stereotypes. Industry censors never raised the issue of possibly denigrating working people. They worried more about suggestions of excessive drinking, sex outside marriage, and "unpunishing thieving." The Breen office told the producers that "it should be possible to tell this story without having the characters continually poring wine down their throats." And censors did fear that the box office in Latin America could be hurt if audiences did not realize that the men were not recent immigrants from south of the American border but native-born Americans who had lived for generations around Monterey.[17]

The farming community of Cat-Tail, Florida, houses hard-drinking men but also some earnest immigrants, greedy capitalists, and a woman independent enough to take care of herself in *Juke Girl*. Economic life in Cat-Tail is controlled by an entrepreneur named Henry Madden, who pays low prices for locally grown vegetables and then sells them for a profit in distant cities. The discourse over a fair economic system is merged with one over the need for gender harmony in the larger narrative. Steve Talbot, played by Ronald Reagan, is a migrant whose father lost his farm in the Depression and who likes the ardor of a local Greek immigrant, Nick Garcos. The hard-working newcomer is looking for ways to transport his produce directly to cities, bypassing Madden. Talbot is also attracted to Lola Meyers, a girl who sings and dances for hire at the local "juke joint." Narrative resolution in this story promises to bring more economic justice to small growers and domesticity to a man and a woman living on the economic margins of American society.

Talbot, who asserts that he "just don't like to see a man kicked around," hatches a scheme to help Garcos gain his ends. They recruit field hands and raise a crop of their own, which they manage to sell in Atlanta. With cash in his pockets, however, the immigrant quickly reverts to old habits by getting drunk in the "juke joint" and storming off in a rage to confront Madden. This common man, who cannot control his emotions, is killed in the fight that ensues. Talbot and Lola do find happiness, however, and they begin to work the immigrant's farm as a couple.

*Pittsburgh* (1942) is a film that reflects the pressures of war culture and makes a more determined effort to sublimate discourses over class and gender into one about the need for patriotic consensus. Thus, it tends to locate these social tensions in the past and to discredit the importance of group and even individual desire. The narrative acknowledges the existence of capitalist avarice and plebeian aimlessness as well as the brutal reality of inequality, but ultimately it calls for greater efforts at self-denial for the sake of national unity.

Pittsburgh Markham and Cash Evans are two laborers who begin their work lives in the coal mines of western Pennsylvania. They are moral opposites. Markham is a free-wheeling, hard-drinking man who seeks to escape a life in the mines and in the working class altogether. He tells a date that he will not be swinging a pick forever and that in time all the world will know who he is. To a miner who is optimistic of the union's getting him a six-cents-an-hour raise, he replies, "You'll never get fat on that kind of dough." Markam's alter ego is Cash Evans, a person who feels an obligation to the needs of others and a desire for fair-mindedness in the relations between labor and capital.

Markham embarks on a path of self-realization that will destroy his relations with Evans, his co-workers, and a "hunkey" girl from a local coal town, Josie. At first the woman shares his desire to get out of the working class, seeing it as simply a dead end. The way out for both of them, in typical cinema fashion, is not through political mobilization but through entrepreneurship. Markham conceives of a plan to start his own enterprise by selling coke to steel companies and promising to bring the aspiring female along with him when he rises. Once established, however, the successful businessman ruthlessly forces out partners who invested with him and marries the daughter of one of his former upper-crust colleagues. Later he admits to the girl from the coal town that the marriage was purely for business reasons, a statement that causes her to lose all respect for him.

Pittsburgh does bring Evans into the venture, but this proves to be a troublesome decision. Evans, still sensitive to the needs of working people, wants to improve wages and make safety improvements. He even considers the idea of profit sharing, a suggestions that prompts Markham to force his old friend out of the business completely. When the two men trade punches, the audience is treated to a symbolic expression of class conflict in American society.

Eventually the selfish Markham stands alone. He has no partners or friends, and his wife divorces him. His frustrated workers present him with demands and threaten violence if they are not met. A union leader tells him he has "forgot the human element." But the contest between capitalism and labor—and for that matter, the politics of the thirties—is resolved, not through negotiations, but by Pearl Harbor. In a sense, the Japanese attack served as a cultural marker that not only signaled the beginning of the war but also the end of the thirties and the power of the discourse over class conflict to command a significant narrative attention. Suddenly the demands of war forces workers and managers to put aside differences and strive for victory. Markham even finds some sense of redemption by leaving his entrepreneurial pursuits behind and toiling in a war plant for a larger cause. Ironically, the plant is run by Evans, who now resists an idea to bring his old friend back into an administrative role. But Josie returns to make a plea for these men—and for the entire audience—to put the discord of the past behind. She tells him that personal feelings should be put aside and that "the only emotion that should guide each and every one of us today [is] devotion to our country."

The logic of wartime narratives discredited attitudes that promised to disrupt the massive effort to generate unity. In this cultural period personal desire, whether cast within the discourse of class relations or gender relations, was severely restrained and often castigated. In *Valley of Decision* (1945), the point was made again that disparate classes could find common ground in America and that heroes and heroines were people devoted to the cause of love and harmony. Paul Scott is the son of an Irish immigrant who built a thriving steel mill in the Pittsburgh region. He is driven by a desire to do what is best for the business and for its workers, many of whom respect him because he toiled with them for a time as a young man. Scott's siblings, however, do not share his vision of cooperative capitalism and want only wealth. Disinterested in the family nature of the enterprise, they seek to sell the plant to the highest bidder.

Below the hills on which the Scott mansion stands is the "flats," a section populated by Irish mill hands and their families. Here live the Raffertys, led by an angry old man named Pat, who blames the Scotts for the industrial accident that has confined him to a wheel chair. Pat Rafferty's anger is the counterpart to some of the greed in the Scott household. Fortunately, there is also a source of goodness and reconciliation in the "flats" in the figure of Mary Rafferty, Pat's daughter. A model female who allows for no personal desires, she is content to serve as a domestic to the rich family on the hill.

Avarice and anger threatened to destroy this industrial world. At one point labor agitation becomes so intense that it leads to the death of old man Rafferty and Paul Scott's father. But love and reconciliation do triumph. After a tortuous course, Paul is able to express his love for the low-born Mary Rafferty. And his mother, now a widow, leaves her share of the mill to the lowborn domestic, knowing that, unlike most of her children, she had best interests of the mill and the workers (and Paul) at heart.

There is no promise in Alfred Hitchcock's *Lifeboat* (1944) that the emotions of the lowborn can ever be integrated into an American society that is harmonious. The story explores the connection between human nature, democracy, and fascism by looking at survivors of a German submarine attack who cling to life on small boat. American society is depicted in the cast of survivors who included an aristocratic woman, an African American, men of distinct working-class backgrounds, and a fascist figure in the form of a German submarine captain who has been plucked from the sea. The Americans are depicted as more democratic than the German, but their commitment to democratic ideals is highly tenuous. The white workingmen in the film actually appear to be more interested in violence and dominance. One, who is from the Chicago stockyard district, wants to control the boat himself. And these men beat the Nazi captain to death when they learned how he has betrayed them by getting them to sail toward German lines. Indeed, their impulses are only moderated by the more cosmopolitan woman and by the African American, who is a symbol of virtue and religious devotion.

## THE BATTLE OF PRODUCTION

The concerns expressed in *Lifeboat* or the complex social conditions expressed in a story like *Juke Girl* did not dominate wartime representations of ordinary Americans, however. In *Wings of the Eagle* (1942) "the people" are suddenly removed from migrant camps and economic struggles and are placed in factories consumed with the manufacture of tanks, ships, and planes. Using actual footage of the Lockheed Vega plant in southern California, this story is set in 1940 as Americans are slowly drawn into World War II by building war goods for England. Common people still speak with the accents of the lower orders as they did in many Warner Brothers films of the thirties, but now their interests turn from crime or despair to winning the war.[18]

In a familiar approach, it takes an immigrant in the film to teach native-born Americans the true meaning of patriotism. The representative newcomer, Jake Hanso, is a foreman at the plant and completely devoted to the building of bombers. He suggests that all workers donate overtime to building an extra bomber that will be given to England as a Christmas present (an event that actually took place at the plant in 1940). Hanso's American-born son Pete also works in the plant but is anxious to enter the Army Air Corps. Family dreams involve Pete's flying the planes that Jake builds. The boy's eventual death in war only stiffens the resolve of the earnest newcomer to produce even more planes and help America win.[19]

Corky Jones, a young man from Chicago, is less certain of his commitment to the war effort. He is more interested in working in the aircraft plant as a way to avoid the draft and not as means to serve the nation. Audiences are treated to numerous visual images of the massive plant and the extraordinary effort that is going into military production, but they also hear Jones tell a friend that "there are only two kinds of guys these days. The fellow who figures the angles and the jerks who end up in a parachute battalion." Because loyalty, like violence, was examined on a continuum in the cinema, we are not surprised to learn that Jones also finds it difficult to commit to a woman as well. He is not converted until he learns of the news of Pearl Harbor and the death of Hanso's son. Suddenly he gives up his plant job and his pursuit of his friend's wife and enlists in the Navy to take the fallen warrior's place.

*Joe Smith, American* (1942) was another tribute to the common men who assembled the aircraft needed to defeat America's enemies. In this story, set again in a California plant, workers hang American flags from the rafters and are portrayed as totally dedicated to the quest for perfection in building bombers. Joe Smith is a crew chief in the final assembly department but is given a special assignment to install the new Army bombsight in planes. The bombsight is a "secret weapon" that no other nation has and, as suggested in other films of the era like *Air Force* (1943), it will help the United States defeat its enemies. Joe, the son of immigrant parents himself, is entrusted with this assignment and cannot even tell his wife about it.

Smith is not only a skilled worker and a patriot but also a contented

Robert Young as the devoted worker and citizen in *Joe Smith, American* (1942). During World War II the representation of working people became highly romantic and idealistic. Credit: Film Still Archives, Museum of Modern Art, New York

breadwinner. Audiences can see that he owns his own home and a car, and can watch his wife prepare him a dinner after work, a reminder that the Depression is over. Husband and wife express affection for each other and enjoy going to the movies together. In this model working-class home, his son even studies American history and tells his father about Nathan Hale and his regret that he had but one life to give to his country.

Joe Smith's devotion to duty is tested, however, when he is kidnapped by men who want to learn about the secret work he is doing. They threaten to harm his wife and child, and they beat him, but he survives the ordeal by dreaming about the time he met his spouse and how lovely she looked. Just as GI's would be encouraged to hold on to memories of women back home to endure the rigors of war, Joe clings to images of love and home life in his effort to be a patriot. Eventually he escapes his captors, leads police back to the men who are trying to undercut the war effort, and eagerly returns to the plant to resume the job he had started. The common man now had a place of honor in the culture and his priorities in order: nation, home, and family.

Alfred Hitchcock's *Saboteur* (1942) continued the project of remaking common people into dedicated patriots in 1942. A review in the *Motion Picture Herald* claimed that the drama showed "a people's growing realization of themselves and their responsibilities." In this instance "the people" are represented by Barry Kane, a man who witnesses an act of terrorism in the aircraft plant in which he works. Unfortunately, officials suspect Kane of treachery and force him to find the perpetrators on his own if he has any hope of exonerating himself. Kane thus embarks on a cross-country search for the villains.

Hitchcock uses his flight across America, from California to New York, as a means to present a debate over the relative merits of democracy and fascism. For instance, at one point Kane is forced to travel with a group of misfits in a circus troupe, including a midget and a pair of Siamese twins. When the group is faced with a decision to hide Kane from authorities or turn him in, they take a vote and express their need to be treated with fairness rather than with the type of discrimination they face all too often in their own lives. They protect the man in an act that suggests that neither he nor they would have any chance for justice in a totalitarian regime.

Finally Kane infiltrates an American fascist organization in New York. One of the fascist leaders tells him that he is one of the "moron millions" but that a "few" Americans long for the order and efficiency a totalitarian state can offer. Kane charges them with sabotage, however, and warns that their kind will lose the war. In a struggle with Kane at the top of the Statue of Liberty, the fascist saboteur falls to his death, and the common man turned patriot stands vindicated. Industry censors worried about depicting citizens taking the law into their own hands and disregarding established legal procedures. They even objected to language that suggested that the police often did a better job of frightening people than protecting them. But such "antisocial" expressions in no way contradicted the main patriotic thrust of the feature.[20]

The cultural embrace of the nation by ordinary workers and immigrants was central to *American Romance* (1944) directed by King Vidor. In an early version of the screenplay for this film, the highly conservative

Vidor had represented industrialists as heroes, and unions as violent and subversive. But the Office of War Information, concerned that any partisan view would damage attempts at wartime unity, forced him to moderate this approach and to emphasize wartime labor and management cooperation. The central character, Steve Dangos, is in fact a lowly immigrant worker who worships America because he feels it offers him more opportunity than he could ever hope for in the old country. There is no hint in this story that he ever plans to return to the land of his origins as many of his contemporaries actually did or that he has demanded rights in return for his toil in the Depression.[21]

The film presents the immigrant worker as an individualist and a patriot. Dangos actually walks from Ellis Island to the iron ore ranges of Minnesota, a plot device that allows the camera to record the material and industrial might of the nation. Dangos takes it all in and exalts over the possibilities he sees for making money. He also loves a woman as much as his new nation. He tells Anna O'Rourke, a Minnesota teacher who gives him instruction in the English language, that he will never leave her. He even accepts her suggestion that someday he could "climb to the sky" and run his own steel company.

Eventually Dangos takes Anna to Pennsylvania and toils in a mill in order to learn the steel business. This ardent patriot even gives his sons names like George Washington Dangos and Thomas Jefferson Dangos. And through it all, Anna remains a dutiful wife who will see most of her dreams come true. The loyalty of this immigrant family is tested in World War I when George Washington Dangos is killed in action. Anna shed tears, an act that suggests the possibility of regret over paying such a price for membership in the nation, but her husband only reaffirms his pride in his son and recites the "Pledge of Allegiance" as he becomes a new citizen.

Hard work and faith do lead to success for Dangos, but he is faced with a crisis when one of his sons, who manages his business with him, expresses sympathy for an emerging union in their plant. The elder Dangos, believing only in the self-initiative that fueled his own success, has little patience for labor unions. His son and the company's directors want to avoid the production delays that a strike could bring, however, and decide to cooperate with the workers. Again the OWI acted on the final script here by getting producers to delete a sit-down strike, which officials feared would remind workers of strategies they wanted them to forget. At the end, Steve and Anna fulfill a long-held dream to see California and then return to make planes rather than cars during World War II.[22]

## WOMEN WERE PEOPLE TOO

Women were needed in theater audiences and war factories as much as men, and consequently they drew a significant amount of cinematic attention. Gender accord was considered essential for the war effort, if only to reduce GI anxiety over female faithfulness at home. Thus, a film like *Tender Comrade* spoke to this issue by, in the words of one reviewer, "extolling our brave American girls who are keeping the home fires burning." The film's opening presented the most popular rationale for women to remain devoted to the men who defended them. In a dream sequence, actress Ginger Rogers imagines a conversation with her soldier-husband in which they outline their plans for the postwar. After professing love for each other, they discuss how they will "get a little place on the edge of town," have children, sleep late, and have barbecues. Ordinary family life was the goal; it was the home that would be the site of gender harmony and the social peace.[23]

Ginger Rogers (middle) reminded audiences of the need for women to be completely loyal to the needs of the nation and the men in their lives in *Tender Comrade* (1943). The reality and complexity of individual emotional life was essentially constrained in the culture of wartime. Credit: Film Still Archives, Museum of Modern Art, New York

This film centers on the domestic situation of a group of female factory workers who live together and pool their resources while their men are away at war. Jo Jones (Rogers) stands as a exemplar for American women because she is completely loyal both to her husband and to the American cause. Her housemate, Barbara, cannot match her level of devotion, however, and stands as the moral opposite of Jones. The women support the ideal of democratic participation by taking a vote among themselves to resolve issues within their house, but Barbara is more intent on exploring the new freedom the war offers her and is unwilling simply to wait for her husband to return. She dates other men and tells her housemates that she is "sick" of all the talk about sacrifice.

Ultimately, the narrative affirms female devotion and submission to the needs of men. Barbara renounces her interest in sexual experimentation when she hears that her husband has been killed. The report turns out to be inaccurate, but it still forces her to exclaim that she would "knuckle down to him" once he returned. Jones, however, learns that her spouse will never come back from the war. Wartime movies often treated battle deaths indirectly by portraying the news of such an event rather than the actuality. But grief only gives Jones a chance to express her patriotism; it is a burden she is willing to carry. Her burden is made bearable, moreover, by the fact that the dead soldier left her a son. At the end, she informs the child that his father died for a just cause: "He only left you the best world a little boy could grow up in."

Although Claudette Colbert's character of Anne Hilton is more firmly located in the middle class in *Since You Went Away* (1944) the film offers further proof that the restoration of harmonious gender relations and the traditional home were central features in the popular understanding of the war. These films tell us that when ordinary people joined the war effort they thought they were fighting not only against totalitarianism but also for the creation of a more harmonious and democratic society in which class and gender accord would replace hard times and troublesome relationships. More than any other symbol, this dream of a society without violence and betrayal was represented by the image and the idea of home. In a romantic sort of way, American men and women imagined that they would be united in a prosperous, peaceful, and secure home, much like the one that commanded so much attention in this film.

Anne Hilton is the perfect representation of American womanhood at this time. She is completely devoted to her husband who is away at war and is reluctant to abandon her domestic role until she eventually takes a job in a war plant. She clings to his explanation of the events that dominate their lives, articulated on the night before he went away, that they are embarking on the greatest adventure of their lives. And she is convinced that her task is to "keep the past alive" by maintaining a "warm" home to which he can return after the fighting. Hilton does all that she can by raising two daughters, budgeting her government allotment check, and rejecting romantic overtures from a male friend, Tony, who visits her periodically. In fact, a scene in which Tony makes suggestive advances to her in a car perturbed industry censors. They feared that "any suggestion . . . that an officer of the U.S. Navy could intend any illicit relations with the wife of a fellow officer in the Army, who is absent from home, would prove extremely offensive."[24]

Scholars like Robert Westbrook have noted that a liberal state like America had to appeal to the private interests of citizens if it were to convert them to the war crusade. Loyalty in the liberal state was premised on the notion that patriotism would result in the granting of individual rights and the protection of individual interests. Thus, a male could be convinced to fight, not simply because he loved America, but because an American victory was the best bet he had for ensuring that he would have a warm and loving home, a decent job, or "freedom from want" in the future. Westbrook nicely extend this idea to an explanation of why Betty Grable was by far the most popular of American "pinup" girls during the war. There were women who appeared to be more sexual, but men wanted to protect not so much the erotic female as "wives and sweethearts on the home front" that they could settle down with once the war was over. In other words, Westbrook argues, there was more to the pinups than the sexual exploitation of women.[25]

In the 1944 film *Pin Up Girl* Betty Grable plays a working-class girl, Laurie Jones, who pursues private interests under the guise of wartime service. Grable's character joins a USO tour, ostensibly to help her country, but her real goals are more personal: to get out of a small Missouri town and to find excitement in places like Washington, D.C. In the nation's capital, she falls for a soldier who tells her that he is not interested in marrying a "pinup" but a girl who is "sincere and honest." On getting to know her, however, he reconsiders his original position and attempts to help her start a singing career. But the story makes it clear that if she were ever forced to choose between being a pinup and being a wife, she would not hesitate to elect the latter.

# THE PEOPLE GO TO BATTLE

Women were also elevated to the status of brave combatants in a film like *So Proudly We Hail* (1943). This story of Army nurses trapped with American men on Bataan and Corregidor presented women who were dedicated to serving the wounded and the nation. A reviewer in *Variety* was impressed with the fact that the women dealt closely with death but stood by the defeated men "with something invincible." The film took pains to establish that these women are from the ranks of average American families and are simply pulled into a war they do not want. As they embark from San Francisco just before Pearl Harbor, they have boyfriends, worry about their make-up, and have parents who speak with immigrant accents. The unexpected attack of December 7, 1941, forces their ship to divert to the Philippine Islands, where they find American forces trapped in tragic circumstances.[26]

Janet Davidson, played by actress Claudette Colbert, is a dedicated nurse who attempts to avoid any personal relations with servicemen because "she has a job to do" and has no time for romantic diversions. Resistance to one suitor declines one night, however, when the couple finds themselves together in a foxhole. Trapped on Corregidor, she eventually decides to marry the man. In a subsequent wartime scene, which deploys the image of Americans as God-fearing in a world threatened by evil forces, the two are married in a ceremony where a marriage under the eyes of God is considered sacred. This common man and woman exchange vows to forsake all others and to honor and love each other. The two even dream of someday going to his uncle's farm, where "everything is simple," and raising kids. When orders arrive to evacuate the nurses to Australia, this dedicated American woman refuses to leave both her husband and the battlefield. But other nurses pull her away after she is injured in a blast. While suffering from depression on a ship bound for home, she receives a letter from her lover with a copy of the deed to the farm. It is the possibility that they will be reunited that starts to pull her out of her despair, and the words she reads in his letter say that this is not just a war for soldiers but also a "people's war" fought to allow individuals to live in dignity and freedom.

These women can fight as well as love. When they are trapped at one point by a Japanese patrol, they come face to face with death. But Davidson, cool under fire, instructs them to create a diversion and get away. She even manages to crawl to the body of a dead enemy soldier and get the keys to a truck that carries them all to safety. At the same time, another nurse gives her life to facilitate the escape. Other nurses continue to treat the American wounded even when afflicted with malaria. One caregiver not only witnesses her son's death but affirms that the war must go on and that she is proud that "like his father he died for what he knew was right." These women wear pants, suffer through primitive conditions, hate the Japanese, and exhibit bravery and valor. Men want to protect them. A colonel promises he will evacuate them when the time comes because he will never be able to look his wife in the eye again if he does not. But they do not seek special treatment and generally are willing to defer loving relationships with men until after the conflict is over. Men, women, citizens, and nation are all in perfect alignment in this version of the national culture.

Inevitably, of course, common men became uncommon soldiers. They were defined not only as against the Japanese, who were shown as barbaric and treacherous, but in opposition to forms of American manhood that had no place in the wartime imagination. In numerous combat movies American men were seen as religious, respectful of women and marriage, inherent believers in social equality, and easygoing. Their sense of democracy is marked by both their hatred for totalitarianism and their belief that they all roughly hold a place of equality—which they seem disinterested in leaving—within their home societies. This identity, of course, masked any significant discussion of violent impulses on their part either in the pursuit of material wealth or in the control of women. These were men who got along with most everyone in their society and demanded little in return. Such an idealization can be seen clearly in a character like "Taxi" Potts, played by William Bendix, in *Guadalcanal Diary* (1943). Potts is a happy-go-lucky cab driver from Brooklyn who dreams only of resuming his ordinary life and watching Dodger baseball games. It is the Japanese who are attracted to political fanaticism and domination. Potts exclaims, "I'm no hero. I'm just a guy. I come out here because somebody had to come, [but] I don't want no medals. I just want to go back home."

Other men in the film mimic Potts' ordinariness and his desire to do what it takes to defeat the Japanese. In an opening scene from the film, men are seen on a troop transport in the South Pacific heading into what they know will be a bloody battle. Various religions come together to worship on deck, and a favorite pastime is simply sitting around and "shooting the breeze." Different ethnic and racial backgrounds are evident, and all are elated by mail from home. Indeed, home again became the antithesis to war in these films. It was an imagined place of nonviolence, where men and women loved each other and simple things—like having a child—prevailed. Ideology and politics were little discussed. On the eve of their first encounter with the brutality of war, men think of women not simply as sexual partners but as wives with whom they can start a family. In this film they sing, "I want a girl, just like the girl that married dear old Dad." And when one GI is shot on a beach, he reaches for a photo of his wife and children he carries in his helmet.

In *Bataan* (1943) the same sense of conformity prevails. Men from various ethnic and racial origins agree that they can work together to win the war. An African American serves the group as an engineer. And Jewish-American, Mexican-American, and Polish-American characters are evident. The men even benefit from the services of a Philippine scout who also hates the Japanese. Even past grievances are put aside in this story, as a former murderer and a sergeant who hated him now find common ground against the enemy and die together in a desperate stand to delay a Japanese advance.

There is an important modification of the concept of teamwork and ordinariness in the story, however. Some men are more vital to the war effort than others. The unit, which is assigned the task of restraining the Japanese at a key bridge, is led by a commanding figure, Sergeant Bill Dane, who is clearly more capable of leadership than most of the others. Ethnic types like F. X. Matowski from Pittsburgh or Alex Ramirez from California simply do not have the emotional control and experience of Dane, who has been in the Philippines for two years. Even Dane's captain, who is killed early in the tale, defers to him. When a young sailor wants to play "Taps" over the grave of a dead comrade, it is the wise Dane who counsels him not to let the enemy know of their losses. Audiences also learn that some consider the lone pilot in the group more valuable than infantrymen because they cost more to train. There is even a hint of the uneven nature of the sacrifice required between men in the field and civilians back home who only have to worry about rationing goods. Differences within military and civilian society can be aired, but ultimately the narrative resolves them in its glorification of the heroic sacrifice that all these men willingly undertake. Some think briefly of retreat, but Dane holds them together, and the group remains defiant against overwhelming enemy odds. In an act of heroic sacrifice, the pilot even manages to put his plane in the air and crash it into a bridge carrying Japanese troops. As the film's narrator proclaims at the end: "It don't matter where a man dies as long as he dies for freedom."

In *Air Force* (1943) American men from different backgrounds find a way to come together as an effective bomber crew. The story makes another valiant attempt at generating support for the war and melding the diverse components of American society together. A preamble frames the story and, to the music of "The Battle Hymn of the Republic," restates the call of Abraham Lincoln's Gettysburg Address, that the nation must continue the project to build a government "of the people, by the people, and for the people." Regional and ethnic differences are clearly marked among the crew, moreover, but are quickly overcome as the men fly further and further into the Pacific theater of the war.

John Garfield, who plays a Polish American named Winocki, is the most reluctant of the warriors. He harbors a good deal of anger against the plane's commander, who cut him from a pilot training program. Garfield's character is convinced that enlisted men like him simply do not get fair treatment in the Air Force. His commanding officer argues that he is not the only person that "washed out" of flight training and that he should now realize that everyone must work together as a crew. After seeing the results of Japanese attacks at Pearl Harbor and at Clark Field in the Philippines, however, this ethnic outsider quickly concludes that his commander is right, and more than anything he wants a chance to pay back the Japanese for their treachery. Even after a confrontation with enemy planes that results in the death of the commander, the crew eagerly repairs the plane and returns to the war with Winocki now serving heroically as a tail gunner.

Finally, near the war's end, a family of modest means is simply glorified in *The Fighting Sullivans* (1944). The real war deaths of five Sullivan boys in a naval battle off Guadalcanal served as the basis of this motion picture. Their grieving parents were at first reluctant to see the story move to the cinema but were persuaded that the film would show millions of citizens "the American way of life" and "the kind of life for which our boys were fighting." Indeed, before the film, the parents of the five Sullivans toured war plants and spoke of their loss and the fact that their boys might still be alive if the Air Force had even more planes.[27]

The "way of life" in the movie is nothing short of a glorification of traditional American family life and perhaps the most softhearted portrayal of a proletarian household ever put on the American cinema. Most of the narrative is located in the prewar lives of the boys and the warm upbringing they enjoyed in a devout Irish-Catholic home in Waterloo, Iowa. No doubt the film contributed to the overall integration of Catholics into the culture during this period, but it also shows a plebeian family that is loving and cooperative. The household consists of parents who love each other and siblings willing to stick together even in neighborhood fights, a trait that will put them on the same ship in later years.

The Sullivans are a family of modest means and proud of it. Tom Sullivan is a faithful train operator on the Illinois Central Railroad, and his spouse devotes all of her time to running a nine-room house. Childhood for the boys is idyllic and revolves around fishing, chasing trains, and taking the sacraments at the local Catholic church. The oldest boy, in typical working-class fashion, has to leave school early to help with the family economy, but he wants his younger brother to stay in school. When one brother loses a job, another promises to try and find him another. The father instills discipline, and the mother teaches love and respect. She does not hesitate to intervene and restrain her husband's violent impulses when he is tempted to hit the boys. But she always tells them that they must respect their father because he is a "fine man."

The five Sullivans join the Navy to defend their idyllic life as soon as they hear the news of Pearl Harbor. Their father only regrets that he is too old to join them. When all five are killed on a ship in the South Pacific, they are portrayed as still thinking of each other. The film suggests that four of the men may have been able to abandon ship, but that they went below deck instead in an attempt to save their brother who was in sick bay at the time, an action that allowed them to fulfill a promise they made to their parents to look out for each other. Shortly after he receives the devastating news of their deaths, the grief-stricken father continues to run his train because it is carrying vital war materiel; the lowborn man is still willing to continue the fight his sons began. As the film closes, the five sailors are depicted, not as corpses at the bottom of the sea, but as apparitions in the clouds on their way to a form of redemption higher than any nation could possibly bestow.

## REACTIONS

In a commentary in 1944 on the way in which some wartime films treated the subject of death, writer James Agee observed that Hollywood had basically sidestepped a true confrontation with the horror and pain of the killing. He noted that the many films that portrayed parents as having no regrets at all over the deaths of their sons and seeing such sacrifice as simply necessary for the maintenance of an ideal American community were just not believable. In *Tender Comrade*, where women shared expenses and a home together while the men they loved were away at war, Agee thought he saw nothing but a kind of "sorority-house democracy" that glossed over the real feelings and problems of most women on the home front. Agee thought the film offered a "comfortable realism" where women had almost no qualms about the war or their lack of goods, male companionship, or sex. The ending, in which Ginger Rogers tells her newborn son that his father died simply to give him a better life, struck Agee as simply too "fantastic." No one or no idea, he thought, could fully console people for such losses in their lives.[28]

Some writers shared Agee's lament over the decline of emotional realism in wartime films, but they were in a distinct minority. From time to time, a critic would point out the extravagant nature of images, especially as they pertained to common men and women. A critic in the *New York Times* agreed with Agee about *Tender Comrade*, calling it an "overboard attempt to wring the heart with the anguish of separation and the gallantry of girls who lose their men." In commenting on another story of women dealing with life while the men were abroad, *Since You Went Away*, a writer in the *New Yorker* saw it to be a "wishful post-card version of the home front" and missing the point about how "complicated" things were "among us" during the war. Another critic thought the film offered some realism in its portrayal of individuals who traded on the black market or hoarded goods. But this writer also thought the main characters were treated in a more fanciful way, especially in their devotion to the men in their lives and to the war effort. Another observer said that the main female characters, especially, smiled so much through their tears that they were really offered as models to "The People" of what proper wartime deportment should be like. This writer concluded that the film would be the "definitive home-front movie and will continue to be that until a realist comes along to show us what life is really like in America during World War II."[29]

Most commentators on films during the war treated sentimental and idealized versions of America and its people approvingly. Few seemed to expect anything less. Consider the response to *The Sullivans*. Some critics noted accurately that the film was not a war picture but one that told of the warm family and community life five working-class boys from a town in Iowa had before they were all killed on the same ship in the South Pacific. Observers liked the fact that the Sullivan family was religious and generally cooperative. One thought the film was really a tribute to "American parents" who raised their children with the right combination of love and discipline. Bosley Crowther, in the *New York Times*, went so far as to conclude that the Sullivans were "typical Americans, with love of home and love of family" at their core.[30]

*Joe Smith, American* was another film that was effusive about the "commonplace American." In this case, a simple breadwinner proves up to the task of standing up to enemy agents. Reviewers accepted the narrative's point that Joe was "no more phenomenal than any one's next-door neighbor" and so contented with his ordinary life that he was willing to do whatever it took to defend it even at home. *Time* proclaimed that individuals like Smith who toiled on assembly lines were largely forgotten by Hollywood when they were "busy glamorizing World War I doughboys." The magazine said that these workers were crucial to the war effort and that a celebration of their capacity for patriotism was the "kind of propaganda" that the film industry needed to make.[31]

This new-found effort to sentimentalize the image of the lower classes was actually evident even before Pearl Harbor. In responding to *Sergeant York* in July of 1941, the *New York Times* noted that the real York, a World War I hero, reflected the "raw integrity peculiar to simple folk" and the fact that the "American hayseed" who "marches in the forefront of this nation's ranks" was really at heart "proud, industrious, and honest." In fact, reviewers of the 1944 film *Lifeboat* were somewhat disturbed that the story had presented a Nazi character as rather ingenious and clever, and ordinary Americans as frequently opportunistic, cynical, and aimless. In this regard, the *Daily Worker* invoked its traditional call for more positive images of common people by complaining that the Nazi was the only person in the boat with a "plan." The reviewer was disturbed by the fact that the "democrats" were shown as "incompetent" and "spineless."[32]

Even where reviewers attempted to call for realistic depictions of war itself, the idea of realism was used mainly as a way to enhance the veneration of ordinary people and not as a way to expose either their exploitation or their emotional turmoil. That is to say that now the concept of realism was put into the service of fostering heroic and romantic views of Americans themselves. Thus, a reviewer of *So Proudly We Hail* liked the fact that the film alluded to the amputation of a soldier's legs, the hatred of an American nurse toward the Japanese, and the deliberate strafing of a Red Cross hospital by the enemy. It praised these scenes for bringing "realism" to the screen, but it also noted how this reality of war amplified the role of nurses and the Red Cross, showing audiences the "heroism" of the "war-front nurse" and "glorifying" the American Red Cross. Similarly, *Air Force* showed some of the devastation of the Japanese attack at Pearl Harbor and the fall of Wake Island. But critics were more inclined to note how the "team-work" of the plane's crew was "inspirational" for all Americans on the battlefront or on the home front. In assessments of *Bataan*, observers were struck with the fact that the movie "pulls no punches in displaying the realistically grim warfare conducted in the far Pacific" and the "graphic picturization of the actual conditions which fighters of this country face in the foreign fields." But the review hastened to add that in showing this side of war, audiences would welcome the "strong underlying current of bravery of American soldiers" and the women in the audience would like the "front line adventures" of their sons, husbands, and sweethearts." In fact, in a review of the film in *Commonweal*, the writer claimed that despite the scenes of "hundreds of people—white, black, yellow, and brown—being killed," the film still teaches an important lesson that in spite of the relentlessness of the Japanese, "our men are tough too and will fight to the bitter end."[33]

The tendency to endorse the move away from emotional realism was matched by a nearly full retreat from any discussion of what in the thirties might have been called social realism. Americans did not seem interested in viewing critical accounts of American society and its problems. There was some of that, to be sure. A film like *Double Indemnity* certainly portrayed Americans as willing to do just about anything for money. Interestingly, a crime drama like this one was generally praised for its entertainment value and not subjected to the standards of realism or patriotism that films more explicitly about the war were. Even sentimental films often had characters who were less than honest and were disinterested in the fight for the four freedoms. *Native Land*, a documentary-like feature that came out in 1942, did attempt to combine a thirties' call for unionism with a new campaign of anti-totalitarianism and did not hesitate to point out where Americans themselves opposed these democratic agendas. But essentially, little was said of social problems or the battle between labor and capital. In *American Romance*, there was segment that involved a contest between a immigrant industrialist who hated unions and his son who sided with men in his plant that wanted to organize. But reviewers paid much more attention to aspects of the story that idealized American myths like the one that said immigrants could come here with nothing and amass great wealth and come to love their new homeland. And they were impressed with scenes that conveyed the "vast size and beauty of the nation" itself. Again, it was left mostly to publications like the *Daily Worker* to hold such films accountable to the "realism" of the classic labor/capitalist struggle. The newspaper regretted that *American Romance* failed to show the "terrific exploitation of labor" in the Minnesota iron range and in steel mills and doubted the representativeness of the immigrant steel worker who rose to the top and turned his back on labor. But the war against fascism had muted some of the rebellious tendencies of even the far left, and the *Daily Worker* could only conclude that the film did show labor and management working together "for the common good of our country" and thus "deserves the wholehearted support of every one who loves America."[34]

## CONCLUSIONS

The penchant during the thirties to see the environment and soul of the lower classes as complicated was not as evident during wartime. Working-class types tended not to be aggressive gangsters or women on the rise but model citizens like Knute Rockne, Joe Smith, or Jo Jones, who were capable of putting aside their personal desires for the sake of helping the larger society of which they were a part. Democratic instincts prevailed over those that were more liberal. During this time when the nation and its inhabitants were somewhat idealized, the unsettled relationship between capitalism, individual desire, and democracy was not so clearly depicted as it was in the thirties. Men and women tended to get along. Class conflict was minimal. Movie critics and even the radical press gave evidence of suspending their normal critical stance for the sake of winning the war. Films discussed in this chapter like *Sergeant York, Wake Island, So Proudly We Hail,* and *Since You Went Away* actually were among the top box office hits of the wartime period, suggesting that audiences were not resistant to the images of men and women devoted to their nation and to each other or to the ideal that national goals should supercede personal ones.[35]

Cultural representation during the war offered a portrait of a nation that worked. Democracy appeared possible, liberalism less problematic. It remained to be seen if this confidence could last.

# THREE

# WAR AND PEACE AT HOME

It comes as no surprise to learn that the sentimental overlay on American culture did not survive the war. Never far from the surface, realistic portrayals of ordinary individuals and the social life of common people returned with a vengeance once the pressure of wartime conformity had subsided. This meant that liberalism and illiberalism again contested representations of democracy on a widespread basis as they had in the thirties.

Norman Mailer, in *The Naked and the Dead*, his classic novel of World War II published in 1948, demonstrated this quite clearly. Mailer, a vet who had served in the Pacific theater, told a story about the war and the Americans who fought it that was completely at odds with the aspirations of the Office of War Information and wartime Hollywood. For Mailer, many of the American soldiers were actually men who manifested a limitless capacity for dominance and brutality both on the field of battle and at home. Raised in a society in which men struggled with each other for wealth and power, Mailer's main characters were primarily illiberals, consumed with gaining the upper hand, and they would not hesitate to resort to cruelty to get it whether it was against the Japanese or women back home. Their attraction to dominance and brutality was naked and inbred, but it was the naked who survived and not the dead.[1]

Traditional American politics in the late forties was not as pessimistic as was Mailer about the nature of American men or about the competitive individualism nurtured by the American economic system. Rather, there was a general revulsion in political circles against many of the trends of the thirties and forties that had diminished the role of the individual for the sake of mass political mobilizations. Whether American leaders viewed mass movements like the New Deal that were intended to further economic democracy or National Socialism, which was designed to destroy both democracy and liberalism, the conclusion was widespread that a political future had to rest largely on a renewed sense of individual freedom and less organizational control. Arthur Schlesinger, in his classic political tract of 1949, *The Vital Center*, argued this point strongly, claiming that the key issue facing the United States at the time was not Soviet Communism but the "power of organizations over individuals." Schlesinger actually exhibited some of Mailer's pessimism by inferring that the war had undermined the assumption that men were "perfectible," but overall, unlike Mailer, he saw a way out. For Schlesinger, steeped in the framework of left/right politics, the political future had to be fashioned around a "vital center" or a blend of "the maintenance of individual liberties" and "the democratic control of economic life."[2]

Postwar politics, like wartime politics, became essentially consensual. General agreement was expressed over the evils of communism, a stance that tended to reinvigorate positive idealizations of capitalism and individualism and reinforce disillusionment with mass political mobilizations. Moreover, the sacrifices of the thirties and of wartime had created a tremendous desire for consumer goods in their infinite variety. A "business-orchestrated" campaign to sell the "American way of life" after the war convinced Americans of all ranks that free enterprise and the protection of individual rights would be the best guarantees for social harmony and abundance. Historian Roland Marchand has explained that the postwar period was marked by a dream of a "classless prosperity" in which everyone in society could participate in consumption and leisure activities. Marchand was able to demonstrate, for instance, that this dream was fostered in part by the nationalization of American advertising and its message that past class affiliations were by no means permanent. Everyone was encouraged to realize personal dreams and the benefits of democracy and liberalism through consumer goods like automobiles and new suburban housing. Depression-era images of struggling working-class families and militant labor organizations were being quickly put aside inside and outside the labor movement.[3]

The resurgent force of liberal and capitalist political visions was not good news for organized labor. Labor membership continued to increase in the thirties and forties, and workers had certainly gained a measure of respect during the war with their no-strike pledge, but in 1946 the initial instinct of large unions was to reassert their power and make up for sacrifices in influence and wages that they had made during the war. Led by auto workers in Detroit and longshoremen in New York, more strikes took place in the year after the war ended than in any other year in American history.[4] Yet the pressure to move toward the center and rising consumer expectations was strong. Business leaders and values had regained much of the influence they had lost in the thirties, and this allowed conservatives to speak out more aggressively against labor unions.

Certainly the antilabor animus of a reinvigorated Republican Party and a growing anticommunist crusade that railed against government-sponsored reform and labor militancy changed the climate of politics in ways that made it more difficult to sustain social democratic agendas from the thirties. Harry Truman himself was often reluctant to initiate government economic controls in the way Roosevelt had, although he did go further in promoting the democratic thrust toward civil rights. But eventually even labor leaders like Walter Reuther, the head of the powerful United Auto Workers (UAW), began to abandon the militant language of class conflict and promote goals like increased "buying power" for "the People" rather than to demand that labor receive a greater share of the "national wealth." And the Congress of Industrial Organizations (CIO) began to purge left-wing unions from its rolls in 1949 in an effort to demonstrate the anticommunist leanings of the labor movement and join the vital center of an emerging consensus in American politics. Inevitably, labor paid a price for joining the postwar acceptance of consensual politics, capitalist leadership, and consumerism in the form of decreased militancy and democratic activism that had marked its rise during the Depression.[5]

## BREAKING AWAY

Many of the images that circulated in the mass culture of postwar America did not readily endorse this new political consensus or the optimism that Schlesinger had expressed that a new American man could be created who was both a throwback to the rugged individual of the nineteenth century and a concerned social democrat. Hollywood, in particular, endorsed some of this faith but also did not hesitate to say again that liberalism and democracy might not be in store for the common man. When mass culture came to telling stories about ordinary people, in fact, it was likely to move away from issues like the celebration of consumer capitalism that had preoccupied national politics. It was inclined to pay special attention to the fears and anxieties of women or to offer outlooks like Mailer's that were essentially bleak. In part, this was due to the fact that mass culture quickly broke from its wartime pact with traditional political authorities to conceal the realism of American life and returned to its original project of probing the conflicted dimensions of human emotions and of society. Countless stories and debates circulated in postwar culture that ran counter to the impulses of the anticommunist or procapitalist crusades to eschew rigorous national self-analysis. Even the idealized notion from wartime that American men were natural-born patriots came under assault.

Mass culture, in part, simply could not leave behind issues raised by the recent encounter with unprecedented levels of violence in ways that traditional politics did. The problem for those who might have expected a proliferation of optimistic films about common people and everyday life in America in the aftermath of a victory, however, was that the impact of the recent war left a tremendous legacy of cruelty that cried for explanation, especially from a medium that was highly sensitive to the range of human emotions. Conventional politics was caught up in an effort to restore traditions like free-market enterprise and rugged individualism. It was left to mass culture to ponder more fully the lessons of the recent past. Mailer offered one when he argued that the constant struggle to succeed in a capitalistic society made many American men brutal and domineering. But after 1945 there was a growing perception that the problem of brutality in society was not simply about economic struggles but also had something to do with the very nature of men themselves. Pushed by suspicions that all men—including Americans—were capable of atrocities, mass culture began to probe layers of emotional realism that were simply off-limits in the mainstream political debates of the postwar period.[6]

Even a cursory review of postwar culture will suggest that victory on the battlefield and dreams of prosperity did not bring peace of mind. The atomic bomb brought both a sense of relief that the invasion of Japan would not be necessary and a fear that the United States could someday be vulnerable to such a weapon as well. The joy of victory and the resurgence of the economy could not hide what the war had done to the American psyche and the image that Americans now had of themselves. World War II definitely reaffirmed many positive notions Americans held about their country, especially when compared to the insidious nature of totalitarian regimes in other nations. But lessons from the war also disclosed the troublesome prospect that brutality resided in the nature of people everywhere. The postwar discovery of German concentration camps, Japanese atrocities in China, and the gradual revelation of the deaths of innocent civilians in Hiroshima and Nagasaki at the hands of Americans themselves reinforced the belief that violence was not peculiar to totalitarian regimes but lived in the hearts and souls men everywhere. Cruelty, in other words, was of human and not national origin. And although this point was not so evident in the early public commemoration or interpretation of the war, it quickly became a staple of the narratives that circulated throughout American culture in the late forties as official commemorations and popular remembering of the event moved in opposite directions.[7]

If one were to look solely at mass culture, the evidence is substantial that the most pervasive uneasiness of the postwar period was grounded, not in the potential for class conflict or an atomic explosion, but in the explosive temperament of American men, a point that made this issue particularly sensitive for women who had to live with them. John Hersey's interviews with Hiroshima survivors, published in the *New Yorker* in August of 1946, certainly suggested that Americans were capable of inflicting considerable harm to innocent civilians. Two years later, in June of 1948, readers of the same magazine could ponder a short piece of fiction that told of citizens who gathered annually in a small American town to stone to death one of their own. The bloody ritual was presented as a practice that was never questioned and a reminder that the threat of violence at home was eternal.[8]

From clues like these, historian William Graebner concluded that postwar America was a "culture of profound contingency." If brutality resided in the hearts of all men, then optimistic projections of the future in any form could always be upset. We can elaborate on Graebner's point to say that domestic peace as well as world peace was now contingent not simply on holding back the proliferation of military weapons or restraining foreign enemies but on the containment of dangerous men in the American homeland itself. Inferentially, the ability of the reigning paradigms of American political culture—liberalism, democracy, consumer capitalism, militarism—to elicit unequivocal support was weakened. How could anyone say that a political ideal or even a political organization like a labor union or a party could improve the future until assurances were made that the potential for domestic violence could be restrained? The idea of contingency, especially when rooted in an unstable human temperament rather than in foreign ideologies, stood as a massive obstacle to the effort of coherent and dominant narratives to persuade. And just as before the war, it was mass culture that took up this discussion of uncertainty.[9]

But mass culture in general and Hollywood in particular had a problem: how do you represent the disorder that was at the heart of American society, and how do you explain its origins? The general sense that human nature was dangerous did not prescribe in any way how this anxiety might be demonstrated in narrative form. Hollywood did not enter a period of unlimited free expression and euphoria, moreover, once the war was ended. Government restraints over film content were certainly loosened, but movie studios faced a steady decline in box office receipts in the late forties as Americans slowly turned to other forms of entertainment. Labor factionalism was rampant in Hollywood in 1946 as several organizations struggled for control in production facilities, and the House Un-American Activities Committee set up shop in Los Angeles in 1947, convinced that communists, intent on inserting their propaganda into films themselves, were active in the Screen Actors Guild. Thus, one would assume that films would not be in a position to make broad indictments about the evils of American society or the nature of some Americans themselves. Yet that is exactly what they did. Censors enforced a code of personal morality, and government investigators monitored expressions of left-wing ideology, but films were able to weave a critique of capitalistic society and ideas of the inherent brutality of many Americans into complex stories that eschewed any single point of view. They did this in at least two strategic ways. First, they tended to frame larger ideological and social issues into personal stories that muted the powerful implications they had for larger political entities like the nation. Second, they perfected the technique of constructing narratives that were contradictory in nature rather than centered and uniform. Respectable Americans appeared alongside dangerous ones. Films that pictured ordinary Americans as peaceful and loving could be found as well as those that saw the real America in much darker tones.[10]

Human relationships were already upset by the war itself. Moving from hometowns and traditional families, American society was marked by new forms of sexual freedom, long separations between men and women, the call for women to enter the workplace, and even the formation of homosexual communities in cities where massive numbers of service personnel were mobilized. Suspicions between people increased the longer they were apart; male workers often resented women who entered the workplace. In fact, gender relationships may have been destabilized more than any other set of associations during the period. Thus, marriages were often entered into hastily or ruptured for good. Much concern was evidenced in society over the impact of absent fathers on the well-being of young boys and over the incidence of juvenile delinquency. Interestingly, when asked to recall the war years, people in Orange, Texas, indicated that they thought the period was marked at home mostly by moral decay and increasing sexual promiscuity. And if one pays attention to postwar films, there was a hint that Americans were growing tired of the idea of constantly repressing personal desires in the thirties and forties for the good of larger institutions and the nation itself. The widening exploration of personal desire in the culture, in fact, had ominous implications for ideals of mutualism and the institutions that fostered them like labor unions and political parties. Perhaps this is why Dana Polan suggested that by 1945 there were signs that "discourses of commonality" had reached the limits of their ability to persuade.[11]

Some of the uneasiness over strained social relations and the explosion of violence in the war years was manifested in the "panic" over sexual deviance that characterized the immediate postwar period. George Chauncey has astutely noted how police press coverage of sex crimes increased despite no apparent rise in police statistics covering assaults or murders. Chauncey linked this sense of panic to an increased attack on homosexuals, but we can also suggest that it grew from a heightened sensitivity to the brutal nature of many human beings. In reporting on similar forms of anxiety, Susan Gubar learned that many women had not seen the war itself as simply a heroic crusade against tyranny—in the fashion of the larger political narratives—but as an excuse for men to practice misogyny. Thus, she found in the writings of female novelists of the time the idea that war was a "blitz" on women, who were now expected to be sexually accessible and a "prize" for the victorious men when they returned home. Mailer suggested some of the same points. If gender referred to the "social organization of the relationship between the sexes" and the fact that male and female identities are culturally constructed, then we can see that the impact of the war threatened to intensify discussions over gender relations perhaps even more than over class.[12]

The worry that American men could inflict violence at home was actually a relatively new national concern for twentieth-century Americans. Historian Elizabeth Pleck has argued that there was virtually no public discussion of wife beating, for instance, from 1900 until 1970, in part because of the lack of a strong feminist movement and because of the way in which the Great Depression and World War II tended to privilege the needs of men over women. Pleck shows that the major sociological journal of the study of marriage and the family published no article on the subject of family violence between its founding in 1939 and 1969. Pleck does note some professional discussion over the problem of rape in the

1940s, but much of it focused on the treatment of a women's "unconscious desire" to be brutalized and dominated. She found this theme not only in professional journals but in a postwar film like *Adventure* (1948), in which a working-class male subdues a "sexually repressed librarian."[13]

The postwar debate over the violent nature of humans in general and over the emotional state of the returning vet in particular, carried out more in mass culture than in traditional politics, included three crucial dimensions. First, there was a widespread effort to restore traditional gender roles of male breadwinners and female mothers. This meant women were often forced to leave the workplace and urged to do all that they could to comfort the returning servicemen. Second, the desirability of the heterosexual marriage was strongly reinforced. Although this point has too often been seen merely as an attempt to restore patriarchy, it was also done in order to force men to leave the brutality of war and misogynist values of the military behind. And finally, there was a pronounced rebellion against the first two positions in the culture. Ideas accentuated by the war that women could not be trusted (while men were away), that true manhood was best realized through individual acts of aggression rather than love, and that male independence was preferred to marriage were now articulated fairly regularly.

Examples of all three positions abounded in a culture that was filled with powerful crosscurrents in the late forties. Traditional notions of motherhood and female loyalty to men were venerated, to be sure, both before and after the war. Wives and mothers were constantly instructed to assist vets in making the transition back to civilian life and to help him to feel that he was "head man again." But social practice drifted from ideals as postwar levels of female employment rose consistently; in 1949 twice as many women worked outside the home as in 1940. Fathers were not only expected to resume domestic roles but were seen as crucial to restoring emotional stability for children. The logic of the times suggested that fathers had the potential to teach girls how to respect a man and to provide young men with a sense of discipline—if they were not overly authoritarian.[14]

In a postwar political world that devoted much effort to reviving dreams of prosperous, heterosexual families led by sensible breadwinning fathers and in castigating both liberated women and homosexual men, however, there was evidence of considerable opposition to these ideals. Not all men were ready to put the war behind them and give themselves over to a loving relationship with a women. Timothy A. Shuker-Haines has insightfully labeled this resistance to domesticity as "reactionary masculinity" and traced its expression to pulp magazines such as *Argosy* and *Blue Book* in the postwar period. It was the defense of this form of masculinity that stood at the heart of the postwar success of the novels of Mickey Spillane. Raised in a working-class neighborhood in Elizabeth, New Jersey, Spillane's major fictional hero, Mike Hammer, exhibited disdain for the emerging ideal of a middle-class father who provides reason and prosperity for his wife and children. Hammer stood outside the vital center of postwar politics and with that strain of postwar culture that venerated domination over democracy and independence to the exclusion of a social conscience. Hammer was an illiberal private investigator who pursued his version of justice (and his indifference to democracy and liberalism) anyway he saw fit. He was avowedly sexist, racist, anti-intellectual, homophobic, and an exemplar of a "brand of jack booted fascist vigilantism in the guise of preserving order." Spillane's 1947 novel, *I, the Jury*, in which Hammer kills the female object of his lust in cold blood because she is unwilling to commit to one man, turned the illiberal detective into a cultural hero to many.[15]

This expanded debate over violence and gender, however, was ominous for the cultural position of workingmen in American society, coming when it did in a period of growing antilabor feeling. The image of the ordinary GI, which tended to mute class distinctions in the representation of American men, was now giving way to a tendency to see men further down the social rung as potentially the most savage and least desirable men of all. In the immediate postwar years, this point was not so clear in the overall culture. By the fifties, however, as we will see in the next chapter, the cultural burden of indigenous violence and antidemocratic attitudes was disproportionately assumed by blue collar men and women.[16]

## THE RETURNING VET

The heroic common man with the capacity to defeat the German war machine needed assistance once the war was over. The returning soldier, brutalized and injured by the devastation of war, quickly became the subject of some films. Struggling to sustain elements of optimism for a better postwar world, the creators of these stories placed the future of the vet and the building of a cooperative society, not in the hands of government planners, capitalists, or even rugged individualists, but squarely in the hands of women who could render love and understanding. Again, the images of film forced a consideration of gender tensions in ways conventional politics did not.

Common women played central roles in offering Americans hope that the brutality and pain of the war could be put aside, a necessary step if optimism in democracy and liberalism was to be sustained. Female characters in movies like *Pride of the Marines* (1945), *Best Years of Our Lives* (1946), *From This Day Forward* (1946), and *Till the End of Time* (1946) all exhibited a willingness and a capacity to forgo personal goals for the sake of creating domestic harmony. In *Pride of the Marines*, the challenge for a loving wife was steep, for she had to restore the self-confidence and emotional stability of a soldier who had been blinded by Japanese gunfire. Film scholars have argued that this story shifted the emphasis on larger social problems that could be found in many thirties films to a discussion of individual roles and identities, although personal roles and identities were already widely debated in the Depression era.[17]

Actor John Garfield plays a real-life foundry worker, Al Schmid, who fought valiantly against the Japanese in the Pacific and became a national hero. Schmid is attracted to Ruth, a woman he meets just before he leaves for the service. Even in their prewar relationship, he constantly asserts his view that men are superior to women and likes to brag about how much better he is at hunting and handling a gun. And he relishes his freedom: "I like to live independent. . . . Right now I'm sitting pretty, first class burner at the foundry making forty bucks a week and trying hard to spend it all." When the more cautious woman reminds him of the need to save for a "rainy day," he replies that he envisions only days with "no responsibilities, no worries, no waiting around on women." His married landlord also fantasizes about a hunting trip to Canada for both of them, although he eventually has to relinquish this dream due to the wishes of his wife.

Americans were told in this narrative, of course, that they were fortunate to have men like Al Schmid once the Japanese attack on Pearl Harbor pushed them into war, an assertion that heroic and independent men have a place in wartime. Initially Schmid even thinks shooting the Japanese might be more fun than hunting, and he is impressed by the spirit of colleagues at the foundry who are eager to enlist in the armed services. He is quick to follow, declaring that one has to be "real rugged to get into the Marines." At this point the narrative sanctions Schmid's version of masculinity as Ruth tells him that if she were a man she would feel the same enthusiasm for war and violence that he does. She even promises to wait for him, calling herself the "sticking kind" and assures him that she will "wrap myself in cellophane" and not date other men.

Rugged manhood and a staunch sense of individualism are traits that

John Garfield plays Al Schmid, a wounded vet in *Pride of the Marines* (1945). In this story the heroic warrior was rendered dependent upon the love and kindness of a woman, a sign that many Americans were willing to put the veneration of common men and their military exploits behind them. Credit: Film Still Archives, Museum of Modern Art, New York

serve this factory worker well and help to make him a war hero on Guadalcanal, where he kills hundreds of Japanese with his machine gun. But a grenade explosion ruins his eyesight, sending him to a naval hospital in California to recuperate. Culturally, the hospital serves as a symbolic decompression chamber where wounded vets and caring female nurses discuss the needs of a postwar world. In this sense, the film serves as a surrogate for real civic discussion. The nurses stand as representations of the need for all women to care and nurture men scared by battle. One nurse even takes the initiative to contact Ruth in Al's hometown of Philadelphia to encourage her to write to her boyfriend. This model of postwar femininity certainly constrained the possibilities for female self-realization in the era, but it also constituted a direct assault on the type of male independence that a person like Schmid enjoyed before the conflict.

The wounded soldier does not appear to think much about independence while recovering from his wounds. Rather, he now laments the fact that his disability prevents him from assuming a more traditional role as breadwinner and proper husband for Ruth. "I was going to buy her things she never had," he exclaims. "I was going to see that she never had to work again. What good can I do her now? I can't even get married. I'll never earn enough money to keep her. I won't have her being a seeing eye dog for me."

Talk among the hospitalized vets further reveals how deeply gender anxieties run. Some men express skepticism over the ability of women to be faithful. Others think of tender reunions with sweethearts. Many contemplate the nature of the postwar economy, a topic that speaks directly to the felt need of men to take up roles as providers and to keep women at home. Some are sure that there will be no more need for "apples and bonus marches." And in a clear rejection of many of the ideals of postwar working-class organizations to enhance worker benefits, one sailor expresses his ideal future: "You ask me what I want out of life. Well I'm not an ambitious guy, thirty bucks a week. Enough to take my girl out on a Saturday night, a ball game on Sunday. That's about all I ask or is that too much?"

The men also have some concern for the very survival of democracy, just as Mailer did. Wounded vets in the film promise that if things do not go well after the war, they will strive, in a vague sense, to see that changes are made to ensure that a democratic community prevails. Lee Diamond, Schmid's fighting comrade from Brooklyn, says that he went to war primarily to protect the ideal of democracy in the first place. With "America the Beautiful" playing softly in the background, Diamond insists: "Don't tell me we can't make it work in peace like we do in war. Don't tell me we can't pull together." To emphasize the heroic and sentimental emotions of the feature, Warner Brothers arranged for the premier to be held in Schmid's hometown, where more than four hundred veterans from the Marine division that landed on Guadalcanal gathered for an event that was broadcast over radio to American armed forces around the world. The real Mrs. Schmid even told a magazine that having Al back was the "most wonderful time" of her life and that she now wanted to have his child.[18]

Schmid is eventually convinced to return to Philadelphia to receive a Navy Cross. A fellow officer argues that he has to go back and see if the people who cared for him before the war still feel the same way. On the eve of his homecoming, audiences can see Ruth praying in a church (a practice widely attributed to Americans during the war) for the wounded warrior "to know that he is wanted." Divine intervention is reinforced by the urgings of Diamond that he use the same "guts" he demonstrated on Guadalcanal to face Ruth despite the fact that he is now less than the man he wants to be. In a scene of home as a stable and warm place with a decorated Christmas tree, Schmid admits to the woman in his life that he realizes he can no longer do everything for himself, a sign that some of the male independence that Schlesinger longed for may not be obtainable. But Ruth elects to emphasize, not his newfound dependency, but his past achievements and their future together. She tells him:

Why shouldn't two people need each other? We can have a family. Sure we will have a problem, but everyone has problems. All married couples do. . . . Oh, sweetheart, don't you realize that every single guy who fought is no longer ordinary? Don't you realize that millions of people were looking to Guadalcanal while you were fighting there? . . . It wasn't any ordinary guy who kept the Japs back that night. You are one of the most extraordinary fellows in the world.

As the film ends, the postwar couple rides away in a cab with an image of Independence Hall looming in the background. Stable gender relations, democracy, the rehabilitation of the wounded male, and the containment of male independence—a sizable domestic agenda—all appear attainable. For political leaders, a reinvigorated capitalism and the atomic bomb would insure a peaceful future; in the popular imagination, the key to domestic peace resided in the dream of peaceful coexistence between men and women.

The most famous and powerful call for female support in putting the devastation of war behind us and building a stable and democratic future was certainly to be found in *The Best Years of Our Lives* (1946). Since the connection between gender harmony and future stability was important, the film began by first restating the promise of classlessness and prosperity that marked much thought in aftermath of the war. Three veterans from different social backgrounds fly over America and see for themselves (and for the audience) signs of the growing prosperity like automobiles and golf courses. Quickly the narrative joins the discussion, however, about the need for female love and understanding for men who have been both emasculated and wounded by their sojourn in the military. Marriage is central to the reconversion of the men to domestic life, but women are not subordinate in this formulation. They have vital (domestic) roles to play in soothing the scars of war. The veterans in this story can never get to the point of making a decent living or building a democratic community if they do not receive the understanding and support of loving women. Kaja Silverman has inferred that this film actually deviated from the pervasive theme of female dependency by showing how important women were to restoring the "wounded male subject to his former potency." But it should be stressed that overall ordinary women were not all that dependent in postwar features discussed here.[19]

Two of the veterans in the story, Fred and Homer, are clearly lower-class men. The third member of their group, Al, is a banker who lives in distinctly middle-class surroundings. Despite their varied backgrounds, however, all three find the return to civilian life troublesome and clearly need female assistance. Homer's plight is the most difficult because he is a double amputee. Thus, this former sailor is as despondent about prospects for a normal life as was Al Schmid and as unwilling to make himself a burden to anyone else. His girlfriend, however, is a model of postwar feminine understanding. In one of the pivotal cultural moments in the postwar discussion over gender, he takes her to his bedroom, a place where he might be expected to assert his masculinity, and tells her that he is really no man at all. Standing before her as neither heroic warrior nor self-made man, he admits that he can not even dress himself for bed and that he is as "dependent as a baby." This adoring female is more than ready to assist the emasculated male and the nation by helping him and by promising that she will never leave him. Homer's postwar life, in other words, is contingent, not on political activism or individual struggle, but on a loving and supportive relationship with a woman.

Fred also struggles with his war experience and, to a greater extent, with the fact that he is from the working class. His readjustment is hampered by the psychological scars of flying bombing runs over Germany and by the fact that his wife has postwar ambitions of her own that do not include him. In 1946 he is frustrated over the fact that his war service has led him back only to his menial job as soda jerk and over the realization that his spouse has been less than faithful. During the war his wife came to value her independence, and she is not inclined to submit to his needs now that he has returned. And clearly he has come to expect more for his toil than a life of low status and low pay.

He finds his path to readjustment through a combination of female love and liberalism, although the former point commands much more screen attention. Support and affection come from Al's daughter, Peggy. In another bedroom scene, the young woman cradles him in her arms when nightmares from his bombing runs over Germany make him cry out in the night. She even tells her parents that if his wife will no longer help him she will. Production code censors were uneasy about a scene in which a woman did not respect an existing marital arrangement, but the needs of the vets and the nation took precedence over concerns such as these.[20]

Again, some explicit references to democracy and liberalism are made in the film. Back at his post in the bank, Al complains that last year it was "kill the Japs" and this year it is "make more money," an association of the connection between violence and capitalism worthy of Mailer. Al fights particularly hard at his bank for easier loan policies. He defends a decision to grant a loan to a vet who had been a sharecropper before the war but now wants to own his own land, arguing that during the war men had come to rely on each other and that postwar society needed the same sense of solidarity. At the end of the story, Fred imagines that he might be able to create a business by building prefabricated housing from old aircraft parts, although no assurances are given that he can lift himself and his new wife, Peggy, out of the lower classes. The return of market capitalism had some ominous overtones after 1945. Certainly there was optimism, as Fred's defense of investing in individuals affirms. Yet fears were still widespread that another depression might return, although they were not as powerful as the concerns over the potential turmoil that still resided in the emotions of ordinary American men.

Postwar mandates for a better life through marriage also punctuated the narrative of *From This Day Forward* (1946). Again, the future of common people was articulated, not in terms of increased plebeian mobilizations or rugged individualism, but in terms of loving relationships and steady jobs. Indeed, the absence of a narrative of class relations in this film is even more curious because the original story was written by Thomas Bell, whose 1941 novel *Out of This Furnace* celebrated the mobilization of immigrant workers and the triumph of a union in Braddock, Pennsylvania, the community in which he lived.

Like other movies about returning vets, *From this Day Forward* elected to discuss couples rather than classes. It told the story of Bill and Suzie Cummings and their endeavor to create economic security and a loving relationship in the forties. Bill, in particular, is haunted by the memory of losing his job before Pearl Harbor and the possibility that another depression will prevent him from assuming his role as a breadwinner. The ending is hopeful, although no one knew for sure in 1946 what the future would be.[21]

The creation of a democratic community in film was always more dependent on an idea of gender harmony than was the case in the world of mainstream politics. Thus, the association in the popular mind between the restoration of stable marriages, economic security, and the future of a democratic community—and the fear that these goals would not be realized—was made repeatedly. *Till the End of Time* (1946) offered another twist on this discussion by locating the obstacles to harmony not only in the problems of returned vets but in the disposition of women as well. Most of the story centers attention on Marines recently returned from the Pacific like Cliff Harper, played by Guy Madison, and Bill Tabeshaw played by Robert Mitchum. Harper finds postwar employment on an assembly line that manufactures radios but is uncertain that he wants to remain in a working-class occupation. He appreciates the pride his parents show in his wartime accomplishments but expresses bitterness over the fact that the war took away an opportunity he had to gain a college degree in engineering. Ultimately, his readjustment will be facilitated by the love of a woman he meets more than by the job he gets.

Tabeshaw's destiny is left unresolved in this story precisely because he is less interested in building a loving relationship with a woman and more inclined toward gambling, drinking, and some distant goal of ranching. During production, movie industry censors recommended that more of an effort be made to reduce the amount of scenes showing soldiers drinking and the use of "brutal commando tactics" in a barroom fight because such images appeared to be a jarring change from wartime idealizations of such men.[22]

Audiences see here a woman who also carries scars from her wartime experience. When Harper expresses a desire to marry her, she does not respond by affirming a belief in the need to help vets readjust. Rather than displaying an overwhelming desire to serve the needs of men, she voices her own set of desires and forces the former Marine to care for her for a time. At one point she elects to date another man, a move that angers Harper considerably. He confronts her and calls her a "tramp," but she retaliates by asserting that she too is not clear about her life choices after the war and that she has psychic scars from the conflict, having lost a spouse in France. She feels that she has sacrificed enough, in other words, for the nation and its men, and her postwar future is filled with doubt and anxiety. As she breaks into tears, Harper suddenly turns from confused veteran to caregiver and comforts her.

Again explicit political messages like the promise of a postwar free of intolerance are given less attention than the need for gender harmony and emotional comfort. In one of the movie's final scenes, the two Marines join a paraplegic comrade and start a brawl in a barroom with men who have asked them to join hate groups that exclude Jews, Catholics, and African Americans. Tabeshaw, who "sweated out the four freedoms" on Guadalcanal, where he saw a Jewish friend killed, is now enraged by the existence of such attitudes in America. The fight scene suggests that the struggle for democracy still remained but that it would be more about tolerating diverse races and religions than about classes, a point that has been made by historians looking at the transformation of American political outlooks after the war as well. But if the structure of this narrative and others like it insinuated anything about postwar culture, it was that all was not right among the people, that the war had raised serious issues that still had to be worked through, and that political agendas that moved quickly toward the restoration of optimism and consensus at home were ignoring much of what the people still felt.[23]

## NOSTALGIA FOR THE WORKING-CLASS FAMILY

The dream of gender harmony that dominated many postwar films contained the hope that a peaceful and just future might begin at home. It was a dream that simultaneously reasserted visions of domestic confinement for women and lowered the independent and dominant standing of men. The seeds of a more democratic conception of gender relations and of a society that was more cooperative (less liberal) than competitive, in other words, could be extracted from such formulations. These hopes were also found in a group of movies that looked with some longing to lower-class families and the way they were imagined to be incubators of selflessness and love. Nostalgia is often driven by a need to recapture what seems irretrievably lost, and these stories did just that. In their sentimental overtones, they even kept alive some of the romanticism of wartime. In the period before the war and before the Depression, Hollywood suddenly discovered proletarian households devoid of incipient gangsters and fallen women in which morally upright individuals struggled to help and care for each other.

*Our Vines Have Tender Grapes* (1945) is a story of moral longing for a nation now worried about the explosion of brutal behavior in the world— and possibly about the return of competitive capitalism. This narrative focused its lens more on the desire for a warm community than on the fulfillment of individual dreams. It was a tale set in an idyllic rural community of caring and loving Norwegian Americans in the upper Midwest. Communal harmony and generosity marked this symbolic reconstruction of common people in a world where genuine fears existed that such values could not be maintained. One newspaper review of the film said it was about "neighbors helping neighbors." At countless turns, the story emphasized the need for cooperation and love in a society that could be brutal and unpredictable. In the development of a relationship between a father and a daughter in the film, audiences were especially reminded of the capacity of men for love.

Martinius Jacobson, played by Edward G. Robinson, punishes his daughter Selma early in the story for her selfishness when she refuses to let a friend use a pair of her roller skates. Averse to physical violence, however, and fearing his strong hands might hurt her, he takes the skates away rather than strike her, a reminder that disputes can be resolved by means other than force. In fact, after disciplining her, he is so concerned for her happiness that he wakes her up at four o'clock in the morning to take her into town to see a passing circus troupe and let her enjoy the sight of elephants. This farmer of modest means even digs deeply into his pocket for five dollars to persuade a man to bring the animal off of a truck to do tricks for the youngster. In return, Selma expresses appreciation for this act of love and generosity and tells her father that this is the best summer of her life.

Generosity is also extended on a communal basis. When Selma and a friend are swept into a raging river while playing in an old bathtub, men from the settlement gather to enact a dramatic rescue to save the children. The destruction of a farmer's barn by fire offers the community another opportunity to help one of its own. At a local church meeting, the community discusses the fact that the family lacks insurance for the structure, and Selma then reminds them of their communal obligations when she offers to sell her precious nine-month-old calf to help the family in need. The local newspaper editor, Nels Halvorsen, even delivers a speech reinforcing the need for a spirit of giving. He quotes from an old editorial written by his father:

We are all children by adoption of the land in which we live. The earth is here and the water and the sunlight and the labor to make it yield. The only thing that can make a land evil is the people who inhabit it. If we have within ourselves the nobility to share in times of stress and need with those who are destitute, then we can raise our heads with dignity among the princes of earth.

The film not only articulates a clear position in the postwar controversy over unrestrained individualism and capitalism but joins the growing argument over the darker dimensions of human nature. In one scene Selma walks through unspoiled countryside with a young friend, Arnold, who expresses a desire to someday use a rifle and become a soldier. Selma counters his dreams with an assertion that girls can fight just as well as boys. On impulse, she picks up a stone and hurls it at a squirrel, killing the animal instantly. But this confrontation with death saddens both of them, and Selma reasons that a newborn calf on her father's farm will somehow replace the life that she took. When Nels Halvorsen does go off to war, she thinks out loud about the bombs that are dropped and tells her father that she does not "think it's true about peace on earth, good will toward men." Her father argues that some things have to be defended at all costs, but this is a position the young woman never fully accepts.

A reconstructed world of ordinary working people is again invoked as a symbol of love and caring in the 1945 film *A Tree Grows in Brooklyn*. This sympathetic portrait of working-class family living in a small tenement early in this century extends compassion rather than condemnation to "the people." More importantly, like *Our Vines Have Tender Grapes*, it positioned the prewar world as a place of love and unity—despite its flaws—opposite a world of brutality and destruction that was now presumed by some to have been born in the early forties. Here a family is described from the point of view of a young girl, Francie Nolan, who loves her parents despite their faults and who recalls countless acts of kindness.

The pursuit of loving and supportive relations is constantly hindered in prewar Brooklyn by harsh economic circumstances. Kate Nolan recognizes the realities of a limited income for her family and attempts to face these conditions realistically through hard work, saving, and sacrifice. Her spouse, Johnny Nolan, is an Irish-American dreamer, who sings at social affairs for a living and hopes for a big break on the Brooklyn stage. One night he tells his daughter Francie that eventually he is going to bet on a horse and win enough money to take her away. In the meantime, however, Kate scrimps to save pennies just to pay on insurance policies that will at least give them decent funerals.

The film's director, Elia Kazan, later explained that he had hired actor James Dunn for the role of Johnny Nolan because he too had a problem with alcohol that had hurt his career. Kazan thought he saw a trace of pain in Dunn's face that indicated he had "failed the test of life" and wanted to bring that "pain" to the screen. Again, however, industry censors were unconcerned over unflattering representations of working people. They accepted the image of excessive drinking by members of the working class, although they had recoiled when such images were attributed to soldiers in *Till the End of Time* (1946). They spent more time trying to get Kazan to change the portrayal of Kate's sister, Sissy, who was depicted as a woman who had been married several times and apparently had never been legally divorced. They felt that this suggested bigamy and that the story did not sufficiently condemn these "illicit relationships."[24]

Some in Kate's family argued that love was more important than money. Her sister, who had been divorced and had troubled relations with men, told her how fortunate she was to have a guy "you care clear overboard about." But the struggling housewife was ambivalent about loving this blue-collar provider. She told her sister:

> Yeah, where does crazy over somebody get you? You don't put no pennies in the bank. You don't buy no clothes to send the kids to school in. Maybe you got it better not sticking to one guy. I wish sometimes I wasn't so crazy over him. I won't have the kids taking after him either. Him and those dreamy way of his I used to think was so fine. Not if I got to cut it right out of their hearts.

The loving father makes one last attempt to make the world better for the woman he loves. Realizing that his daughter longs to be a writer (and not a working-class housewife), he attempts to help her by finding steady employment on a New York construction project, a task for which he is completely unsuited. The family's plight is made more difficult by the fact that Kate is pregnant again, and they must move to a smaller apartment. Kate is inclined to see Francie's dreams to stay in school and for a better life as unrealistic; her idealistic husband, however, dies trying to prove that they are attainable. The blue-collar community of Brooklyn renders assistance to the saddened family. Neighborhood people offer jobs to Francie and her brother in order to help the family survive and out of the respect they had for Johnny Nolan. And in a scene that ultimately condemns an economic system that makes victims out of good people, Francie reads a tribute she wrote to her father that challenges those who would have claimed he was a failure. "He had nothing to give but himself," she exclaims, "but of this he gave generously like a king."

The romantic view of the blue-collar world and caring community was not a staple of postwar film (or politics) by any means, but it would receive one more effective treatment in 1948. These cultural narratives were clear on what they valued in the memory of the prewar world of workers and what they despised. Values of sharing and generosity were to be admired; a life lived on the economic margins was not. This was certainly the case in *I Remember Mama* (1948). Director George Stevens, who spent the war filming actual combat scenes in Europe and saw the horrors of the concentration camps after the war, found it impossible to make a movie about the war just after it ended. He could not directly confront the violence and devastation he had seen until the late 1950s, when he made a film about the life of Anne Frank. In 1948, he choose to retreat to prewar San Francisco and tell the story of an immigrant family in which a mother demonstrated exceptional acts of love and generosity. It is no wonder that reviewers noted the "deeply moving nostalgia" of the film and the "poignant tender tribute to the family institution."[25]

This is a narrative not about heroic soldiers but about self-sacrificing women, a key symbol in the growing argument against male violence and unrestrained competition that was on the minds of the American people in the late forties. Supported by a dutiful spouse who works as a carpenter, "Mama" manages the household finances, distributes resources, and provides leadership and stability. She is the cultural contradiction to Mailer's warriors.

The opening scenes venerate the memory of family solidarity. Nels, the oldest son, expresses an interest in attending high school, a decision that threatens to reduce total household income in the same way that Francie Dolan's wish to stay in school and become a writer did. The immigrant parents discuss the sacrifices they would be willing to make to enhance their son's chances in American society. His father decides to do without tobacco; his mother elects to forgo a winter coat she needs. A sister offers to babysit, and Nels himself plans to seek employment at a local grocery store after school. It is this symbolic and collective self-sacrifice that allows "Mama" to declare that her son can not only have the education he desires but that the family will not have to go into debt, a statement that venerates the old working-class value of thrift on the eve of a revolution in consumer spending and debt.

A mother's devotion to her children is expressed again and again in the story. When her daughter Dagmar needs an operation, "Mama" refuses to have the girl taken to a county hospital for poorer families and insists that she will find a way to pay for her to be taken to a clinic. When clinic rules restrict her ability to fulfill a promise she made to the child to visit her, the mother worries that her daughter will feel abandoned. Driven by maternal love and almost totally lacking in personal desire, she sneaks into the facility, posing as a cleaning woman. As audiences watched this woman scrub floors on her knees just to be near her daughter, they were reminded that society's future was not necessarily in the hands of brave warriors or astute businessmen, but of loving mothers who could offer the best human nature had to give. "Mama" ends the scene in the sick ward by bringing her child a toy and singing a sweet Norwegian melody to soothe her fears and the worries of an audience in a postwar world. The working class has no capacity for political protest or collective action in narratives like *I Remember Mama* or *A Tree Grows in Brooklyn,* but at least it still retains some standing as a source of moral values in the imagined nation.

Family cohesion and cooperation are continually positioned against the raw pursuit of wealth in this film, another reminder of how widespread was the fear over the return of liberal capitalism in the postwar. In one instance, "Mama" sells a treasured broach in order to buy her daughter Catherine, through whose voice the story is told, a graduation gift. When Catherine learns what her mother has given up, however, she secures the return of the heirloom and vows to "keep it forever." In response to this act of selflessness and devotion on his daughter's part, Catherine's father pours her a cup of coffee, a sign that she has now earned the right to drink what had been reserved only for mature adults. Coming of age in this family involves the capacity to restrain personal desire, not to realize it.

Individual goals are certainly acknowledged. "Mama" goes to great efforts to help Catherine attain her dream of becoming a writer, and there is some discussion of the fact that Nels may someday become a physician. The point is that in smoothly functioning families headed by selfless women, individuals learn to balance the needs of the democratic community with those that are more personal. "Mama" even interprets the great immigration streams into America at the turn of the last century as attempts at finding family stability rather than material gain (a highly defensible argument). She tells her children that she came to America with her husband because so many relatives were already here and that what she liked most about San Francisco was that she could rejoin a larger familial unit.

## LOVE AND MONEY

Common men faced an insoluble dilemma in the film culture of the late forties. Since their plebeian neighborhoods and occupations were not imagined to hold much of a future, they were still faced with the need to find more justice and, for that matter, more money in their lives. In the postwar—as in the prewar—period, Frank Capra addressed this issue by exploring ways American society and its economic system might be made more democratic. His normal recourse was to deploy the character of a concerned middle-class leader capable of fighting against the corruption and greed that stood in the way of a better life for all. As always, however, audiences were more likely to see films about lowborn men who simply took it upon themselves to find a path toward a more prosperous life by employing the competitive and forceful instincts they learned on city streets where only the strongest and fittest survived. The problem was that these very qualities of toughness and independence threatened to destroy the aspiring man because they prevented him from establishing loving connections to others. This point was made repeatedly in boxing narratives, for instance, which reevaluated the relationship between manhood, violence, and capitalism that was so central to postwar culture. The boxer was a symbol of all people in the lower classes who struggled to rise in American society through grit and determination.

After 1945, Capra's concern for the fate of the democratic community—something that was at the heart of his features in the thirties—was complicated by an intensified concern over the future of individualism. Capra's male leads in the postwar films like *It's a Wonderful Life* (1946) and *State of the Union* (1948) were not so single-minded in their focus on saving democracy. Instead, characters like George Bailey and Grant Matthews fought personal battles over how much they were willing to sacrifice their own desires for the good of community and nation. Capra's Depression-era tales tended to celebrate the individual agency and leadership of male heroes in conjunction with a generalized sense of neighborly or collective action as a means of solving economic and political problems. In a sense, they represented something of a blend of liberal and democratic sentiments. But after years of hard times and war that had forced millions to relinquish private agendas, even Capra reflected something of the popular exhaustion with the democratic notion that personal interests were inevitably secondary to national or collective ones.

Although *It's a Wonderful Life* is remembered today as a "Christmas story," it was above all a restatement of the apprehensions that pervaded American culture in 1946. The burden of years of sacrifice, the return of capitalism, and the future of democracy were very much subjects at its core. Its central character, George Bailey, is not a veteran but a middle-class male who lives in a small town, the symbolic center of American democracy. But contentment eludes Bailey. He finds some satisfaction and the love of a woman in the community, but he retains some bitterness over the fact that he can never leave to go to college or see the world. In the end, he turns out to be a traditional Capra hero (with regrets) by fighting to save his family's savings and loan business and to help proletarians get the loans they need to become homeowners in the face of a greedy capitalist who attempts to take complete control of the town's economic life. Importantly, this troubled middle-class leader cannot resist monopoly capitalism by himself. Plagued by self-doubts over the course of his life, in the end he needs the cooperation of a loving wife and neighbors who care for him. The final scene of the picture, in which family and friends rally to Bailey's cause and rescue the savings and loan with their contributions, constitutes a powerful moment in the film of the immediate postwar in which hopes for a society based more on reciprocity than individualism are powerfully articulated. The problem for the image of democracy in mass culture was that such moments were increasingly rare.

Two years later, in *State of the Union*, even this brief moment of optimism is gone. Grant Matthews, a vet and a self-made businessman from the West like Capra himself, contemplates running for the presidency and abandoning his economic pursuits because he is upset over what he sees as a lack of cooperation and a preponderance of self-interest in postwar society. He is angry at labor leaders who call for wildcat strikes, corporate managers who are too inflexible in dealing with their workers, and even veterans for demanding too much compensation for their service. Fearing social chaos and a rising tide of communism, Matthews explores a run for the White House. Interestingly, movie censors may have shared some of Capra's fears, for they expressed no reservations about portraying labor or political leaders as corrupt and worried only about suggestions of excessive drinking or an adulterous affair in the story.[26]

There are two women in Matthews' life, and each serves to point him in a different direction. A rich and ambitious woman who is attracted to his quest for political power encourages Matthews to strive for the presidency as a way to fulfill dreams of power for herself. She tells him that he has an ideal combination of "sincerity and drive that the common herd will go for." His wife, played by actress Katharine Hepburn, is more interested in holding him to his obligations to his marriage. She also thinks he might make a fine president, but she reminds him that he needs to think less about power and money and more about his responsibilities at home. In the end it is her voice that prevails over the goals of power and wealth.[27]

The fear that the uncontrolled pursuit of money and power could only lead to moral decay and social chaos was rooted in an older political discourse that centered on the reform and regulation of capitalism and capitalists that had been a central part of American political life since the nineteenth century. Capra had often given audiences some hope that love and cooperation could win out over unbridled ambition. Many postwar films continued to take up this political question—the promises and pitfalls of liberalism—without making such promises. Thus, a good number of films, like *Saturday's Hero* (1951), in which a young man's plan to rise through sports met only failure, still reminded audiences that a wonderful life may very well not be attainable for the lowborn. This point was certainly at the heart of *Body and Soul* (1947) and *Force of Evil* (1948), two stories that drew upon Popular Front critiques of capitalism as a source of ruinous behavior. In these particular movies, both shaped substantially by Abraham Polonsky, whose communist and socialist sympathies would eventually result in his being blacklisted and denied work in Hollywood by 1951, social forces took precedence over subconscious ones in explaining personal behavior.[28]

In *Body and Soul*, Charley Davis, played by actor John Garfield, whose career was also hurt by the film industry's attack on suspected radicals, is a Jewish kid who hangs around the symbolic center of many film versions of the working-class neighborhood—the pool room. After his father dies at the hands of local gangsters and his mother is forced to apply for charity, Davis decides that boxing is the only way he can escape poverty. His girlfriend Peg, a good woman who wants only a traditional family, dislikes the corruption and violence associated with the sport and asks him if his long-range goals include boxing or becoming president. Davis responds, "I just want to be a success."

The story makes it clear that Davis is not simply chasing money and fame but can find no sense of self-esteem in his working-class world. His parents are frustrated by their lives, and his mother laments, "Twenty years ago I wanted to live in a nice place so our Charley would grow up a nice boy and learn a profession. But instead we live in a jungle so he can only be a wild animal." Her spouse responds by blaming their difficult life on pressures outside their control: "Do you think I picked the east side like Columbus picked America?" He settled there because it was the least expensive place he could find to live and bought a small candy store to support his family.

Polonsky's radical outlook, nurtured in his Communist Party activities in the thirties, comes through forcefully in this feature. Capitalist America creates not opportunity but a moral dilemma for this lowborn male when the boxing industry forces him to sacrifice his sense of honor and integrity by throwing fights and hurting innocent people in his quest to get ahead. This competitive struggle takes him away from a virtuous female, eventually throwing him into the arms of a nightclub singer. Morals and plans for a wedding to Peg were put aside for fame as a fighter; Peg's admonitions that boxing only perpetuates cruel and heartless values and that their relationship will be in endangered are ignored.

The film's moral critique of capitalism, which put it clearly within the realm of traditional leftist politics at the time, was reinforced by the attention it directed to America's racial problems. A black boxer in this film, played by actor Canada Lee, who was yet another victim of the anticommunist hysteria of the late forties, emerges in the story as a voice of moral reason. Lee's character argues strongly against the corrupt practices of boxing and therefore against the unfairness of American society. More importantly, because unscrupulous promoters contribute to his eventual death by forcing him into fights when he is in poor physical condition, he becomes a symbol of how society mistreats all African Americans. This was a theme that would soon gain even greater filmic attention in the postwar era.[29]

Near the end of the film, Davis is offered an opportunity for a big payoff if he will take a dive. Lee's character, however, makes him realize that he is not only capable of winning the bout but that it would be foolish to sacrifice his sense of honor more than he has. On the eve of this pivotal match, he also exhibits some regret over the damage he has done to his relationship with Peg. He returns to the neighborhood and the family he has abandoned to see her and his mother. Suddenly the prospects of an ordinary working-class existence in a home filled with love appear much better than the brutal world of capitalist struggle that, like wartime, is marked by moral ambiguity. He quickly realizes that the promoters have deceived him and that the other fighter is out to destroy him whether he takes a fall or not. Self-respect now becomes more important than money, and Davis decides to fight to win back all that he has lost. At the film's climax he does just that, walking away with an uncertain economic future but with the woman he loves.

In Polonsky's *Force of Evil* (1948) men again are impelled by the almighty dollar. John Garfield, who by the late forties was so identified as a performer who had emerged from an urban and working-class background that he was often called the "people's star," played a leading role in this film as Joe Morse, a highly successful lawyer for a powerful crime syndicate who has used his brains to move up from lowly origins. He does much better in the story than his fictional brother, who remains in the old neighborhood running a small time gambling operation.

Although in true postwar fashion there is little idealism in the film,

Garfield feels a tinge of moral responsibility to help his brother "back in the slums where we were born." He does this by trying to convince him to fold his betting operation into a larger one run by Garfield's boss, Ben Tucker. The lowly sibling, struggling with poor health, somehow feels it is more virtuous to survive off the gambling dreams of ordinary people than to affiliate with a big-time operator like Tucker, who gives these people much less of a chance to win.

In the end, Garfield's brother is killed by Tucker and his mobsters, causing the upwardly mobile lawyer much regret and remorse. Feeling somehow responsible, he goes to the police with revelations of the criminal activity in which he is involved, an act that pleased censors who were continually looking for personal misbehavior to be punished. Overall, working people are weak or greedy in this film and reveal almost no potential for effecting meaningful social change. Censors even persuaded Polonsky, who professed to enjoy the good income he made from the film industry even while he indicted capitalism, to remove suggestions about possible corruption within the New York City police department. They also convinced him to revise his portrait of Garfield's brother to show that he entered the gambling racket under a delusion that it was an activity in which he could put to use business skills he had previously acquired. In this way they hoped to slightly mitigate the censure of capitalistic America as a "force of evil."[30]

Midge Kelley in *The Champion* (1949) is another blue-collar male interested in doing whatever it takes to become a success in postwar America. This boxer's father is much less supportive of his son's ambitions than his counterpart in *Body and Soul;* Kelley, in fact, was abandoned at age four and sent to an orphanage. It is here, rather than in the streets of the city, where his ambition is nurtured. All he can think about in the orphanage is "getting rich someday, rich enough to hire detectives to find my father" and "beat his head off." He reasons that in this society it is every man for himself: "Nice guys don't make money. That's the way things are."

Kelley decides to pursue wealth with the only resource at his disposal: his brute strength. He is not deterred by warnings from a boxing promoter who tells him that the sport is corrupt and that he could be seriously hurt. Alternative jobs available to men like him, like being a soda jerk, a fry cook, or a ditch digger, are dismissed with contempt. To the promoter he replies, "You told me there was money in the fight game. You take me on and I'll make plenty for both of us."

Women who can remain devoted to one man regain some moral ground in this working-class world. But Kelley does not hesitate to sacrifice his relationship with his wife, Emma, in order to become a boxing hero. He had married her after they met in a small restaurant in which she worked. After the couple began an affair, the girl's father coerced them into matrimony because he (like film censors) could not stand the thought of his daughter having sex outside marriage. Embarrassed by her father's actions, Emma still insists that she will make Kelley happy. Love is not enough, however, and Kelley bails out of the relationship, charging that the wedding was a "frame-up" and that he is tired of being "pushed around."

In the climactic event of his life, Kelley fights for the standing and glory that elude most common men. A radio announcer informs audiences that he represents "a story of a boy who rose from the depths of poverty to become champion of the world." And in a brutal fight whose very ferocity denotes the potential of American society and all men for cruelty, Kelley wins the championship, only to die from injuries he sustained in the match and lose everything in the end. Again, film censors asked producers to tone down some of the depictions of violence in the fight scenes and punish Midge and Grace for their "immoral conduct." Records reveal that censors, preoccupied with personal moral instruction, never mounted any objection to the scathing critique of open market competition that marked this film and many others.[31]

*Knock on Any Door* (1949) presents another story of contrast between one man who makes it out of the lower orders and another who does not. Andrew Morton, played by Humphrey Bogart, becomes a successful lawyer, although he still remains tied to his old neighborhood. When he goes back one day to help a friend named Nick Romano, who is suspected of killing a policeman, an elderly man warns him that the smart kids get out of the ghetto and stay out. Indeed, Morton's law partners had urged him not to take this case because it might bring unfavorable publicity to their firm, which concentrates on settling estates for wealthy clients. But Morton, at the risk of damaging his prospects for a full partnership in the firm, feels he has ignored the human needs of his class of origin for too long.

Romano is clearly a victim and is ultimately not responsible for whatever evil he may perpetrate. His father, a lowly immigrant who spoke little English, was unfairly sent to jail for defending himself against an attacker. When the man died in prison, his mother was forced to raise her sons with little income and live in one of the worst neighborhoods "in any American city." Nick Romano was thrown into a life of petty crime, the lawyer tells a jury, where he profited from selling stolen goods and cars. Morton contends that such an upbringing led only to a desire "to get out and get even some day."

The story gives Romano some credit for making an attempt to live a respectable plebeian life. Encouraged by Emma, a woman who believes in him and wants to "live on top of a hill in a big white house," Nick marries and tries to hold a steady job. He tells the woman that he wants her to be proud of him, and he tries his hand at the manual labor of loading sacks in a warehouse. But his past has taught him that he can earn more by gambling than by menial toil, and his neighborhood pals decry his attempts at respectability. When he announces to Emma that he can no longer ignore the rewards of a life of crime and that he does not want the child she is carrying, she is devastated and commits suicide, so strong is her desire for love and motherhood.

Despite Morton's best attempts, Romano finally admits that he was responsible for the murder of the police officer and receives a death sentence. But the lawyer recites again the tragedy of this man's life and reminds the courtroom of the pernicious effects of living in poverty (whether one gets a "push" or not). He tells the court that Romano is guilty but that society is ultimately to blame "for what they have done to him." He warns American audiences that "until we do away with the type of neighborhood that produced this boy, ten will take his place. . . . Until we wipe out the slums and rebuild them, knock on any door and you may find Nick Romano." Hollywood censors, always more willing to punish individuals than to blame society, were not inclined to let such a liberal view of moral transgressions stand. They argued for fewer shots of garbage piles and drunks sleeping in urban neighborhoods, not because they felt such images demeaned the world of the working classes, but because they wanted audiences to see "less behavior of a low moral tone." They also made an effort to eliminate suggestions that urban youth would actually engage in drunkenness and illicit sex.[32]

## A PEOPLE WITHOUT POLITICS

Many postwar films identified problems like the return of troubled vets or ruthless competition that could rupture the American community. They also offered solutions like strong and loving women and democratic-minded men who were capable of restoring health to the state of the union. The narratives of film noir, however, offered no such assurances. If there was a politics at all in the world they created, it was a dark and dangerous illiberalism disinterested in building a better life by either democratic or liberal means. These films rejected the notion that antisocial impulses could be regulated, that life could ever become wonderful, that love could triumph over hate, and that the future would be better than the past. Indeed, they envisioned a world without a future. The realism they offered was certainly more emotional than social, but the portrait of emotions they offered was severely skewed toward a darker set of drives like treachery, hate, and brutality. In a film like *Out of the Past* (1947), audiences saw a man and a woman who could never enter a traditional marriage or hold a regular job because they were never able to put behind them their deceitful and murderous ways.

Even the returning vet faced an uncertain future in film noir. Consider the 1946 film *The Blue Dahlia*. The script was by Raymond Chandler, who had co-scripted (with Billy Wilder) the story for the noir classic *Double Indemnity* (1944) from the James M. Cain novel. We can speculate that, unlike Capra who had memories of a warm, lower-class family life, Chandler carried more despair into his work because he was raised by a "drunkenly violent father" in Chicago. Certainly people in his film scripts were interested mostly in sex and money and were beyond redemption. This was certainly the case in both *Dahlia* and *Indemnity*. In *The Blue Dahlia*, a vet comes home only to discover that his wife has betrayed him. She spent the war years running around with the owner of a nightclub, the Blue Dahlia, and was even responsible for the accidental death of their son. Marriage offers no hope for social stability because this female is incapable of suppressing her desires for the sake of preserving a union with the returned soldier. In fact, in this story the vet actually ends up in a relationship with the estranged wife of his spouse's wartime lover, as relationships are represented as eternally problematic.[33]

The popularity of film noir exemplified the underlying sense of pessimism that pervaded the key discourses of postwar America and a real inclination to contest dominant myths that had been crucial to Hollywood and to America itself. James Naremore has suggested that this genre of films was preoccupied with themes like decadence, sexual violence, a sense of loss, feelings of insecurity, and a fascination with new forms of subjectivity. Thus, some of these features presented stories of men, often vets themselves, who were simply disinterested in repairing damaged relationships or in attaching themselves to any social institution, an image that tended to reaffirm fears that human nature ultimately could not be civilized. Evil and violence pervaded this narration of the nation. Moreover, because such forces could not be located in particular class, these stories tended to blur such distinctions and the political claims they had formerly engendered. Perversion and brutality rooted in an unstable human nature ruled the lives of people best described as ordinary. These films actually contested impulses in society to celebrate the return of free market forces, to honor war heroes, and to celebrate the American victory. Hopes for reestablishing patriarchy, social cohesion, or almost anything else were exploded. Thus, in the opening scenes of *The Blue Dahlia*, the wayward wife expresses a fear that her spouse will probably want to "beat me up." And in a film like *Dead Reckoning*, a returned soldier, played by Humphrey Bogart, must fight a woman and an Italian-American gangster from the "slums of Detroit" so intent on getting money that they are willing to kill another veteran who has been nominated for the medal of honor. It is no wonder that Bogart's character refers to postwar society as a "sick world."[34]

American hopes that the violent male that won the war could temper his brutal impulses once he was back home were put to rest in the 1946 feature *The Killers*. Certainly industry censors tried to mute some of the depictions of violence displayed there. Joseph Breen, director of Hollywood's Production Code Administration, asked that no sawed-off shotguns be used in the film because they were illegal, that the emphasis on murder be reduced, and that a prize fight scene not be made "unduly brutal." But the final product certainly made its point about the violent potential of American citizens in unmistakable terms. The tale opens with menacing men entering a small American town with nothing but murder on their minds. They are after Pete Lund, a man who is also unable to leave a disreputable past behind him. The killing of Lund early in the film is performed brutally in a hail of gunfire and, as the rest of the film makes clear, for no good purpose. Lund took eight "slugs" that "nearly tore him in half" according to the coroner, but local police express little interest in the entire matter because they do not see Lund, a drifter, to be part of their community. Broad social concerns cannot transcend the narrow bounds of fear and indifference.

Originally an unrefined kid from the streets of Philadelphia, Lund dreamed of elevating his standing in American society through boxing, an occupation that continually served as a key metaphor for explaining how individuals could break away from the lower classes. An injury to his right hand, however, ends Lund's ring career and forces him into an alternative path of crime where he meets a mobster named Kofax and a woman called Kitty, a sultry singer played by Ava Gardner. In film noir fashion, the attraction to a woman will lead to his destruction.

Indifferent to the benefits of domestic life, Lund prospers from gambling and crime and relishes the wealth and female attention it brings. After one daring heist of a payroll in New Jersey, however, Kitty tricks him by convincing him that other members of their gang plan to steal his share of the proceeds. Reacting as Kitty anticipated, Lund makes a pre-emptive strike against his colleagues by taking all of the proceeds from the robbery and fleeing with his female companion. But eventually Kitty is able to appropriate all of the funds for herself and disappear with Kofax to start a traditional life of her own. Later we learn that it was Kitty and Kofax, in fact, that sent men to kill Lund in the beginning of the story in order to end any possibility that he would ever testify against them. If the unpredictability of the free market was one thing Americans worried over in 1946, this film gave them something more: the suggestion that many of their fellow citizens were basically dishonest.[35]

A common man is again misled by a woman interested more in money than love in *The Postman Always Rings Twice* (1946). Dramatic tension turns on the relationship between a handyman and the wife of the man who employs him at a small gas station and roadside café. One day the aggressive plebeian grabs the attractive woman and demands to know if her husband satisfies her sexually. Soon the adulterous couple plans to run away. However, interestingly enough, his lower-class status gives her some pause. She is not sure that this poor man can really ever give her a life she wants, and she makes it clear that she is not interested in living like a "couple of tramps."

Upward mobility is pursued here not through hard work or dedication but through a scheme whereby the handyman murders the husband so that he and his lover can take over the business. Their partnership proves unsatisfying, however, especially because the female is in charge of the enterprise and frustrates this male's desire for dominance and respectability. Eventually, the woman is killed in an auto accident and the workingman is sent to the gas chamber since police believe he killed both his lover and her husband. Film censors insisted that moral transgressions be punished, and in this picture both the male and the female lead die. But their demise did not diminish the powerful statement left behind that neither democracy nor liberalism offered a way out for millions of individuals trapped in a world of greed, deceit, and lust.[36]

It followed that if traditional political ideals were unable to guarantee a better future, steps would have to be taken to regulate the dangerous people that occupied the lower regions of American society. The masses of people living in the crowded tenements of cities were beyond the reach of traditional reform politics, for many of their problems were simply not

John Garfield and Lana Turner play ordinary people capable of greed and betrayal in *The Postman Always Rings Twice* (1946). Such depictions of the nature of working people in the postwar era reinforced concerns raised by the war itself that there were dangerous impulses at the core of individual Americans. Credit: Film Still Archives, Museum of Modern Art, New York

of an economic or social nature. They were innately antisocial and unable to construct stable emotional lives. Thus, in *Anna Lucasta* (1949), a working-class family is ruined by the alcoholism and brutality of its Polish-American patriarch. In the aftermath of the war, this point was repeated endlessly.

It was *The Naked City* (1948) that reaffirmed in a graphic way that cruelty and emotional turmoil was congenital and was actually fortified in a society that fostered the unregulated pursuit of personal desires for material gain. On the surface this may have been seen as an obvious critique of unfettered capitalism, and it was. Yet this film and others suggested that there was something in the makeup of the lower classes that made them seem incapable of managing their emotional drives. Because of this genetic defect, the film made clear, they had to be governed by dedicated public servants like policemen and detectives, who devoted their lives to the domestic war against brutality of all kinds.

In the same year that Mailer suggested that naked violence permeated the essence of American culture and of many citizens themselves, this film actually accepted that reality and focused on the attempt to limit its expression. Now that evil had been defeated in the larger world, law enforcement agencies and officers had to continue the battle at home. Were it not for the wise police detective, played by Barry Fitzgerald, and the dedicated father and investigator, played by Don Taylor, honest citizens would again be threatened by dangerous people among them. Interestingly, the idea for the story came from a book authored by Arthur "Weegee" Fellig, who was the son of humble Jewish immigrants in the Lower East Side of New York and who made a career out of photographing the violence and pain he saw all around him in the urban milieu.[37]

Jean Dexter and Willie Garzah are key figures in this tale. The young woman has fled her working-class, Polish-American household in New Jersey for the "bright lights" of New York and the dream that she can transform herself into a person of higher standing. She has even cast aside her given name. Audiences never see Dexter because she is murdered early in the film as a result of a "wild" lifestyle and an encounter with a physician who happens to be involved in a burglary ring with Garzah, a brutish man who lives in an Italian-American section of town.

The film resorts to many of Hollywood's established practices in depicting the lowborn. In one scene in which Dexter's immigrant, working-class parents come to the city to identify their dead child, some stereotypical notions of such people are reasserted. These modest folks are morally upright and desirous of no more than the hand that life dealt them. They represent "the people" as respectable but meek and do not seem plausible participants in any of the "classless prosperity" of the postwar. The grieving mother expresses anger over the dishonor that her daughter's lifestyle and death has brought to the family back in New Jersey. She claims that she hated the girl's decision to change her name and that she had warned her that she would turn out to be "no good." "I hate her for what she has done to us," the heartbroken mother exclaims as she hugs the body of her offspring.

Although Hollywood often told (but did not guarantee) the working class that the only way out was through individual struggle, they were reminded that it was best to play by some set of moral rules. In the character of Garzah, however, we are advised that many in the lower classes are already dangerous—even before they strike out on any upward ascent. Garzah is responsible for the murder of the young woman but appears more interested in crime as a way to make a living than as a path to upward mobility. He lives in a rundown apartment in a lower-class neighborhood where people can be heard speaking Italian. At times he has made a living as a wrestler, and he is generally portrayed as another in the long line of blue-collar brutes. He is not some communist subversive but a common man with an inbred propensity for brutality that can be found in almost any urban neighborhood. With such fury and cruelty inborn, committed and highly trained police stand as the first line of defense for those who hope the postwar era will be better for traditional families and domestic peace. Censors saw the film mostly as an opportunity to demonstrate a traditional theme: that crime and moral transgressions do not pay. Thus, they objected to the eventual suicide of the physician who was involved with Garzah as an act that allowed a guilty man to avoid punishment at the hands of society. But prominent representations of police work in this story added the point that traditional morality was now insufficient to stem the rising threat of male violence.[38]

In a very incisive analysis of the place of the city in American culture, Kevin McNamara demonstrated that earlier in the twentieth century the city was sometimes viewed positively as a place in which people could move beyond the narrow moral views and intolerance of rural villages and remake themselves into more enlightened and cosmopolitan individuals with a greater respect for differences. However, he rightly saw no such optimism in *The Naked City*, where police forces worked tirelessly to limit "the ills of unrestrained desires and immigrant populations." McNamara correctly saw that much of the film was meant to reinforce the idea that "wanton desires" on the part of any class must be regulated by bureaucratic law enforcement agencies and that any hope for a new sense of tolerance for others—a democratic community—was in serious jeopardy.[39]

Lowly origins were not as important as insanity in *White Heat*, a 1949 Warner Brothers film about a criminal gang leader who had inherited his madness from his father. Crime boss Cody Jarrett, played by James Cagney, runs a highly efficient outfit that includes his devoted mother. The narrative contains many of the key elements of the late forties: widespread betrayal, untrustworthy women, and highly organized law enforcement organizations. In fact, the police in this story rely more on sophisticated technology in pursuing mean-spirited criminals than those in *Naked City*. Much effort is expended, for instance, to show new electronic devices that law officers can now use to track the movements of gangsters. In this story both sides—criminal and police—are highly organized in the pursuit of their goals, a sign that violence and the campaign against it will involve significant resources and planning in the future.

Jarrett's ruthless quest for money and power is certainly driven in part by his family's history of deprivation. He complains that "my old lady never had anything." But (like Garzah) he has no real consumerist desires, despite the dreams of his girlfriend for expensive goods. Unlike the thirties, where Cagney's gangster character aspired to expensive clothes and uplift from his social origins, here he appears to be more interested in the planning and execution of the crime itself. This may be due to the fact that he is largely driven in his quest by some form of insanity rather than by his social environment. Bouts with emotional rage are frequent for this dangerous man, who is also tied excessively to his mother, the only woman he really trusts. He complains about headaches that feel "like a red-hot buzz saw inside my head." And prison doctors who study his case inform audiences that his father had been "insane" and that Jarrett has a "psychopathic devotion to his mother." When he hears of her death while in prison, he flies into an uncontrollable fit. Whatever the exact nature of his mental disorder, Jarrett's life of crime is clearly rooted more in his subconscious than in his lack of standing in the material world.[40]

## THE NEW DEMOCRACY

Democratic politics before 1945 had dreamed of a national community that held a respected place for a vigorous working class that participated actively in shaping political affairs and in winning the war. Postwar culture, driven by fears of human and atomic violence, however, moved quickly to raise doubts about the capacity of many common people to participate responsibly in any democratic community or that such a community was even possible. This negative appraisal of the working class could not have come at a more inopportune time, for it flourished just as Americans came to realize that they had for too long accepted ethnic and religious prejudice in their midst. The horrible lessons of National Socialism in Europe and of the Holocaust taught Americans that ethnic and religious intolerance must be resisted at all costs. A steady stream of scholarly studies now explained how ethnic and religious (but not class) prejudice led to negative stereotyping and hatred. Writers were quick to point out that elements of such intolerance existed in the United States and had the potential to lead to the type of ethnic violence that had marked Nazi Germany if they were not eliminated. The upshot of this sudden confrontation with intolerance was that class politics came to take a back seat to an increasing concern with ethnic and racial tolerance.[41]

A few films like *Gentlemen's Agreement* (1947) and *Crossfire* (1947) confronted the problem of social discrimination directly. A story like *Crossfire*, in fact, was not only grounded in the postwar turn to greater racial and ethnic understanding but was also affected deeply by the era's concern over male violence. Most accounts of this film stress the fact that it represented a pioneering attempt to confront the existence of anti-Semitism in America. In the story a drunken soldier, played by Robert Ryan, beats a Jewish man to death in a Washington apartment. Ryan's character dislikes Jews in general because he feels they profited by the American war effort, and the man he killed had not served his country. Audiences were reminded, however, that the victim had, indeed, served on Okinawa, that Jews had served the American nation as had all ethnic groups, and that the United States still had serious problems of intolerance of its own.

But the film also linked expressions of violence in America to the experience of the recent war. One man, falsely accused of the murder, is a womanizer and a drunk because of the impact of his military service. Before he dies, the murder victim actually exclaims to this soldier, played by actor Robert Mitchum, that America now faces social turbulence at home because it does not have enemies to hate anymore and "now we start looking at each other again. . . . You can feel the tension in the air, a whole lot of fight that just doesn't know where to go." Fortunately for Mitchum's character, he is helped by a women—his wife—who forgives his wrongdoing and affirms her love for him. Censors again worried over the sexual tone of the film more than the discussion of intolerance. They did urge care in the depiction of ethnic hatred and argued against the use of terms like "kike." In *Crossfire* the less inflammatory term "Jew-boy" was used. But they also worked to minimize suggestions of sex outside marriage and any hint that the Jewish man was a "pansy" who may have had unconventional sex with other soldiers.[42]

The treatment of American soldiers in this film as hateful and mean-spirited, moreover, was also a reminder that the sentimental image of these patriots that graced the wartime screen was in trouble as well. The association between brutal behavior and the military, a point that would not have been widely sanctioned during wartime, began to seep into a number of postwar stories. The good-natured common man of World War II, charging into combat only because he had to defend his nation and his loved ones, was not so apparent in films that expressed disillusionment with patriotic devotion. In *Battleground* (1950), ordinary American soldiers were seen as confused about the role in the war; some sought a "clean wound" that would enable them to go home. In *The Sands of Iwo Jima* (1950) an American sergeant is ridiculed for placing his devotion to the Marine Corps above the need to care for his wife and son.

Any discussion of bigotry in American culture, of course, could not avoid the issue of racism. A leading scholar of the depiction of African Americans in the cinema has argued that the postwar world "became the occasion for a freshened liberal culture that restored racial issues to national prominence." Before the war a distinctive black subjectivity or well-rounded African-American characters seldom appeared on the screen. Thomas Cripps demonstrated effectively how such figures tended to be compliant to the wishes of whites and how the exploitation they encountered was brushed over by nostalgia. The impulse to mute black anger and the harshness of their treatment was reinforced by goals of the Production Code to omit any remarks that would be considered offensive to ethnic and racial groups. Even the government's documentary wartime film, *The Negro Soldier* (1944), glossed over the cruelest parts of our racial history by focusing on the progress of a black soldier from basic training through officer's candidate school and African-American achievements like Joe Louis's victory over the German boxer, Max Schmeling.[43]

*Home of the Brave* (1949) is important not only because it marked a new recognition of America's severe racial problems but because it contributed to a gradual erosion of the heroic memory of the American war effort by promoting a memory of war as trauma rather than victory. James Moss, the black character in the story, is in emotional turmoil after the war not only because his sense of self-esteem has been destroyed by years of bigoted treatment by white Americans but because of the suffering that men of all colors carried from their encounter with war. Moss is still scarred by the knowledge that some of his fellow soldiers did not want to go on an important mission with him because of the color of his skin. He also tells a military psychiatrist treating him that he is haunted by the feelings of relief he had when a close white friend was killed; he experienced a sense of joy that his boyhood friend had died instead of him. But the psychiatrist convinces him that he is no different than other men who experienced survivor's guilt and that he must put both wartime trauma and racist scars behind him if he is to live a normal life in the future. At the end we get a hint this might happen when Moss and a white buddy plan to open a bar of their own.[44]

The new sensitivity to racial issues received full treatment in *Pinky* (1949). This relatively popular film fit nicely into the groundswell for toleration that marked the late forties. Most importantly, the script was able to offer a more developed African-American point of view because it was the result of a collaboration between its producer, Darryl Zanuck, and the National Association for the Advancement of Colored People (NAACP). Cripps demonstrated that the NAACP was able to force the portrayal of a larger degree of African-American power in fighting intolerance. This more compelling assertion of black pride and agency led to a story in which *Pinky*, a light-skinned woman who could pass for white when she wanted, elected to affirm her African-American heritage. Before production Zanuck even replaced a potentially more conservative director, John Ford, with one who leaned toward the left, Elia Kazan. The complex array of forces that can shape a film is further revealed in this case by the employment of the black actress Ethel Waters, who resisted playing the role of a "conventional black menial" that Ford wanted her to play. Thus, Waters' role became one of a strong African-American woman who was a source of wisdom and strength.[45]

The narrative of *Pinky* may be liberal in its confrontation with American racial intolerance, but it moves away from the liberal-democratic paradigm of the thirties and forties in two significant ways. In a large sense, much like *It's a Wonderful Life*, the story raises doubts about folding individual desire into the larger needs of the community. The female protagonist ultimately elects to fight for the well-being of the black community, but her decision is still portrayed as an agonizing one, not a natural one, reached after much personal turmoil because she relinquishes a chance to lead a materially better life. Moreover, the film joins the postwar effort to denigrate lower-class white males. In this case, ordinary police deputies are out-and-out bigots, who drink more than they should and attempt to rape Pinky Johnson one night on a dark rural road.

Although Pinky is an African American, she discovers that when she goes away to school in Boston her light skin allows her to pass for white almost at will. Upon her return to the South and the black grandmother who supported her, the newly trained nurse is forced to decide if she will use her new professional skills to help the impoverished black community or return to the North for a better life with a white physician who loves her.

The film portrays African-Americans in the South as living in run-down conditions. The shack that Pinky's grandmother inhabits stands as an anachronism in a postwar American culture expecting material improvement. In this regard, the film represents the racist South overall as a backward region in a nation moving forward to a more enlightened future. The story also makes it clear that local police forces treat minorities unfairly, although the American justice system is vindicated at the end of the story when a Southern judge grants Pinky the property she inherited but that local whites tried to take away from her.

At the end of the film, Pinky decides to use the house and property given her by an elderly white woman for whom she cared to open a clinic for local minorities and a school to train black nurses. The narrative infers that the old woman had already sensed Pinky's racial pride and inclination to serve her people when she decided to leave the property to her. There are whites who support her in her campaign to uplift her people, but the story also involves African-American nurses and a black physician at the end, a reminder that blacks would now play an active role in shaping their own destiny and bettering their lives.

In 1950 *No Way Out* became another attempt of the immediate postwar to show Americans that racial intolerance was not confined to totalitarian regimes. The plot confronted audiences not only with the continued existence of white hostility toward blacks but also with the specter of additional race riots that marked the wartime era itself. Not surprisingly, the film had no doubts about where to locate the most virulent form of racial hatred in American society: squarely in the working-class districts of major American cities.

In this tale, actor Sidney Poitier portrays a dedicated physician who exhibits the highest standards of professionalism and tolerance. When a man who has been wounded by police dies while under Poitier's care, his brother spits on the black doctor, seeking to blame him for his death. The film makes it very clear that the Biddle brothers, Johnny (who dies) and Ray, are from the poor white neighborhoods of urban America. White workingmen are further defamed in the film when we learn that the former wife of Johnny Biddle has sought to escape her lowly origins because she was abused by her father.

The only way that Poitier can prove that the man died of natural causes, in this case a brain tumor, is to have an autopsy performed on his body. Thus, he falsely admits to charges of murder in hopes that a mandatory autopsy will reveal that the man died of natural causes. The coroner's examination confirms the cause of death as a brain tumor, but the furious brother is not placated. As he plots to kill Poitier himself, angry working-class whites meet in a local pool hall to plan an assault against an African-American ghetto. Although the actual attack was later edited out due to white protest, the final version of the movie leaves a clear impression that a riot took place. At the end, Biddle's attempt at killing the object of his hatred fails, and he is wounded in the leg. Although filled with rage, Poitier manages to place professionalism above anger and treat his wounded attacker. In control of his emotions, the physician sneers at Ray in the end and says, "Don't cry, white boy, you're going to live."[46]

## REACTIONS

It comes as no surprise to learn that commentary on films in the immediate postwar actually showed some exhaustion with the sentimentality and dreamy quality of wartime culture. To be sure, nostalgia for a prewar, pre-Depression past existed and was welcomed. Thus, critics even referred to characters in stories of working-class families set in the past such as *A Tree Grows in Brooklyn* as "beautiful." *Our Vines Have Tender Grapes* was described as "heart-warming Americana." And one writer felt that *I Remember Mama* brought to the screen "a layer of warm and deeply moving nostalgia that plucks at that special heart-string." Even the *Daily Worker* found *A Tree Grows in Brooklyn* to be "deeply moving" when it told the story of a common man who failed to make an adequate living for his family, although it wondered why there was no protest from among people who lived in such "sub-standard living conditions."[47]

Overall, however, there was a sense among critics that the culture had sustained enough sentiment and nostalgia for the time being. Some of this could be seen in the responses to Capra's *It's a Wonderful Life*. A writer in the *New Yorker* complained that George Bailey was simply not believable as a banker because he appeared to be thinking of only "doing good" all day long. This reviewer found the film "silly" at times and some of the language so sweet as to appear as "baby talk." Another observer felt a weakness of the picture was its "sentimentality" and "its illusory concept of life"; it simply did not reflect "average realities."[48]

To be sure, not everyone was willing to flee into a cultural world of harsh realism. Letters preserved by Capra from fans of *It's a Wonderful Life* generally thanked him for presenting an essentially hopeful and optimistic story. One viewer wrote and thanked him for freeing people "momentarily from fear, rapacity, greed, intolerance, and confusion that seems to encompass us." This fan felt that too many postwar films were already emphasizing "destructive emotions" to such an extent that they were "sowing the seeds of another war." A woman who saw the feature told Capra that the world wanted to believe in the "dignity of the human soul" and was "sick of the violence" of the recent past. Many praised the director for offering a positive view of family life and religion and for rising above the "sordid melancholy" of other Hollywood productions.

Capra himself responded to one letter by arguing that his aim in making the picture was precisely to counter postwar fears and anxieties with a more optimistic portrayal of human nature and potential. "To hell with romanticizing gangsters, villains, whores, and pimps! To hell with communism and fascism! To hell with Hemingway, Cain, Steinbeck and the whole four-letter word cult! To hell with psychosis, neurosis and halitosis," he complained, "I'm going to make a picture about good people. People who eat, work, hope, dream and make love in the normal way." And there were even critics who shared the director's point of view. *Variety* liked the fact that the film featured "wholesomeness and humanism" after a "clammy cycle of psychological pix and a tortured trend of panting propaganda vehicles."[49]

The social and emotional realism held in check in depicting the people during wartime returned, to be sure, but the issues were not completely what they had been in the thirties. The simple pursuit of wealth or status on the part of lowly men and women was now a story complicated by the need to probe the lingering affects of the war. This included not only a desire to portray the war experience in more ironic terms than seemed possible during the conflict itself, but also recognition of the emotional scars that had to be healed. At times the solution to these problems was to be found in the relationships between men—especially vets—and women. In some cases, such as the existence of prejudice in American society, the problems were social. There was certainly some willingness to escape the present and to retreat to moments that were more hopeful or even nostalgia for families and communities that were harmonious, but the predominant view of the people and their prospects in the late forties was grim, clearly resistant to Capra's hope that people could be depicted as essentially good.

The response to films about ordinary soldiers coming home reinforces this general willingness to move beyond the fanciful stories of wartime. Veterans were still seen in heroic terms, and there was much appreciation articulated for the fight they gave. Thus, reactions to *Pride of the Marines* accepted the film as one of "American patriotism" and one that captured "American pride in defending our way of life" with "American guts." And some saw in *The Best Years of Our Lives* a "warm glow of affection" for the recently arrived veterans and the American community who supported them. Yet, films like this were more likely to be praised, not for their affectionate delineations of America and its people, but for the frankness in which they discussed the problems faced by citizens during the war and its aftermath. Thus, a writer in *Commonweal* lauded

*Pride of the Marines* for showing the "anger toward life" possessed by a wounded marine and the fact that the film exposed the fears of the future that vets felt as they returned with physical and emotional scars. In part, this reviewer felt that this openness about the feelings of veterans actually helped to make them more heroic. But this sort of emotional realism was also praised as a desirable alternative to the "sentimental propaganda" that had circulated in the culture about the fighting men. The reviewer, in fact, was disappointed at the end of the film because of a suggestion that a blinded vet might see again. He thought this was simply too much of a retreat from all the blunt portrayal of anxiety that came before it. The *Daily Worker* found the film to be "truthful" about veteran problems but focused most of its praise on efforts in the story to articulate postwar dreams for "jobs, social security, tolerance, and peace." David Platt, the newspaper's reviewer, reported that when he watched an actor proclaim in the film that Americans could "pull together" in peace as they had in war to make their country prosper a "great roar of applause" filled the theater.[50]

*The Best Years of Our Lives* was seen in a similar way. Commentators liked the fact that the characters and the setting in an American town (really Cincinnati) made the entire story "lifelike." The fact that women betrayed men in the story, that vets worried about uncertain futures, and that a real amputee from the U.S. Navy played himself were all cause for strong praise. *Variety* exclaimed that "the people live" in the feature and that "the realism is graphic; the story compelling; the romantic frailties and the human little problems confronting each of the group are typical of the headlines concerning postwar readjustment." Another commentator felt the film fully reflected "the delicate tensions, the deep anxieties and the gnawing despairs that surely have been experienced by most such fellows" just home from the war.[51]

The postwar longing for a more genuine representation of everyday life and ordinary people and the appreciation of expressions of cynicism paved the way for a good number of features that raised larger doubts about the ability of the people in the postwar period to build a life that was wonderful and prosperous. The optimism never went away, but the hard-boiled plots today usually referred to as film noir certainly proliferated. There was a realization in the forties that these features reflected the cynicism that Capra sought to counter. An observer of *The Blue Dahlia* noted that the story seemed to stress violence for its own sake and noted that "brutality" appeared to be at the center of a number of recent "mystery" movies. While this critique came close to describing noir features in words we might read today, it would be incorrect to say that these dramas were seen as simple expressions of cynicism and hopelessness at the time. The cynicism and brutality was certainly noticed. But they were also appreciated for their entertainment value and reincarnations of older crime and punishment narratives. Thus, a reviewer of *The Postman Always Rings Twice* was a bit surprised by the "matter-of-fact" look it took at lust and murder but thought that the sensational treatment of these topics would lead to certain box office success. The commentator even thought the audience would sympathize with "little people too weak to fight against passion and the evil circumstances it brings." Similarly *The Killers* was praised for its ability to maintain "high tension" and "keep audiences on the edge of their seats." The *New Yorker* called the film one of the best of the current "gangster films" that was now appearing and expressed admiration for its "intensity" and the "naturalness" of its dialogue. And a reviewer of *The Naked City* in the same publication actually decided that the film gave something of a "sentimental" portrait of the large city because it tended to look at New York too much as a vast abstract place dominated by crime and did not capture at all the "real complexities" of the metropolis.[52]

The strain of pessimism generated by the war quickly merged with the ongoing tendency of American film to depict the world of the lower classes as unpredictable and vexing. In part, this point could be made rather easily by the reassertion of older forms of social realism such as were found in stories that saw the mean streets of urban America as incubators for the unbridled and often unprincipled quest of the boxer. Together, these strands simply pleased many for their ability to replicate the harshness and capricious nature of everyday life. Thus, James Agee liked *Body and Soul* not only for its portrayal of the gritty experience of the boxing trade but especially because it offered a "sense of meanness" of the world in which these people lived. *Variety* said that the film gave viewers an "authenticity" by showing how boxers can be cheated and "punched into unconsciousness." The journal concluded that this tale "might have been the real-life story of any one of a flock of New York eastside or Brooklyn street fighters" who sought to rise in American society. And, clearly, the origins of the "meanness" in their world and their own ambitions were seen as mostly environmental in many of the films of the immediate postwar period that treated the ordinary struggles of proletarians. Thus, films like *The Champion, Force of Evil,* and *Knock on Any Door,* as well as *Body and Soul,* were seen as tales of the lowborn caught in a society of excessive competition, greed, and social turmoil.

*Knock on Any Door* was viewed as a story of the problems associated with "skid rows and wild youths." *Force of Evil* located the source of the film's social problems in "racketeers who fatten off the little person's nickels and dimes." The fact that the main boxer in *The Champion* showed character defects like abandoning his wife once he became successful was attributed to his "boyhood poverty."[53]

This desire for social realism, grounded in the older politics of workers versus capital, always promised to enhance the discussion of democracy, and in the immediate postwar period, this dream resulted in wide acceptance of films that dared to raise the issue of racial and ethnic prejudice in the nation. Certainly the democratic rhetoric and pervasive nature of the sacrifice in the war helped to lay the foundation for this approval. In fact, one of the few criticisms these features received was that they often did not go far enough in discussing this issue. Thus, in talking about *Crossfire*, James Agee certainly endorsed its attempt to reveal the ugliness of anti-Semitism in America but claimed the story could have been even more "fearless" if it had substituted African Americans for Jews, a decision Agee attributed to Hollywood fears of offending the box office in the South. And a critic of *Pinky* in *Commonweal* liked the fact that the film condemned "anti-Negro prejudice" but wanted movies to someday "go the whole way in blasting the false notions of white supremacy." Most everyone who wrote about the films concerning race, however, celebrated their frankness and agreed that they deserved a good box office because of their important message. Thus, *Home of the Brave*, originally a play whose anti-Semitic theme was altered to a racial one for the movie, was praised for "directly and honestly" coming to grips "with the evil of racial defamation, which is one of the cruelest disturbers in our land."[54]

Although support for the attack on racism was widespread, a debate raged in the public mind over the origins of racism itself, a controversy that was grounded in the mingling of social and emotional realism that flowed through mass culture. The issue was what to blame: the conditions at the bottom of society or some deep and disturbed layer of human nature? A critic in *Commonweal* seemed to take the side of the those who thought the origins were psychological and pointed out that the hatred described in *Crossfire* emanated from the war and the fact that there was still "a lot of fight and hatred with no place to go" once the conflict had ended. Another writer felt that such animosity came out of human fears we all have of things we do not understand. But others saw the causes of racism as socioeconomic. In analyzing *No Way Out*, several critics noted the lower-class origins of the men who hated a black physician. One actually expressed dismay over suggestions that such hatred could be "psychopathic." But others stressed that the "narrow, warped mentality" of the men who shot a black physician was tied to the fact that they were "slum bred with all the prejudices of such an environment."[55]

## CONCLUSIONS

The postwar cinema of the people was torn between images and stories of hope and doubt. Driven by desires to restore realistic appraisals of American society after the dewy-eyed features of wartime, a number of films revived the argument that common people in American were threatened by the unbridled pursuit of money and power. Thus, boxers like Charley Davis and Midge Kelly took up again the unpredictable cause of the striving individual; men like Pete Lund were killed for the faith they placed in women. In the aftermath of World War II, this sort of realism was supplemented as never before, however, by the gut feeling that selfish and destructive passions ruled the very hearts and souls of average Americans; illiberal men like Cody Jarrett and Willie Garzah could strike at any time. Certainly films about women showing their love and support for returning vets, and families pulling together to overcome life's obstacles attempted to counter the pessimism over unregulated liberalism and illiberalism. Kate Nolan, Selma Jacobson, and George Bailey all fought to preserve a cooperative view of social relations.

A new and fresh look at the problem of race and prejudice in this country offered some optimism that forms of intolerance would be eradicated and democracy sustained. Thus, James Moss and Pinky Johnson appeared to overcome the heavy burdens of racial discrimination and find ways to build a constructive life. Indeed, among the films examined in this chapter that attained the biggest box office success—*The Best Years of Our Lives*, *Gentlemen's Agreement*, and *Pinky*—there was a sense that emotional and social problems could, in fact, be overcome.[56] The long list of evil characters that moved across the screen in features like *The Killers*, *White Heat*, and *The Naked City*, however, suggested that the quest for a better future faced an uphill battle.

# FOUR

# BEYOND CONTAINMENT
# IN THE FIFTIES

Historians have debated the political and cultural aspects of the 1950s intensely. Most acknowledge the creation of a powerful political consensus aimed in a broad sense at stemming the spread of communism in the world. This was a period in which political figures like Senator Joseph McCarthy appealed to the "hyperpatriotism" of many Americans and gained some political advantage by conducting searches for communist sympathizers and accusing fellow citizens of subversion and treason.

The political effort to fight communism in the world and to defend democracy and liberalism, in other words, also involved a simultaneous campaign to regulate the behavior of Americans at home. McCarthy saw the communist threat not only in the shape of Soviet dictators abroad but in the form of bureaucrats in the American state department or even directors on a Hollywood sound stage. In the culture of the Cold War, many who backed the Wisconsin senator also exhibited suspicion toward homosexuals, independent women, and militant labor organizations. In other words, the defense of democratic and liberal ideals also involved strong expressions of illiberalism and intolerance.[1]

Scholars like Stanley Nadel have argued that culture during the earliest years of the Cold War was ruled by the idea, or the "privileged American narrative," of *containment*. Aspects of this culture like its veneration of capitalist values or its disdain for state planning exhibited powerful strains of liberalism but could also give evidence of illiberalism in attacks on strong labor organizations or individuals who deviated from standard sexual practices. Containment, in other words, was intended to govern worlds that were both public and private, social and emotional. As such, it desired to restrain thought and behavior that were at odds with the dominant institutions of the United States after World War II, institutions that were deemed responsible for helping to pull the nation through the recent war and for sustaining the American way of life: patriarchy, capitalism, the military, and organized religion. Thus, as Nadel brilliantly explains, the fetish with domestic security in the fifties was not only about curbing political subversion but about "deviant" sexual practices as well. In a sense, he also suggests, the dominant thrust of the culture was congruent with the center of politics much as it had been during World War II. Corporate production, biological reproduction, military forces, and televised espionage hearings were all "deployed" in a vast attempt to mobilize public thought, ensure consensus, and shape the production of culture.[2]

Although Nadel's study is not particularly interested in the working classes, it offers much to ponder on how Hollywood narratives of the decade may have imagined a nation with little tolerance for deviance or opposition to traditional institutions. Nadel uses the film *The Ten Commandments* (1956) to illustrate many of his points. In a political culture where religion became very important in defining Americans in their struggle against atheistic communism, he notes the popularity of biblical epics. In the case of *The Ten Commandments*, the story was framed by a preamble from director Cecil B. de Mille, who called the movie "a story of the birth of freedom." The extended treatment was necessary, according to de Mille, because the central theme of the picture was "freedom"; it was about whether men ought to be ruled by God's law or "by the whims of a dictator like Ramses." Containment is further venerated because the story infers that freedom is not only compatible with deep religious faith but with corporate enterprise (but certainly not working-class agency) as well. Thus, Nadel relates how Moses gained status in Egypt the American way—by earning it through his military exploits and his ability to organize a large mass of workers to efficiently build a city and monument to the Egyptian leader. Nadel is even able to detect the promotion of domesticity in this film and to explain how a prospective marriage partner made herself appealing to Moses by promising to "serve him."[3]

The policy of containment had special relevancy for Hollywood. The House Committee on Un-American Activities (HUAC), which had conducted an initial search for subversion in the film industry in 1947, announced in 1951 a new and broader inquiry into the relationship between the movies, its profits, and the Communist Party. In a series of hearings from 1951 to 1954, more than two hundred individuals connected with the industry were named as communists and consequently denied the opportunity to work in various aspects of motion picture production. Congressional investigators, recalling how effective films had been in molding public opinion during the war, now accused directors, writers, and actors of attempting to "communize the country." Prominent members of the film community like actor Humphrey Bogart and John Garfield created a Committee for the First Amendment, which sought to defend the ideals of free speech. Many studio heads failed to support them, however, and insisted that "subversive germs" had infiltrated the industry. As a result of the hearings, studios created a "blacklist" of directors and writers who were suspected of communist sympathies and denied employment. Ten who refused to testify under oath before the HUAC were sent to federal prison. Certainly these actions contributed to a climate of fear and repression in the film industry and, one might presume, an aversion to make cinematic statements that were critical of America and its basic institutions.[4]

This drive toward political and cultural conformity embedded in the vision of containment was reinforced by the spreading appeal of consumerism. In 1950 the studio-sponsored Motion Picture Alliance for the Preservation of American Ideals endorsed a pamphlet written by novelist Ayn Rand that encouraged producers and directors not only to keep their films free of communist influences but to avoid attacks on American business and the free enterprise system and on wealth and success, another indication that the illiberal dream of privileging some interests over others was part of the Cold War defense of liberalism itself. Consumerism, of course, not only constituted a defense of free-market capitalism but also fostered notions that discredited patterns of life as it was normally lived by the lower classes. To state the obvious, it certainly militated against any celebration of thrift or personal denial that had been at the heart of the working-class family economy for decades.

Less appreciated is the fact that the new consumer economy also called for an end to authoritarian models of parenthood, something that some films and other forms of cultural expression had long associated with the lower classes. Television and advertising encouraged mothers and fathers to be nurturing rather than controlling and to provide the type of comfortable existence that simply did not exist in the urban neighborhoods and industrial districts where most working people lived. Some psychiatrists at the time actually worried that men who were unable to shoulder this new burden of being a good provider might actually slide into forms of deviant behavior. And such outlooks converged nicely with expanding (but unauthenticated) concerns expressed by many intellectuals that the lower orders were likely to support antidemocratic political movements like McCarthyism.[5]

Television more than any other medium in the decade promoted the values of middle-class consumption. By 1953 one in five Americans lived in suburbs and had television receivers. Popular shows about affluent families promoted father figures who were able to give their families nice suburban homes and material comforts without obvious physical exertion or angry impulses. Tensions were minimal in their households, domestic violence was nonexistent, and a reasonably good future seemed assured. Affable parents represented a retreat from the world of the production line, incessant toil, and anxiety and betrayal that marked many of the narratives of the lives of common people in the late forties and fifties. Clearly the future belonged to wise and supportive middle-class individuals like James Anderson on the television show *Father Knows Best*. But this gentle and affluent man also represented an escape from the politics of the past; he expressed no concern for a fair and democratic society and no anxiety over atomic weapons. It is no wonder that in a study of early-fifties television, George Lipsitz discovered that networks slowly replaced shows about working-class families with ones about more affluent ones. Where blue-collar images remained, as in *The Honeymooners*, they were men and women living a life without prospects. As government loan policies encouraged suburban flight from crowded working-class neighborhoods, television further attempted to efface the memory of "the people" and the politics they had launched during the Great Depression.[6]

Despite its central status in American political life, however, the power of Cold War and procapitalist ideology taking shape in the fifties was limited. Protest movements that exploded in the 1960s, such as those dealing with racial equality, generational anger, and female unrest, actually took firm root at this time. W. T. Lhamon has argued effectively that there was a certain exhaustion with the "doctrinal struggle" in the decade and a sense of fatigue with the idea of curbing personal desires, a notion that was already prominent in American film. He sees in the decade not so much overt rebellion as indifference toward established canons and the rise of activities that would allow people new ways of expressing themselves and constructing identities. Thus in his view, there were citizens who moved with "deliberate speed" away from "inherited ways of being in the world" or received identities such as fatherhood, dutiful wife, and even subjugated racial minority. Lhamon believes this process was initiated in part by a sense after the war and Hiroshima that everyone was a victim to some extent. Inferentially, we can speculate that leaving the city for the suburbs or the working class for the middle class was not just about consumerist dreams but was also about abandoning a world dominated by concerns over personal sacrifice, suffering, and even violence.[7]

The striking thing about political and cultural expressions outside the accepted boundaries of containment culture was not so much that they were ubiquitous but that they were more likely to be found in the realm of mass culture than in traditional politics. With "deliberate speed," many Americans embraced magazines like *Playboy* that celebrated a life for men outside marital commitments and musical styles that challenged standard norms of sexual restraint. Margot Henriksen has documented an extensive discussion in many films of the era that articulated "psychological confusion" in American society and the widespread existence of insanity in the population. She sees this discourse as essentially representing a form of dissent from American political and military strategy. Her point is that Americans worried about the irony of Cold War policies that promised a progressive future contingent on the spread of atomic weapons. Unlike Nadel, she argues that the contradictions of at least this part of the dominant American narrative could not be masked. To be sure, new challenges to American orthodoxy in the world of traditional politics took place in the form of a rising civil rights movement, although this process was actually reinforced by a Cold War that forced America to come to terms with its policy of white supremacy in order to win adherents in non-white nations in its ideological struggle with the Soviet Union. But frequently dissent moved through the channels of mass culture and was carried along by its project to survey the fate of the individual and reproduce the landscape of the human heart.[8]

Containment culture sought to manage the domains of emotional and social realism; mass culture divulged their possibilities and excesses. In the working-class world that Hollywood imagined during the height of the Cold War, the influence of containment culture was certainly evident: labor leaders found market rather than political solutions to employment problems; at least one film was denied most of its theater bookings because of the political sympathies of its makers; and a dockworker and a boxer found deliverance in America from their wayward ways. To a startling extent, however, its imprint was considerably less than one might expect; countless figures were deployed in search of liberal and illiberal dreams that were at odds with positive renditions of the nation and its institutions. Ordinary life was incessantly depicted as contingent and therefore insulated from any easy assumptions that capitalism or

America itself would bring a wonderful life to most of its citizens. The presence of millions of females in the audience would ensure a continued discussion about male violence and about the frustrations of living with men who could not provide all the emotional and material happiness a female might want. Working-class men appeared as brutes but also as rebels who shook their fists at the established conventions of their times. The "male rebel" of the early fifties like Stanley Kowalski was an adult, not a teenager, and was symbolic of public displeasure with any sort of containment. If some Americans were caught up in the project to save the world from communism and others were moving with "deliberate speed" toward new identities, the men and women playing in filmic version of plebeian life were still boxed in by the unpredictable swirl of human emotions and economic chance. Congressional hearings and moral censors were helpless when it came to taming the thrust of American mass culture to sell tickets by exposing the contradictions of master narratives and political ideologies—even at the height of the Cold War.[9]

## CONTAINMENT IN BITS AND PIECES

The overall focus of film on the individual always modified any effort to represent the interests of groups like labor or capital. In the early fifties this longstanding conflict continued to attract some cultural attention but in ways that did offer some support to the era's political stance against plebeian radicalism. Consider *I Married a Communist* (1950) (also known as *The Woman on Pier 13*). This picture attempted to sustain ideals of containment in a number of ways. It not only linked working-class protest with ruthless communism, but it effectively trivialized the memory of worker calls for a more democratic community in the thirties. The story centers on a former radical from the Depression era who has now become an enlightened labor leader on the San Francisco waterfront. The hero, Brad Collins, played by actor Robert Ryan, is now part of a successful management team and commands the respect of all who know him. His wife, Nan, admires his self-confidence and the way he pursues goals. His workers appreciate him because he was once a stevedore himself and knows how hard such men toil.

Collins is a reasonable manager who succeeds because he occupies a middle ground. He ignores the extremes of class conflict: the impulses of managers who want to dismiss the rights of labor and of workers who want only to resort to militant action. Although he has abandoned his blue-collar world, he is willing to compromise with his men. When he attempts to mediate a dispute on the docks, however, the local communist party threatens to expose his radical past. They want him to recommend a decrease in wages in his negotiations in order to provoke a strike rather than reach a settlement.

Audiences learn that Collins was once part of the "lost generation of the thirties" and had been a member of the Young Communist League as an unemployed man during the Depression. When communist operatives threatened him with public humiliation for his past activities, however, he rebuffs them with the threat that "it's dangerous to call a man a communist unless you can prove it." He even manages to resist the temptations of a former girlfriend who works for the party as well. She reminds him that they had shared not only an affection for radical causes but also for each other, and that she held him responsible for disrupting their relationship. But this true American does not submit to her powers of persuasion or to communist intimidation. In one scene Collins is wounded by gunshot from a communist agent but remains unmoved in his desire to effect a reasonable settlement to the strike.

The heroic Collins even risks death when he is forced to try to rescue his wife after she is kidnapped by communists. In a statement that ridicules much social protest in the thirties (and probably pleased anticommunist zealots), Collins tells his wife that he only joined the party because he "was a kid out of a job" and "wanted to get even with somebody, anybody." But he hastened to add that he discovered the party "was no good." In the end, communists kill Collins in a gunfight and stand as embodiments of evil and viciousness. Workers and all Americans must do all they can to resist their influence.

The debate over the acceptable terms of working-class protest is continued in *The Whistle at Eaton Falls* (1951). Again the narrative centers on an intelligent and moderate working-class leader, Brad Adams, played by actor Lloyd Bridges. In many ways Collins and Adams turned out to be among the most capable working-class leaders ever mounted on the screen. The setting for this story is as important as the tale itself: the small town—the recurring symbol of the idea that communal life was still viable. There is hope in this film that capitalist leaders and consumerist impulses will not render the working class redundant. And the veneration of that hope is found as much in the narrative structure of the picture as in the loving shots of the small mill town and the people who work in it.

A preamble to the film sought to minimize any doubts about its meaning: the stable nature of the community has everything to do with the success of the capitalist venture. The tranquil portraits here of community life with postmen delivering mail and boys playing baseball can only be sustained if the local mill can continue to offer steady jobs. Thus, the opening recalls the thirties, when a shoe company shut down and the factory whistle, which had come to signal stability, went silent. Luckily, the town was saved by more capitalism (and not worker protest) when a new firm opened a plastics operation that restored the jobs that had been lost. To contest capitalist initiatives was to risk a return of hard times.

Brad Adams is now in charge of machine maintenance at the mill and the head of the local union. But the new firm is faced with economic turmoil. In an effort to stay competitive, the company president informs Adams that new machinery will be ordered to increase production and decrease current levels of employment. Adams does not buy promises that men laid off will be hired back if production increases, and he astutely argues that a surplus employment pool will lower the wages of those still holding jobs. A local woman reinforces a working-class point of view by claiming that many families would be "sunk" by missing paychecks for even a short period.

Working people still have a legitimate voice in this story, and they argue intelligently among themselves over the best course of action. Adams is cautious about the merits of violent protest. Another worker, familiar with previous strike action in Seattle, contends that "you have to fight or you don't eat." Adams's moderate plan to negotiate with management is further jeopardized when the head of the company is killed in a plane crash and replaced by a man who holds virulently antilabor sentiments.

A standoff takes place when the men refuse to operate the new machinery that will lead to the dismissal of some of their colleagues. Soon more militant leaders are able to launch a wildcat strike, despite Adams's warning that such an action violates the terms of the existing labor agreement. In a battle between moderation and militancy, Adams attempts to restrain anger on the part of management and pleads with them not to make good on threats to close the plant and sell it.

The narrative now stands at the type of crossroads that many in the audience may have concluded characterized the state of class relations in postwar America. Could labor and management reach some sort of accord, especially now that both sides were evolving into larger and more impersonal organizations? In this story the widow of the dead company president is presented with an opportunity to sell the plant and invest the proceeds of the sale into a trust fund that would insure a comfortable income for her. She can only recall, however, that her late husband valued the plant's ties to the town and the feelings of mutual respect that he felt existed between the workforce and its managers. He had dreamed of the company, the workers, and the community moving ahead together, a vision that would be seriously weakened in the culture of the 1950s. In a last-ditch effort to preserve both a cooperative form of capitalism and a democratic community, she decides to hire Adams to run the plastics firm, betting on his sense of moderation and overlooking his lack of experience.

The men immediately accept the authority of their former colleague and present him with a briefcase that they declare to be "better than a dinner pail." Adams attempts to settle problems, not through union militancy, but by increasing production so that the mill can have both new equipment and more workers. Economic growth, in other words, is presented as the best alternative to either unauthorized strikes or stubborn owners. But the working class does not appear all that understanding of what is needed to make this system work; it needs enlightened leaders like Adams. Thus, the middle-class manager is now depicted as working late into the night, looking for solutions, while happy-go-lucky workers are pictured dancing the night away. It is clear who will best shape the American future.

Business conditions eventually deteriorate, and the plant closes. In scenes reminiscent of the Depression, idle men stand around the loading docks and appear menacing. Unemployed people carry bags of coal and suffer through cold weather. Images of workers as weak and irresponsible, however, persist as well: one man loses his unemployment check on a horse race and another attempts to set fire to his house to collect insurance money. Men jeer at Adams and scrawl the words "scab" and "traitor" on his car. At the union hall, radicals attract a following. Some men still place their hopes in Adams, but others fight among themselves, and one laborer is killed in a knife fight. All of this unrest prompts a town physician to make a public plea against labor violence, which he claims will only destroy the community.

Finally, a way out is found, not through collective action of the people, but through individual ingenuity. A young man offers Adams the break he is looking for in his search for increased production and larger markets—a machine able to make new products as well as increase overall production. This allows Adams to consider making a new product—channel selectors for all the television sets postwar Americans would buy. Suddenly postwar consumer capitalism—not militant action—represents the best way to sustain prosperity and community. Adams announces a huge new order for television receivers and that there will be work for everybody.[10]

In one graphic instance where the proponents of containment culture were unable to alter film content, they worked effectively to limit the [illegible] ld see a story about a successful strike. *Salt of* [illegible] sition even while it was be- [illegible] erman, had worked for the [illegible] ne of Hollywood's black- lisu [illegible] larmed because the film was supported by a unio. [illegible] nion of Mine, Mill, and Smelter Workers—that had been ex[illegible] the CIO in its purge of radical unions. Conservative union leaders in Hollywood—now in an alliance with their capitalist employers—and the American Legion worked tirelessly to disrupt the production process, and they forced enough theaters to reject showing the feature that it became a financial failure. Members of Congress feared that it would harm the image of the United States during the Cold War struggle to win the hearts and minds of people everywhere, and even millionaire Howard Hughes attempted to prevent its final distribution.[11]

This film was based on an actual strike of a local of the International Union of Mine, Mill, and Smelter Workers against a zinc company in Hanover, New Mexico, but centered much attention on the relationship between a married couple: Ramon and Esperanza. In so doing, it sustained the tendency of film to frame larger issues of class, violence, or national politics in the stream of an ongoing debate on gender. Ramon and the men go on strike over issues of safety, seniority, and wages. They are insensitive, however, to female concerns for better homes, clean water, and consumer comforts such as a radio.

The progress of the strike is hampered by tension between the men and the women. The men are unwilling to allow the females to join in the protest and are slow to recognize their concerns as legitimate issues of protest. One woman complains at a union meeting that the men might as well put a sign outside the hall indicating "no dogs, no women allowed." Eventually the females, including a pregnant Esperanza, force their way into the strike action by bringing coffee to the men on the picket lines.

Capitalist managers are ruthless rather than reasonable in this tale. Ramon is beaten by police—an action that was considerably more frequent in real labor history than in films—and company doctors deny Esperanza their services when she delivers her child. When a court injunction ordering the men back to work makes it appear that their cause is lost, it is the women who find a solution. Recognizing that the injunction only restricts striking miners, they decide to carry pickets themselves. In this single moment they are able to contest not only capitalism but traditional gender thinking as well. These women are shown clearly ignoring both the resistance of their own men to their public actions and the police who try to intimidate them. Meanwhile, Ramon and many of his colleagues are dissatisfied because they are now forced to stay at home and assume traditional domestic duties.

The resolution of the story represents a victory for the ideals of worker protest and female equality. Esperanza tells Ramon that he should not fear having a spouse as a friend and insists that she wants "to rise and to push everything up with me if I go." When he attempts to strike her, she stands defiantly, admonishes him never to hit her again, and insists that he sleep elsewhere that evening. The fact that the mine owners also capitulate to worker demands reaffirms the value of strike action and worker (and gender) solidarity in capitalist America. Although the film was not seen widely by the Cold War public, its rhetorical appeal certainly challenged fundamental pillars of containment ideology.

## SO MUCH FOR GENDER HARMONY

American film never became propaganda. It could certainly reinforce dominant views of the postwar era that validated capitalism and anticommunism. Yet in the cinema of emotional and social realism, challenges to positive idealizations of American life were abundant. The imperative to serve traditional authorities and roles—so much a part of political culture during the early Cold War—was particularly questioned in features that divulged the difficulties of marriage and the ongoing disputes between men and women in the lower classes. The camera lingered for hours in these features on drab plebeian neighborhoods and tenements that were vivid reminders that many in Cold War America were not sharing in visions of "classless prosperity." In a sense, this frame on real life sabotaged a fundamental tenet of containment culture: the absolute moral and political value of a traditional marriage. Recall that the early fifties were a period of rising rates of marriage and childbirth after years in which depression and war had forced a delay in such practices. Certainly there was evidence that all Americans were not pleased with the celebration of strict adherence to marital roles and to the desire to contain sex to marriage, but there was no mistaking the point made over and over again that good Americans were not only anticommunists but bread-winners and housewives. Yet the fulfillment of these roles in a number of films appeared difficult at best, despite the efforts of movie censors to tame the representation of sexual longing. The men and women in these features not only struggled with each other but seemed completely indifferent to the baby boom and the anxiety over world communism.[12]

Consider the narrative of *Clash by Night* (1952). There are no heroes in this exploration of relationships in a fishing village in California. Gender tensions outweigh the concerns of class or national politics as men and women struggle with conventional forms of sexual and moral behavior. The leading female character has a very difficult time accepting any domestic roles at all. Studio promotional materials had it right when they exclaimed that the movie was about "clashing desires, mixed motives, and the hungry yearnings of the human heart."[13]

Connections between men and women are in a continual state of disarray. A young woman, played by actress Marilyn Monroe, works in a fish packing plant and tells her boyfriend about a female colleague who received a black eye when she refused to live with her former husband again. Monroe's character informs her beau that "he just beat her up awful" and warns him that he had better not try anything similar with her. Later she tells a girlfriend that she enjoyed the prospect of freedom more than marriage to an ordinary workingman. She feared that in such an arrangement money would be short and she would be "stuck" working in the cannery forever.

The female center of this film, based on a play by Clifford Odets and directed by Fritz Lang, however, belongs not to Monroe but to actress Barbara Stanwyck, who plays Mae Doyle. She has just returned to the village after a failed affair with a man who had been married to someone else. With her future uncertain, she now desires only "a whiskey with her coffee in the morning." Doyle's overt expression of sexual desire troubled censors during the production of the film, especially a later adulterous relationship. Censors did allow the story but attempted to ensure that "actual physical contact between the adulteresses be held to the absolute minimum."[14]

Upon her return to the town, Doyle meets two men, one virtuous and the other undependable. Jerry, the earnest son of an Italian immigrant, owns his own fishing boat and believes a man should work hard and be devoted to the woman he loves. Earl, on the other hand, although interested in ties to a woman, is uncertain about both the regimentation of work and marriage. These two versions of working-class manhood allow

Mae to explore not only her own emotional identity but her level of interest in committing to a man.

The earnest fisherman believes someone like Mae is too sophisticated for him because she has traveled widely and "is used to nightclubs." When he professes his love for her, she indicates some uneasiness with the idea of marital commitment: "I wouldn't make a good wife for you. I'm one of those women who were never satisfied. But it would be nice to be married to someone like you. I'd be safe. . . . But you find someone who likes pushing a baby carriage and shopping in the market and changing the curtains in the bathroom window. I'm bad for you."

Earl reinforces Mae's doubts about a traditional relationship with a guy like Jerry. While they are dancing, he tells her that "Jerry is the salt of the earth, but he is not the right seasoning for you." He exclaims that he cannot envision her "hanging out the family wash." And although she realizes she has an attraction to Earl, she still worries that he would be unable to provide the sense of stability she occasionally desires and to temper her longing for freedom. Finally, she tells Earl that he is a man who does not know what he wants and that she has decided to give marriage with the fisherman a try.

Domesticity for Mae takes the form of a baby and a home with Jerry and his elderly father. But this arrangement is soon disrupted by Earl, who comes to her home in a drunken state one evening and tells Jerry how fortunate he is to have his "castle," his wife, and a child. Earl's appearance stirs old feelings in Mae, and soon she strikes up an affair with him. The explanation she gives her husband for her betrayal not only constitutes a female attack upon "containment" but tends to expand the notion that the lower classes have more difficulties in sticking to conventional moral standards. She tells the fisherman she is simply tired of being a housewife and doing things for him all of the time. "It's no good. Nothing changes. The days go by, down to the grocery store, back to the house, hang out the wash. . . . Without love there is nothing."

An enraged Jerry calls Mae and Earl "animals." When he tells Mae that she is "rotten," she agrees but insists that she cannot stay married. Monroe's character returns at this point and expresses sympathy for the female point of view. She feels Mae has a right to pursue love instead of marriage. Jerry threatens to take away her child, while Earl pleads for her to follow her sexual emotions. He makes the point that the child will grow up someday and leave home anyhow. But Mae Doyle cannot relinquish her identity as a mother even if it means staying with a man she does not love, and she returns to her husband.

*Clash by Night* ultimately upheld the dominant social values of marriage and motherhood but only after the alternatives were given full exposure. Its ending gave censors—and, ultimately, the guardians of conventional behavior and containment culture—what they wanted. It also allowed men and women to explore for a brief time options to the gender roles that most of them filled in their daily lives. As such, it was subversive on at least two levels. Its challenge to gender roles most adults were expected to assume was obvious. But by revealing that loyalty and goodness were always susceptible to the varying impulses of human nature, the story hinted that no belief system could ensure that disorder and betrayal could be avoided.

*Human Desire* (1954) was another cultural story that both affirmed and discredited the values of containment. Fritz Lang, who directed this film as well as *Clash by Night*, again explored the dangerous drives that emanated from the souls of ordinary people but located much of this turbulence in a plebeian world. In this film centering on the passions of railroad workers, homes are modest, neighborhoods are bleak, and men and women flounder in the daily attempt to establish loving and loyal ties. These characters do not suffer from some form of insanity but simply from the emotional turmoil of being human—and blue collar.

Narrative tension revolves around three individuals: Jeff, a Korean War veteran just home from Asia; Carl, a yardmaster for the railroad, who has enjoyed some job improvement while Jeff was away; and Vicki, Carl's wife, who has become disenchanted with the demands of marriage and the limitations of a working-class town.

Problems rather than progress dominate the lives of Carl and Vicki. When the yardmaster loses his job, he convinces his spouse to use her feminine charms on a powerful businessman in order to help him. When she visits the man for an unexpectedly long period of time, however, Carl becomes suspicious and jealous. Vicki does nothing to calm his anger upon her return and rebuffs his advances. In a moment of madness he strikes her and bangs her head against the wall, in what amounts to another public revelation of female abuse at the hands of workingmen. The angry husband then articulates a lament of lowborn men when he charges that she only married him because wealthier men did not want her. "I got his leftovers, didn't I? . . . It went on after we were married didn't it?" Fusing class and gender tensions, the angry spouse plots the murder of the businessman, forces Vicki to assist him, and uses knowledge he has of her relationship with the dead man to blackmail her into staying with him.

In this film, working people are neither getting ahead nor living honorable lives. Unlike the televised image of the middle class at the time, they are unable to control their basic instincts. Again, a director like Lang was able to draw attention to the imperfections in human nature and its potential for fury. This was an appealing theme for intellectuals, who sought to understand the explosive manifestations of brutality in the world wars and, perhaps, for citizens uneasy about the "insanity" of Cold War militarism. But in the early fifties, whether conscious or not, the merging of a brutal human nature with the frustrations of working people did little to help their standing in a culture that was finding it difficult to imagine for them a place of honor and respect.

Discourses over cruelty, human nature, and the lowborn came together in an explosive fashion in *A Streetcar Named Desire*. The story, which introduced the quintessential blue-collar brute in the character of Stanley Kowalski, first came to life in a 1947 play by Tennessee Williams. Some would argue that Williams' homosexuality led to a sense of alienation from conventional behavior and an inclination to expose the full range of deviance in life as it was lived. Moreover, his personal belief that he was a person that most people liked less the more they came to know him could have also fostered a drive to explore characterizations outside the American mainstream where he tended to locate himself.[15]

The film version of the play appeared in 1951. The story centers on a working-class couple, Stanley (played by Marlon Brando) and Stella, who live in a seedy section of postwar New Orleans. When Stella's emotionally troubled sister comes to live with them in their cramped apartment, tension between the three adults escalates. Unlike movie censors, Williams was less interested in containing the representation of desire and punishing those who indulged their fantasies. In this respect, he joined a larger cultural project that was, on the one hand, thinking out loud about matters of deviance, and on the other hand, acknowledging that its manifestations were much more widespread than previously believed. Life for these people and for the audience was no longer marked by clear distinctions between good and evil, a point that dramatically contested the assumptions not only of movies censors but also of the architects of containment. Thus, Stanley Kowalski is a man capable of desiring his wife and beating her at the same time. Neither of the main characters, moreover, reveals any real interest in consumer goods or winning the Cold War. These are not model citizens but ordinary Americans disinterested in politics and floundering in a prosperous nation.

Kowalski is a war hero, a decorated master sergeant who appears unconcerned about the "four freedoms" or the GI bill, although the couple display prominently a photo of him in uniform in their home. Rather, he is intrigued by sex with women, a good game of poker, and drinking beer. Interestingly, both Stanley and Stella seem to have an attraction to violent behavior. In a classic moment from a classic film, Stanley beats his wife and then runs to find her after she flees to an upstairs apartment. Standing in the street, shirt torn, Kowalski yells for his battered wife to return, and she runs down the steps ready to soothe his rage and enjoy his rough sense of masculinity. As she takes his head into her lap, he cries like a child, "Don't ever leave me, Baby." Here is a workingman who is neither a gangster, a self-made man, a patriot, nor a radical. He stands disconnected from the dominant genres of film and the reigning ideologies of Cold War America. Elia Kazan, who directed both the stage play and the film, scribbled in his notebook after reading the story that Kowalski was a man not only driven by carnal desires but completely detached from the religious and political ideals of his time. To Kazan he represented the "basic overall cynicism of today."[16]

Most of the men in Stanley's world have a limited vision of their futures. They are immersed in personal interests like card playing and bowling. Some look for ways to get away from their wives. Mitch, a co-worker played by Karl Malden, actually wants to build a loving relationship with a woman. Although he still resides with his mother, he carries a memento that a dying girlfriend once gave him, and he offers Blanche a sensitive understanding of her own emotional struggle when her brother-in-law offers only contempt and suspicion.

The sentimentality of American culture in wartime and the idealized life of the democratic village is not possible in this filmic world overwhelmed by scornful and sensual emotions. Blanche is especially tormented by the memory of her young husband, who turned out to be gay and who committed murder. In one scene she fantasizes that a young man who comes to the apartment door to collect a bill is really her former lover. Stanley tells Stella that he has heard rumors that she may have even engaged in prostitution. When Mitch finally rejects her for what he thinks is her promiscuous past, she can only run into the street screaming.

While Blanche goes insane in a society that is looking for a better life, Stella learns that she is pregnant. Unfortunately, when his wife leaves to give birth to the child, Kowalski asks Blanche if she would be interested "in a little roughhouse" and rapes her. This act fixed the image of the working-class brute firmly in the mind of movie audiences and was repeated in a number of films throughout the decade like *No Down Pay-*

In *A Streetcar Named Desire* (1951), Stanley and Stella Kowalski, played by Marlon Brando and Kim Hunter, helped to expose the deep and complex emotional drives that existed among common people and that threatened optimistic projections that liberalism and democracy could work in America after World War II. Credit: Film Still Archives, Museum of Modern Art, New York

*ment* (1957) and *Peyton Place* (1957). The rape not only brings about the final breakdown of Blanche but ruptures the marriage of Stanley and Stella. Blanche is carried away to a mental institution, remarking that she can only rely "on the kindness of strangers" and thus not the love of intimates. In the 1947 stage play, Stella decides that Blanche is simply fantasizing about the rape. But in the film she penalizes Stanley by running away from him with the baby to a neighbor's apartment. Movie censors wanted the brute punished.[17]

Censors were consistent during the production of the film in worrying more about the portrayal of unconventional sexual behavior than about the denigration of any class. They argued that suggestions of rape and sexual deviance in Blanche's past life were "unacceptable" and suggested that the rape scene from the play could again be presented as something she imagined since she was so desirous of male love. The film's producer, Charles Feldman, even argued at one point during the production that the rape could not be suggested because it would be incomprehensible that Stanley would violate an unstable person and that such an act would close off all hope that Stanley and Stella could have a normal family life. But Kazan continually fought for the scene and told the head of Warner Brothers Studios that sex would help sell the picture. Censors also continually expressed dismay to Kazan over acts of wife beating and suggestions of perverse sexual behavior. Records indicate that Kazan and Williams fought for the inclusion of these vital parts of the narrative. Williams told Breen, in words that spoke to the heart of postwar anxieties, that the "rape of Blanche by Stanley is a pivotal, integral truth in the play, without which the play loses its meaning which is the ravishment of the tender, the sensitive, the delicate by the savage and brutal forces of modern society."[18]

In addition to industry censors, Warner Brothers had to confront the fears that the Catholic Legion of Decency would give the film a low rating, thus discouraging the attendance of some. Jack Warner, the studio head, met with church officials who expressed concern over what they felt was a "gross emphasis on sex and carnality." This forced Warner to make some cuts over Kazan's objections in order to avoid condemnation by Catholic censors. Some shots of Stella's face that were felt to reveal strong sexual desire on her part were removed and, of course, an actual rape scene was not included but only suggested. The Breen office also got Kazan to suggest that Stanley was punished for what he had done; consequently, Stella exclaims in the movie that she is never going back to him.[19]

Marriages proved no more satisfying in *The Rose Tattoo*, based on another play by Tennessee Williams. The wife of a truck driver turns out to be a devoted partner willing to take in sewing to help sustain her family and to do all that she can to please her spouse sexually. Her loyalty is not returned, however, by a husband who becomes engaged in illegal activity and an adulterous affair with a blackjack dealer from Texas. After he is killed in a shoot-out with police, the grieving woman retains his ashes in her house and lets her neighbors know how much she cherishes the memory of a man she thinks never loved anyone but her. When she learns that he had an illicit affair and that his former lover now wears a rose tattoo as he did, the married woman is crushed.

As in *A Streetcar Named Desire*, Tennessee Williams proved a challenge to movie censors. Exchanges between the author and the Breen office suggest the scope of the problem. Williams felt that the "basic values" of this story were its "warm humanity" and the devotion of a woman to the memory of her spouse. "Unless humanity itself has begun to fall under the censor's ban, there should be no serious difficulty in making a film out of this play that will not violate . . . [the] essential truth of the characters." Breen was uneasy about granting Williams' point that the full range of human emotions should be displayed. Yet this objective was central to postwar mass culture, despite the efforts of the Breen office and most of the institutions of Cold War America to suppress it. Movie censors were quite upset with frank displays of female sexuality in the story. And Breen argued that he did not know what Williams meant when he talked of "humanity" falling under the "censor's plan." "If Mr. Williams' idea of the humanity of his characters involved their absorption in questions of sex and lust, as it does in the stage play, and if it involves the pitiful treatment he accords religion, he should be made to know that these are still very definitely and basically code problems."[20]

Eventually another truck driver, played by actor Burt Lancaster, appears in the woman's life. He struggles to support a grandmother, father, and sister on his meager wages and lives in a house without even an inside bathroom. Yet his muscular body reminds the woman of her departed husband; he even gets a rose tattoo to improve his chances of winning her affections. His promise that he could give her "love and affection in a world that is lonely and cold" stands in stark contrast to the treachery she experienced in her marriage and raises again the specter of contrasting forms of working-class manhood between those who are tender and those who are brutes. He also offers her "human comfort" and an enduring relationship after a long and difficult period. If the economic future of this couple is still in doubt, we still get some assurance that they can build a life together.

Married life and relations between the sexes were not always seen as a hassle. In *Marty* (1955) a lowly butcher ultimately finds happiness only when he encounters a woman who loves him and nourishes his fragile sense of self-respect. In this film, interestingly, the prospect of marriage is presented not as an act of conforming to traditional expectations but one that allows two working-class individuals to start a life of their own free of domestic restraints imposed by the extended families that dominated the households of the immigrant working class during the first part of the twentieth century.

The marital struggle was quickly renewed, however, in *A Catered Affair*. Tom and Angie Hurley, played respectively by Ernest Borgnine and Bette Davis, bear hardships but do not advance or enjoy any sense of freedom in the small apartment they share in the Bronx. The Hurley family has clearly not benefited from postwar prosperity, and to invalidate the patriotic thrust of the times, they grieve over the loss of a son in Korea. Tom, a taxi driver, has been saving for years to buy his own cab, but his spouse feels defeated by the couple's inability to improve economically. She is also bitter over her own upbringing as the daughter of a humble painter and her present status as the wife of a workingman who still cannot afford to purchase a refrigerator. It was easy to feel sympathy for this plebeian couple and to realize that American capitalism did not bring satisfaction to all citizens.

Angie's distress explodes when her daughter informs her that she plans to marry. The young couple want only a modest affair, but the disappointed housewife sees the wedding as an opportunity to give both her daughter and herself the type of lavish event their lowborn families never had. When the hardworking breadwinner realizes that the event could deplete his entire savings, however, he is forced to object. His wife's retort only reinforces the notion that for many in postwar America there is really no end to their economic problems. She argues:

Look, Tom, we had it hard between us, but I'll haggle with you now. This girl is going to have a wedding [to remember] until the day she dies. She's going to have a big white satin photograph album that she can look at when the bad years come and maybe then she will have a kind thought for her father and mother. You've never given her nothing at all.

This stab at the taxi driver cuts deep. He regrets that he was unable to support his daughter's wish to go to college and, ostensibly, assist her in getting out of the class into which she was born. He also reveals his anger over what he feels is a general lack of support from his spouse. "You always ragged me about what a miser I am," he complains to his wife. "Well, I found dollars hard to come by . . . and I am sick and tired of being put up in front of my children as a penny pinching miser."

Their marriage and their self-esteem receives a further blow when their daughter tells them that she has never heard them profess their love for each other and contends that she wants a marriage based more on romance. The plight of the working-class couple seems even more hopeless when it turns out that the parents of the prospective bridegroom are able to provide the newlyweds with a year's free rent to a new apartment, a proposal that only intensifies Angie's wish to throw a large wedding.

In the end, however, the blue-collar housewife relinquishes her dream and accepts the need to use the family savings for a new cab. She tells her

Ernest Borgnine and Bette Davis play a working-class couple in the 1950s torn between their desires to save and to spend in *The Catered Affair* (1956). Their story reflected both sympathy for the plight of the lower classes in a consumer society and the idea that their lives held little hope for a prosperous future. Credit: Film Still Archives, Museum of Modern Art, New York

daughter that her actions should serve as a lesson in what marriage is all about: "You gotta start making sacrifices," she contends. "You can't throw money around." And again she contributes to the cultural project to imagine a bleak future for plebeians. She warns her daughter that if she is not exceptionally frugal, "one day you wake up finding a lot of time [has] gone by and you'll wake up knowing this is the way its always going to be, just like this, day after day."

## TRANSFORMING THE WORKINGMAN

*On the Waterfront* (1954) and *Somebody Up There Likes Me* (1956) actually offered more hope that violent men could be made moral and that conventional ideals could ultimately be sustained. Solutions to the problems of lower-class men in these stories, however, were not to be found in militant political struggles, but in personal transformations nurtured by supporting individuals in their lives, and they were to some extent the rewards of liberal individualism. The notable story of a longshoreman, again featuring Marlon Brando, showed, in fact, what *A Streetcar Named Desire* did not: that redemption was possible for the blue-collar brute. When Kazan and writer Bud Schulberg, who had researched the subject of waterfront corruption before writing the script, approached major studios with the idea for a film, they were told that there was little interest in "waterfront radicals" and that the tale seemed "pretty communistic." The head of Twentieth Century Fox, Darryl Zanuck, compared it unfavorably to *The Grapes of Wrath* and suggested that the story could not so easily be inserted into the traditional narrative of American nation building like that of the Joads who had reminded him of "pioneers."[21]

The story, however, contained much that would please defenders of containment culture. Labor union dishonesty was again raised as a serious issue. The point in this film and others like *Inside Detroit* (1955) and *The Garment Jungle* (1957) was that obstacles to working-class progress were not to be found in the actions of capital but in the nature of some working people themselves. In *The Garment Jungle,* local hoodlums extort profits from a factory owner and prevent him from granting worker wishes for unionization and more benefits. In *On the Waterfront,* dishonest practices by hoods who extort kickbacks for jobs is finally eliminated by the heroic action of Terry Malloy, Brando's character, who decides to break a code of silence that pervades his culture and inform police on such illegal practices. Scholars ever since have interpreted this act as a symbolic defense of Kazan's own act of naming Hollywood subversives in front of the House Un-American Activities Committee in 1952.[22]

Actually, too much analysis of the film and of Malloy's character has focused on Kazan's encounter with HUAC. The origins of the story itself go back to Kazan's collaboration with Arthur Miller on another project of waterfront workers that sought to expose the way they were victimized and the efforts of some of them to resist the methods of racketeers. Malloy is also much more complex than a mere informer. He is a working male in postwar culture struggling with both the hand society has dealt him and his inner emotions. He is both violent and tender, victim and hero, and as such he is inscribed by the contesting cultural discourses of cynicism and hope that may have been as influential in molding the postwar world as those that focused intently on communism and capitalism. If he stood as a rationale for informing, he also exemplified the difficulties of finding a way out of a turbulent world and of living without any real expectations of material improvement.

In preparing to film the story in 1953, Kazan prepared notes for Brando that told the actor to consider Malloy the opposite of Kowalski. Kazan felt Malloy lacked Kowalski's confidence and struggled with his loyalties and emotions. To the director, Malloy was the "opposite of destructiveness; he wants approval." Even after he helps to stem the tide of corruption in his world (and gains some approval) his life still has tragic features, for he remains consigned to the backwaters of Hoboken, New Jersey, and, as such, a symbol that Cold War America is not creating a better life for all of its citizens.[23]

In his autobiography, Kazan praised Brando's sensitivity and training as a method actor, which allowed him to convey a sense of personal emotions to the larger story that Schulberg had acquired originally by talking to real people on the docks. Thus, when Brando sees his dead brother hanging from a meat hook, according to Kazan, he chooses not to yell but merely to slump in grief, a characterization that evokes sympathy for the people living the life that he does. Indeed, Kazan thought the capacity of the film to draw attention to the sorry plight of these proletarians inferred that the film was about much more than "snitchin."[24]

The exploitation of dockworkers is engineered by Johnny Friendly, another corrupt union boss who fought his way to local power from modest beginnings as the son of man who tried to raise ten kids on a "stinking watchman's pension." He has opponents killed and can decide who actually gets to work on a given day. Interestingly, his ruthlessness is grounded in the memory of past deprivation that much of the larger culture was trying to forget.

With most workers immobilized by fear, the drive to reform the docks originates outside the working class in the mind of a local priest (played by actor Karl Malden). The priest calls a meeting in the basement of a local church, which is attended by a few of the dock workers and Edie Doyle, the sister of a man who was recently murdered by Friendly's operatives.

Malloy hears the priest talk but is unmoved. He does show some interest in Doyle, however, and tries to get to know her. Ironically, her working-class parents have grave reservations about any relationship she might have with someone from her own neighborhood. They have saved for years to send her to college in order to get away from the waterfront; this part of America simply has no future. And despite signs that Malloy is capable of tender feelings, her father calls him a "bum" and affirms the futility of working-class life: "See this arm? It's two inches longer than the other one," he tells the dockworker. "That's years of working and sweatin', liftin' and swingin' a hook. And every time I heisted a box or a coffee bag I says to myself, this is for Edie, so she can be a teacher or something decent."

But Edie feels an obligation to help the community and serve its need for justice and fairness. She tells her father that she cannot simply run away to things that are in books and that she wants to find those responsible for her brother's death. She also defends Malloy, arguing that she has detected a capacity for kindness in him, a point that the film reaffirms by highlighting the attention he gives to the care of pigeons that Edie's brother left behind.

Malloy may be capable of loving a woman, but he is cynical about the possibilities of reform in America. He does not see suburbs or consumer comforts in his future at all, and he assumes that any attempt on his part to end the exploitation of men on the waterfront will only lead to his death. On the docks he feels that it is "every man for himself." It takes a dedicated priest and a caring woman to alter his pessimism. He is moved by the priest's argument that families suffer when breadwinners do not get the work they need and his call for remembering that "every man is your brother in Christ."

Transformed by conventional symbols of moral goodness—religion and women—Malloy decides to testify before a crime commission investigating corruption on the docks. He recalls that he has failed at much in his life, including his dream of being a boxing champion, and is stung by Edie's charges that if he fails to confront corruption he will be the "bum" her father says he is. Thus, Malloy does name names, but he also stands for the idea that ordinary people can take steps to resist forms of victimization and degradation that impinge upon them in a political climate reluctant to acknowledge that such degradation takes place.

*Somebody Up There Likes Me* (1956) also reminded viewers that improvement for men from crime-infested tenement districts was difficult but not impossible. Based on the autobiography of boxer Rocky Graziano, this feature told the story of a common man who overcame the drawbacks of his environment to become a champion fighter. Before he could rise, however, Graziano managed to make his own contribution to the ongoing disparagement of the working-class family by revealing the cruel nature of his Italian-American father. When the elder Graziano asked his son when he was "gonna be somebody" in life, Rocky retaliated with a stinging rebuke of the old man: "Whadda ya mean, like you, huh? How much did you make this week? How much did you ever make? I didn't have to go and rob bread and steal coal from the blind man. What did you ever give us around here except your wine breath and the back of your hand?"

The film basically follows the plot of Graziano's published autobiography, which tells the story of a wayward youth who, despite rough treatment at the hands of his father, rises from a life of petty crime. When he beats a guard while in a juvenile reformatory, his fellow inmates suggest he take up boxing and put his violent impulses to good use. At first the young man rejects such advice because his father had tried it and his old man "was a bigger bum than I was."[25]

Once free of the reformatory, he joins the Army but has a difficult time accepting the regimentation of military life. While serving a sentence of hard labor for going AWOL, he finally decides that boxing is the only route in life open to someone like him with antisocial instincts. At this point in his life he is a man incapable of any kind of adult relationship, and he tells a date that he even finds it uncomfortable to sit in a theater and watch a romantic movie. What excites him, he tells her, is the boxing ring and the screams of a crowd urging him "to kill off the other guy." "Where else can a guy like me be something if it ain't in the fight business?" he asks rhetorically.

As the working-class tough becomes a successful boxer, he also comes to enjoy the responsibilities of a breadwinner as well, an indication that fatherhood comes easier to those with better incomes. His manager tells him that being a spouse and father will give him another source of motivation to succeed. In fact, the boxer actually appears to enjoy his new domestic life and is eager to buy ice cream for his pregnant wife and walk through his old neighborhood pushing a baby carriage. But boxing is also a way to maintain traditional gender roles of breadwinner and housewife. When he fights Tony Zale at Yankee Stadium, the women in his life, his wife and his mother, listen to the match on the radio and bear witness to his manhood and his capacity for struggle. They shudder at the punishment he takes, but his wife exclaims, "He is hard and tough and can take anything, but I can't." And his mother urges her daughter-in-law to accept the fact that he is a boxer and to "support him."

As in many boxing films, Graziano eventually faces a moral dilemma. He can lose a match in return for $100,000 or face public disclosure of his dishonorable discharge from the service. He cancels the fight entirely in order to avoid committing an illegal act and the ruin of his reputation, but the press learns of his past misdeeds anyway. The public debate that follows these actions stands as a postwar forum on brutal behavior in the working class. Some call him the "scum of the slums," while those with more sympathy feel he was simply a product of his environment.

For this boxer, as for Terry Malloy, a woman intervenes at a crucial point to set his course right. Rocky's supportive wife tells him that he has struggled too long not to fight again. And a visit to his old neighborhood allows him to see old acquaintances still involved in petty crime and going nowhere. Suddenly he remembers that his father was bitter for years because his mother never allowed him to explore his boxing potential. He tells his father, in words that make the quest for middle-class family life worth any effort, "It's all over for you no matter how much booze you take. But it ain't over for me. I got a wife. I got a kid. I got a home in Ocean Park (outside the slums). I'm fighting Tony Zale for the championship of the world." His father can only break into tears and urge him to "be a champ, like I never was."[26]

## CAPITALISM AND LIBERALISM AGAIN

In the optimistic version of American liberalism, the struggle of the ordinary individual resulted in social and financial success. Yet Hollywood continually disputed this promise and reminded audiences that the struggle for upward mobility held no guarantees. To question liberal capitalism in the thirties could be accepted as a statement of what had helped to cause the Depression. To do so in the fifties amounted to a direct challenge to containment culture and its defense of capitalist ideology. Cold war politics failed to deter the film industry from turning in a mixed report on the structure of opportunity in America and the cost involved in trying to climb up the ladder of success. This was clear in features like *The Harder They Fall* and *A Face in the Crowd*.

The quest of the boxer for a stable family life and middle-class success went unfulfilled in *The Harder They Fall* (1956). This film, based on a novel by Bud Schulberg, is another account of how unfair and abusive American society can be. The victim is Toro Moreno, an immigrant from Argentina, who thinks that America will give him the opportunity to make the money he needs to improve the condition of his family in his homeland. Moreno is a huge physical specimen but wholly lacking in the business and boxing skills needed to become successful. Thus, he is vulnerable to the greedy ambitions of fight promoters.

Moreno is befriended by a promoter named Nick and a sportswriter concerned about corruption in boxing named Eddie. Nick wants to use a publicity blitz and rigged matches to turn Moreno into a boxing contender, but Eddie has doubts about such ventures. He learns of many old boxers who are now in pain and poverty because they were cheated. One boxing manager tells him that if you gave fighters more of the profits "some broad will marry him and put him to work in a factory." Another tells the reporter that most of these men are "lazy, worthless bums, who won't take a decent job."

Moreno eventually grows angry over the extent to which he is controlled and expresses a desire to return to Argentina. But Nick plans one more big fight in Chicago and tells him he owes it to the men who have invested in him. Moreno now realizes that most of his wins have been fixed, and he worries that he is not nearly as good as he thought he was. Eddie tells him that at least he could take his winnings from the match and "get out of the rotten business." When Moreno is knocked down by a champion, however, he refuses to follow instructions to remain on the canvas. In a scene in which a common man suddenly decides to regain the self-respect an unjust society took away, Moreno goes after his opponent, only to get bloodied in the process. But the exploitation never stops. And through a series of complicated accounting procedures, the broken fighter is left with almost nothing from a total gate that exceeded one million dollars. Out of sympathy, Eddie gives him his own share of the profits so that he can buy a house for his mother in Argentina and get out of America, where money is more important than people's pride and dignity and "where the little people sit and get fat and fall asleep in front of the television set with their belly full of beer."[27]

The lowborn man fares better materially in *A Face in the Crowd* (1957) but does not reach the level of moral goodness envisioned for some men like Terry Malloy or Rocky Graziano. The leading character, Lonesome Rhodes, is a drifter and guitar-picker who ends up in jail in a small town in Arkansas for drunk and disorderly conduct. Rhodes is smart enough to see that he can turn his life around by using his talents on radio and television to build a successful career. In the process, however, he comes to adopt a cynical view of the media that made him famous, for it causes him to believe that "the people" can be persuaded to buy just about anything from products to political ideas. One can watch this feature, in fact, and not be sure what to fear most—the media or the ignorance of the vast American proletarian class.

In the end, Rhodes makes money but cannot control his drinking or his lust for women, and he proves completely incapable of sustaining a stable adult relationship. It is clear that his media success and fame prompt him to despise the very people from which he rose, and he resorts to calling them "rednecks, crackers, and hillbillies." Ultimately, he becomes a representation of all men and women, carrying in this tale a modest promise for good and an immense appetite for power and self-satisfaction. As the hero proclaims, "Lonesome Rhodes is the people; the people is Lonesome Rhodes."[28]

Film director Kazan claimed that this film was intended to unmask the power of television to control citizens' thinking. Again, however, neither he nor censors who objected to the fact that Rhodes was "inordinately ambitious" and had "no sense of sin" appeared to have had concerns for the poor light in which they portrayed ordinary people. And again, as in *Meet John Doe* and *Fury*, we get the idea that the people can be easily led. Disregarding the concerns of censors and the overall image of common folks, Warner Brothers simply went ahead and attempted to sell the feature as the story of a man's quest for power at all costs. "Power," the film's press book proclaimed. "He took it raw like his bourbon and sin."[29]

## THE BREAKDOWN OF THE AMERICAN COMMUNITY

Films that stressed community dynamics as much as individual perspectives—such as *It's a Wonderful Life*—promised to raise the issue of democracy more explicitly, for they allowed for a discussion of social relations and what various classes owed each other. In the fifties, however, Hollywood undermined sentimental notions of American community life. Thus, from portrayals of the fate of working people set in a newly developing suburb as they were in *No Down Payment* (1957) or in a traditional American town as they were in *Peyton Place* (1957), audiences received a suggestion that democracy and communal stability were simply not possible in Cold War America. Part of the problem was that lower-class people still had a difficult time earning respect in these films and were seen as inherently troubled and dangerous. They were not, however, the only threat to a democratic community. Clearly, they also faced prejudice and exploitation at the hands of those in the classes above them. In any case, American society was simply not working as the proponents of containment culture would have liked.

In *No Down Payment*, a proletarian couple moves to a new world of suburban housing and backyard barbecues only to be ultimately turned away. Four couples purchase homes in the new town of Sunrise Hills after the war. This narrative finds fault with middle-class suburbanites as well as blue-collar people, although it will leave no doubt which group will be unable to adjust to the new postwar world. White-collar salesmen drink to excess, and parents worry that their children are watching too much television. The new suburbanites still exhibit old racist ideas when Asian Americans think about moving into their enclave. But one housewife still defends their new lifestyle: "We have so much in common. We are all about the same age; we all have nice homes; all our husbands are doing very well."

Narrative tension is again rooted in the savage nature of men. Dave Martin and Troy Boone are both war veterans, but one has clearly managed to regulate his emotional drives better than the other. Martin is college educated and acquired valuable skills while working at Los Alamos during the war; he never saw actual combat. Boone, on the other hand, is an unpolished Marine who survived the rigors of combat in the Pacific region. He and his wife, Leola, have moved from Tennessee with the hope of putting their country origins behind them. They dream of becoming part of a new culture in which, as one of their new neighbors explains, everyone has more security than their parents and where "there's not many guys who have to sweat to get a decent living anymore."

Boone wants to be part of Sunrise Hills by becoming its chief of police, a role that will allow him to continue to be the defender of homes and families as he was in the war. Not surprisingly, he longs for his past as a warrior; he admits that the worst day of his life was the one in which he left the service. In fact, his friends think he runs his gas station "like a Marine outpost on Guadalcanal" and find his garage crammed full of war medals and souvenirs taken from the Japanese. This encounter with brutality has carried over into his domestic life, where his wife infers that he has beaten her in the past and will do so again when he drinks. Boone tells his neighbor, Jean Martin, that if he didn't have his memories of battle, he would "crawl in my car and turn on the exhaust pipe. You think it makes me feel like a man greasing cars and cleaning toilets in gas stations?" he protests.

Troy and Leola Boone dream of a future like the Martins. With college and valuable experience, mild-mannered Dave Martin worries only about whether he should concentrate in sales or engineering. The Boones, on the other hand, find it difficult just to emulate middle-class conventions. They cannot hide their overt interest in sex, and Leola is not as good as her neighbor at keeping her house in order. She is also haunted by a past like her husband. In her case, she bore a child out of wedlock and gave it up when she could not pay the medical bills. Troy, the father of the child, was nowhere to be found when she was forced to decide whether she could keep it or not.

In the end, Troy's quest for inclusion is doomed to fail because he is

In *No Down Payment* (1957) the character of Troy Boone (left) represented the difficulty of men with lower-class backgrounds and promilitaristic attitudes (note the collection of medals) in adjusting to lives of contentment in postwar suburbs. Credit: Film Still Archives, Museum of Modern Art, New York

unable to fulfill the mandated requirements for entry into the postwar middle class. He cannot forget the pleasures associated with violent behavior and is unable to shed his working-class ways. When the local city council rejects his application to head the police department because he lacks a college degree, he becomes furious and screams at town officials that Sunrise Hills would have been controlled by the Japanese if it were not for veterans like him. He returns to his home in a frenzy and tells his wife that they are "dirt" and accuses her of having someone's else's child. She retaliates by reminding him of his past abuse and argues that his cruel temperament was one reason why she gave the infant away. A drunken Troy then wanders into Jean Martin's house and assaults the symbol of the status that eludes him by raping her. Censors worked to shorten this scene and urged that Troy's abuse of his wife be limited only to an extent necessary to give her reason to kill him in the end. But overall, Boone comes across as another in a line of blue-collar brutes.[30]

*Peyton Place* (1957) also maligned both working-class and middle-class people (and thus Cold War America) but still managed to identify brutal behavior most closely with the lowborn. Both the book and the subsequent film exposed the repressive nature of American society and the desire of women for sexual enjoyment and careers outside the home. The fact that rape is depicted as an act of violence toward women and abortion as an act that served the interests of a woman underscored how much the story expressed a female point of view at odds with some of the masculine notions of containment culture. Even reviewers at the time noted the discrepancy between the positive view of America set in the beauty of the New England landscape and town, and the portrayal of rape, violence, abortion, and hurtful gossip.[31]

The author, Grace Metalious, drew heavily from her own experience in creating this story. She hated the working-class life of her childhood among mill hands in Manchester, New Hampshire. In fact, she became a dental assistant at a young age specifically to move away from the mill district. Her distaste for hardship was matched by her suspicion of men. Abandoned by her father and raised by a grandmother, Metalious was aggravated by the fact that her husband had gone off to World War II close to the time when she was due to deliver a baby. When she realized that she had to support him again so that he could attend college after the war, she "screamed silently" and felt "trapped in a cage of poverty and mediocrity." Drawing on her own sense that traditional marriage and wartime sacrifices were overly restrictive for women with creative drives, Metalious crafted a story that discredited the domination of men over women and overly sentimental views of postwar America.[32]

Set in a small New England town on the eve of World War II, *Peyton Place* was indifferent to aspirations in American culture to link ideals of a democratic community with domesticity. By the late fifties, moreover, even industry censors had lost the much of their ability to curtail expressions of illicit sex and brutality in the land. Some effort was expended by code officials to remove suggestions that women might be flattered by statements that they were "oversexed," but clearly the force (if not the language) of Metalious's novel survived. Also persisting in the film were her hatred of traditional gender arrangements and dislike for life in the working class. Her personal sentiments and prose are graphic illustrations of how badly many postwar Americans wanted to leave their lower-class origins behind.

There are glimpses of a democratic community in the story when people greet each other on a typical day or when dedicated professionals like the local physician and a teacher named Elsie Thorton demonstrate commitment to the welfare of others. But the full realization of such a community is blunted by the pervasiveness of male privilege. Usually located in the middle class, this power is expressed in the symbol of the competitive male who can provide leadership and assume responsibility. Thus, when the men who run the town meet in the office of the community's leading industrialist to select a new school principal, they decide on a man with professional training rather than choosing Thorton, who has served town students for years. College degrees count for more than devotion, however; and Leslie Harrington, a leading industrialist, calls Michael Rossi, Thorton's competitor, a "qualified man who has done graduate work." When Rossi stands up and asks for a higher salary than the local group had planned to pay, he is able to present the image of an assertive male that Thorton cannot match.

Workingmen in *Peyton Place* have no potential for leadership. Lucas Cross does not live near the center of town with its park and greenery but on the margins of society in a run-down shack. He works as a janitor at the high school, while his wife, Nellie, is employed as a maid. Cross tells Thorton, after she has learned that she has lost her bid to become the school principal, that fairness is not part of society in Peyton Place. "Like everybody else in this here town, they really give it to you," he bemoaned. "[You] work yourself to death and then they bring in an outsider to pick the plum off the tree." Thorton defends the idea that American society can still be fair by admonishing Cross for drinking too much and for not applying himself when he was in school. But the janitor refuses to accept personal responsibility for his lowly status and claims that nothing he learned in school prepared him for the cutthroat nature of the real world: "I'll tell you something, Miss Thorton, something you can teach your class someday. The minute they walk out that door, they walk into a dog-eat-dog world. It's crawl in front of the big dogs if you want to eat, get a job. . . . Shakespeare didn't do me no more good than Washington Crossing the Delaware."

But educational deficiencies are the least of this common man's problems. To his wife and stepchildren, he is merely a barbarian and a source of pain. He takes money his stepson has been saving for a correspondence course to support his drinking habit. In fact, the young man can not understand why his mother ever married him, since "he has been hitting everybody, even you." Eventually the boy leaves the town "to make something of himself" by getting away from Cross and the prospect of working at the local mill.

The situation is even more ominous for his stepdaughter, Selena Cross. The girl attempts to live a respectable life and is even elected vice president of her senior class. At home, however, she is the object of her drunken stepfather's lust. He yells at her for "parading" around the house in a slip. "Just because we don't live in a palace, it doesn't mean we have to act like we are pigs," he roars. One night when he is at home alone with her, he tells her that he has never had a beautiful woman, and despite her vigorous resistance, he impregnates her. When the young woman pleads with a local doctor to abort the fetus, she is forced to reveal the hideous origins of her pregnancy in order to persuade the physician to act. But the physician gets Cross to sign an admission of guilt and forces him to leave Peyton Place by threatening him with public disclosure and the wrath of the townspeople. When Nellie Cross learns what happened, she also becomes a victim of male violence by electing to end her life.

Several years later, Cross returns to the shack as a sailor. But servicemen were not heroes to Metalious, and the esteem they enjoyed during the war was rapidly eroding in the mass culture of the 1950s. When Cross tries to rape Selena again, she manages to kill him. In order to save her when she is tried for murder, her doctor produces the document that proved how Cross had violated her, and the town is forced to confront the existence of homegrown evil in its midst. The physician's admonition to the courtroom crowd that Peyton Place had failed to "watch over one another" is a striking revelation that hopes for a democratic community in America were on the decline.

But the dysfunctional nature of the Cross family was not the only example of how the film demeaned common people. The figure of Betty Anderson also invoked a theme already established in films such as *A Streetcar Named Desire* and *A Place in the Sun* (1951) that plebeian women had less self-esteem than women in higher social stations and had only limited control over their sexual drives. Whereas Allison MacKenzie, a middle-class woman, has the confidence to explore a life away from Peyton Place as a writer, two working-class girls have more limited horizons. Selena Cross only wants a traditional marriage, and Betty Anderson feels all she has to offer is sex in return for something better in life. In a discussion over the merits of formal schooling, Anderson says that "a low-cut neckline does more for a girl's future than the entire Britannica Encyclopedia." She proves her point by attracting the attention of Rodney Harrington, the son of the local mill owner. His father tries to dissuade him from marrying "the local tramp," arguing that he would have to marry someone "on your own level." But even the middle class can be castigated in this tale, and Rodney exclaims that he does not want to wed "a cold fish from Boston" and cheat on his wife like his father had. Eventually the young man defies his father's wishes, marries the common girl, and chooses to work at the local mill instead of attending Harvard. When he is killed fighting in World War II, the elder Harrington finally accepts his daughter-in-law and his grandchild, in an act that demonstrates how much it actually took to overcome class differences in the United States.

## RACE OVER CLASS

In the immediate postwar era, some films, like *Crossfire* (1947) and *No Way Out* (1950) began to unmask ethnic and racial tensions that saturated American society. This project, stimulated by the immediate reaction to some of the lessons of National Socialism and to the contributions of minorities to the American war effort, moved along slowly in the fifties but did promise—along with female concerns—to replace class as a matter of concern in both cultural and political life. The portrayal of a bright and ambitious African-American youth in *The Blackboard Jungle* (1955) furthered the attempt to offer blacks a realistic point of view in mass cultural narratives. And at the end of the fifties and the start of the following decade, it appeared that this effort was gaining momentum. There is no doubt that the African-American perspective had to be made palatable to audiences that were largely white. As the scholarship of Thomas Cripps has suggested, films of this period could explore a black subjectivity and point out America's racial problem, but black individuals were always restrained rather than avowedly angry or out of control. In fact, Cripps points out, correctly I think, that the thrust of late forties "message" movies was lost somewhat in the subsequent decade. As an example, he notes that the movie *Paris Blues* (1961) began with a suggestion of interracial dating but soon cast the four adult characters as simply "color-coded pairs."[33]

Sidney Poitier was the key black actor and symbol of the fifties and early sixties, but in Cripps's opinion, he was "a bland antidote to racial tension." In the 1957 film *Edge of the City*, there is at least some affirmation of the possibilities of "racial brotherhood." Poitier and John Cassavetes play two dockworkers who strike up a friendly alliance to ride out the corruption and racism of a labor boss who dislikes both of them. Poitier is certainly restrained and better able to control his emotions than the other leading working-class characters in the story—just as he was in *No Way Out* and *The Blackboard Jungle*.[34]

Tommy Tyler (Poitier) and Alex North (Cassavetes) toil on a labor gang that is continually exploited by a character named Charlie, who extorts money for jobs and hates blacks. It is Tyler who continually tries to protect North from abuse on the docks and who eventually gives his life for such an effort. The film not only exposes the violence and racism of the waterfront but manages to sustain a familiar portrait of the world of American workers as one that is populated by menacing and corrupt people.

During happier times, Tyler and North manage to double date and go bowling. Over dinner, they chat about the unfair manner in which Puerto Ricans are treated in America and the "submerged" status of women. After his friend is killed, however, North is reluctant to inform on the murderer and break waterfront conventions of silence. But women, including Tyler's widow, express outrage over his unwillingness and eventually force him to go to the police. At the end, North tells Charlie that he plans to testify against him, and in an ensuing fight—the preferred form of justice in the blue-collar jungle—the menacing boss is killed.

Things appear to be getting better for African Americans, however, in *A Raisin in the Sun* (1961). The oppressive nature of American race relations is unmistakable, but this story depicts a younger generation of blacks less willing to remain impoverished and more determined to rise. African-American aspirations are aired in this story when the Younger family, living in a crowded apartment in Chicago, debate what to do with a $10,000 life insurance check. Walter Lee Younger, played by Poitier, wants to abandon his lowly job as chauffeur and invest the funds into a liquor business. But his newly widowed mother is determined to move Walter, his wife and son, and her daughter into a nice house in a white section where Walter's young son can have room to play. The maternal head argues that it is a nice home that will give the family pride. Walter Lee feels only frustration, however, that his mother is standing at the head of the family instead of him and preventing him from realizing his economic dreams.

African Americans demonstrate mainstream values in this story, which essentially points the way to their inclusion into postwar America. Walter wants to earn enough money to gain dignity in America and stand tall within his own home. His mother, Lena, however, takes the position that the quest for material advancement, even after years of subjugation, cannot be made by abandoning the traditional values and dignity that have marked her family. She is concerned that the generation that follows her worships dollars more than God, especially after her daughter tells her that she is tired of God getting all the credit for gains that people make. She reminds her children that when she lived in the South, her family worried about lynchings and just getting to the North. Now she fears that they have forgotten their family and religious loyalties and are only "consumed in money."

Eventually, Lena decides to put some of the funds into a down payment on a suburban home and give the rest to Walter to invest. But Walter's business partners betray him, and he loses his entire share, a setback that threatens to ruin household finances and the move to a new house. The family is further tested when a group of white homeowners offers to pay them to flee the home they have just bought. Walter at first wants to take the money; they need it desperately. But his mother again invokes the call for black pride and dignity when she says, "We have never been that poor. We have never been that dead inside." Persuaded to do the right thing, Walter turns the money down and argues that the family comes from a "long line of proud people" who will find a way to pay for the house and succeed. Unlike many working-class families depicted in the fifties and early sixties, the Youngers inspire hope. They share postwar dreams of abundance but still try to earn their way with dignity and

Sidney Poitier as Walter Lee Younger argues for a chance to invest family resources and lead a black family into the prosperous mainstream of postwar America in the 1961 film, *A Raisin in the Sun.* Credit: Film Still Archives, Museum of Modern Art, New York

hard work whatever the obstacles. In the movie culture of the fifties, they were one of the few lower-class families with a promising future.

But prospects for the lowborn of any race were by no means assured in mass culture, partially because film narratives were never prepared to hide the unpredictable nature of the capitalist economy or the hateful tendencies lurking in the nature of Americans themselves. In *West Side Story* (1961), two gangs of urban boys confront squarely the dilemma of holding high expectations in America. Unfortunately, those choosing optimism and love are beaten back, and the future is anything but certain. A Polish-American youth, Tony, desires a steady job, the love of a woman, a house in the country, and fatherhood. He even imagines that racial walls can be breached when he declares his love for Maria, a girl who has just emigrated from Puerto Rico. The immigrant girl shares his hopes and looks forward to being a "young lady of America."

Obstacles to love and understanding in America abound, however, in this dangerous place of city streets and rival gangs. The film takes a clear position on the cultural debate over whether the problems of the working classes are rooted in an unfair society or in the temperament of the lowborn themselves. When Tony is killed for trying to prevent a gang fight, Maria declares that "it's not us, it's everything around us" that gets in the way of their dreams. And in one song, members of one of the gangs, the Jets, condemn society for offering them only jobs without a future and the stigma of being called juvenile delinquents. They cynically claim they must be "psychologically disturbed" because "my daddy beats my mommy, my mommy clobbers me, my grandpa is a commie [and] . . . my brother wears a dress." The rival Sharks share some of the same concerns. When their girlfriends declare that they prefer America to Puerto Rico because they are able to escape male domination and can buy on credit in New York, their male counterparts respond that there "are lots of doors slamming in our face" and that life is only all right in America "if you are white." At the end of this story, as American culture stood on the eve of the social upheaval of the 1960s, film culture was offering no real promise of advancement for most of these people.

## REACTIONS

Printed reactions to fifties films about working-class life appeared to be almost completely indifferent to the aspirations of containment culture. They were absorbed mostly in another cultural conversation about the promises and drawbacks of human passions that promised to sweep away the political concerns of the Cold War. In many ways, people talked about these films as if the mental state of individuals stood above the concerns of the nation-state to arrest the spread of communism or to nurture the growth of consumer capitalism. In the political imagination of mass culture, however, there were few certainties. Communists were not always the enemy; human desires might be. Working people could be cruel but were capable of love and kindness as well. And America was not simply a land of promise where material success and moral certainty would reign. Looking through the lens of emotional and social realism, America was often seen as a place with squalid tenements, rapists, and frustrated people.

Letters to Warner Brothers from individuals who had seen *A Streetcar Named Desire* reflect the popular preoccupation with individual emotional life. Some felt films should represent life in all of its complexity and be free of censorship. Others articulated the belief that the expression of emotional realism had gone too far and that the explicit portrayal of human desire and emotions was unsuitable for many in the audience. When it became known that the movie studio had censored some of Kazan's scenes for fear of incurring the condemnation of the Catholic Legion of Decency, several people objected. A man from Long Island wrote that he hated "this kind of censorship . . . which is keeping a large number of movie goers away from the theater" and could not understand why the Legion of Decency had such influence. Other writers, however, strongly objected to what they saw as the film's moral transgressions. A woman from New Jersey told Warner Brothers that censorship was needed for the "welfare of children." She claimed that moviegoers like her were not "fanatics" and did not object to films showing the "realities of life." She did disapprove, however, of movies that emphasized "sordidness, vulgarity, brutality or an anti-religious spirit." Another critic objected to the sexual frankness of the film and argued that people went to the theater to be entertained. He argued that he could go to "skid row" and see the "ugly way of life" for free rather than spend money on films like Kazan's.[35]

Reviewers, however, uniformly praised the picture that they said "throbs with passion." They did not necessarily like the fact that a woman in this film descended into insanity or that another was raped by her brother-in-law, but they accepted this representation of the world in which they lived because they believed it to be true and because the dramatic presentation was so well done. Thus, a writer in *Commonweal* lamented that fact that the film was "depressing" and "not hopeful for mankind." He realized, however, that "it's story of a woman's loneliness and desperate need for love and of man's misunderstanding and cruelty toward his fellow men" and that it was told with "intense feeling and poetic insight." This review paid grudging respect to emotional realism at its dramatic best. At one point the reviewer, Philip Hartung, questioned whether such a "soul-searching story is really material for motion pictures." And yet he admitted that Marlon Brando's performance was "outstanding for its realism" and that a study of "Blanche's demoralization and the need for charity merit understanding." In a similar way, a review in *Variety* admitted that the film was an "escape from escapism" and offered "brutal reality" but admired the fact that it held audience interest with its "sensitivity" and "poignancy."[36]

Many of the films about working people in the decade focused on individuals beset by emotional turmoil and offered no way out of their predicament as the stories ended. Generally, this frame on plebeian and American life was accepted. Reviews of *Clash by Night* saw the film as one mostly about a frustrated woman "buffeted by life's realities" and torn between her desire for security with one man and sex with another." Almost no condemnation of the woman's adulterous affair can be found in the reviews. Even the *Catholic World* praised the acting of Barbara Stanwyck and only asked rather meekly if it might be possible to have someone "do a picture about nice, moral people." The disappointed wife of a cab driver in *A Catered Affair* does not cross moral boundaries in her desire to spend meager family savings on a lavish wedding for her daughter, but her plight failed to evoke much sympathy. One reviewer saw the woman not as deprived but as simply trying to "keep up with the Joneses." Another felt that the "dominant emotion aroused" by watching the story was one of feeling sorry for the woman's daughter because she never got the wedding she wanted. In films like these, reviewers do note the realistic settings of a fishing village in California in the former film and the Bronx in the latter one, but they are inclined to discuss the stories in terms of the emotions and desires of the characters and not their social station.[37]

The capacity of human emotions to bring bleakness and oppression to everyday life and the declining attention given to social realism were key ways in which critics discussed *The Rose Tattoo*, *Peyton Place*, and *No Down Payment*. One writer was struck by the "spectrum of emotional alterations" exhibited by the female lead in *The Rose Tattoo*. In this story a woman mourned the loss of her dead husband, grew angry when she realized he had been unfaithful to her, and then found "booming joy" with a new man near the end. When critics expressed disapproval, it was because the emotions or actions displayed were not believable. Thus, a reviewer in *Variety* had trouble accepting the point that the woman missed her departed husband solely because he had been "a robust, virile mate." *Peyton Place* did evoke some comments on the fact that it inferred a sense of larger social changes in American society. Many reviewers noted the contradiction between the presentation of a peaceful New England town as a setting and the tale of lives marked by violence and moral decay. Mostly, however, discussion focused on the duplicity of the town's elites and the blunt accounts of sexual matters. As expected, the *Catholic World* argued that *Peyton Place* was "no place" for Catholics because of its moral tone. In a short review in a publication for parent-teacher groups in the United States, a writer chose to focus only on the part of the film dealing with a plebeian family and said the movie was about an "impoverished family on the outskirts, living almost like animals under the domination of a drunken and irresponsible stepfather." Finally, reviewers saw suburban couples in *No Down Payment* as "pitifully naturalistic" and saw the couple from the hills of Tennessee as plagued by "unrequited desires." In fact, the review in *National Parent-Teacher* expressed regret that the story did not explore the problems of the suburbs more fully. The opinion here was that the tale evolved into "too much melodrama" and revealed a "classic set of neuroses among the various couples as will be found in a Tennessee Williams plot."[38]

Films that blended some depiction of the real conditions of working-class life with extensive character development brought widespread approbation. *On the Waterfront*, a film that in our times is often talked about in terms of Cold War politics, was almost never reviewed as a story that justified Kazan's "naming names" to HUAC. Contemporaries tended to value its stark depiction of the life and work of longshoreman and the emotional and personal transition of the lead character, Terry Malloy. *Variety* said the fact that the film was actually shot on location in Hoboken, New Jersey, and in the "blue-gray early morning" gave the feature a "chilly realism." Another reviewer felt the film brought a "graphic dimension" to existing newspaper accounts of "the personalities and evils of our waterfront." It was the fullness of the working-class personality and the hopeful transition to respectability of Malloy that drew most of the acclaim, however. Consider this description in *The New York Times:*

> Terry Malloy is a shatteringly poignant portrait of an amoral, confused, illiterate citizen of the lower depths who is goaded into decency by love, hate, and murder. His groping for words, use of the vernacular, care of his beloved pigeons, pugilist's walk and gestures, and his

discoveries of love and the immensity of the crimes surrounding him are highlights of a beautiful and moving portrayal.[39]

Malloy became, in other words, a symbol not only that harsh social conditions could be overcome but that common American men could mend their violent ways. This was a line of analysis very much grounded in the postwar concern over inner drives and violent emotions, despite the obvious claim here that religion and love could do more than unions or strikes. Even *National Parent-Teacher* recommended the film for teens, noting that it was a "moving drama of a young dockworker's painful growth into responsible maturity." *Commonweal* saw the story as one of a man who could change from a "tough bully in his youth" to a "man of courage who commands respect in his later years." Not surprisingly, the *Daily Worker* paid little attention to Malloy's personality. The radical journal certainly appreciated the "element of truth" in the film's depiction of "mobsters" on the docks, of the "degrading" scramble for jobs that took place each day on the waterfront, but it could not accept the suggestion that the rank and file longshoremen were so reluctant to challenge a crime boss and needed a priest to stir them to action. The newspaper claimed that in the real story on which the film was based, longshoremen actually held a rally on their own to mobilize against the racketeers.[40]

Emotional realism attracted considerably more comment than accounts of the social environment. However, when social realism was confronted more explicitly through older questions of labor-capital relations or newer ones of racial matters, approving responses were evident. For instance, it is striking that *Salt of the Earth*, a story of labor strife, was not seen by mainstream reviewers as subversive of America's Cold War battle against communism. Most critics saw it simply as a straightforward realistic story with a strong pro-labor stance and some sympathy for the position of women in the Mexican-American community in the mining campus in which it was set. *Variety* actually attacked those who wanted to prevent the showing of the film, argued that "one would have to be quite analytical to read the alleged 'Red line' into the production," and viewed it as "reminiscent of the social problem pix Hollywood used to put out in the thirties." The *Daily Worker* not only praised the movie for being pro-labor and attaining a high level of "depth and realism" but liked its advocacy of female equality. The paper offered an extensive amount of testimony from ordinary people who had seen the film, all of it filled with praise. Thus, a "cabdriver" was quoted as saying that the film should be shown to everyone "who works for a living"; a "machinist" claimed he had never seen a film that dealt with workers as this one did; a "secretary" traveled from Philadelphia to New York to see the film and now wanted to return home and tell her friends how good it was; and a "repairman" felt it was a "true picture of how one man's relationship toward his wife changed through struggle." Another film about a labor strike, *The Whistle at Eaton Falls*, was generally endorsed for its plea for class harmony and its indictment of extremism and uncompromising attitudes on the part of some managers and workers. And critics saw *The Garment Jungle*, with its story about corruption in unions, as a "realistic and intense dramatic documentary," since it was not only "forceful dramatic screen fare" but reasonably faithful to a series of articles on "labor warfare within the needle trades" that had appeared in *Readers Digest*.[41]

Cold War politics was actually conducive to messages that promoted racial equality and understanding in America. Thus, when a rare film brought forward graphic accounts on matters of race relations or the plight of African Americans (something that was done by Hollywood with the expectation that theaters in the South might not show the feature), favorable opinion was widespread in the mainstream press. *Edge of the City* was praised as a "social document" that was "never preachy" and for showing "the Negro" not as a "problem" but as a "fully-integrated first-class citizen." Similarly, *A Raisin in the Sun* was endorsed for looking beyond the African American as simply a national dilemma or a "theatrical stereotype" and allowing him to be "an all-too-human being." Other commentators liked the fact that the film conveyed the "economic reality" of an urban black family with expectations for better housing in the suburbs similar to whites. Finally, *West Side Story* received much acclaim not only for its music and choreography but for its "stark approach to a raging social problem" of juvenile delinquency. Some viewers certainly liked the romantic aspects of the love story in the movie but felt its "preachment against juvenile delinquency" was "more potent" than it would have been if it was simply a "message picture."[42]

## CONCLUSIONS

Films treating aspects of working-class life in the fifties adhered to some aspects of containment culture, to be sure. Communism was vilified and resisted by characters like Brad Adams in *The Whistle at Eaton Falls*, and labor organizations were usually seen more as vehicles of corruption than of progress. The Grazianos and the Youngers showed that social mobility was still an attainable dream. American faith in religion and the need for personal morality were endorsed in pictures like *On the Waterfront,* in which the figure of Terry Malloy was ultimately one that ratified traditional values and the dream of containing human desire.

Yet the imagined world of Hollywood's lower depths turned out to be a real problem for those who would have hoped for a stronger defense of Cold War ideals or a more sentimental picture of America. Determined to continue its probe of human emotional life and, to a lesser extent, social conditions, the film industry clearly acquiesced to the demands of its audience and the dictates of its own traditions to imitate life. And because it did, the portrait it offered of ordinary people, while not flattering, ultimately discredited many of the most cherished verities of Cold War America. Stanley and Stella Kowalski reinforced the idea that Americans could be lustful and violent. The Cross family—Lucas, Nellie, and Selena—was in complete disarray. Female characters like Meg Doyle and Angie Hurley insisted that marriage was unsatisfying. Troy Boone gave evidence that some World War II veterans would not be welcome in the postwar world despite what they had done for their country. A boxer like Tony Moreno proved again that the liberal dream was likely to end in failure. In its insistence that marriages did not always work, that ordinary Americans were constantly beset by emotional and economic problems, and that liberal capitalism and democracy were simply not available to many individuals, mass cultural products like film continued to move further and further away from the assurances of traditional political organizations and closer to acknowledging that personal longings and frustrations were what mattered most. Moreover, while not flocking to all of the films examined here, audiences showed some approbation toward this more critical view of their world when they placed *A Streetcar Named Desire, On the Waterfront,* and *Peyton Place* among the top-grossing films of the years in which they appeared.[43]

# FIVE

# THE PEOPLE IN TURMOIL

Although Americans moved in various political directions in the thirties, forties, and fifties, there was always a master plan that sought to push the expression of democracy and liberalism in some directions and not others and to limit the full exposition of personal desire in political debates. Since political life in these decades tended to emphasize the power of institutions over individuals, the concerns of men over women, and the power of whites over blacks, the expression of democracy and liberalism was generally distorted to serve this political reality. Thus, in the thirties, democratic rights were sought mostly for workingmen and pursued through strong union and governmental organizations. Discussions of liberalism were tied mostly to the fate of capitalism and the need to balance an ideal of personal uplift with one that called for restraint. The full access of women and minorities to work, unions, capitalist enterprise, and political influence was minimized.

During World War II the need for unions, capitalist enterprise, and white male hegemony was not forgotten, but a broader political vision was articulated by political leaders that included a defense of democratic and liberal rights for all citizens. This more inclusive understanding of political rights was driven to a great extent by a reaction to the images and threats of fascism. However, organized politics changed after the war. American political leaders still defended the concepts of democratic and liberal rights, male power, and capitalist expansion, but the capacious language of wartime, which was more welcoming to women and unions, was curtailed. A dawning recognition of the problem of white supremacy was indeed recognized, although this was still not a topic that commanded considerable attention from major political parties. The crusade against communism certainly defended democratic and liberal ideals in the postwar era, but in a way that continued to weaken the labor politics of the thirties and the democratic and liberal rights of many citizens who were viewed with suspicion.

The ability of mainstream politics to sustain master plans such as the New Deal or the Cold War was weakened considerably in the 1960s. Obviously, events like the war in Vietnam and the civil rights movement had much to do with the splintering of white male authority and the demise of traditional political alliances that marked this fall. Yet it must be stressed that many of the stories, images, and characters that circulated through American culture in the middle decades of the twentieth century had already cut away at authoritarian and dominant political values as they were constituted. Changes that took place in the sixties and beyond were not only the result of the well-known political controversies of the time but were also induced by the growing ability of mass culture to dominate both cultural and political expression. Thus, by the decades of the 1970s and 1980s, with the power of political, moral, and even film authorities in some decline, the disorder, confusion, and anger that existed in the emotional and social worlds of common people was transferred more directly to the screen than possibly at any time in the era of sound pictures.

In a sense, the imagined life and politics of the lower classes now had a complexity and a grounding in social and emotional realism that were unprecedented. Democratic and liberal aspirations were still imagined to exist among the people, and in a few instances they were realized, but they were challenged effectively by depictions that showed the ire of ordinary individuals and even more "grim antagonisms" of lower-class life than was normally the case. Common people were now portrayed as wrestling with the demise of male authority, the ebbing of union-sponsored democracy, the war in Vietnam, the rise of racial tensions, and the new possibilities for women. The congruence between political and cultural expression that marked the years of World War II returned, but now the collective story of working-class life in film was much more elaborate and was riddled with conflicting streams of liberalism, democracy, and illiberalism—much as it was in real life.

The sixties were harder on the Democrats than the Republicans, and therefore damaging to the interests of organized labor. The problems are well known. The coalition that had forged the party and the New Deal in the thirties began to come apart over its policies in Vietnam and over civil rights. The Great Society initiatives of Lyndon Johnson were viewed in many working-class neighborhoods as signs that Democratic leaders favored blacks over whites. Some traditional Democratic voters resented what they felt was a shift of domestic reform from union issues to matters of racial equality. Nelson Lichtenstein also notes that over time unions themselves moved away from older issues of shop floor control and strike actions and began to bargain merely for more benefits as a way of allowing their members to play a greater role in the consumer economy. With unions less interested in mobilizing their workers for political action and many workers unhappy with their traditional political leaders in Washington, serious signs of decay became evident in the alliance between organized labor and the Democratic Party.[1]

Vietnam hurt the working class in a number of ways and gave many of its members more reason to feel alienated from their traditional political moorings as well. The war contributed to an overall sense of distrust toward government and weakened the concept of national loyalty. Consider that working-class support for the New Deal, for the war government of the forties, and for the Cold War was always embedded in an ideal that their patriotism would be rewarded in terms of union legitimacy, economic security, and the unquestioned needs of male breadwinners. The manner in which troops were recruited to fight the Vietnam war, however, turned out to be a tremendous source of alienation for many working people, for it suggested that their loyalty was now a source of maltreatment rather than of benefits. They resented terribly the fact that many middle-class kids enjoyed college deferments and that most of the draftees, and therefore the soldiers that died, were from the lower classes. The fact that many college students openly challenged the war and the government that had brought them new and improved lifestyles since the thirties only aggravated the situation further. By no means did all working people in America support the war in Vietnam, however, although this is a common assumption sustained by images of construction workers attacking anti-war protestors in New York City in 1970 and the fact that some prominent labor leaders like George Meany continually backed the American effort. Some studies show clearly that many of the rank and file actually opposed it and differed with many union leaders on the issue. Where working-class support for the war appeared strong, moreover, it was often grounded less in political arguments like stopping communism and more in a feeling of outrage against privileged protestors and college students who marched as their sons and relatives died. They were united more in anger than in a sense of patriotism.[2]

Working-class loyalty to the Democrats was also severely tested by racial transformations that were taking place in many urban neighborhoods and schools. In South Boston in the 1970s, white working people engaged in ugly acts of violence toward blacks and expressed hatred toward middle-class professionals who designed school integration programs by day and fled to affluent white suburbs at night. Similarly, in the Canarsie section of Brooklyn in the same decade, one scholar found that "house-proud" working families who had moved up since the Depression into the respectable domiciles now felt "molested by formidable powers: blacks, liberals, and bureaucrats." For their part, blacks too were experiencing dramatic changes as better-paid black workers and a rising black middle class moved from older neighborhoods and left behind an African-American community that was increasingly poor, angry, and disadvantaged.[3]

Deprived of its normal political allies and clout, working-class politics began to exhibit greater signs of illiberalism by the late sixties. Many blue-collar voters began to look with more interest to political leaders like George Wallace, Richard Nixon, and Ronald Reagan, who acknowledged their fury and frustration over political efforts to achieve racial integration and over countercultural attacks on traditional values that for them included parental authority, religion, and patriotism. These politicians also promised "law and order" instead of additional social reform to solve America's problems. In the beginning of the Wallace campaign for the presidency in 1968, polls among working-class voters in the North showed very high (sometimes as much as 40 percent) support for the campaign of the Alabama governor. Although effective counterattacks on the Wallace campaign by Democratic strategists helped to keep most of these voters in the party ranks during the November elections, he still managed to win a respectable (for a third party candidate) 8 percent of voters in the North. Lower-class voters were also attracted to Richard Nixon's defense of ordinary Americans as good and honorable people—"the silent majority"—who did not protest in the streets but (according to Nixon) stood solidly behind his war policies at a time when young protestors and dissidents appeared to be mocking traditional values. In the 1972 presidential election, Nixon clearly made inroads into the traditionally Democratic rank and file because of the way he acknowledged their anger. And in 1980, Ronald Reagan continued to attract support from lower-class people with a philosophy that eschewed New Deal visions of government assistance or working-class democracy and concentrated more on a promise that pride in traditional institutions and authorities, morals, and political values like national loyalty and capitalism that had been discredited in the sixties could now be restored.[4]

The place and politics of working people after the sixties would be altered not only by political transformations but by economic ones as well. The impact of a massive amount of plant closings and deindustrialization further undermined the traditional place the blue-collar class had come to hold in American politics and society. Between 1965 and 1990, American companies built more than 1,800 plants employing over a half-million workers in Mexico alone. At home plant shutdowns eliminated more than 22 million jobs. New positions were created to be sure, but generally they paid less and were nonunionized. In the aftermath of the decline of the Democratic Party, the foundation of the industrial unions that had helped to sustain working-class political influence for decades was rapidly eroding. With their unions and party now in a weakened state, America's workers were unable to mount any sort of truly effective resistance to the assault on their lives that deindustrialization constituted. In instances where workers took militant action, they often failed to receive meaningful support from national union leaders, who had grown indifferent to many of the concerns of their locals. And the federal government offered almost no resistance at all to the plague of plant shutdowns.[5]

Working people had already lost much of their cultural standing, of course, even before their political and economic situation eroded. Countless images had filled the cinema in the forties and fifties of plebeians whose lives were in emotional turmoil and whose communities were drab and dangerous. Television continued this unflattering portrayal of blue-collar life with the wildly popular series *All in the Family*. This highly politicized comedy repeated the point that lowborn men were inherently illiberal and that they would find it difficult to live outside the lower regions of American society even if they moved upward. In this show a white, working-class bigot, steeped in the traditions of patriarchy, blind patriotism, and white racism is challenged and ridiculed repeatedly by all of the symbolic figures that had been denied power in the traditional political world of the thirties, forties, and fifties: women, young adults, and blacks. Archie Bunker was not Stanley Kowalski—although he often seemed insensitive toward the needs of his spouse—but he was clearly an anachronism in a modern American revolution devoted to overturning the political culture of the middle century that had restrained full expressions of female, minority, and personal desire.

In fact, the celebration of individual agency and personal fulfillment was not new in American culture but was reinvigorated after World War II at a time when alternative ideas like moral restraint, collective politics, and democratic—as opposed to liberal—visions began to erode. Peter

Clecak has argued that the quest for self-fulfillment was the "central metaphor of American civilization" in the sixties and seventies. Moral and political issues certainly became more about private rather than social or national issues than they had been in previous decades. The goal of many government programs became the creation of equal opportunity for individuals and the meeting of "enlarged psychic expectations" for abundance and personal liberty. Women, for instance, took decisions on abortions away from medical experts and claimed them for themselves. Politics came to be more about the need to claim individual rights than about transforming society or saving the world from dangerous forces. Clecak argues that such a culture did produce some nostalgia for old ethnic and working-class families that were unaffected by ideals of personal desire and where a sense of security could be established in a small community, but he also notes that such dreams merely served the conservative tenor of the era by erasing the history of working-class militancy and showing that the ideals of cooperative families and communities were aspects of the past rather than the present.[6]

## THE NEW HOLLYWOOD

A new society now faced with the weakening of its primary institutions and fixated on personal rather than collective goals did not prove to be a problem for Hollywood to represent. The working-class world imagined by film for decades compared quite closely to this new political and social reality where women, minorities, and even personal fury accounted for more, and institutional authorities and conventional values counted for less. Moral censorship was effectively ended by the early sixties—even before Vietnam and civil rights had become raging issues—and there was no more insistence in the industry that crooks be punished, adulterous women be condemned, or authorities be respected. The heightened interest in violence and violent men after 1945 could now be explored more fully.

At the same time, the centralized power of movie studios and their ability to orchestrate movie production declined. The amount of money required to make films grew to such an extent that studios could not launch film projects with their own resources—although they had always been dependent on a few key bankers and investors. Now "deals" were struck between investors, independent producers, agents, directors, actors, writers, and studios. With a decentralized system of control shaping the content of film, directors, writers, and actors obtained more freedom in self-expression. Stories of personal transformation and revolt against traditional institutions proliferated. Antisocial visions of the nation now coexisted to a greater degree with those that were pro-social. Ironically, the existence of more representational possibilities allowed Hollywood to offer a fuller and more diverse treatment of working-class life. This meant that common people now became more complex individuals, struggling with personal transformations and emotional problems, attached to a wider variety of political outlooks, and capable of bringing hope to America as well as extravagant doses of brutality and despair.

The first wave of this new freedom of expression moved quickly to sustain the high degree of faultfinding with American institutions that had marked the sixties. In a 1975 film like *Nashville*, for example, director Robert Altman advanced the idea that there was pervasive "disillusionment" in America. Altman, who had already questioned favorable representations of the American war efforts in *M\*A\*S\*H*, portrayed numerous characters in the capital of country and western music as preoccupied with the pursuit of fame and generally indifferent to the needs of others or lacking in any sort of basic integrity. Films about Vietnam provided no more assurance of a more orderly or democratic future. Many of these features argued that the war only degraded those it touched and produced nothing of value and no men who could be considered heroes.

The very popular *Godfather* films of the 1970s, directed by Francis Ford Coppola, continued the massive cultural project of denigrating the nation and many of the men who ran it. Like the gangsters films of the thirties, Coppola's criminals were creatures of capitalism and the drive for wealth and power in America. But in the fashion of post-1945 culture, they were also motivated by inner drives for control and honor that predated capitalistic society and, by implication, emanated from the eternal problem of human nature. There was little hope offered in these stories that such men could ever be contained, although Michael Corleone's wife certainly tries in *The Godfather, Part II*, when she aborts his son in order to end one particular line of brutal men. Not surprisingly, authorities like the Catholic Church and the federal government are pictured as corrupt; they are certainly not working for the ideal of justice for all. Coppola told an interviewer in 1972 that he had always wanted to use the Mafia as a metaphor for America and its profit-driven culture. But along the way he also managed to castigate powerful religious institutions and patriarchy. And mob leaders (read capitalists) like Corleone were duplicitous: protecting their families on the one hand, and destroying them on the other.[7]

Yet Hollywood continued to mount a defense of conservative values as well, although such a position would never be all that conservative political leaders would have liked. Certainly the possibility existed that a resurgent conservatism and mass culture might find some common ground in their mutual obsession with individualism and their shared skepticism of governmental power. Such conjunctures were, in fact, evident in films like *Dirty Harry* (1971) and *Rambo: First Blood, Part Two* (1985), in which the heroic actions of individual Americans gave voice to the ideals of "law and order" and anger over the critique of Vietnam. The 1975 film *Death Wish* told a story of a successful architect who avenged the murder of his wife by a racially mixed group of hoodlums. Moving through the streets of New York, this angry man began killing and wounding young punks indiscriminately. Rather than being punished or censored in any way, however, police authorities simply told the man to get out of town.[8]

By the 1970s, the imagined characters of the lower-class world had acquired a highly complex set of political views and emotional conflicts. In the thirties, gangsters were troubling but ultimately liberal capitalists riveted to a narrow quest for wealth and power; fallen women wanted many of the same things. During World War II, common citizens were mostly one dimensional: intent on serving their nation. In the postwar period, with its bow to emotional realism, common people were displayed as having a wider range of political thought that included democratic aspirations (*Home of the Brave*), liberal dreams (*Somebody Up There Likes Me*), and indifference and brutality (*A Streetcar Named Desire*). But their political and social conscience was still rather narrow in most of these features, confined to the immediate issues of their own lives, dreams, and neighborhoods. During the decade of the sixties itself, there was a noticeable drop-off in the production of stories featuring working-class protagonists. Stereotypes of lower-class whites as bigots were stressed in *To Kill a Mockingbird* (1962). A lower-class man was simply consumed with his own private project to defy authorities of all kinds and appeared disinterested in issues pertinent to a larger society in the 1967 picture *Cool Hand Luke*. *Bonnie and Clyde* (1967) revealed common people during the Depression who were desperate and who were plagued with personal troubles but detached from the mainstream political community. The 1969 film *Midnight Cowboy* repeated the theme of lower-class men struggling to survive on the margins of economic and political life. This story also made it clear that the two male leads in this feature were victimized by their upbringing in lower-class households; one was abandoned by his mother, and another was the son of a man who shined shoes and could not write. In both instances, these men led lives completely detached from the prospect of either democracy or liberalism.

## ANGRY MEN, MEAN STREETS

The figure that emerged in the seventies of the common man as a complicated political man often detached from any organized political effort was not always a likeable character, especially when he took it upon himself to restore lawfulness in a world devoid of moral certainty and trustworthy authorities where democratic and liberal aspirations no longer survived. In this second coming of a postwar America, common men were forced to take political matters into their own hands. They were gunfighters of a sort, but they plied their trade and vented their anger not on some distant frontier but right in the middle of their social world and against fellow citizens rather than against savages. This was clear in movies like *Joe* (1970) and *Taxi Driver* (1976).

*Joe* marked the beginning of an attempt to express some of the displeasure of lower-class whites against the transformations that took place in the sixties. Joe Currant works in a factory, respects his country, and is proud of his service in World War II; he hates blacks and despises "hippies." He is a colorless man, watching television at night, collecting guns, and dreaming mostly about punishing those in society who do not share his desire to defend the world that shaped the life he leads. He explains his understanding of recent politics in America to a local bartender, claiming that "the niggers are getting all the money." "You tell me why the fuck work," he complains, "when you can screw, have babies, and get paid for it." In a tavern where a large photo of the American flag being raised on Iwo Jima hangs on the wall, he also assails the counterculture. He is disturbed by white kids with college educations and fancy cars who take drugs and have orgies. "They're getting away with murder," he complains. "Sex, drugs, pissing on America. . . . I'd like to kill one of them." And while he is at it, he throws a punch at the "liberals," claiming that a good many of them are "queer."

Life changes for Curran the day Bill Compton walks into his favorite bar. Compton draws Curran's respect when he learns that he has murdered his daughter's long-haired boyfriend for leading the young woman into a life of drugs and sex. He admires a man who takes matters into his own hands, and he compares Compton's murderous act to the killing of Japanese soldiers in World War II. The two men soon forge an alliance to search for Compton's missing daughter and, in the process, to purge America of its unruly youth. Curran is actually enthusiastic about crossing the border into this strange world and seeing "these animals and where they live." Along the way, however, he exhibits considerable duplicity by taking part in a drug and sex party with the "hippies" he despises in Greenwich Village and expresses a desire to repeat the experience once it is over. Eventually, the two vigilantes find a rural counterculture commune and start shooting at its occupants with abandon. "These kids shit on you," he yelled. "They shit on everything you believe in." In the chaos, however, Compton unknowingly kills his own daughter. In the painful and tragic ending there is no sense that these men or the nation in which they live can restore any kind of moral or peaceful society.

The aftermath of the sixties and the shadow of Vietnam also framed the politics and fury of *Taxi Driver*, Martin Scorsese's 1976 film about a deranged former marine who had served his nation in southeast Asia. A director like Scorsese, born in 1942 and imprinted with many of the fault-finding impulses of the counterculture himself, moved easily toward a critique of established politics and institutions in America and concluded that without authorities and institutions that could be trusted, futures were problematic and widespread cynicism was inevitable. The result was the character of Travis Bickle, a lonely and ill-tempered common man who embarks on a personal crusade to restore moral and political order to America. Bickle is no Stanley Kowalski. He does not inflict violence on others simply to satisfy his own lust. He is also completely disinterested in the politics of men like Joe Radek or Lonesome Rhodes. He may have served conservative interests at the time when he dreamed about improving society's morals, but he exhibits no faith in established institutions. He lives a life free of any attachments or expectations for upward mobility. He is an illiberal like Joe Curran, positioned in a netherworld between democracy and liberalism where authorities are untrustworthy, futures uncertain, and friends nonexistent. Disgusted by what he feels is social and moral decay around him and by his isolation, he drives his cab each evening through city streets, repulsed by the "whores, scum, pussy . . . dopers [and] junkies" he sees around him. This picture is not only a depressing portrait of American society but a meditation on the idea of despair, a theme Columbia pictures thought they could sell because they thought the image of struggling and desolate individuals now pervaded the culture. Studio pressrooms saw the feature as one that described the "all too human condition of loneliness" and the plight of "a human being who moves through the madding crowd, jostled, brushed, ignored [and] abused."[9]

Like many of Scorsese's leading male characters, Bickle exhibits only a tenuous attachment to conventional practices. He demonstrates some interest in a stable and loving relationship with a woman and, we can infer, some other career besides self-appointed moral crusader. He is attracted to a blonde named Betsy, who represents a level of respectability that appears unattainable in his world. In a visit one day to the offices of a political campaign where she works, he brings her a gift, hoping to establish some sort of relationship. He tells the candidate that she supports, moreover, that the city is like an "open sewer" but declares some faith that the president will eventually cleanse society of its moral decay.

The community metaphor that stood at the heart of numerous cinematic stories such as *Happy Land* (1943) and *It's a Wonderful Life* as a way of evaluating the state of democracy and social stability is not evident in this film. The people Bickle meets in his cab are living without any moral or political center. One rider is a young girl who has turned to prostitution; another is a man who announces his intention to kill his wife for her infidelity. Clearly, social decay is weighing heavily upon Bickle, but so are his own inner demons. He has constant headaches, and he tells a friend that he is contemplating bringing violence to bear on all of the turmoil he sees around him. Bickle's solution to remove his frustration and rectify social ills is to be found, not in the realm of traditional politics, but in acts of personal vengeance. He writes in his diary that his life has been nothing but one continuous chain—"one day indistinguishable from the next." He now senses, however, that he can break the dull repetition of his existence and purify society by buying a gun—"a real monster"—and killing off what he sees as the source of the problems.

Regenerated through the acquisition of violent outlooks and weapons, Bickle shaves his head and swallows pills as he prepares to appoint himself an army of one to restore law and order. First, he shoots a black man who is holding up a store in his neighborhood. Then he plots the assassination of a the political candidate who admits in a speech that the nation has taken some "wrong roads" that have led to war, poverty, and unemployment. The man does promise that the nation will not let "people suffer for the few," but we know with certainty that Bickle no longer believes that such commitments will be kept. Only the intervention of security men force him to abandon his assassination plot.

At the climax of the story, the taxi driver obtains some degree of moral reform when he kills the pimp of the young prostitute who had ridden in his cab and the operator of a cheap hotel where her sexual encounters took place. In the aftermath of the shootings, the camera lingers on the bloody scene and presents audiences with an interpretation of American society and human nature that is grim and pessimistic. We also learn that Bickle has parents somewhere from whom he must conceal his real life. He writes and tells them that he cannot send them his address because he is doing secret work for the government; he also mentions that he is making a good deal of money and dating a girl named Betsy. This crusader for moral reform must remain apart from a society that is corrupt and from loving relations if he is to accomplish the task he has set for himself. His issues are both social and personal. As to his fate and that of his nation, audiences get no clue or reassurance. As we watch him drive off into the night, we can presume there will be further assaults against evil in the only manner he knows—individual action. His image verifies a point Scorsese made in a 1976 speech: that films could no longer be made "where everything seems to fall into place and make sense." "There are deep, dark things in all of us," he claimed in words that went to the heart of a postwar project to undermine utopias, "and they come out in different ways."[10]

## CAUGHT IN A TRAP

Scorsese played an instrumental role in bringing the angry man to the screen, but he was also capable of repeating older stories of ordinary males who were completely devoid of larger political interests and incapable of building loving relationships and leaving the violent, lower class worlds that he imagined had created their troubled personalities in the first place. Such men lived in a realm beyond mainstream values and politics, and there did not seem to be much they could ever do about it. Stories like *Mean Streets* (1973) and *Raging Bull* (1980) inferred, in a sense, that democracy and liberalism were never going to be part of the life of these people.

In his "semi-biographical" story of *Mean Streets*, Scorsese followed young men coming of age in New York's Little Italy. The lives and nature of these men are ultimately determined by the web of crime and violence that shapes their neighborhood. Actor Harvey Keitel plays a young Italian American named Charlie, who is trying to do something that is almost impossible in his world as it is imagined by the director: looking for love with a woman named Teresa and pursuing wealth through crime all at the same time. Established institutions are of no help to him and are actually under attack in this story, as they are in most of Scorsese's work. The Catholic Church lacks any capacity to advance the cause of a compassionate and caring society, and Charlie rejects many of its practices and traditions in favor of a religion grounded more in personal forms of penance and emotional expression. In later interviews, the director made clear that he was displeased with the church as he knew it and wanted this film to focus on "inner lives" as a way of reforming a violent and corrupt society. Scorsese recalled organized crime figures in his neighborhood tipping their hats to prelates and participating in church rituals; however, violence, street crime, and the mistreatment of women persisted in his neighborhood, and the church did little to oppose it.[11]

The young men in this story devote much of their daily existence to making bets, fighting in pool rooms, bribing local police (another authority discredited), drinking, and looking for sex, often with sophisticated women from Manhattan. Completely alienated from traditional institutions and political life, they desire to flee the responsibilities of patriarchy by fashioning lives outside familial and religious spheres. No hope is offered here that these men will ever be regenerated morally. Teresa represents one chance for Charlie to escape his violent and disorderly world. Like working-class women before her, she dreams of flight from the lower-class neighborhood and movement to an "uptown" apartment away from the controlling influences of her parents. She invites Charlie to move in with her, but he claims he would be unable to meet the expectations of a relationship because he is "moving in on something in his neighborhood right now." Charlie cannot conceive of a future outside his lower-class world. When Teresa challenges him by demanding to know just what it is he really likes, his response is evasive. He reveals that he likes "spaghetti and clam sauce. . . chicken with lemon and garlic and John Wayne." When she tells him he is afraid to commit to a woman, he replies, "For me, all I got is the neighborhood . . . and those guys, that's all that is important to me right now." Here is a lower-class male consigned to his station in life, not by an unjust society or the failings of capitalism, but only by his own immaturity and his attraction to a life of small-scale crime.

Some men from the lower order simply could not manage the central projects of American life; they were incapable of becoming either democrats or liberals. Their lives and their worlds were filled with skepticism, in part, because traditional institutions had let them down. More significantly, they had a wide range of personal problems that were not easily recognized or solved. Thus moral reform, which conservatives in the seventies and eighties would have argued was a way to solve some social and emotional problems, resulted, in the hands of illiberals like Curran and Bickle, in ruinous and destructive behavior. Struggles for upward mobility and respect on the part of boxers like Jake LaMotta in Scorsese's 1980 film *Raging Bull* demonstrated as well how much these men were incapable of keeping their personal desires from turning into ferocity.

Gerald Early has argued well how boxing has always been a popular way of exploring the plight of lonely individuals trying to get ahead in a mean-spirited culture of "bruising." In the 1950s the story of Rocky Graziano reinforced positive views of liberalism by depicting the fighter's struggle to successfully climb out of the working-class ethnic ghetto. But narratives of mass culture have always contained antisocial potential; Early acknowledges that boxing stories allowed audiences the chance to review the "ritualization of triumph and defeat, [and] the expression and thwarting of the sheer ambiguity of masculine aggression." Graziano's ebullience over his rise is contradicted in *Raging Bull* by LaMotta's madness and destructiveness. He is ungovernable and lives beyond the reach of both liberal and conservative (or moral) dreams of reform. LaMotta carries memories of his own father's brutality toward his wife and children into his adult life and, consequently, is imprinted by his blue-collar past. As Early notes, however, he is also an embodiment of the "male temperament in post–World War II industrial society. . . the prizefighter par excellence of the modern world." He hates his father, toils in a machine-like fashion, and is fixed on the modern search for a sense of self through the "base instincts of survival, war, and sex through the artifices of game and sport."[12]

The dark and somber LaMotta uses his innate capacity for violence to lift himself from his Italian-American world and its complex web of familial obligations to the middleweight championship. In the film's beginning, the boxer lives unhappily with his wife in a small apartment in the Bronx. Insensitive to her needs and overly demanding, he pushes her around and generally makes her life miserable. He spends more time running around with his brother Joey and trying to meet a pretty blonde named Vicki that he had first seen at a local pool. When his spouse threatens to go out on him as he does on her, he tells her only that he does not care. His brother's response to her warning is more menacing; he tells LaMotta to kill her.

Sex and violence go together in LaMotta's illiberal world. Thus, the director shows the boxer taking the blonde to an apartment for sex and

In *Raging Bull* (1980), actor Robert De Niro played a boxer who was an illiberal, seeking to use his violent temper to lower the standing of those around him. The liberal dream of individual advancement was shattered by this common man's inability to manage his violent drives. Credit: Film Still Archives, Museum of Modern Art, New York

then immediately cuts away to a match between the boxer and Sugar Ray Robinson. LaMotta inflicts punishment on the black fighter with his brute strength, but the more polished and agile Robinson wins a ten-round decision. After the fight, the bruised boxer needs Vicki to soothe and console him but is able to restrain himself from having sex with her in the belief that it will preserve his strength for what matters more—the next fight with Robinson.

For a time LaMotta appears able to put his destructive impulses behind him. He marries the young blonde, another symbol of leaving the ethnic ghetto, and reestablishes a family life of sorts in the Bronx again, although even in this period he appears to spend most of his time discussing boxing with his manager and his brother Joey. And his temper is never far from the surface. Insanely jealous, he reacts angrily when Vicki comments that the next man he is to fight is handsome. In the ring, the primitive LaMotta sets out not only to win but to bloody the face of a man he sees as a potential rival for his wife's affections. Ultimately, he cannot sustain loving relationships with anyone: wife, brother, family, or nation. He is a solitary warrior, using all his instincts only to satisfy his cruel drives. Frustrated by his desire for brutality over love, Vicki finally tells him she is tired of all of his control and feels like a prisoner. She complains that she can not look at someone the wrong way without getting "smacked."

Joey tells a local gangster one day that Jake plans to make it "on his own," but nobody makes it on their own in a world where life and futures are so contingent on the containment of male fury and exploitation. LaMotta himself becomes a victim when he is forced to throw a fight in return for a promise of eventually getting a shot at the championship bout. Frustrated by the cruelty and complexity of the boxing profession and the fact that he has to incur a loss, LaMotta turns his anger against his wife and his brother, incessantly accusing them of sleeping together. In one savage outburst, he beats them both. After his fight career ends, the boxer opens a nightclub in Miami, where he lives with Vicki and his children. Tired of the ring and trying to stay in top physical shape, he gives some evidence of enjoying the solitude of family life and relaxing by a pool in the hot Florida sun.

LaMotta cannot be domesticated for long, however, and he begins to spend more time at his club, where he performs as a stand-up comic and, unfortunately, gets in trouble for serving liquor to minors. Sadly, he tries to get money to pay his fines by selling his championship belt, but he ends up in jail anyhow. In a scene where audiences see the former boxer hitting his head against the stone wall of his jail cell, we finally get a glimpse of the torment of the lower-class man raised on mean streets and riddled with hostile emotions. At the end of this modern tragedy, a lowly man loses his family and his sense of self-esteem. He can only repeat the lament of Terry Malloy that he could have been a contender and instead sees himself as merely a "bum."

## MOVING UP

In a culture centered on the fate of the individual, some men and women could still rise from their lowly origins even as others were going nowhere. The liberal dream lived in the seventies and eighties even as it died, such was the capacity of the cinema to reveal the contradictions of liberalism. Classic tales of pulling oneself upward in society were offered in *The Last American Hero* (1973), *Coal Miner's Daughter* (1980), and *All the Right Moves* (1983). The first of these films was a tale about auto racing in which a young man named Junior Jackson was suddenly forced to find money to help pay the legal expenses of his father, who had been arrested for making moonshine. The elder Jackson only turned to an illegal means of making a living when he tired of his low-paying job in a saw mill. Racing, however, becomes more than a way to make a living for his son. He quickly discovers that he can excel at it and find fame and fortune. He becomes a true liberal capitalist by showing that he can be competitive and take risks on the racetrack. He tells his brother, a garage mechanic, that "there ain't no profit in playing it safe." With some corporate sponsorship and heroic individualism, Jackson quickly moves out of his plebeian world.

*Coal Miner's Daughter* reveals aspirations for upward mobility on the part of a wife and husband who were dirt poor. It tells the real-life story of country music star Loretta Lynn and how she overcame an upbringing in squalid conditions in the coal mining regions of Kentucky and a marriage at the age of fourteen. Pushed into a singing career by her husband, who bought her a guitar and who never tired of sending her recordings to local radio stations, Lynn eventually lifted her entire family out of poverty and became a major star. In the beginning of the story, the drive for success appears to be rooted mostly in the male spouse. As it evolves, however, the film makes it clear that Lynn sees the possibilities for personal transformation and wealth in what she is doing. Success creates some marital problems for the couple—as it did for Lonesome Rhodes in the 1950s—but the central point about the glorious rewards of the individual struggle is unmistakable.

In *All the Right Moves*, another working-class boy finds a way to escape a dead-end life in a dying Pennsylvania mill town. The route out of the steel mills for Stefan Djordjevic is not auto racing but football. His family has toiled in the mills for years, but this young man dreams of getting out, not through boxing, but through a college scholarship that will allow him to become an engineer so he can have "something to say about steel after it is made." Even his high school coach aspires to flee the place and get a college job in California. There is certainly support for the ideal of cooperative action in this story. It is clear that the football team can not win without racial harmony, and the entire community offers support for a victory in the big game against a highly ranked team from a middle-class school. The coach, in fact, uses the players sense they are all working class to build harmony. He tells the players that they have been

Tom Cruise (left) played a young man in *All the Right Moves* (1983) who managed the liberal project of the realization of individual desire much better than Jake La Motta did. Credit: Film Still Archives, Museum of Modern Art, New York

called "Dagos," "Polacks," and "niggers" long enough. "All right, that's what you are. That's what I am. That's what we are together," he shouts at them. "That's how we're going to win this game—together."

The team loses the big game. In the end, however, the coach gets his chance to move to a college in California and gives Djordjevic a scholarship to come with him. Both men can now look forward to a future outside the limited confines of the mill town. For others in their lives, however, like Djordjevic's girlfriend, brother, and father, life will simply go on with no signs of improvement or change. Listening to the film's sound track played at the feature's end, audiences hear that America offers "blue skies" for some of the lowborn but only a life in "dying towns that take away your soul" for others.[13]

*Rocky* (1976), one of the most popular of all films of the seventies and eighties, again invoked the dream of uplift for the common man through individual initiative. Rocky Balboa is a character from the underside of American life—the gritty neighborhoods of South Philadelphia—who merges the politics of liberalism and illiberalism. In this film a vision of self-improvement is attached to a desire on the part of the white working class to strike back at African Americans who are perceived to have benefited at their expense in the sixties. In a sense, *Joe* and *Rocky*, both directed by John Alvildsen, served the project of some filmmakers to give white working people a political voice in the period and even a dose of revenge. Joe went after the counterculture; Rocky tried to punch out Apollo Creed.

Boxing films were always more about liberalism than democracy. The boxer was a driven individual, intent mostly on his own personal quest; if he served larger goals along the way, so be it. There is seldom a hint in such stories of the need to defend family, community, or class as there was in *Black Fury* or *The Grapes of Wrath*. Balboa is a two-bit fighter who gets a chance to win the heavyweight championship of the world. As the film opens, however, he appears to be anything but a potential contender. He fights in small gyms for forty dollars a night, dates a girl who sells pet supplies, and makes ends meet by extorting money from weaker people for a local crime boss.

It is Creed, the current champ, who offers Balboa an unlikely chance at his dream. When his scheduled opponent is hurt, the black boxer announces that he will give a "local underdog fighter" a chance to beat him on the occasion of the nation's bicentennial. Balboa, a blue-collar man who is sensitive to the needs of women and to the limitations his background has placed on him, tells his girlfriend that his "old man" told him that since he was not particularly smart, he would have to use his body to get ahead. And he informs the promoter interviewing candidates to fight Creed that he still believes America is a "land of opportunity" where everyone has a chance to win, citing the victories at Valley Forge and Bunker Hill. Rocky does not win the fight, but he goes the distance, proving to himself that he is not just "another bum from the neighborhood." What he gains in this event is a measure of self-respect that has been denied to most men of his class.

Tony Manero, a young man from Brooklyn played by John Travolta, seeks to leave his neighborhood in *Saturday Night Fever* (1977) through dancing rather than boxing. This picture, unlike *Rocky*, spared almost no effort to discredit the blue-collar neighborhood, characterizing it mostly as a place that inhibited individual ambition and spawned violence. Manero finds little satisfaction working in a hardware store, and, like many similar characters before him, he is deprived of a sense of self-esteem by his parents. His mother lavishes most of her affection and hopes on his older brother who becomes a priest; his unemployed father is prone to hitting Tony or even his spouse more than offering support. When the older man is unimpressed by a modest raise his son has earned at the hardware store, Tony responds angrily that he has been told only twice in his life that he is any good: when he received the raise, and when he was dancing at the disco. Later Manero tells his brother he has always felt like "shit" in the family.

It is on the dance floor rather than the shop floor that Tony chooses to earn the respect of others. Dancing here is not about social reform or articulating working-class grievances. It is a site for self-expression and personal transformation. Winning does not bring the satisfaction he had hoped for, however, because he and his partner are chosen over a Puerto Rican team that they feel was superior but victimized by racial discrimination. Shortly thereafter, a friend is killed in a gang fight in his neighborhood. Encounters with unfair treatment and brutality leave the young man despondent. Rocky Balboa tried to restore faith in classic liberalism and overcome this cruel and unfair world; Travis Bickle used hatred to purge it of some of its worst elements. At the end of this story, Tony Manero has no hope for liberalism and is not an illiberal by nature. He slips into depression rather than seeking reform. Audiences are left wondering if common men like him can ever really get away from their despair and find justice and self-respect.

## THE UNIONS

The return in the seventies to depicting the problems of plebeians on a wider basis than had previously been the case included some renewed attention to labor unions. These organizations were never represented in a positive manner in the films analyzed in this study, and the two decades after the sixties proved to be no different. There were some exceptions, to be sure, but generally their contributions to democracy were assigned to the past; their penchant for corruption was a continuing theme. The 1979 movie *Norma Rae*, of course, was a special case and depicted union drives as meaningful ways to improve the life of common people. But this story was also an account of the personal transformation of a woman that it is treated below in a section on stories about blue-collar females.

Another rare but affirmative glimpse of union action was to be seen in *The Molly Maguires* (1970). In one sense the film is rather remarkable, because it offered an unambiguous view of the abusive side of capitalistic enterprises and the need for militant protest on the part of coal miners, although the impact of their complaint was muted by the fact that it was set in the nineteenth century. The solidarity and class consciousness of the coal mining community in American history, however, something that had rapidly receded from the real world of sixties and seventies politics, was central to this story. Irish-American miners banded together, both historically and in this tale, into a secret organization called the Molly Maguires in order to respond to the unfair treatment they received from local mining companies in nineteenth-century Pennsylvania. Led by a strong man named Jack Keough, these men built a communal spirit by organizing sporting events, mobilizing their vote, and inflicting damage on company property by burning the hated company store that commandeered their wages.[14]

Ultimately, the Mollies are betrayed by one of their own. James McKenna, an informer, infiltrates their ranks on behalf of the police, who always favor the owners, and testifies in court against the workers after they have attempted to murder the mine supervisors. These men are not trying to climb a social ladder or flee their lowly origins as much as they are attempting to claim some fairness and justice for their fellow miners. McKenna even asks Keough at one point why he leads protests instead of trying to get out of the coal fields completely. The response of this union leader is a direct indictment of the state of inequality in America in both the past and the present. "And how would it be different?" he reasoned. "There is them on top and them below. Push up or push down. Who has more push. That's all that counts." But in this instance the miners who pushed up lost, and their leaders were hanged.

Worker militancy is set in the past again in *F.I.S.T.* (1978). This film is centered on the rise of a strong labor leader in the thirties but ultimately offers a narrative of declension as both the union head and the union itself grow increasingly complacent and corrupt over time. Johnny Kovak, a character played by Sylvester Stallone, is the dynamic labor leader that was missing from most films about workingmen in the previous forty years. Coming of age in the working districts of Cleveland, this man is attached to his working-class community, capable of leading struggles to help his neighbors during the Depression of the 1930s, and even interested in loving a woman. In fact, the picture offers one of the warmest and most loving portraits of a plebeian district ever presented in an American film. In scenes where Kovak, the son of Hungarian immigrants, brings flowers to his Lithuanian-American girlfriend and walks down the crowded streets of Cleveland on a summer evening in the thirties with people relaxing on their front porches and music drifting from taverns, audiences get a rare glimpse of a place in which a person could build a life rather than of a neighborhood one wants only to escape.

Kovak is a true believer in union militancy. He tells men in the Depression that they need an organization to gain better wages and benefits as he leads a fight to establish the Federation of Interstate Truckers (F.I.S.T.). Unlike some films set in the thirties, this features makes a special effort to show how poorly management treated its employees. It is the brutal repression that the men receive at the hands of industrialists that forces leaders like Kovak to seek assistance from national labor organizations that, unfortunately, have ties to organized crime. Eventually Kovak moves up in the union organization and into a middle-class lifestyle in Washington, D.C. Sitting in a plush office in the nation's capital, he tells a senator, "You can get anything you want in this country with a little bit of push." The story makes it clear, however, that his elevation and worker affluence in America has been achieved through dishonesty. At a national convention in Miami set in the 1950s, union officials are depicted as engaging in unscrupulous tactics like the misappropriation of union funds. Kovak and F.I.S.T. are soon subjected to Senate investigations for questionable loans they have made to mobsters. And the entire union movement is held up to ridicule for betraying the noble goals of the Depression decade.

Unflattering portrayals of unions are mixed with problems of race in *Blue Collar* (1978), a story in which plebeian lives fall apart completely. Action centers on two auto workers, one black and one white, a rare admission of the possibility for multiracial cooperation in the industrial workplace. Zeke Brown, played by actor Richard Pryor, and Jerry Bartkowski, played by Harvey Keitel, toil in a plant where frames for cars are welded but where the company pushes them to work at a furious pace. In one scene men on the assembly line have to run just to get a drink or take medicine in order not to slow production.

These men are completely deprived of sources of pride in their work or their lives and lack any concept of a meaningful future. They are victims, not citizens, preyed upon by the company, government tax collectors, and their own union. Brown and Bartkowski even refuse to distribute pamphlets for their union because they do not feel it serves their interests and because they are too busy holding down additional jobs to make ends meet. Moreover, blacks feel the union favors whites, and many share the view that it cannot be trusted. Bartkowski reveals that unions had actually betrayed the men in a previous strike. And the two leading characters plot to steal funds from their union, reasoning that they would only be taking back what the union has taken from them.

Utter confusion—and no coherent politics—reigns in this plebeian world. Brown and Bartkowski argue about turning over information to the FBI that would incriminate union leaders. Brown is reluctant to cooperate because he is convinced that African Americans can never get fair treatment from law enforcement officials. Closure to the story is reached when a narrator tells the audience that all unions do is pit black workers against white workers and keep working people in their place. Viewers are left not only with another anti-union statement from Hollywood, but more importantly, with impressions of a world in which no one would really want to live.

## THE FEMINIZATION OF THE WORKING CLASS

In the seventies and eighties, the representations of working people came to feature women in a more significant way than they ever had before. Women appeared as powerful leaders of unions and of families instead of as simply individuals desperate to flee the lower regions of American life—although desperate women continued to be seen as well. These newly emergent figures stood strong at the center of movies like *Norma Rae* (1979), *Silkwood* (1983), and *Places in the Heart* (1984) and attempted to right the wrongs of their time and place. The democratic and liberal tendencies inherent in these newer depictions, however, did not mean that these political ideals were now imagined as a given in the future of the lower classes. The fate of these people, whether they moved forward as groups or as individuals, was still recognized as highly uncertain. This point was made clear in stories like *A Woman Under the Influence* (1974), *Alice Doesn't Live Here Anymore* (1975), and *Looking for Mr. Goodbar* (1977).[15]

Unions gain a more positive rendering in *Norma Rae*, but the story is ultimately as much about the personal transformation of a woman as it is a tale of the attainment of working-class democracy. Martin Ritt, who had directed *The Molly Maguires*, believed that a successful picture stressed personal stories over issues and stated that he intended the film to be primarily about a woman fighting for her children and for what she believed. In a southern textile plant, Norma Rae Webster confronts a daily struggle for survival as a single mother whose husband was killed in a "beer joint" and who is now forced to raise two children and make ends meet. The young mother recalls that work in the mill destroyed the health of her mother, and she is intent on improving the conditions of her fellow workers. Confronting management is difficult for her, however, for she works as a "pusher" in order to gain higher wages. This makes her responsible for urging other workers to strive continually for more production and thus in a sense an extension of management.

Norma Rae's aspirations to help workers is grounded in her strong affiliation to her community and to the people that she loves. She is not inherently anticapitalist and knows little about unions until she meets a labor organizer from the North who tells her how people of different faiths and races had come together in the past to attain common ends. Her father expresses distrust toward outsider organizers, labeling them "communists, agitators, crooks, or Jews." But when Norma Rae hears the man explain to an audience how someday they would all inherit the earth only if they took it upon themselves to do so, she is encouraged to start mobilizing workers of all races in her plant.

A scene of an organizing meeting in her home where blacks and whites and men and woman gather to express their grievances is among the most sympathetic accounts of a pro-union position mounted on the American screen since the thirties. Suddenly plebeians are not cast on a lonely and highly singular struggle as gangsters, fallen women, or boxers, but they are now part of group seeking measures of justice and respect that rightfully belonged to them. Indeed, images like these make clear much of what had been repressed from the screen for so long. A black man explains how his race has been "pushed, poor, and scorned." And several white women tell stories of how they can not even sit down on the job when they have menstrual cramps or how their spouses had died of "brown lung."

Norma Rae soon becomes consumed with the idea of organizing and even begins to neglect her domestic duties. Union business comes to stand for more than just a struggle for economic justice. Union work becomes a way for a woman to quickly gain self-confidence and see how her life as a wife and mother has really limited her potential for self-realization. When Norma Rae defiantly raises a sign proclaiming "union" within the mill, it is the female operatives that stop their machines first. At a moment in American culture when solidarity and a working-class leader are finally venerated, the hero turns out to be a heroine discovering her own sense of empowerment as much as leading a movement to ensure workers' rights.

*Silkwood* is a similar story that blends a narrative of female self-realization with a struggle against corrupt corporate practices. The real-life story of Karen Silkwood demonstrated once again that corporations could engage in corrupt practices in America even as they created jobs. Driven by a sense of outrage over safety violations at the nuclear processing plant

Sally Field played *Norma Rae* (1979), a figure who offered a positive image of a union organizer and a powerful example of how a woman could transform her life. Credit: Film Still Archives, Museum of Modern Art, New York

in which she works in Oklahoma and a "moral imperative" to expose dangerous business practices that could endanger the lives of millions of people, Silkwood joins forces with union officials in order to gather information that could expose the evil practices of her employer. Gaining a new sense of independence, she begins to place her pursuit of justice ahead of her traditional relationship with a man. Her quest ends tragically and mysteriously, however, when she dies in a car crash before she can fully expose the nuclear corporation. Silkwood paid a high price for democratic and personal aspirations, although the company was actually forced to close its doors one year after she died.

In *Places in the Heart* (1984), a woman leads a successful quest for justice and for the well-being of her lower-class family. Action was again set in the past—Texas in the 1930s—in this feature in which a homemaker is forced to take over the running of a family farm after the breadwinner, an officer of the law, is killed trying to arrest a black teenager. The woman faces a difficult time in planting her crops because banks threaten her with foreclosure on her debt and hateful whites intimidate a black drifter trying to assist her with planting her crop. Yet by making a supreme effort, this household manages to bring in the cotton and pay the bills. The woman, played by actress Sally Field (who had also acted the role of Norma Rae), is so taken by her initial success in a capitalistic venture that she begins to think of planting an even larger crop next season. Attaining a better life is still difficult, however, because the local Ku Klux Klan decides to drive away her African-American farmhand, a household member her enterprise cannot afford to lose. In the movie's final scene, a dream sequence is presented. The proud woman is seen sitting in a church with her husband, children, the black man who helped her, and the one who was killed for shooting her husband in the first place. This scene is only a vision, however, of what a society free of violence and prejudice might look like. All who watched it knew that it was the exact counterpoint of what the past and the present had been.[16]

Women from the lower classes also struggled with a wide assortment of issues besides those located in the workplace. Traditional family life was oppressive for Mabel Longetti, a character in *A Woman Under the Influence* (1974). In *It's a Wonderful Life* Frank Capra suggested that the working class could lead purposeful lives and avoid moral degeneration if capitalism simply worked fairly and gave them the chance to become responsible homeowners. But Capra's formulations, for both working men and for women, did not recognize the potential for disruption emanating from inner emotional drives—impulses that could not be eliminated from the post–World War II cinema. Mabel and her spouse, Nick, were at one time apparently normal blue-collar Americans, working hard and raising their children. Nick, the foreman on a construction crew, is forced to spend increasing amounts of time on the job, however. Mabel becomes overwhelmed by having to take on more responsibilities of parenthood on her own. These pressures simply drive her out of the home one night as she flees to a local bar where she drinks the night away with a strange man. Eventually, her mood swings become more pronounced, and she begins to drink and take pills with increasing frequency. She discloses to her husband her frustrations with simply being a wife and mother, declaring that she feels she is free to do and be anything she desired. And she tells the children that she feels she has never done anything worthwhile in her entire life except give birth to them.

Nick tells Mabel, after a period of institutionalization, that her problems are past and there would only be "good times" in their futures. But soon she tries to slash her wrists, an act that evokes only rage from her blue-collar spouse, who simply can not understand the depths of her pain.

Seeing her self-destructive impulses as a rejection of him and the life they have created, he at one point simply knocks her down. The children, equally insensitive to her distress, continue to make demands on her as if nothing has happened. Nick, driven by his wish to see patriarchy work, proclaims that they really all love each other and that there is nothing for any of them to worry about. Final scenes bring not optimism or resolution but only a suggestion that Mabel—like many in the audience—will continue to struggle with her emotions and with her life in a plebeian household.

A single mother copes with economic difficulties more than with emotional ones in *Alice Doesn't Live Here Anymore* (1975). After her truck-driving husband is killed in an accident, the female lead is forced to find a way to survive and raise her young son. Since the only job she ever held besides that of being a housewife was as a singer, she begins to look for employment in bars in the Phoenix area. She is quickly frustrated, however, because tavern owners show more interest in her body than in her abilities, and she realizes that the profession she is trying to enter is dominated by younger women. Eventually she is able to earn a modest income from small clubs that allows her to move into a motel room with her son and fight off the advances of wolfish males. In these difficult times she fantasizes about getting back to her childhood home in California and buying a pair of "gold high heel slippers." Reality returns quickly, however, when an unemployed man in the next room threatens his wife with a knife. Reminded of her precarious situation in a threatening society outside the preserve of the patriarchal home, she flees southward to Tucson and finds work as a waitress.

Improvement and progress continue to elude her. She argues with her son constantly and, when he runs away with a friend, is forced to exclaim, "I don't know how to live without a man." Near the end, she meets a fellow who professes to care for her. His support causes her to think that she may be able to have both a career and a domestic relationship and that, no matter where she might move, she could not have one without the other.

A more gruesome fate awaited a single woman trying to forget her lower-class past in *Looking for Mr. Goodbar*. In this feature a woman rebels, not against corrupt management practices, but against a childhood in which she suffered from polio and chafed under the heavy restrictions of her father and his Catholicism. Coming home late one night, she is lectured by her tyrannical father about how she has to conform to his rules while she lives in his house. He reasons that he has earned the right to set standards of conduct for her by working in a coal yard for years and supporting his family, even if his ideas run against the "holy crusade" of women's liberation.

Seeking personal independence and sexual pleasure, Teresa Dunn, played by actress Diane Keaton, moves out of her father's house to an apartment of her own. A new lover tells her one day after having sex that she is now a "fallen women." "Thank God," is her quick reply. Sensitivity to the handicapped motivates her to become a teacher of the deaf by day. At night, however, she cruises bars and seeks sexual gratification. Her problem is not capitalism but motherhood, and she takes steps to insure that she can never have children. But the freedom to do what she wants carries a high price in this story. The "fallen women" of the thirties was punished by losing the wealth she had obtained. Dunn loses her life when she is murdered by a man frustrated over his inability to satisfy women sexually. This film offered little hope that liberalism could work in a society marked by brutality and emotional unrest.

## COMING HOME AGAIN

In the seventies and eighties, any attempt to imagine a more hopeful future for the people was not only undercut by the continuing dramatization of the emotional turmoil of individuals and the excesses of powerful capitalists but also by the legacy of an unpopular war. Hollywood quickly picked up on the fact that Vietnam was a working-class war in which blue-collar men were not only destroyed in battle but were abandoned by their country once they came home. Cynicism survived in the narratives about this conflict and the men who fought it. In *Coming Home* (1978), the lives of ordinary American men were seen as simply shattered by the brutality of the conflict. Heroic images were difficult to mount, although few heroes were to be found in the wide assortment of characters that stood for ordinary Americans in the entire period under review. In this film, former soldiers who fought in Vietnam become simply emotional casualties who come to see their homeland as an evil place that offers them no promise for fairness or respect. One of the men simply decides to swim into the sea out of despondency, so painful are his recollections of war. Another tells high school students not to listen to Marine recruiters and movies that promise glory in combat. "I'm here to tell you that I have killed for my country, " he exclaims, "and I don't feel good about it."

*The Deer Hunter* (1978) also subverted a heroic view of war and a sense that it offered common men an opportunity to realize a strong sense of male identity. The story centers attention on three mill workers from a steel town in Pennsylvania: Michael, Nicki, and Stevie. Michael is a solitary gunfighter whose sense of identity and place within society is based more on his capacity to kill than on his ability to support women and children. He can bring down a deer with one shot and stands as an exemplar of men who do not need women or the help of other men. His buddies not only lack his shooting skills but manifest a need for females, a weakness that would stand in the way of their ever becoming good soldiers—or proud, independent liberals, for that matter.

Confidence in the future and stable relationships do not come easily in this dying town. The lives of its people are portrayed as unsatisfying and revolve around an endless cycle of drinking, pool playing, sex, and betting on football games. As in *The Godfather, Part II*, the immigrant past of these people, with its faith in nation, church, and labor union, is rendered archaic; only the elderly make their way anymore to the cavernous churches in the town. Old men still wear veteran's hats and demonstrate a belief in ideas that are proclaimed on a banner in a local auditorium: "Serving God and Country Proudly." The dying embers of an old and warm immigrant community flicker sporadically in wedding celebrations and in a large mural in a wedding hall that evokes faint memories of some distant homeland. Men and women in this town, however, are really adrift somewhere in a time zone between a past marked by supportive communities that worked and a future bereft of any promises at all for lonely individuals skimping by on the economic margins of American life. Beliefs in a future where democracy and liberalism coexist and thrive are hard to detect.

War as a verification of manhood rather than as an ideological crusade is the essence of the story. Men who lack the self-reliance of Michael find the transition from shooting deer in Pennsylvania to killing a foreign enemy difficult. Stevie, who is married and is dependent on female companionship, is devastated by the experience of combat. Nicki, who once asked a woman to marry him, becomes suicidal and despondent in Asia. Only the expert deer hunter is up to the challenge of confronting violence at every turn. Michael shows what independent men can do when he and his friends are captured by the Viet Cong and forced to play a dangerous game of Russian roulette, a metaphor for the insanity of war itself. The deer hunter instinctively recognizes the game for the test of manhood that it is and tells the weaker Stevie to pull the trigger when he is forced to put a gun to his head to "show 'em you got balls." He knows that the enemy would kill him if he did not. As Stevie took his turn, the deer hunter prepared. When given the chance to put the weapon to his head, he asks his captors to put even more bullets in the gun, a sign that he is willing to take even greater risks than the others. Armed with the additional ammunition, however, Michael turns the gun, not on himself, but on the enemy, and frees his comrades.

Not surprisingly, only Michael comes home a hero of sorts. Stevie returns as a paraplegic, and Nicki can not even muster the fortitude to leave Saigon, eventually killing himself in another game of roulette despite efforts by Michael to save him. In many ways the emotional constitution of these men explains the manner in which they react to war itself. Back in Pennsylvania, Michael avoids events planned to welcome him home because he has always felt estranged from the community and because he is unable to bring himself to celebrate anything connected with Vietnam. He moves in with Nick's former girlfriend but gives no hint of ever intending to commit to a long-term relationship. He never tells her that he cares for her in the way he told Nick he cared for him in Saigon when he tried to help him out of his depression. However, when he hunts again, he intentionally misses the deer on his first shot, an indication that he is actually questioning forms of male identity that he has held for so long. As the movie ends, Michael appears in a tavern with his medals and joins friends in singing "God Bless America." Perhaps he would eventually find a home at last in the community and the nation. Yet, just as clearly, such a home could never offer again what he missed— the male brotherhood and sense of personal power he once felt. His form of rugged masculinity and liberalism died in Vietnam. He seems to care very little for the working-class community around him that is rapidly disappearing as well.

Director Oliver Stone's interpretations dominated cinematic interpretations of Vietnam in the 1980s. Stone, a veteran himself, followed the thematic leads of *The Deer Hunter* and *Coming Home* and readily took up the lament of what was lost in the war rather than what was gained— a direct refutation of the heroic memory of any war. To a great extent, however, he also probed questions of how the nation came to Vietnam in the first place, and his answers served to bolster the growing tide of pessimism and anger that was evident in late-twentieth-century melodramas about ordinary people. *Platoon* (1986) was a partially autobiographical tale of Stone's own experience in the war and featured a protagonist who went to battle to reject the respectable world his parents had offered him. Chris Taylor, played by actor Charlie Sheen, is struck by the lowborn status of most of the men with whom he fights. In a letter to his grandmother, he expresses amazement that soldiers from the "bottom of the barrel" with only a factory jobs waiting for them when they come home still manage to serve as proud and strong warriors. Taylor thought that if he could become more like these guys that "nobody cares about," he might be able to acquire a greater degree of self-confidence and purpose in his own life. In demonstrating respect and sympathy for these common men, these Vietnam films (as had World War II films) actually helped to moderate the continuing assault on the abilities of blue-collar men that had punctuated American culture for so long.

Ultimately, however, Stone was not as interested in rehabilitating the image of the common man as he was in attacking the ideals and powerful leaders that pushed America into war in the first place. In *Platoon* this issue is explored in the contest between two sergeants who lead men into battle: Elias and Barnes. Both are skilled warriors, but Elias has a sense of compassion and is able to place some limits on his brutal impulses. Barnes is like a figure from *The Naked and the Dead* who places no boundaries on his dangerous drives and, in the end, actually kills Elias in cold blood. As he becomes a man and a soldier in Vietnam, Taylor opts for the style of manhood represented by Elias and shoots a wounded Barnes. Norman Mailer argued in 1948 that most American men were inherently violent. Stone endorsed Mailer's point and told audiences in 1986 that it was the nature of men like Barnes that drove the nation into Vietnam in the first place.

In *Born on the Fourth of July* (1989), Stone told the story of a young man from a working-class family in Massapequa, New York. In this film Ron Kovic is led to war, not by the dark side of his nature, but by the misguided leaders and ideologies that dominated America in the 1950s. The picture reconstructed a version of everyday American life in the decade that was actually more coherent and orderly than the one that could be seen in many of the films of the fifties. In the Kovic family and in their town and nation, there was general agreement about the basic need to validate patriotism and fight communism. Kovic's sense of duty was reinforced by a mother who was a devout Catholic and who strongly supported the anticommunist crusade. In other words, American political culture turned the young boy into a loyal soldier willing to accept dreams of becoming a man and a hero through war.

When Kovic's actual experiences in Vietnam transform him into a disillusioned, antiwar protestor, audiences got Stone's central message that American leaders and the views that they had articulated could not be believed. Kovic's life is a mess after coming home. He is confined to a wheel chair and stripped of his sexual potency. There is a hint at the end that he will find his way back into the American mainstream through participation in politics, but overall his encounter with Vietnam did to him what the struggle to get ahead in capitalist America did to countless cinematic figures—it made him a victim rather than a hero.[17]

## AFRICAN AMERICAN FANTASIES AND REALITIES

In the aftermath of the sixties, characterizations of African Americans became more complex and mature, just as they did for lower-class whites. This process had taken place rather slowly since World War II but now appeared to move forward with greater speed. Movies began to depict the realism of the black ghetto in ways that had not been possible in earlier decades when the political culture had largely avoided a serious examination of African-American life. Blacks were now seen wrestling with many of the same issues that faced white plebeians, such as the daily struggle to survive and prosper on mean streets and the need to figure out how dangerous neighborhoods could be left behind. The many ways in which white racism had an impact on their lives was now given a much more complete exposure.

This new confrontation with race, however, was still inscribed with many of the political traditions that had long marked the American cinema. Thus, in the seventies, many of the black figures that commanded screen attention could be described as strong, independent individuals who could meet all of the challenges that life in the ghetto threw at them. In features like *Sweet Sweetback's Baadasssss Song* (1971), *Shaft* (1971), and *Superfly* (1972) black men emerged as fantastically clever and powerful persons, capable of overcoming the forces that oppressed them. Strong doses of emotional and social realism did manage to counter these hypermasculine fantasies, however, in pictures like *Sounder* (1972), *Do the Right Thing* (1989), and three 1991 pictures: *Hangin' with the Homeboys*, *Boyz N the Hood*, and *Jungle Fever*. In these films the problems of lower-class blacks—and whites, for that matter—simply continued to cause pain and suffering.[18]

The African-American hero of the early seventies was an image that redressed centuries of oppression. He could stand against the white power structure and sexually gratify white women nearly anytime he wanted. Unencumbered by inner demons and political agendas, he simply pursued African-American dreams of power. In a sense, he was the gangster again, hell bent upon domination and indifferent to calls for a more democratic or moral society. Disconnected from the politics of Vietnam, unions, and even civil rights, his present and future looked considerably better than that of most of the men who inhabited the imagined world of the white working class at this time. These characters had little difficulty negotiating a morally uncertain world where the police were brutal and corrupt and where money was made through petty crime and dealing in drugs. They could outsmart the police, the Mafia, and almost any other obstacle in their path. Films which featured these characters, like *Shaft* and *Superfly*, did not hesitate to let the camera linger on scenes of a destitute African-American community, where streets were littered with trash and where people had to find ways to survive day after day. But this black hero had risen above the devastation of the ghetto and now inhabited a higher ground of sex, money, and personal power in a netherworld between white society and black impoverishment. Crime was usually their way out, but they claimed that the amoral society they inhabited was not of their own making. In *Superfly*, one successful drug pusher tells another, "It's a rotten game," but it is "the only one the man left us to play."

There is almost no hope of a democratic future expressed in these pictures, an attitude that infiltrated stories of white plebeians as well. American society is corrupt, and blacks have no choice but to find ways to survive within such an environment. For the most part, the black heroes have to be vigilant, for they are in constant battle with both law enforcement officials who tend to treat minorities unfairly and criminal elements. In *Sweetback*, a black crowd burns a police car (and contributes to the larger attack on traditional authorities in the decade) in order to help the leading character escape the clutches of the law. Sweetback's only offense was to free another black man from being beaten by the Los Angeles police.

In *Superfly*, a high-ranking police official, whom the hero calls a "redneck faggot," is actually at the top of a massive drug ring. The black hero/drug pusher only avoids death at his hands by resorting to a clever scheme of taking out a contract on the official's life in the event he is killed. The lead in this story does dream of abandoning his life of crime and living a normal life with a woman, but for most of the story he effectively turns drugs into dollars. In *Shaft*, John Shaft is somewhat more compliant with police authorities because his work as a detective encourages such cooperation. Eminently capable of taking care of himself, however, this "superhero" contests crime bosses in both the black and white communities who threaten him. When he engineers the escape of a young African-American woman from the clutches of the Mafia without any assistance from the police, audiences get a hint that the only way blacks can defend their interests and endure in a world of unregulated liberalism and illiberalism is to be as strong and cagey as Shaft.

As the camera moved more deeply into the heart of the ghetto, however, African Americans were suddenly thrown into the type of hopeless, unpredictable, and turbulent world that had confronted the white working class in film for decades. Political elites and the larger society seemed disinterested in their plight. Personal ambition and the struggle to hold families together existed in the ghetto, but happy outcomes were difficult to achieve in the face of widespread drug use and white hostility. In *Hangin' with the Homeboys*, for instance, good jobs, college, and the respect of women appear to be unattainable goals for four young men living in the Bronx. All these boys have is each other and the fear they share that their lives might turn out to be like those of the unemployed and despondent men that populate their neighborhood.

In *Boyz N the Hood*, American dreams of a future better than the past barely survive at all in South Central Los Angeles. Drive-by shootings and unemployment are pervasive, and murder and brutality are a way of life in this story that was partially based in the personal experience of the film's young director, John Singleton. Some individuals still retain a hope for an improvement in their lives. Tre Stiles, the central figure, is no "superhero" but a young black man who follows the rules. He works hard, listens to his father, and hopes to leave the ghetto for college. In a sense, the figure of his father, who also attempts to promote black home ownership and businesses in the ghetto in an attempt to keep "outsiders" from bringing guns and drugs to the neighborhood, represents a dream of restoring African-American patriarchy and the community structure that was rapidly disappearing in the real world of African-American neighborhoods as well.[19]

Dreams of personal uplift also hold the attention of Tre's good friend and star football player Ricky Baker. The contradictions of life in this neighborhood—which can never be resolved—are never more apparent than when college recruiters come to the area while police helicopters circle continuously overhead. Eventually Baker's dreams are destroyed when he is killed in a senseless act of gang violence. His murder solves nothing, however, and his friends only retaliate and kill the perpetrators in an act that suggests that the cycle of uncontrolled violence is endless. This film makes no clear statement as to whether brutality is rooted in social or emotional problems, although racial segregation is clearly a force in the lives of these people. Near the end, Ricky Baker's brother watches a television show about "living in a violent world" and expresses amazement that the production depicts problems in foreign countries and never mentions the murder of his sibling. "They don't care what is going on in the hood," he explains. Two weeks later he too is killed. Tre Stiles, however, does get to enter college in Atlanta.[20]

Daily life in the Bedford-Stuyvesant section of New York was put under the microscope in *Do the Right Thing*. Like many of director Spike Lee's films, this feature reaffirmed the point that many Americans found progress and democracy elusive. Indeed, everyone is victimized in this tale about relations between African Americans and white ethnics. The owner of an Italian restaurant, Sal, is proud of the family business he has built in a black neighborhood over the years. After one particularly prosperous day, he tells a black employee, Mookie (played by Lee), that he will always have a place at this pizzeria. These were not words Sal's son, Pino, wanted to hear. His daily toil for his father has caused him to become hateful toward Mookie and all blacks, and he has urged him to move the business to an Italian neighborhood.

Long-simmering racial hostilities finally explode one day when Sal tries to quiet some black youths who are playing rap music in his place. A small disturbance soon turns into a full-scale riot, however, in which police shoot a black male and African Americans burn down the Italian shop. There is no coherent politics here, only uncontrolled fury driven by racism. As Sal and his sons watch their family enterprise go up in flames, people in the street yell "Burn it down!" The film's climax advances neither solutions for racial problems nor hope that they will go away. Lee offered two quotations on the screen at the end that simply contradicted each other. One from Martin Luther King made the point that violence was "immoral" because it promoted hatred rather than brotherhood. But King's words were followed by those of Malcolm X, who said that he did not want to advocate violence but that it was often justified as a means of "self-defense."

The possibility of racial harmony, now a prerequisite in the cultural imagination if a future of democracy was to be envisioned in America, was explored more extensively in Lee's movie *Jungle Fever* (1991). In this story, love across racial boundaries does blossom for a time in a professional office. Back in working-class neighborhoods like Harlem and Bensonhurst, however, the races and individual families are completely unable to regulate their emotions and create stable and trusting relationships. Alienation is pervasive between races, genders, and generations. Parents, unable to understand the estrangement of their children from traditional values like marriage, react with anger and brutality. For their part, younger blacks and Italians live lives that are devoid of any guarantees of love, uplift, or stability. Democracy and liberalism are in ruins.

Interracial love flourishes for a time between a married black man, Flipper, and an Italian-American girl named Angela. Despite his interest in the woman, Flipper understands that racial antipathy on the part of Angela's father and brothers would prevent him from ever setting foot in their home. Angela has grown tired of the racism of the men in her family, however, and the control they exert over her after her mother died. Eventually the couple's affair proves to be destructive for both of their families. Flipper's marriage ends when his wife learns of his involvement with a woman she considered to be "low-class white trash." Angela's father brutally strikes his daughter when he discovers the identity of her boyfriend and calls her a "disgrace" to their family and a "nigger lover."

Racial emotions now blended comfortably into mass cultural productions that were already attuned to the idea that people were driven more by passion than by reason. So did generational ones. Flipper's father becomes increasingly angry over the behavior of his two sons. The older black man is a firm believer in the Bible and in traditional forms of married life, and he expresses disapproval of his son's adultery. He is even more upset with another son, Gator, who has acquired a drug habit and an inclination to steal in order to support it. In this Harlem neighborhood, small-scale capitalism is perfected by drug dealers who work the streets incessantly. When Flipper finds his brother one day at the "Taj Mahal," a neighborhood crack house, audiences see one of the most powerful scenes of hopelessness and despair in America ever mounted on the screen. There is no hint that political traditions could work or improve the lives of people, black and white, who simply sit on the floor of an abandoned building in a drug-induced stupor. In the end, Flipper's father can only react to his addicted son out of anger rather than love, and he shoots him because he sees him as the incarnation of evil. Director Lee may have decided to portray the tragedy of drug addiction more fully in this film because some critics had castigated him for failing to reveal the full extent of exploitation and suffering that existed in the ghetto in *Do the Right Thing*. Certainly *Jungle Fever* considered the decomposition of American society in more complete terms than his earlier work, but in doing so, it joined an even larger project of American mass culture to confront positive idealizations of both the nation and the nature of the people who inhabited it.

The Italian-American family fares better in the story but is still left with a troubled future. After living with Flipper for a time, Angela returns home to her father, who complains that contemporary women do not know their "wifely duties" and that young people "treat marriage as a joke." Her brother Paul is even beaten by men in his neighborhood who are upset over the fact that he dated a black girl that came into his store. Since these men also manifest a distinct prejudice against extended schooling and against intellectuals and do not appear interested in entrepreneurship of any kind, one is left with the impression that they will remain frustrated and angry forever.

## REACTIONS

Despite the range of plebeian characters displayed in the America of the seventies and eighties, lonely and angry men dominated the period's imagination. Traditional hopes that liberalism and democracy could in some way prevail in American life commanded rather little attention. The lonely and obsessive illiberals—like the kind offered by Martin Scorsese—dominated much of the imagery of the period and carried the cultural burden of the idea that American political conventions and traditional authorities could no longer bring hope and order.

Interestingly, reviewers almost never disputed this sense of gloom and argued the opposite: that a viable future for the people was possible. Rather, they worked in the same frame of reality that Scorsese and others did. They shared the disposition of culture makers to examine the torments and passions of the individual in the here and now, and they were often displeased when the films or the common people in them were not complex and relatively authentic. In this focus on the singular person, the broader social frame was narrowed; the past and the future were treated only minimally. Thus, most observers noted the contradictions of Travis Bickle and sought ways to explain them. A review in the *Miami Herald* claimed Bickle was both a "potential killer and a crusader for moral reform." Several critics noted how he was both drawn to the city and the characters that inhabited it and at the same time prone to destroy them. Others felt his murderous drives were rooted in a desire to "cleanse" society or that he was insane. Some, of course, looked with disfavor on the violence in the picture—including Tennessee Williams, who had argued passionately for the depiction of brutal forces in society when helping to produce *A Streetcar Named Desire.* Generally, however, observers were approving of the film, since they tended to be enmeshed in the massive public discourse themselves over the fate of the solitary individual, and in the possibility that anyone could drift into aberrant behavior.[21]

Jake LaMotta, too, was widely accepted and, despite his cruel and brutal nature, praised as a characterization. In his autobiography, LaMotta had explained his drive to be a champion in terms of his poor background and his desire for a better life. Certainly that point was not so clearly enunciated in the film or in the film's reviews. Vincent Canby, in the *New York Times,* pondered the question of LaMotta's rage and the motivation for it and declared that the movie refused to "explain away in either sociological or psychiatric terms" the boxer's behavior. In fact, he felt the movie, which he considered the director's "finest," never clarified this point at all. Another observer went further in noting that the film seemed uninterested in making any point at all about the boxer's "social milieu," inferring again that his drives are unexplained. Indeed, where critics ventured to guess what LaMotta was about, they tended to invoke the sense of social decomposition that characterized contemporary society rather than anything from the boxer's real-life social origins. The *Toronto Sun* reviewer felt the film succeeded because the movie had created an "uncompromising portrait of a man of action" who participated in the central rituals of "our society" at a time when those rituals (such as the struggle for success or the realization of manhood through violence) had been discredited. The *New York Daily News* moved in a similar direction, linking LaMotta's character to the demise of the image of "macho" created by Vietnam, and the rise of the women's movement and the "purified moral majority."[22]

In the seventies and eighties, it was expected by many that the imagined individuals at the lower depths of American society would be working their way through a number of emotional, personal, and sometimes social problems. *All the Right Moves* was particularly praised for this reason. The story of a young man in a dying mill town trying to devise a way out by getting a football scholarship in order to become an engineer was seen as a welcome relief from stories that depicted adolescents as interested only in "sex, drugs, and rock" and totally lacking in powers of analysis. Reviewers also liked the "reality" of the mill town setting and the fact that the young man's working-class father treated his son like a human being. Some also liked the fact that there were winners and losers in the town—those who were able to leave, and those who could not.

Similarly, one reviewer liked *Mean Streets* precisely because it was not a simplistic story but showed its characters "trapped in a tiny world [New York's Little Italy] whose manners and morals are a jumble of things" and unclear of the choices they had in their lives. A critic in *Time* approved of the fact that *Joe* conveyed "honestly" the "anguish" of its aroused male leads and even the motivations of its "flower-children." No matter that the ending was murderous and bleak.[23]

Stories about the daily hassles of lower-class women were also seen as part of the effort to get at the facts of working-class existence. Certainly everything about *Alice Doesn't Live Here Anymore* did not evoke a positive response, but many liked the way the story sympathetically portrayed a "knocked-about lady trying to figure out what went wrong" with her first marriage and "whether it's possible to do better a second time." Its director, Scorsese, was lauded as a "fine young recorder of social reality" by the *Los Angeles Times*. And the *Time* reviewer believed that the portrait of a young woman in *Looking for Mr. Goodbar*, who was alienated from her autocratic father and took delight in sexual pleasure, was very much a "fact of our time."[24]

Conversely, significant departures from social and emotional realism continued to draw criticism. Writing about film in the seventies that dealt with labor unions, Stanley Kauffmann charged that *F.I.S.T.* (and, in his opinion, *Rocky*) took the "materials of naturalism" like scenes of working-class protest in the thirties and "exploited" them for the sake of "romance." Thus he looked with disfavor on the fact that the story "fiddles fictitiously with its subject," which is apparently the life of labor leader James Hoffa, and absolves the individual union head of any responsibility for the eventual corruption of the union by blaming everything on society. Interestingly, *Newsweek* made the same complaint, refusing to accept the romantic view that the labor leader remained "pure of heart" after his ascendancy. Similarly, comments on *Norma Rae* generally praised the performance of the female lead but often pointed out that the story was not believable. One observer noted that Norma Rae herself demonstrated no hint of a moral longing for justice early in the story that would explain her eventual decisive action to help her fellow mill hands, and the roles of an outside labor organizer who comes to her mill town and her rather dull spouse appeared to some viewers as too formulaic.[25]

Stories about African Americans were also held to the same standards of authenticity. One critic called the main character in *Shaft* a "fantasy idol" who went around paying back everyone who had "shafted" African Americans in the past. A writer in *Time* called *Superfly* a "racial slur" and was outraged that the picture portrayed all black men as "daddy-boppers or street corner hustlers," white men as "craven criminals," and women of all races as "whimpering sex machines." The critic felt this sort of formulation effaced the "dignity" of these people (a hint as to why realism and liberalism were so valued) and the value of "good action melodrama." Conversely, later features like *Jungle Fever, Do the Right Thing*, and *Boyz N the Hood* were widely praised for investigating the feelings and attitudes of their characters and the social space in which they lived. In *Jungle Fever*, director Spike Lee was praised for his talent and for his ability to explore the tragic and the comedic aspects of life. One reviewer especially liked the way the story looked not only at the issue of interracial love but at the various reactions parents, friends, and entire communities had to such a situation. Others endorsed the director's decision to analyze an aspect of experience rather than judge it and appreciated the treatment of the impact of drugs and drug addiction in a black neighborhood. A commentator on Lee's *Do the Right Thing* liked the fact that the filmmaker preferred "abrasion and ambiguity to comfort and tidiness." Another looked with favor on the fact that the story had no heroes but only "complex human beings" who seldom "do the right thing." John Singleton, the director of *Boyz N the Hood*, was compared to Lee for being a realist as well—or, as one writer put it, "a chronicler of the frustration faced by young black men growing up in urban settings." Janet Maslin wrote in the *New York Times* that in the setting of the "hood" actors could easily become stereotypes, but "the film's strength is that it sustains an intimate and realistic tone." Another observer commented that the movie offered "a rich tapestry of diverse characters" and noted how much "strength" it took to break out of this environment and "what it takes to become in a man in this society."[26]

The project to place Vietnam in some sort of political frame, such as the crusade to arrest the spread of communism, was doomed from the start in a culture concerned more about personal than national futures. In part, this may explain why films that treated the war as destructive and ruinous to the lives of the ordinary men that fought in it tended to be respected. A realism heavily laden with emotional content was by definition less national or collective in its orientation. This approach certainly tended to sustain critical views of the war, but it also endorsed a stereotypical view of the political mindset of the lower classes to which, incidentally, no one seemed to object. That is to say, critics recognized but did not object to the fact that in *The Deer Hunter* and in *Born on the Fourth of July*, for instance, men went off to war without ever questioning it. In the former film, the men seemed to simply move into the war as the next stage of their lives; in the latter feature, the protagonist is a true patriot. Reviewers realized that in many of these films some men lose their loyalty to the nation in the war and become politically radicalized by the conflict. But in evaluations of *The Deer Hunter*, many critics tended to affirm the goal of the film to look beyond the politics of blaming the United States for the conflict and seeing it as a universal problem that emanated from the "murderousness" of men on both sides and as an event that forced individual combatants to face an assortment personal problems and traumas. Thus, Vincent Canby in the *New York Times*—in true liberal style—felt that what was "best" about *Born on the Fourth of July* was that the lead character had to fashion for himself a personal transformation from an "innocent and clean-cut" youth to a "angry and exhausted" man with a "headband around his forehead and hippie-length hair." Reviewers noted, to be sure, the overwhelming focus on men rather than women in these features, but they tended to value and accept the running commentary these stories made on the damaging effects of the war on individuals and the resulting struggle with "what it means to be a man" after Vietnam.[27]

## CONCLUSION

Images of disaffection and cruelty were pervasive in films about the lives of common people in the seventies and eighties. In part this reflected the inability and unwillingness of the movie industry and of traditional authorities to censor the grim side of human nature and everyday life. It also demonstrated the extent to which the shadows of the sixties loomed over these decades and reinforced longstanding currents in mass culture that exhibited misgivings about the ability of government, capitalism, or conventional values to ensure stable futures. Ambiguity and apprehension (along with certainty and optimism) were not new ideas to anyone who had been going to the movies most of their lives, but now their presentation was intensified and, for a time, relatively uncontested. In the political world, leaders like Richard Nixon and Ronald Reagan struggled to counter alienation and restore faith in authority and various political traditions like the idea of a strong nation and the potential for improvement in individual lives. Some movie characters, like Junior Jackson, Loretta Lynn, Stefan Djordjevic, and Rocky Balboa, emerged to back their positions. Others, like Ricky Baker, Travis Bickle, Terry Dunn, Ron Kovic, Jake LaMotta, and Karen Silkwood, suggested their confidence was misplaced. By continuing their probe of social and (especially) emotional realism, numerous films about ordinary people continued to take a more critical view of America and raised questions about whether liberalism or democracy could truly be made to work in the face of the pervasiveness of illiberal tendencies.

When a feature did attempt to restore faith in liberalism, it could do very well at the box office. *Rocky* was the top grossing picture of 1976; *Coal Miner's Daughter* was number six in 1980. But *Joe, Taxi Driver, Saturday Night Fever, Looking for Mr. Goodbar, The Deer Hunter, Coming Home,* and *Platoon* were all among the twenty highest grossing films of the years in which they appeared.[28] Films about ordinary working people in this era did not rule out the possibility that singular persons could escape oppressive situations or better themselves, but improvement took place only sporadically in a dreamed-up world whose fictional plots, ironically, were monitored constantly to see that they remained true to life. In a political world dominated as much by mass culture as by political parties themselves, the biting commentary of the sixties was sustained but in a way that served neither the left nor the right. Yet what else could one expect from a liberal discourse preoccupied with surveying the landscape of the human spirit?

# LIBERALISM AT THE MOVIES
## A Conclusion

A vast array of working-class types moved across the Hollywood screen in the half-century after 1930. In every decade, the American cinema constructed plebeian figures that allowed audiences to think about vital issues of their times and explore a range of possible identities and fates. It is true that these films almost never celebrated the labor radical or the power of the militant union, and it took Hollywood too long to break free of the hold of white supremacy that marred American society and to explore aspects of the social and emotional condition of African Americans. But at no time would terms like pro-capitalist, anti-labor, or even white racist have been an accurate way to describe the ideological orientation of these characters or the films in which they appeared.

Eschewing both dogmatic coherence and utopian projections when it came to telling stories about lower-class life, the proletarian images studied here represent a complex assortment of people and beliefs. In various decades gangsters, poor women, and boxers revealed a faith in liberal capitalism. Miners, mill hands, and soldiers tempered personal dreams and fought for democracy in their lives and in the world. Brutes, cab drivers, vets, and small-time hoods were often intent on taking away opportunities and rights from others, exhibiting almost no interest in either liberalism or democracy. At times individual striving worked as a solution to deprivation and frustration. Often it did not. Narrative resolution upheld moral behavior and sometimes implied that such standards of conduct were impossible to achieve. Working people could be imagined as proud patriots, fervently devoted to their country, or they could be pictured as trapped in a corner of American society with no prospects for a better life. Contradictions abounded; mood swings were pervasive in this fictive world of melodrama and "realism."

At one level this diversity of meaning might be explained by the existence of varying interests that had a stake in the final product that appeared on the screen. Certainly, studios were run by corporate leaders who viewed unions with some disfavor. These men were also intent on affirming their loyalty to American traditions; consequently, they rallied eagerly to the crusades against fascism and communism. Directors too exercised an enormous influence in the shaping of film, and the outlooks of men like Frank Capra or Martin Scorsese definitely affected the way common people were portrayed in their stories. During and just after World War II, the government joined the effort to alter film content. For a long time moral authorities in American life like the church wielded enormous power and worked assiduously to uphold a specific set of standards designed to constrain the expression and realization of human desire. And although their leverage is difficult to assess, there can be no doubt that audience expectations also mattered a good deal. The attention paid to female desire was perhaps the greatest verification of this.

Clearly, the representation of common people emanated from a very broad discussion in society that crossed class, gender, political, and racial lines. It involved understandings and debates about many issues, but the immense scope of its content and the wide variety of people and institutions that took part in its production, consumption, and evaluation suggests that something broader than the simple expression of the interests of any one studio, class, or political group was ultimately at work here. To ask the question another way: What were all these people talking about?

I would suggest that, amidst the unending assertion of financial, emotional, and political concerns, these films—and much of American mass culture—were continually inscribed by the powerful current of liberalism and (to a lesser extent) democracy that flowed through the American imagination. In 1955 Louis Hartz made a widely circulated argument that America was essentially a liberal society bereft of any meaningful alternative political ideologies throughout its history. Hartz saw in American history a story of the rejection of an old European feudal order that had rested on the sovereign power of kings and the inordinate influence of clerics. He argued that influential conservative or socialist parties (in the European sense) never took root in the United States because there was never a need to defend or overthrow an old order as there had been in Europe. Consequently, for him, the ideals of liberalism and the liberty of the individual became so strong that they appeared to be natural components of the political culture. Hartz made the interesting argument that liberalism was so central to America that it was more or less taken for granted; no one ever thought of the need to organize a liberal party.[1]

To say that liberalism dominated American politics and culture is not to say that alternative outlooks did not exist. Hartz saw some alternatives himself, although for him they emanated from the very nature of liberalism. He argued that liberalism was entrenched so strongly that it often could not tolerate any deviation from its ideals and had a "tyrannical compulsion" that manifested itself in hostile (or anti-liberal) movements. As he wrote in the 1950s, when fears of totalitarian regimes were pervasive, McCarthyism struck him as such an event. Modern scholars have moved beyond Hartz by noting the power of democratic and conservative political movements in American history that expressed a desire to place moral and civic responsibilities on the free individual and to temper the liberal dream of self-fulfillment. They have also given evidence of an antipathy toward the acceptance of modern society with its celebration of the liberated person freed from the claims of traditional moral constraints. Others have argued that racism and sexism and other forms of illiberalism are pervasive in America and quite incompatible with liberalism in the purest sense. Liberalism, therefore, did not stand alone; but certainly the core issue for American politics still seemed to be about the individual and just how free he or she should be allowed to be.[2]

Writing at around the same time, Reinhold Niebuhr probed the nature of America's liberal philosophy as well. Niebuhr too appreciated the need to resist systems of tyranny and injustice in the world, but he worried that the United States now pursued those goals through the use of "evil" weapons of destruction. This concern led him to speculate about the secular and ironic aspects of a "liberal society" and to look for reasons why destructive impulses persist even in societies committed to justice and happiness. His basic point was that modern political ideologies—whether they were about American liberalism and capitalism or about Communism—had essentially turned their backs on what he felt was a fundamental assumption about human nature embedded in Christianity. Niebuhr astutely saw that in the political regimes of both liberal democracies and communist states the source of evil was located in society (or in powerful organizations), and therefore it was assumed that it could be eliminated or managed. In the liberal-democratic world, social problems were usually corrected by reform movements that frequently brought about more democracy or restrained illiberal forces that had denied rights to various individuals. Often moral regulations were effected to govern the excesses of individuals. In a sense, both democracy and illiberalism were offshoots of the exercise of the liberal ideal. The New Deal, for instance, pragmatically sought democratic solutions to the Great Depression in order to save liberal forms of capitalism. Communist doctrine ascribed the origins of evil to the "institution of property" and to the actions of the capitalists elites. Eliminate property and you would eliminate evil. Niebuhr claimed that for the liberal idea of the natural goodness of men, communism simply substituted the exclusive virtue of the proletariat. In the end, for this philosopher, both liberal and communistic political doctrines led to the "heady conclusion" that "man was the master of is own fate and the captain of his soul."[3] I would add that it would be natural, therefore, for any political regime to have a master plan as long as that regime assumed that it could manage and improve the nature of its society and the behavior of its citizens. Master plans leaned in the direction of a creating hope—and, perhaps, utopias.

In a society saturated by the stories and representations of mass culture, however, no such "heady conclusions" could prevail—and thus optimism in the political world was subverted even if it was ratified from time to time. Framing his study within the confines of the political (rather than cultural) realities of his time, this was a point that Niebuhr did not see. But unless a political regime could exert a tremendous amount of control over cultural expression, it was simply not possible to embark on a political project centered on the desires and fates of individuals without facing the ambiguous dimensions of their longings and lives. Richard Rorty has argued convincingly that utopian politics usually set aside questions about both the will of God and the "nature of man." It did not take more than a few hours of watching movies about ordinary Americans in any decade to see that the issue of the nature of men and women was never set aside and remained highly problematic.[4]

The contingency of human life—the extent to which it was dependent on emotional drives or historic events—was increasingly central to the representations of mass culture in a liberal society, and as such, liberalism, illiberalism, and democracy all competed for cultural space. It was not that these concerns were new. Even John Locke and John Adams worried over the basic instincts of human beings; Adams thought the answer was government by wealthy and intelligent men. For centuries people realized that human emotions were unpredictable. Thus, the Hollywood films discussed here did not tell people something they did not already know. They were challenging because they told them exactly what they did know to an extent that undermined the assumptions of political and moral leaders that individuals could be regulated and futures insured. Instabilities of meanings were the price one paid for a culture saturated with liberalism and its cultural products.[5]

Interestingly, a recent probe of liberal politics in twentieth-century America discovered, in part, a reluctance on the part of most of the liberal political leaders and reformers to confront liberalism in a full-blown fashion. Gary Gerstle insightfully argues that before World War II reformers, including many New Dealers, tended to pursue liberal ideals like the emancipation of the individual through rational organizations like schools, government agencies, or even labor unions that could mitigate the worst effects of economic exploitation or immoral activity. Gerstle says these reformers shied away from confronting problems in the "cultural arena" like racial and ethnic hatred because they involved too much irrationality and were therefore difficult to manage. For Gerstle it was World War II that forced a change in attitude on the part of liberals and a recognition that they could no longer ignore racial and ethnic prejudice and concentrate only on reforming capitalism.[6]

We can elaborate upon and modify this argument by suggesting that all along, mass culture was tackling dimensions of liberal thinking that traditional politics tended to ignore by promoting a heated discussion of the range of desires and wants in human nature. Often rejecting the hope and rationalism of Progressives, New Dealers, and even Cold Warriors that paths to progress could always be found, mass culture faced up to the dilemmas of human nature—both its rational and irrational aspects—experienced continually by all kinds of individuals and turned them into subjects for discussion when political leaders tended to sidestep them. This is what made it so powerful.

Film and mass culture had less fear of exploring the social and, especially, the emotional life of individuals because they were born in a liberal political culture bent on asserting the need to review the full extent of individual desire and freedom in the face of longstanding efforts by governments or elites to control them. As individuals gained more rights—such as the right to vote or to make consumer choices—in the nineteenth and twentieth centuries, the culture in which they lived took more note of the various dilemmas such independence brought. In a world rapidly emasculating sacred forms of authority and symbols, the locus of politics and culture now shifted increasingly to the singular person as the source of ethical value and political power and away from all sorts of established authority. As long as the liberal political world felt the singular person could be managed, political and traditional institutions had a meaningful role to play. If this assumption were disrupted, however, as it increasingly was in the narratives of the cinema, the faith in liberal-democratic politics could be questioned. A broad cultural discourse, or the exchange of all kinds of outlooks—feminine, working-class, middle-class, black—began to claim space formerly reserved for powerful institutions like parties, churches, and unions and the white men that ran them. Discourse in the culture came to count for as much as debates at election times (maybe more). This did not mean that powerful ideologies such as liberalism and democracy no longer shaped life and thought. Rather, increasingly, it was harder to cast them in coherent or absolute frameworks that were progressive or utopian.[7]

To acknowledge that a discourse dominated by liberalism or the question of individual freedom to pursue wants emerged so powerfully in the twentieth century explains much. Such an undertaking would necessarily be quite concerned with personal life in all of its social and emotional aspects. If democracy had been the preeminent American ideology, I would argue that a quest to delineate social realism and all of the conditions that limited the attainment of a more moral community and society would have been more widespread than it was and would have overshadowed the continuing portrayal of emotional realism. Over time, however, the probe of the emotions and the range of desires that marked ordinary people predominated in the culture. Both forms of realism, moreover, worked against the imposition of any true form of escapism or utopianism. This tendency toward "realism," in fact, was at the heart of the project of mass culture itself to establish a domain for political discourse in a public realm often indifferent to the needs and aspirations of traditional institutions like political parties or religious organizations where citizens could exchange views of what it was like to live in a liberal society. The inclinations of liberal reformers detected by Gerstle actually left open to the mass culture industry many of the emotional and biological issues politics tended to ignore. To study film and mass culture is not to study the tenets of a political dogma or the manner in which political thought is institutionalized, but to see close up how people *experience* ideology and talk about it in all of its complex dimensions.

This point has been made by scholars who have studied the cinema of the Third Reich. Scott Spector has argued well that scholars have not always accepted film as historical evidence because of concerns over the accuracy of its images and stories. Beyond what he calls the "factual base" of history, however, Spector has shown how German films from the Nazi era projected not facts so much as a range of desires and identities within the "ideological field" of Nazism itself. Modifying assumptions that Nazism was simply a top-down ideology in a top-down state, he shows how these German films actually contained a "matrix of multiple meanings." Thus, he saw expressions in these films of Germans exploring alternative longings, such as a desire for the "demonic Other" or the Jew, that would have been forbidden in pure Nazi doctrine or in a meeting of party faithful. In one instance, an actor who played a lustful Jew who raped an Aryan women in the film *Jew Suss* (1940) actually attracted fan mail from many German women in the audience.[8]

If oppositions could be detected in a cinema under the regime of totalitarianism, the potential for "multiple meanings" under the regime of American liberalism was immense. Spector understands that ideology can be realized not only at the level of doctrine and in the material reality of institutions but also in the realm of cultural discourse, where the "subjects" of an ideology experience and discuss the dominant ideals of their time and place. At this level, people in the United States were free to consider where they stood within the ideological field of liberalism and its attendant creeds of democracy and illiberalism. Where liberal ideology met individuals outside the structures of institutional life, a more complete perspective on the individual was possible. With so much riding on the behavior and thought of the singular person, the past, present, and future were suddenly seen as highly contingent—perhaps beyond the reach of moral or political reform. The period after World War II tended to reinforce this sense of uncertainty. Boundaries and traditional verities were rendered unstable. Meditations on human nature competed effectively for cultural space with interests based only in class, gender, and race. As mass culture counted for more in cultural and political discussions, and as the subjective viewpoints of workers, women, and minorities attracted more attention, it was harder to maintain narrow or even derogatory views of common people. To an extent this proliferation of views offered a greater dose of democracy, as women and minorities claimed more cultural and political attention. There was a trade-off for the rise of such realism, however. Faith in traditional institutions and ideals (as well as the hegemony of powerful males) was often replaced by doubt, cynicism, and bewilderment. Scholars have demonstrated how unsettling American films were to European cultures steeped in tradition and class hierarchies. Often forgotten is that fact that they were upsetting to American officials as well, and that both conservative and radical forces in America worried about the potential of the movies to weaken collective mentalities of any kind.[9]

In the films studied here, alternative views of reality abounded. Liberal capitalism could be both affirmed—as it was in *All the Right Moves* and *Places in the Heart*—or undermined—as it was in *Body and Soul*. Workers could appear as angry strikers—as they did in *Black Fury* or *F.I.S.T.*—or as potential entrepreneurs—as they did in *Whistle at Eaton Falls*. Often working people could be seen dreaming about becoming the middle-class Other, as they did in *Baby Face* or *A Raisin in the Sun*. They could also take pride in making the working class a better place to continue their lives, as they did in *Norma Rae*. They could find patriotism both rewarding and debilitating as they did in countless war films. They could reject conventional morals, as they did in *Clash by Night;* or they could look upon them as a source of self-realization, as they did in *Marty* and *On the Waterfront.*

The discourse of liberalism even allowed many of them to struggle openly with the Other within themselves and entertain the possibility of using their freedom to become anti-liberals. In this contest, played out on the uneven field of human emotions, the results were often not promising that dreams of human emancipation and liberal progress would be realized, a point made over and over again in presentation of figures like Cody Jarett, Stanley Kowalski, Lonesome Rhodes, Travis Bickle, and Jake LaMotta. When historic events like World War II or Vietnam disrupted faith in political and social traditions, the stage was set for the mass cultural version of liberalism to explode into political discourse and into the culture in all its profusion.

The traditional history of American working people has been encapsulated within its materialist assumptions. Economic factors, exploitive owners and managers, and conservative political figures mounted continual efforts to defeat a proletarian mass with the potential to generate powerful democratic political movements. Working-class democracy reached its pinnacle in the thirties, according to the standard story, with the emergence of the CIO and the New Deal. This powerful political force remained active but gradually lost its standing after 1941. World War II enforced a culture of unity over the one that sanctioned class conflict. In the war's aftermath, however, a resurgent conservatism effectively attacked radicals in unions and in society and co-opted labor leaders with consumerist dreams. Recent scholarship has reinforced the idea that the working class itself was plagued with internal divisions along lines of gender and race, findings that actually square more directly with the history that Hollywood had been projecting all along.

Before, during, and after the conventional story of labor's rise and fall, however, Hollywood told another tale of working-class life that was affected both by the variables described by historians and by a more intricate set of emotional factors that they seldom looked at. This many-faceted debate—with its "matrix of multiple meanings"—was more likely to be heard and viewed in theaters than in factories and was more likely to be attuned to the outlook of women and the vagaries of emotional life than were most union meetings of the time. It challenged the spirit of the collective with the hopes and fears of the individual, and it did not always verify the dream that men could be the masters of their own fate. It was too realistic to say such a thing on a consistent basis. There were other films about fantasies and romance that could offer audiences pure escapism, to be sure. One could always retreat to a Capra film that held out the hope that reason could still save the American blend of liberalism and democracy, and Scorsese remained for those who feared it could not. In the middle stood Hollywood's portrayal of working people, struggling mightily with everything life threw at them.

# NOTES

## INTRODUCTION: MASS CULTURE AND POLITICAL TRADITIONS

1. Anthony Giddens, *Beyond Left and Right: The Future of Radical Politics* (Stanford, Calif.: Stanford University Press, 1994), 4–8.

2. John R. Hall, "The Reworking of Class Analysis," 1–37, and Margaret A. Sommers, "Deconstructing and Reconstructing Class Formation Theory: Narrativity, Relational Analysis and Social Theory," 82–90, in *Reworking Class*, edited by John R. Hall (Ithaca, N.Y.: Cornell University Press, 1997).

3. Steve Ross, *Working-Class Hollywood: Silent Film and the Shaping of Class in America* (Princeton, N.J.: Princeton University Press, 1998), 111–33. For a summary of many of the labor vs. capital and social problem films of the silent era, see Kevin Brownlow, *Behind the Mask of Innocence* (New York: Knopf, 1990), especially 463–500. See also Lewis Jacobs, *The Rise of the American Film: A Critical History* (New York: Harcourt, Brace, 1939), 149. Jacobs detects sympathy for working people in silent film but not much support for their rights as workers. Michael S. Roth, "*Hiroshima Mon Amour:* You Must Remember This," in *Revisioning History: Film and the Construction of the Past*, edited by Robert A. Rosenstone (Princeton, N.J.: Princeton University Press, 1995), 84–91.

4. Tony Bennett, *The Birth of the Museum: History, Theory, Politics* (London: Routledge, 1995), 17–56; Geoff Eley, "The Family Is a Dangerous Place," in *Revisioning History*, 17–43; Melissa Dabakis, *Visualizing Labor in American Sculpture: Monuments, Manliness, and the Work Ethic, 1880–1935* (Cambridge, UK: Cambridge University Press, 1999), 83–89.

5. Ruth McKenney, *Industrial Valley* (Boston: Houghton-Mifflin, 1939), 96, 100, 150; Barbara Foley, *Radical Representations: Politics and Form in U.S. Proletarian Fiction, 1929–1941* (Durham, N.C.: Duke University Press, 1993), x, 3.

6. Erin A. Smith, *Hard-Boiled: Working-Class Readers and Pulp Magazines* (Philadelphia: Temple University Press, 2000), 5–18.

7. Lary May, *The Big Tomorrow: Hollywood and the Politics of the American Way* (Chicago: University of Chicago Press, 2000), 1–5, 31–60, 273.

8. Michael Denning, *The Cultural Front: The Laboring of American Culture in the Twentieth Century* (London: Verso, 1996), 9, 102–3, 125.

9. May, *Big Tomorrow*, 175–209; Denning, *Cultural Front*, 152–54, 464; Stephen Vaughn, *Ronald Reagan in Hollywood: Movies and Politics* (Cambridge, UK: Cambridge University Press, 1994), 191–218; Robert Sklar, *Movie Made America: A Cultural History of American Movies* (New York: Vintage Books, 1994), 267.

10. Robert B. Ray, *A Certain Tendency of the Hollywood Cinema, 1930–1980* (Princeton, N.J.: Princeton University Press, 1985), 25–27, 31–32.

11. Ibid., 35.

12. Garth Jowett, *Film: The Democratic Art* (Boston: Little, Brown, 1976). See Jeanine Basinger, *A Woman's View: How Hollywood Spoke to Women, 1930–1960* (New York: Alfred Knopf, 1993), 6–7.

13. Paul R. Corman, *Left Intellectuals and Popular Culture in Twentieth-Century America* (Chapel Hill: University of North Carolina Press, 1996), 8; John Howard Lawson, *Film in the Battle of Ideas* (New York: Masses and Mainstream, 1953); Jackson Lears, *Fables of Abundance* (New York: Basic Books, 1994), 138–39.

14. Norman Cantor, *The American Century: Varieties of Culture in Modern Times* (New York: HarperCollins, 1997), 7, 49, 53. On the rising cultural power of melodrama, see Christine Gledhill, "The Melodramatic Field: An Investigation," in *Home Is Where the Heart Is: Studies in Melodrama and the Woman's Film*, edited by Gledhill (London: British Film Institute, 1987), 5–39.

15. Eric Lott, *Love and Theft: Blackface Minstrelsy and the American Working Class* (New York: Oxford University Press, 1997), 80–81; Jim Cullen, *The Art of Democracy: A Concise History of Popular Culture in the United States* (New York: Monthly Review Press, 1996), 67–69; 89–90; Michael Denning, *Mechanic Accents: Dime Novels and Working-Class Culture in America* (London: Verso, 1987). See also Lawrence Levine, *Highbrow/Lowbrow: The Emergence of Cultural Hierarchy in America* (Cambridge, Mass.: Harvard University Press, 1989), 57, 177.

16. Andrew Bunstein, *The Language of Democracy: Political Rhetoric in the United States and Britain, 1790–1900* (Ithaca, N.Y.: Cornell University Press, 1995), 12–17; Michael McGerr, *The Decline of Popular Politics: The American South, 1865–1928* (New York: Oxford University Press, 1986), 148.

17. David Nasaw, *Going Out: The Rise and Fall of Public Amusements* (New York: Basic Books, 1993); Peter N. Stearns and Carol Z. Stearns, "Emo-

tionology: Clarifying the History of Emotions and Emotional Standards," *American Historical Review* 90 (October 1985): 813–36; Nancy K. Bristow, *Making Men Moral: Social Engineering During the Great War* (New York: New York University Press, 1996), xix–19; Leo Charney and Vanessa R. Schwartz, "Introduction," in *Cinema and the Invention of Modern Life*, edited by Charney and Schwartz (Berkeley: University of California Press, 1995), 7.

18. Lears, *Fables of Abundance*, 137–39; Joel Pfister, "On Conceptualizing the Cultural History of Emotional and Psychological Life in America," in *Inventing the Psychological: Toward a Cultural History of Emotional Life in America*, edited by Pfister and N. Schnog (New Haven: Yale University Press, 1997), 17–59.

19. Homi K. Bhabha, *The Location of Culture* (New York: Routledge, 1994), 1, 5, 140. Bhabha is excessively ahistorical in his discussion of the current postmodern world and tends to underestimate the level of contradictions that marked Western society before World War II. He makes a good point, however, when he says that it is more difficult to "totalize experience" today. For him "totalizing language" has been replaced by the "language of ambivalence." On the growing tendency to stress the cultural rather than the materialist origins of class identities, see Sommers, "Deconstructing and Reconstructing Class Formation Theory," 73–105; Terry Eagleton, *Ideology* (New York: Longman, 1994), 147–48, 175–77. Also see James Thompson, "After the Fall: Class and Political Language in Britain, 1780–1900," *Historical Journal* 39 (1996): 785–806.

20. Linda Williams, "Melodrama Revised," in *Figuring American Film Genres: Theory and History*, edited by Nick Browne (Berkeley: University of California Press, 1998), 42–88; Walter Benjamin, "The Work of Art in the Age of Mechanical Reproduction," in *Illuminations* (New York: Harcourt, Brace and World, 1995), 223, 238; Julia Hallan with Margaret Marshment, *Realism and Popular Cinema* (Manchester, UK: Manchester University Press, 2000), 3–10.

21. Cullen, *The Art of Democracy*, 12–14; Tony Bennett, Colin Mercer, and Janet Wollacott, eds., *Popular Culture and Social Relations* (Philadelphia: Open Society Press, 1986), xi–xix. After World War II mass culture was held in low repute by intellectuals in this country, who linked it to the rise of totalitarianism in Germany. See Andrew Ross, *No Respect: Intellectuals and Popular Culture* (New York: Routledge, 1988), 44–46; Michael Denning, "The End of Mass Culture," in *Modernity and Mass Culture*, edited by James Naremore and Patrick Brantlinger (Bloomington: Indiana University Press, 1991), 253–68.

22. Todd Gitlin, "Bites and Blips: Chunk News, Savy Talk, and the Bifurcation of American Politics," in *Communications and Citizenship: Journalism and the Public Sphere in the New Media Age*, edited by Peter Dahlgren and Colin Sparks (London: Routledge, Chapman, and Hall, 1991), 119–36;

Robert W. McChesney, *Rich Media, Poor Democracy: Communication Politics in Dubious Times* (Urbana: University of Illinois Press, 1999), 7, 15.

23. Frederic Jameson, "Reification and Utopia in Mass Culture," *Social Text* 1 (Winter 1979): 130–48; Cullen, *Art of Democracy,* 30; Martha Bayles, *The Loss of Beauty and Meaning in American Popular Music* (Chicago: University of Chicago Press, 1994), 7; Stuart Hall, "Notes on Deconstructing the Popular," in *People's History and Socialist Theory,* edited by Raphel Samuel (London: Routledge and Kegan Paul, 1981), 227–40.

24. Benjamin, "Work of Art," 223–38.

25. David Norton, *Democracy and Moral Development* (Berkeley: University of California Press, 1991), 31–33; Alexis de Tocqueville, *Democracy in America* (New York: Vintage Books, 1990), 2:100–103; Benjamin Barber, "Liberal Democracy and the Costs of Consent," in *Liberalism and the Moral Life,* edited by Nancy L. Rosenblum (Cambridge, Mass.: Harvard University Press, 1989), 54–68. See William Boelhower, "We the People: Shifting Forms of Sovereignty," *American Literary History* 9 (Summer 1997): 364–78, for a provocative discussion of how literature produced by American immigrants has reflected a tension between considerations of the "self" and the myth of "We the People" or the subconscious sense of obligation to an idea of peoplehood. Boelhower argues that today our sense of democracy is based on the notion of "radical individualism" and that we are "paradoxically a community of people without a community."

26. Robert Wiebe, *Self-Rule: A Cultural History of American Democracy* (Chicago: University of Chicago Press, 1995), 15–19; Andrew Bunstein, *Sentimental Democracy: The Evolution of America's Romantic Self-Image* (New York: Hill and Wang, 1999), 2–5.

27. J. David Greenstone, *The Lincoln Persuasion: Remaking American Liberalism* (Princeton, N.J.: Princeton University Press, 1993), 244–54, 284–85.

28. Russell Hanson, *The Democratic Imagination in America: Conversations with Our Past* (Princeton. N.J.: Princeton University Press, 1985), 13, 26, 259; Rogers M. Smith, *Civic Ideals* (New Haven, Conn.: Yale University Press, 1997), 1–11, 473–75; Fritz Stern, *The Failure of Illiberalism: Essays on the Political Culture of Modern Germany* (New York: Columbia University Press, 1992), xxv–xxix.

29. Robert B. Westbrook, *John Dewey and American Democracy* (Ithaca, N.Y.: Cornell University Press, 1991), xiv–xvi, 287–99, 364–65; John Durham Peters, "Democracy and American Mass Communication Theory: Dewey, Lippman, and Lazarsfeld," *Communication* 11 (1989): 199–220. Simone Chambers, "Discourse and Democratic Practices," in *The Cambridge Companion to Habermas,* edited by Stephen K. White (Cambridge, UK: Cambridge University Press, 1995), 233–37, suggested that the realization of democracy certainly rested on the existence of discourse or extensive communications within society. But for discourse to sustain a democratic culture, participants

in that exchange had to pursue "mutual understanding." If participants used discourse for "strategic action," for the attainment of specific behavioral response, then the process was likely to result in less democracy and more domination and control.

30. Benjamin A. Barber, *A Passion for Democracy* (Princeton, N.J.: Princeton University Press, 1998), 4–38, 73–74, 81.

31. See Mary Ann Glendon, *Rights Talk: The Impoverishment of Political Discourse* (New York: Free Press, 1991), 3–14; Barber, *Passion for Democracy*, 81–83; Charles P. Epp, *The Rights Revolution: Lawyers, Activists, and the Supreme Court in Comparative Perspective* (Chicago: University of Chicago Press, 1978), 1–48. On international pressures on the United States to live up to its democratic creed in terms of racial justice, see Mary L. Dudziak, *Cold War Civil Rights: Race and the Image of American Democracy* (Princeton, N.J.: Princeton University Press, 2000), 12.

32. Barber, *Passion for Democracy*, 4–5, 14. See also Susan J. Phair and Robert D. Putnam, *Disaffected Democracies: What's Troubling the Trilateral Countries* (Princeton, N.J.: Princeton University Press, 2000); Robert N. Bellah, et al., *Habits of the Heart: Individualism and Commitment in American Life* (Berkeley: University of California Press, 1985), 50.


## ONE. POLITICAL CROSS-DRESSING IN THE THIRTIES.

1. Barbara Foley, "Renarrating the Thirties in the Forties and Fifties," *Prospects* 20 (1995): 455–66.

2. Raymond Williams, *Modern Tragedy* (Stanford, Calif.: Stanford University Press, 1966), 23. See also Alan Brinkley, *Voices of Protest: Huey Long, Father Coughlin, and the Great Depression* (New York: Vintage Books, 1982).

3. The phrase "grim antagonisms" was drawn from a review of *Angels with Dirty Faces* (*Variety*, 26 October 1938), and referred to the polarity of moral and criminal behavior in the film (clipping in *Angels with Dirty Faces* file, Production Code Authority Records (PCA), Herrick Library). See Garth Jowett, *Film: The Democratic Art* (Boston: Little-Brown, 1976), 272; Norman Corwin, "Our Heroes," *Saturday Review of Literature* 24 (25 October 1941); William Graebner, "Norman Rockwell and American Mass Culture: The Crisis of Representation in the Great Depression," *Prospects* 22 (1937): 323–56.

4. Giuliana Musico, *Hollywood's New Deal* (Philadelphia: Temple University Press, 1997), 102–3. For a discussion of the impact on film of intellectuals who fled Germany and left-leaning intellectuals who left New York in the period, see Saverio Giovacchini, "Democratic Modernism and the Hollywood Community, 1933–1953: The Art and Politics of the Movies in the Era of the New Deal," Ph.D. diss., New York University, 1998. James Agee and Walker Evans, *Let Us Now Praise Famous Men* (Boston: Houghton-Mifflin, 1941); Erskin Caldwell, *Tobacco Road* (New York: Scribners, 1932).

5. Gary Gerstle, *Working-Class Americanism: The Politics of Labor in a Textile City, 1914–1960* (Cambridge, UK: Cambridge University Press, 1989); Lizabeth Cohen, *Making a New Deal: Industrial Workers in Chicago, 1919–1939* (Cambridge, UK: Cambridge University Press, 1990); Josh Freeman, *In Transit: The Transport Workers Union in New York City, 1933–66* (New York: Oxford University Press, 1989).

6. Michael Kazin, *The Populist Persuasion in American History* (New York: Basic Books, 1995), 138. Gerstle, *Working-Class Americanism,* 153–95; Warren Sussman, *Culture as History: The Transformation of American Society in the Twentieth Century* (New York: Pantheon, 1984), 75–85, 150–210.

7. Cohen, *Making a New Deal,* 100–145; Steven Fraser, *Labor Will Rule: Sidney Hillman and the Rise of American Labor* (New York: Free Press, 1991); Lea Jacobs, *The Wages of Sin: Censorship and the Fallen Women Film, 1928–1942* (Berkeley: University of California Press, 1997), 44–45, 56–57.

8. William Brock, *Welfare, Democracy, and the New Deal* (New York: Cambridge University Press, 1988), 271–81.

9. Linda Gordon, "Social Insurance and Public Assistance: The Influence of Gender in Welfare Thought, 1890–1935," *American Historical Review* 97 (February 1992): 19–51. See also Elizabeth Faue, *Community of Suffering and Struggle: Women, Men and the Labor Movement in Minneapolis* (Chapel Hill: University of North Carolina Press, 1991), 83, 126–27; 153. Mirra Komorovsky, *The Unemployed Man and His Family* (New York: Dryden Press, 1940). George Chauncey, *Gay New York: Gender, Urban Culture and the Making of a Gay Male World, 1890–1940* (New York: Basic Books, 1994), 353–54, argued that the growing anxiety over the status of traditional fathers led to "growing revulsion" against gay men in many cities in the thirties. See Michael Kimmel, *Manhood in America: A Cultural History* (New York: Free Press, 1996), 20–21, for a discussion of how comic strips of the decade mocked "fatherly competence."

10. Barbara Melosh, *Engendering Culture: Manhood and Womanhood in New Deal Public Art and Theater* (Washington: Smithsonian Press, 1991), 4.

11. Kimmel, *Manhood in America,* 1. Sherwood Anderson, *Puzzled America* (New York: Scribners, 1935), 4–13, 120–22.

12. Lawrence Levine, *The Unpredictable Past: Explorations in American Cultural History* (New York: Oxford University Press, 1993), 240–41.

13. Robert Warshow, *The Immediate Experience* (New York: Doubleday, 1962), 34–35, 158–59.

14. Andrew Bergman, *We're in the Money: Depression America and Its Films* (New York: New York University Press, 1971), xi–xvi, 3, 9–11.

15. Terry Christensen, *Reel Politics: American Political Movies from Birth of a Nation to Platoon* (New York: Basil Blackwell, 1987); Bergman, *We're in the Money,* 34; Charles J. Maland, *Chaplin and American Culture: The Evolution of a Star Image* (Princeton, N.J: Princeton, University Press,

1989). According to Larry May, weekly patronage rose by about one-third from 1929 to 1939 in part because of the spread of theaters beyond urban areas to small towns and the rural South; see May with Stephen Lassonde, "Making the American Way: Modern Theaters, Audience and the Film Industry, 1929–1935," *Prospects* 12 (1987): 114.

16. Thomas Doherty, *Pre-Code Hollywood: Sex, Immorality, and Insurrection in American Cinema, 1930–1934* (New York: Columbia University Press, 1999), 347–64. Stephen Vaughn, "Morality and Entertainment: The Origins of the Motion Picture Production Code," *Journal of American History* 77 (June 1990): 39–65. Christensen, *Reel Politics*, 40–42. Joseph M. Curran, *Hibernian Green on the Silver Screen: The Irish and American Movies* (New York: Greenwood Press, 1989), 49.

17. Hays was quoted in Richard Malthy, "'To Prevent the Prevalent Type of Book': Censorship and Adaptation in Hollywood, 1924–1934," in *Movies, Censorship and American Culture,* edited by Francis G. Couvares (Washington, D.C.: Smithsonian Institution Press, 1996), 101–17. Timothy E. Scheuer, *Born in the USA: The Myth of America in Popular Music from Colonial Times to the Present* (Jackson: University of Mississippi Press, 1991), 117–18.

18. Lea Jacobs, "Censorship and the Fallen Women Cycle," in *Home Is Where the Heart Is: Studies in Melodrama and the Woman's Film* (London: British Film Institute, 1987), 100–112. Mary Beth Haralovich, "The Proletarian Woman's Film of the 1930s: Contending with Censorship and Entertainment," *Screen* (1970): 172–88.

19. See, for instance, the *New York Daily Worker,* 9 March 1935, 7.

20. Michael Denning, *The Cultural Front: The Laboring of American Culture in the Twentieth Century* (London: Verso, 1996), 12–13, 39–43; Leonard Quart, "Frank Capra and the Popular Front," in *American Media and Mass Culture: Left Perspectives,* edited by Donald Lazere (Berkeley: University of California Press, 1987), 178–83. See also Thomas Allen Greenfield, *Work and the Work Ethic in American Drama, 1920–1970* (Columbia: University of Missouri Press, 1982), 68–73.

21. Darryl Zanuck to William Wellman, 18 March 1933, *Heroes for Sale* file, Box 4, WBA; James Wingate to Darryl Zanuck, 1 March 1933; Wingate to J. L. Warner, 20 May 1933, *Heroes for Sale* file, Production Code Authority Collection (PCAC), Academy of Motion Picture Arts and Sciences Library (AMPAS); *New York Daily Worker,* 9 March 1935, 7.

22. See clippings in *Little Caesar* file, PCAC/AMPAS.

23. See F. Meyer to Joseph Breen, 22 November 1935; Carleton Simon to Will Hays, 1 June 1931; James Joy to E. B. Derr, 4 June 1931, *Scarface* file, PCAC/AMPAS.

24. Darryl Zanuck to Jason Joy, 6 January 1931, *Public Enemy* file, PCAC/AMPAS.

25. For dissatisfaction toward the lack of police involvement in curtailing Powers's activities, see Lamar Trotti to Will Hays, 13 April 1931 and 14 April 1931, Will H. Hays Papers, Indiana State Library.

26. Carlton Simon to Will H. Hays, 1 June 1931, *Scarface* file; *Variety,* 21 October 1938, clipping in *Angels with Dirty Faces* file, PCAC/AMPAS.

27. Joseph Breen to J. L. Warner, 20 May 1938 and 19 January 1938, *Angels with Dirty Faces* file, PCAC/AMPAS.

28. Les and Barbara Keyser, *Hollywood and the Catholic Church: The Image of Roman Catholicism in American Movies* (Chicago: Loyola University Press, 1984), 62. For another film that depicts a broader effort to contain potentially dangerous drives in adolescent boys, see *Boys Town* (1938).

29. James C. Robertson, *The Casablanca Man: The Cinema of Michael Curtiz* (London: Routledge, 1933), 20–25.

30. Christine Gledhill, "Genre and Gender: The Case of Soap Opera," in *Representation: Cultural Representation and Signifying Practices,* edited by Stuart Hall (London: Sage, 1997), 357–60.

31. Bergman, *We're in the Money,* 74–82.

32. A 1994 VCR release of *Our Daily Bread* by Kino Video Productions includes copies of the two "phony" newsreels.

33. Joseph Breen to James Wingate, 26 and 29 March 1936; Breen to J. L. Warner, 12 September 1934, *Black Fury* file, Warner Bros. Archives. See also Francis R. Walsh, "The Films We Never Saw: American Movies View Organized Labor, 1934–35," *Labor History* 27 (Fall 1986): 564–66. On the issue of sharing the available work in Pennsylvania coal fields during the 1930s, see John Bodnar, *Anthracite People* (Harrisburg: Pennsylvania Historical and Museum Commission, 1983).

34. See *Hollywood Reporter,* 26 March 1935, and *Motion Picture Herald,* 3 April 1935, clippings in *Black Fury* file, PCAC/AMPAS. *New York Daily Worker,* 15 March 1935, 5. See also *Modern Times* (1936), a film by Charlie Chaplin that offered almost no hope that working people could make any improvements in their lives.

35. Bergman, *We're in the Money,* 50–52. Ruth Feldstein, *Motherhood in Black and White: Race and Sex in American Liberalism, 1930–1965* (Ithaca, N.Y.: Cornell University Press, 2000) shows how New Deal liberalism placed a great burden on mothers for rectifying social problems. See also Jacobs, *Wages of Sin,* 10–12.

36. "Story Outline," *Baby Face* file, Box 1, WBA.

37. Howard Smith to Darryl Zanuck, 11 November 1932, *Baby Face* file, Box 1, WBA.

38. James Wingate to J. L. Warner, 11 May 1933; Wingate to Will Hays, 28 February 1933, *Baby Face* file, PCAC/AMPAS.

39. Joe Breen to J. L. Warner, 8 February 1937, *Marked Woman* file, PCAC/AMPAS. In this letter, Breen told Warner to soften the scene in which

Vanning strikes the sister and delete a scene of him hitting Mary. He also did not want sounds of women moaning after their beating.

40. Some films did not attempt to blend a discussion of economic problems with gender tensions but used the later to omit any considerations of the former. This was true in *Steel Against the Sky* (1941), a narrative in which two brothers who are construction workers devote most of their energies to the pursuit of the same woman.

41. See Joseph Breen to B. B. Kahane, 8 April 1935, *Alice Adams* file, PCAC/AMPAS. In *Hoosier Schoolboy* (1937), another story of the Depression set in a small Indiana town, the return of prosperity was shown to be contingent on labor peace and on compromise between unyielding capitalists and strikers.

42. Joseph L. Breen to L. B. Mayer, 26 August 1935; *Motion Picture Herald,* 30 May 1936, clipping in *Fury* file, PCAC/AMPAS; *Black Legion* press book, *Black Legion* file, WBA. Lotte H. Eisner, *Fritz Lang* (New York: Oxford University Press, 1977), 164–76; Robert Sklar, *City Boys: Cagney, Bogart, Garfield* (Princeton, N.J.: Princeton University Press, 1992), 65; Michael E. Birdwell, *Celluloid Soldiers: Warner Bros.'s Campaign Against Nazism* (New York: New York University Press, 1999), 35–40.

43. Jeffrey Richards, *Visions of Yesterday* (London: Routledge and Kegan Paul, 1973) 222–52; Quart, "Frank Capra and the Popular Front," 178–83; Abraham Polonsky, "How the Blacklist Worked in Hollywood," *Film Culture* 50–51 (Fall–Winter 1970): 44.

44. On the tendency of the Popular Front to move away from overt leftist partisanship, see Quart, "Frank Capra and the Popular Front," 178–83; Lee Lourdeaux, *Italian and Irish Filmmakers in America: Ford, Capra, Coppola, and Scorsese* (Philadelphia: Temple University Press, 1990), 13, 130.

45. Raymond Carney, *American Vision: The Films of Frank Capra* (Cambridge, UK: Cambridge University Press, 1986), 9.

46. Frank Capra, *The Name Above the Title: An Autobiography* (New York: Macmillan, 1971), xi; Joseph McBride, *The Catastrophe of Success* (New York: Simon and Schuster, 1993).

47. Gerstle, *Working-Class Americanism,* 166–79.

48. On the promotional efforts for this film, see *John Doe* file, Warner Bros. Archives. Also see John Ford's *Young Mr. Lincoln* (1939) for a Capra-like argument that in precapitalist America were to be found values and leaders like Lincoln who could bring about civic harmony and a sense of oneness that America now needed not only to overcome the strife of the thirties but in the coming contest with European dictators.

49. *Variety Film Reviews,* 31 January, 1940.

50. John Steinbeck, *Grapes of Wrath* (New York: Viking-Penguin, 1939), 536–37; 580–81.

51. The original script, dated July 13, 1939, is in the *Grapes of Wrath* file,

WBA. See also Rudy Behlmer, *America's Favorite Movies: Behind the Scenes* (New York: Frederick Ungar, 1982), 120–29; Vivan C. Sobchack, *"The Grapes of Wrath:* Thematic Emphasis Through Visual Style," in *American Film in a Cultural Context,* edited by Peter Rollins (Lexington: University Press of Kentucky, 1983), 68–87; Christensen, *Reel Politics,* 52. In *Sullivan's Travels* (1941), the economic suffering of people is resolved, not through effective political action, but through flights of fancy. In the movie, a prosperous Hollywood producer wants to see what deprivation and suffering are really like. Dressing as a hobo, he is harassed by law enforcement officials and ends up in a convict labor gang. The story even raises the specter of racism in the country and offers a powerful scene of African Americans singing "Let My People Go." But the ending could only call for more entertainment and laughter for the oppressed, and it made no attempt to conclude this story of abusiveness with symbolic calls for justice and retribution.

52. Charles J. Shindo, *Dust Bowl Migrants in the American Imagination* (Lawrence: University of Kansas Press, 1997), 2–9. Richard Pells, *Radical Visions and American Dreams: Culture and Social Thought in the Depression Years* (Urbana: University of Illinois Press, 1998), 253, 274–81, argues that directors like John Ford fled the call for realism by affirming conventional values from the past. Ford, however, injected powerful points about the exploitation of common people that still served as a basis for potential protest and reform.

53. Denning, *Cultural Front,* 259–63; Pells, *Radical Visions and American Dreams,* 214–18. Also see Leah Greenfield, *Five Roads to Modernity* (Cambridge, Mass.: Harvard University Press, 1992), 4–10. In *How Green Was My Valley* (1941) the point that capitalism could be destructive to families was sustained without taking up the cause of radical proletarianism. Set outside the United States in a coal mining valley in Wales, the movie was directed by John Ford, who modified the portrayal of labor unrest during its production. In the original script a scene was planned in which striking miners fired shots at soldiers sent to quell a disturbance. In the final version, however, such a confrontation was removed, and the miners simply flood the mine in protest. See *How Green Was My Valley* file, John Ford papers, Box 4, Lilly Library, Indiana University.

54. *Nation* 133 (16 September 1931): 290; *Outlook* 159 (9 September 1931): 54. For a discussion of realism as historically contingent, see Julia Hallam with Margaret Marshment, *Realism and Popular Culture* (Manchester, UK: Manchester University Press, 1988), x. Amy Kaplan, *The Social Construction of American Realism* (Chicago: University of Chicago Press, 1988), 11–12; William Alexander, *Film on the Left: American Documentary Film from 1931 to 1942* (Princeton, N.J.: Princeton University Press, 1995), 7–19.

55. Kaplan, *Social Construction of American Realism,* 11–12.

56. David P. Peeler, *Hope Among Us: Social Criticism and Social Solace in Depression America* (Athens: University of Georgia Press, 1987), 3–4.

57. *Nation* 134 (22 June 1932): 708; (26 October 1932): 409.

58. *New York Times,* 11 November 1932, 17; 11 April 1935, 27; 13 January 1936, 12; *Variety Film Reviews,* 17 April 1935; *Literary Digest* 119 (27 April 1935): 34. *New Masses,* 1 October 1935, 44–45; 22 October 1935, 29.

59. *New York Daily Worker,* 9 March 1935, 7; 15 April 1935, 5; 6 February 1936, 7.

60. *New York Times,* 25 August 1937, 25; 3 October 1934, 25; *Variety Film Reviews,* 25 July 1933; *New Masses,* 27 March 1934, 30.

61. Fredric Jameson, *Signatures of the Visible* (New York: Routledge, 1992), 162–69; *Variety Film Reviews,* 29 August 1931 and 24 May 1932.

62. *New York Times,* 26 November 1938, 18; *Variety Film Reviews,* 29 April 1931.

63. *Variety Film Reviews,* 27 June 1933; 21 August 1935; 28 July 1937; 22 December 1937; *Literary Digest* 24 (21 August 1937): 26; *Commonweal* 22 (30 September 1935): 427.

64. Fan mail to Capra can be found in the Frank Capra Archives, Wesleyan University, Middletown, Connecticut. I would like to thank Leith Johnson and Joan Miller for their assistance in using this material. In the *Mr. Smith Goes to Washington* files, the following letters to Capra: M. Fry, 23 October 1939; J. G. Smith, 31 October 1939; M. Clements, 3 November 1939; E. Hoefer, 9 November 1939; W. Rehn, 14 December 1939; V. Pinson, 7 January 1940.

65. See *New York Times,* 29 October 1939, and North Tonawanda, N.Y., *Evening News,* 6 October 1939, clippings in *Mr. Smith Goes to Washington* file, Will Hays Papers, Indiana State Library; Joseph Breen to L. B. Mayer, 19 January 1938, *Mr. Smith Goes to Washington* file, PCAC/AMPAS.

66. In the *Meet John Doe* files, Capra Archives, see letters from A. Hall and M. Taber, 18 June 1941; J. Mullowney, 21 July 1941; A. Burkhart, 27 July 1941; Capra to M. Gluck, 8 April 1941. *Variety,* 19 March 1941, 16. See also Eric Smoodin, "This Business of America: Fan Mail, Film Reception, and *Meet John Doe,*" *Screen* 37 (Summer 1996): 111–28; Smoodin, "Viewing for Every Citizen: Mr. Smith and the Rhetoric of Reception," *Cinema Journal* 35 (Winter 1996): 3–23. I thank Eric Smoodin for sending me copies of his essays. See also Herbert Bieberman, "Frank Capra's Characters," *New Masses,* 8 July 1941, 26–27.

67. *Time* 35 (12 February 1940): 70; *Newsweek* 15 (12 February 1940): 37–38; *Commonweal* 31 (9 February 1940): 348.

68. See Tino Balio, *Grand Designs: Hollywood as a Modern Business Enterprise* (New York: Scribners, 1993), 405–6; Thomas Schatz, *Boom or Bust: The American Cinema in the 1940s* (New York: Scribners, 1997), 466–68.

## TWO. THE PEOPLE'S WAR

1. See Gary Gerstle, *Working-Class Americanism: The Politics of Labor in a Textile City, 1914–1960* (Cambridge, UK: Cambridge University Press, 1989), 289, 310; Lisabeth Cohen, *Making a New Deal: Industrial Workers in Chicago, 1919–1939* (Cambridge, UK: Cambridge University Press, 1990), 355. See Wallace Stegner, *One Nation* (Boston: Houghton-Mifflin, 1993) for an example of how unity was celebrated over religious and racial diversity at the time.

2. Benjamin Alpers, "This Is the Army: Imaging a Democratic Military," *Journal of American History* 85 (June 1998): 129–63.

3. Samuel A. Stouffer et al., eds., *Studies in Social Psychology of World War II* (Princeton, N.J.: Princeton University Press, 1949–52), 1:423–34; *Saturday Evening Post*, 17 July 1943, 29; 24 July 1943, 29.

4. John Morton Blum, *"V" Was for Victory: Politics and American Culture During World War II* (New York: Harcourt Brace Jovanovich, 1976), 53–55; Dana Polan, *Power and Paranoia: History, Narrative, and the American Cinema, 1940–1950* (New York: Columbia University Press, 1986), 67. Norman Corwin, "On a Note of Triumph," Audiocassette, Lodes Tone Production, 611 Empire Mill Rd., Bloomington, IN 47401.

5. Michael A. A. Adams, *The Best War Ever: America and World War II* (Baltimore: Johns Hopkins University Press, 1994), 74. On the censorship of photographs, see George H. Roeder, *The Censored War: American Visual Experience During World War Two* (New Haven, Conn.: Yale University Press, 1993), 33, 70; Robert K. Merton, *Mass Persuasion: The Social Psychology of a War Bond Drive* (New York: Harper, 1946), 74–83. *Time* 18 October 1943, 42; 20 December 1943, 63; 11 September 1943, 95.

6. Nelson Lichtenstein, *The Most Dangerous Man in Detroit: Walter Reuther and the Fate of American Labor* (New York: Basic Books, 1995), 195–208.

7. Robert Westbrook, "I Want a Girl Just Like the Girl That Married Harry James: The Problem of Political Obligation in World War II," *American Quarterly* 42 (December 1990): 587–614. *Saturday Evening Post* 216 (3 July 1943): 40. William Graebner, *The Age of Doubt: American Thought in the 1940s* (Boston: Twayne, 1991), 14–15; Adams, *Best War Ever*, 12; John Costello, *Virtue Under Fire: How World War II Changed Our Social and Sexual Attitudes* (Boston: Little, Brown, 1985), 97–98. Susan Hartman, "Prescriptions for Penelope: Literature on Women's Obligations to Returning World War II Veterans," *Women's Studies* 5 (1978): 197–200.

8. Timothy E. Scheurer, *Born in the USA: The Myth of America in Popular Music from Colonial Times to the Present* (Jackson: University of Mississippi Press, 1991), 62.

9. Thomas Schatz, ed., *Boom or Bust: Hollywood in the Late 1940s* (New York: Scribner, 1993), 22, 27, 131.

10. Lary May, "Making the American Consensus: The Narrative of Consensus and Subversion in World War II Film," in *The War in American Culture: Security and Consciousness During World War II,* edited by Lewis A. Erenberg and Susan A. Hirsh (Chicago: University of Chicago Press, 1996), 71–104. Clayton R. Koppes and Gregory D. Black, *Hollywood Goes to War* (Berkely: University of California Press, 1987), 60–69; Koppes, "Regulating the Screen: The Office of War Information and the Production Code Administration," in Thomas Schatz, *Boom or Bust: Hollywood in the 1940s,* 261–81 (New York: Scribners, 1993); Jeanine Basinger, *The World War II Combat Film: Anatomy of a Genre* (New York: Columbia University Press, 1986), 128–29. See Graebner, *Age of Doubt,* 95, on visions of classlessness in war films.

11. Terry Christensen, *Reel Politics: American Political Movies from Birth of a Nation to Platoon* (New York: Basil Blackwell, 1987), 64–65; Basinger, *World War II Combat Film,* 37–52, 71–78.

12. Thomas Doherty, *Projections of War: Hollywood, American Culture, and World War II* (New York: Columbia University Press, 1993), 155–62.

13. Norman Vincent Peale to Jack Warner, 2 July 1941, *Sergeant York* file, Warner Brothers Archive (WBA).

14. "Press book," *Sergeant York* file, WBA.

15. Joseph I. Breen to J. L. Warner, 22 April 1941, *Kings Row* file, PCA/AMPAS.

16. *Los Angeles Daily News,* 14 February 1944; Joseph I. Breen to L. B. Mayer, 10 October 1935; Breen to Luigi Luraschi, 15 March 1943, *Double Indemnity* file, PCA/AMPAS.

17. Production Code Authority to L. B. Meyer, 21 July 1941; 28 November 1941; A. Durland to L. B. Meyer, 10 March 1942, *Tortilla Flats* file, PCA/AMPAS.

18. *New York Times,* 1 August 1942, 14.

19. The gift of the bomber is detailed in the *New York Times,* 11 December 1942, 11.

20. See *Motion Picture Herald,* 25 April 1942; Production Code Authority to Jack H. Skirball, *Sabateour* file, PCA/AMPAS.

21. The New York *Daily Worker,* 28 November 1944, 11; Schatz, ed., *Boom or Bust,* 274.

22. Peter Roffman and Jim Purdy, *The Hollywood Social Problem Film from the Depression to the Fifties* (Bloomington: Indiana University Press, 1981), 263.

23. *New York Times,* 2 June 1944, clipping in *Tender Comrade* file, PCA/AMPAS.

24. Joseph Breen to David O. Selznick, 10 September 1943, *Since You Went Away* file, PCA/AMPAS.

25. Westbrook, "I Want a Girl," 587–614. Feminist scholars have warned that the male protector can quickly turn to the male predator when there is no longer any duty to protect. In some sense, this was a fear of both the war and the postwar periods; see Susan Gubar, "This Is My Rifle, This Is My Gun: World War II and the Blitz on Women," in *Behind the Lines,* edited by Margaret Higonnet et al. (New Haven. Conn.: Yale University Press, 1987), 227–59.

26. *Variety,* 22 June 1943, clipping in *So Proudly We Hail* file, PCA/ AMPAS.

27. Mrs. Thomas F. Sullivan, "I Lost Five Sons," *American Magazine* 137 (March 1944): 17, 94–95.

28. James Agee, "Death Takes a Powder," *Nation* 158 (6 May 1944): 549.

29. *New York Times,* 2 June 1944, 21; 21 July 1944, 16; *New Yorker* 20 (29 July 1944): 42–43; *Commonweal* 40 (4 August 1944): 374–75.

30. *Variety,* 12 January 1944, 3; 9 February 1944, 10.

31. *The Nation* 158 (22 January 1944): 108; *Time* 39 (16 February 1942): 86; *Commonweal* 39 (28 January 1944): 374.

32. *New York Times,* 3 July 1941, 15; 2 April 1942, 27; 13 January 1944, 17; 10 February 1944, 19. New York *Daily Worker,* 15 January 1944, 5.

33. *Variety Film Reviews,* 3 February 1943; 23 June 1943; *New York Times,* 10 September 1943, 29; 4 June 1943, 19; *Commonweal* 11 June 1943, 202–3; 17 September 1943, 538.

34. *Variety Film Reviews,* 11 May 1942; 28 June 1944, 6; *New York Times,* 24 November 1944, 19; *Commonweal* 41 (10 November 1944), 10. New York *Daily Worker,* 28 November 1944, 11.

35. Schatz, *Boom or Bust,* 466–68.


## THREE. WAR AND PEACE AT HOME

1. Norman Mailer, *The Naked and the Dead* (New York: Henry Holt, 1948).

2. Arthur Schlesinger, *The Vital Center* (Boston: Houghton-Mifflin, 1949), 2, 45, 169.

3. Roland Marchand, "Visions of Classlessness: Quests for Dominion," in *Reshaping America: Society and Institutions, 1945–1960,* edited by Robert H. Bremner and Gary W. Reichard (Columbus: Ohio State University Press, 1982), 164–68; Alan Brinkley, *The End of Reform: New Deal Liberalism in Recession and War* (New York: Knopf, 1955), 268; Daniel Bell, *The End of Ideology: On the Exhaustion of Political Ideas in the Fifties* (New York: Free Press, 1965), 175–95; 218–30; Elizabeth Fones-Wolf, *Selling Free Enterprise: The Business Assault on Labor and Idealism, 1945–1960* (Chicago: Univer-

sity of Chicago Press, 1994), 1–11. For a view of consensus in the fifties, see J. Ronald Oakely, *God's Country: America in the Fifties* (New York: W.W. Norton, 1986).

4. George Lipsitz, *Rainbow at Midnight: Labor and Culture in the 1940s* (Urbana: University of Illinois Press, 1994), 99.

5. Kevin Boyle, *The UAW and the Heyday of American Liberalism, 1945–1968* (Ithaca, N.Y.: Cornell University Press, 1995), 61–64. Nelson Lichtenstein, "From Corporatism to Collective Bargaining: Organized Labor and the Eclipse of Social Democracy in the Postwar Era," in *The Rise and Fall of the New Deal Order, 1930–1980*, edited by Steve Fraser and Gary Gerstle (Princeton, N.J.: Princeton University Press, 1989), 122–52.

6. See K.A. Cuordileone, "Politics in an Age of Anxiety: Cold War Political Culture and the Crisis in American Masculinity, 1949–1960," *Journal of American History* 87 (September 2000): 515–35.

7. Paul Boyer, *By the Bomb's Early Light: American Thought and Culture at the Dawn of the Atomic Age* (Chapel Hill: University of North Carolina Press, 1994), 151.

8. Shirley Jackson, "The Lottery," *New Yorker* 24 (26 June 1948): 25–28.

9. William Graebner, *The Age of Doubt: American Thought and Culture in the 1940s* (Boston: Twayne, 1991), 19, 46.

10. See Thomas Schatz, *Boom and Bust: Hollywood in the 1940s* (New York: Scribner, 1993), 1–5.

11. Robert Griswold, *Fatherhood in America: A History* (New York: Basic Books, 1993), 167; Louis Fairchild, *They Called It the War Effort: Oral Histories from World War II in Orange, Texas* (Austin, Tex.: Eakin Press, 1993), 5, 172–83; Dana Polan, *Power and Paranoia: History, Narrative, and the American Dream* (New York: Columbia University Press, 1986), 70–71.

12. George Chauncey, "The Postwar Sex Crime Panic," in *True Stories from the American Past*, edited by Grabner (New York: McGraw-Hill, 1993), 160–78; Estelle B. Freedman, "Uncontrolled Desires: The Response to the Sexual Psychopath, 1920–1960," *Journal of American History* 74 (June 1987): 83–106. Phil Jenkins, *Using Murder: The Social Construction of Serial Homicide* (New York: Aldine de Gruyter, 1994), 37, suggested an actual decline in the rate of serial murders in the 1940s and 1950s. For an argument that marriage tended to restrain male violence, see David T. Courtwright, *Violent Land: Single Men and Social Disorder from the Frontier to the Inner City* (Cambridge, Mass.: Harvard University Press, 1996), 211–12. Susan Gubar, " `This is My Rifle, This is My Gun': World War II and the Blitz on Women," in *Behind the Lines: Gender and the Two World Wars*, edited by Margaret Higonnet et al. (New Haven, Conn.: Yale University Press, 1987), 227–59. In the findings of these scholars, we see important links between the proliferation of violence in society and the state of gender relations and sexual identities. On the continuum between male violence toward women and other

forms of violence, see Anthony Giddens, *The Transformation of Intimacy: Sexuality, Love and Eroticism in Modern Society* (Stanford, Calif.: Stanford University Press, 1992), 121; Joan Wallach Scott, *Gender and the Politics of History* (New York: Columbia University Press, 1988), 6–7, 28

13. Elizabeth Pleck, *Domestic Tyranny: The Making of Social Policy Against Family Violence from Colonial Times to the Present* (New York: Oxford University Press, 1987), 161–62, 181. Although wife beating may not have been discussed in a pointed fashion, the issue of homegrown violence was certainly on people's minds in the late forties. An article in the *Atlantic Monthly* in 1946 concluded from conversations with American soldiers that many American men disliked women. Sociologist Edward McDonagh warned that the personality of discharged servicemen might be less conducive to companionate marriages and that there might be some violent clashes with women after their return from the war. McDonagh thought that military life altered the value system of the ordinary male and led to greater forms of "negativism" like drinking, profanity, and the "egocentric disposition" to use women to gratify "primitive sensual impulses." See David L. Cohen, "Do American Men Like Women?" *Atlantic Monthly* 178 (August 1946): 71–74; Edward McDonagh, "The Discharged Servicemen and His Family," *American Journal of Sociology* 51 (March 1946): 408–13.

14. Mary Ann Doane, *The Desire to Desire: The Woman's Films of the 1940s* (Bloomington: Indiana University Press, 1987); Susan M. Hartman, "Prescriptions for Penelope: Literature on Women's Obligations to Returning World War II Veterans," *Woman's Studies* 5 (1978): 223–39; William Chafe, *The American Woman: Her Changing Social, Economic, and Political Roles, 1920–1970* (New York: Oxford University Press, 1972), 181; Michael Kimmel, *Manhood in America: A Cultural History* (New York: Free Press, 1996), 64–67; Griswold, *Fatherhood in America*, 45.

15. Timothy A. Shuker-Haines, "Home Is the Hunter: Representations of World War II Veterans and the Reconstruction of Masculinity, 1944–1951," Ph.D. diss., University of Michigan, 1996; Kenneth C. Davis, *Two-Bit Culture* (Boston: Houghton-Mifflin, 1984), 180–84.

16. T. W. Adorno et al., *The Authoritarian Personality* (New York: Norton, 1982), 198; Ellen Herman, *The Romance of American Psychology: Political Culture in the Age of Experts, 1940–1970* (Berkeley: University of California Press, 1995).

17. Peter Roffman and Jim Purdy, *The Hollywood Social Problem Film: Madness, Despair, and Politics from the Depression to the Fifties* (Bloomington: Indiana University Press, 1981), 227–29. The point that films of the thirties tended to discuss larger social issues should not conceal the fact that the Depression-era movies had much to say about individual moral behavior as well.

18. See press book, *Pride of the Marines* file, WBA; New York *Daily*

*Worker,* 28 August 1945, 11; Mrs. Al Schmid, "My Love is Blind," *American Magazine* 138 (December 1944): 45–46, 122.

19. Kaja Silverman, *Male Subjectivity at the Margins* (London: Routledge, 1992), 67–89.

20. See *The Best Years of Our Lives* file, PCA/AMPAS.

21. See *From This Day* file, PCA/AMPAS.

22. Joseph Breen to William Gordon, 20 July 1945 and 17 December 1945, *Till the End of Time* file, PCA/AMPAS.

23. Alan Brinkley, *Liberalism and Its Discontents* (Cambridge, Mass.: Harvard University Press, 1998), 96–110.

24. Elia Kazan, *A Life* (New York: Knopf, 1988), 257; Breen to Jason Joy, 26 April 1944, *A Tree Grows in Brooklyn* file, PCA/AMPAS.

25. See clippings, *Hollywood Reporter,* 9 March 1948; *Variety,* 10 March 1948, *I Remember Mama* file, PCA/AMPAS.

26. Breen to Frank Capra, 29 August 1947, *State of the Union* file, PCA/AMPAS.

27. In *The Farmer's Daughter* (1947), a woman runs for Congress against the power of political bosses, who try to manipulate the election, and asserts the need for a greater female voice in politics.

28. Lipsitz, *Rainbow at Midnight,* 281.

29. Robert Sklar, *City Boys: Cagney, Bogart, and Garfield* (Princeton, N.J.: Princeton University Press, 1992), 183–87. Michael Rogin argues that *Body and Soul* represented a challenge to an older cultural idea that immigrant assimilation would come at the expense of African Americans. In films like *The Jazz Singer* (1927) and *The Jolson Story* (1946), Jews gained acceptance in America by adopting blackface, a symbolic act that asserted that they deserved entry into American culture because they were white. *Body and Soul,* according to Rogin, aspired to repudiate this racist path to assimilation by demonstrating an alliance between a Jewish and a black boxer and by disclosing how American society exploited blacks; see Rogin, *Blackface, White Noise* (Berkeley: University of California Press, 1996), 13–15, 87, 212–15. That it also sustained an older critique of American capitalism is made plain in Paul Buhle and Dave Wagner, *A Very Dangerous Citizen: Abraham Polonsky and the Hollywood Left* (Berkeley: University of California Press, 2001), 112–15. This study also argues that Polonsky felt that studio censorship was so powerful at the time that it was exceedingly difficult to insert critical perspectives into film. To repeat a point made often in this study, critical perspectives on capitalism and human nature were repeated endlessly in the American cinema.

30. Stephen Jackson to David Hopkins, 4 April 1948; Abraham Polonsky to Stephen Jackson, 7 April 1948, PCA/AMPAS. Patrick McGilligan and Paul Buhle, *Tender Comrades: A Backstory of the Hollywood Blacklist* (New York: St. Martin's Press, 1997), 485.

31. Joseph Breen to George Glass, 27 October 1948, *The Champion* file, PCA/AMPAS.

32. Joseph Breen to Harry Cohn, 14 December 1948, and Stephen Jackson to B. Smith, 17 February 1948, *Knock on Any Door* file, PCA/AMPAS.

33. Al Clark, *Raymond Chandler in Hollywood* (Los Angeles: Silman-James Press, 1996), 3, 77–90.

34. James Naremore, *More Than the Night: Film Noir in Its Contexts* (Berkeley: University of California Press, 1998), 6–12, 34–43, 139. Naremore gives some credence to World War II as a factor in generating noir ideas (first in France) but also stresses modernist art forms coming out of the early twentieth century that sought to explore personal subjectivity and sexuality as a reaction against impulses to organize and regulate the individual in industrial society. See also Jack Shadoian, *Dreams and Dead Ends: The American Gangster* (Cambridge: MIT Press, 1997), 83; Mike Davis, *City of Quartz: Excavating the Future in Los Angeles* (New York: Vintage Books, 1992), 37; Michael Kimmel, *Manhood in America: A Cultural History* (New York: Free Press, 1996), 69–70. Lynn Segal, *Slow Motion: Changing Masculinities, Changing Men* (New Brunswick, N.J.: Rutgers University Press, 1990), 79, discusses postwar fears of misogyny in a number of nations. See also Graebner, *Age of Doubt*, 25; Richard Slotkin, *Gunfighter Nation: The Myth of the Frontier in Twentieth Century America* (New York: HarperCollins, 1992), 328–30; Lipsitz, *Rainbow at Midnight*, 279–85.

35. Shadoian, *Dreams and Dead Ends*, 85–87.

36. See clipping *New York Times*, 3 May 1946, in *The Postman Always Rings Twice* file, PCA/AMPAS. This film, like *Mildred Pierce* and *Double Indemnity*, was based on an original story by James Cain. It is noteworthy that its origins, while now framed within the concerns of postwar America, resided in the thirties and in Cain's observation of life in Depression-era Los Angeles. Cain noted the anxieties around him over "passion and prosperity"; see Clark, *Raymond Chandler in Hollywood*, 32. See the 1947 film *Desperate* for a story in which criminal elements disrupt the plans of a postwar couple to start a family and a business of their own.

37. Richard Lacayo, "Dames! Stiffs! Mugs!," *Time* 151 (12 January 1998): 85–88.

38. Joseph Breen to Mark Hellinger, 16 May 1947, *Naked City* file, PCA/AMPAS.

39. See Kevin R. McNamara, *Urban Verbs: Arts and Discourses of American Cities* (Stanford, Calif.: Stanford University Press, 1996), 174–208.

40. Sklar, *City Boys*, 253, argues that the environmental and ethnic themes used to explain deviance in the thirties gave way in the postwar period to a greater emphasis on psychological and sexual motivations. The specter of violent working-class men was raised again in *City Across the River* (1949), a

story of wayward adolescents taken from Irving Schulman's novel, *The Amboy Dukes.*

41. Gordon W. Allport, *The Nature of Prejudice* (Cambridge, Mass.: Addison-Wesley, 1954).

42. Joseph Breen to Harold Melinker, 27 February 1947, PCA/AMPAS.

43. Thomas Cripps, *Making Movies Black: The Hollywood Message Movie from World War I to the Civil Rights Era* (New York: Oxford University Press, 1993), chaps. 1, 4.

44. For another story that overturns the wartime narrative of good Americans, see *All My Sons* (1948). In this feature evidence is presented that some Americans were greedy during the war and that the end of war brought not victory but trauma.

45. Cripps, *Making Movies Black,* 232–39; Thomas H. Pauly, "Black Images and White Culture During the Decades Before the Civil Rights Movement," *American Studies* 31 (Fall 1990): 101–19. I would like to thank Michael McGerr for the reference to Pauly's article.

46. George F. Custen, *Twentieth Century's Fox: Darryl F. Zanuck and the Culture of Hollywood* (New York: Basic Books, 1997), 334–35.

47. *Variety Film Reviews,* 24 June 1945; 18 July 1945; 10 March 1948; *Commonweal* 42 (14 Septenber 1945): 525–28; *New York Times,* 8 September 1945, 12; 1 March 1945, 25; 12 March 1948, 29. New York *Daily Worker,* 1 March 1945, 11.

48. *New York Times,* 28 December 1946, 19; *New Yorker* 22 (21 December 1946): 87.

49. E. McBride to Capra, 7 January 1947; S. Jackson to Capra, 28 March 1947; T. Marley to Capra, 13 April 1947; B. Vorbeck to Capra, n.d., 1947; Capra to S. Cornell, 10 February 1947, Capra Archives, Wesleyan University. See also *Variety Film Reviews,* 19 December 1946.

50. *Commonweal* 42 (17 August 1945): 431; *Variety Film Reviews,* 8 August 1945; New York *Daily Worker,* 28 August 1945, 11.

51. *New York Times,* 22 November 1946, 2; *Commonweal* 45 (13 December 1946): 230. See the critique of *Till the End of Time* for its failure to probe more deeply into the emotional problems of returning vets in *Variety Film Reviews,* 12 June 1946. Abraham Polonsky, "The Best Years of Our Lives," *Hollywood Quarterly* 2 (April 1947): 257–60.

52. *Variety Film Reviews,* 16 March 1946; 7 August 1946; *New York Times,* 4 May 1946, 10; *Commonweal* 44 (24 May 1946): 143; *New Yorker* 22 (7 September 1946): 48; 24 (13 March 1948): 80.

53. James Agee, "Body and Soul," *Nation* 165 (8 November 1947): 511; *New Yorker* 23 (15 November 1947): 118; *Variety Film Reviews,* 19 February 1949; 24 December 1948; 11 March 1949; 7 August 1947; *New York Times,* 10 November 1947, 10; 11 April 1949, 29.

54. James Agee, "Crossfire," *Nation* 165 (2 August 1947): 129; *New York*

Times, 23 July 1947, 19; 13 May 1949, 29; 30 September 1949, 28; *Variety Film Reviews*, 4 May 1949.

55. *Commonweal* 46 (1 August 1947): 386; 52 (18 August 1950): 461; 50 (20 May 1949): 149; 51 (14 December 1949): 15; *Variety Film Reviews*, 20 June 1947; 29 September 1949; 28 July 1950; *New York Times*, 13 May 1949, 29; 30 September 1949, 28; 17 August 1950, 23.

56. Schatz, *Boom or Bust*, 466–68.

## FOUR. BEYOND CONTAINMENT IN THE FIFTIES

1. John Rawles, *Political Liberalism* (New York: Columbia University Press, 1993), 9. See Stephen Whitfield, *The Culture of the Cold War* (Baltimore: Johns Hopkins University Press, 1991), for "hyperpatriotism."

2. Alan Nadel, *Containment Culture: American Narratives, Postmodernism and the Atomic Age* (Durham, N.C.: Duke University Press, 1995), 2–4.

3. Ibid., 48, 100–104. For another view of how Cold War culture moved away from the democratic aspirations of World War II, see Whitfield, *Culture of the Cold War*, 10–16.

4. Stephan Vaughn, *Ronald Reagan in Hollywood: Movies and Politics* (Cambridge, UK: Cambridge University Press, 1994), 151–55; Vaughn, "Political Censorship During the Cold War," in *Movie Censorship in American Culture*, edited by Frank G. Couvares (Washington, D.C.: Smithsonian Institution Press, 1995), 237–57; Nora Sayre, *Running Time: Films of the Cold War* (New York: Dial Press, 1982), 21–22; John Cogley, "The Mass Hearings," in *The American Film Industry*, edited by Tino Balio (Madison: University of Wisconsin Press, 1976), 410–26.

5. Robert Griswold, *Fatherhood in America: A History* (New York: Basic Books, 1993), xix–xxi, 9, 178–80; 309. Michael Paul Rogin, *The Intellectuals and McCarthy* (Cambridge: MIT Press, 1967) attempted to discredit this contemporary view of working-class politics by suggesting that support for McCarthy tended to be based more in a fear of communism than in a person's class standing. For another account that rejected the presumption of authoritarian attitudes within the working-class, see Erich Fromm, *The Fear of Freedom* (London: Routledge and Kegan Paul, 1942), 180–81. Fromm noted working-class hostility to National Socialism in Germany.

6. Gerard Jones, *Honey, I'm Home: Sitcoms and the Selling of the American Dream* (New York: St. Martin's Press, 1992), 97. See also Ellen Herman, *The Romance of American Psychology: Political Culture in the Age of Experts* (Berkeley: University of California Press, 1995), 185. T. W. Adorno et al., *The Authoritarian Personality* (New York: Harper, 1950), 267–69.

7. W. T. Lhamon, *Deliberate Speed: The Origins of a Cultural Style in the American 1950s* (Washington. D.C.: Smithsonian Institution Press, 1990), 39.

8. Margot Henriksen, *Dr. Strangelove's America: Society and Culture in the Atomic Age* (Berkeley: University of California Press, 1997), xix–xxi, 9, 178–80; 309; Lhamon, *Deliberate Speed*, 39. See Mary L. Dudziak, *Cold War Civil Rights: Race and the Image of American Democracy* (Princeton: Princeton University Press, 2000).

9. Michael Kimmel, *Manhood in America: A Cultural History* (New York: Free Press, 1996), 247–54; Joanne Meyerowitz, ed. *Not June Cleaver: Women and Gender in Postwar America, 1945–1960* (Philadelphia: Temple University Press, 1994), 229–62; Brett Harvey, *The Fifties: A Woman's Oral History* (New York: HarperCollins, 1993), 51–52, 69, 124; Regina Kunzel, "Pulp Fictions and Problem Girls: Reading and Rewriting Single Pregnancy in Postwar United States," *American Historical Review* 100 (December 1995): 1465–87. See Lee Rainwater, Richard P. Coleman, and Gerald Handel, *Workingman's Wife: Her Personality, World and Life Style* (New York: Oceana Publications, 1959); Graham McCann, *Rebel Males: Clift, Brando and Dean* (New Brunswick, N.J.: Rutgers University Press, 1993), 5–22; Wendy Daminer, *It's All the Rage: Crime and Culture* (Reading, Mass.: Addison-Wesley, 1995), 262.

10. For another film that describes worker organizations as corrupt, see *Inside Detroit* (1955).

11. Terry Christensen, *Reel Politics: American Political Movies from Birth of a Nation to Platoon* (New York: Basil Blackwell, 1987), 94; Peter Stead, *Film and the Working-Class: The Feature Film in British and American Society* (New York: Routledge, 1989), 168–69; Deborah Silverton, *Salt of the Earth* (New York: Feminist Press, 1978); Tom Zaniello, *Working-Stiffs, Union Maids, Reds, and Riff Raff: An Organized Guide to Films About Labor* (Ithaca, N.Y.: ILR Press, 1996), 214–15; James J. Lorence, *The Suppression of Salt of the Earth: How Hollywood, Big Labor and the Politicians Blacklisted a Movie in Cold War America* (Albuquerque: University of New Mexico Press, 1999), 47–54; 123–27.

12. See Jane Sherron De Hart, "Containment at Home: Gender, Sexuality, and National Identity in Cold War America," in *Rethinking Cold War Culture*, edited by Peter J. Kuznick and James Gilbert (Washington, D.C.: Smithsonian Institution Press, 2001), 124–55.

13. See *Clash by Night* file, Production Code Authority files, PCA/AMPAS.

14. Joseph Breen to Harold Melnker, 19 July 1951, *Clash by Night* file, PCA/AMPAS.

15. Tennessee Williams, *Memoirs* (New York: Doubleday, 1972); also see Dakin Williams and Shepherd Mead, *Tennessee Williams: An Intimate Biography* (New York: Arbor House, 1983).

16. See David Savran, *Communists, Cowboys, and Queers: The Politics of Masculinity in the Work of Arthur Miller and Tennessee Williams* (Minneapolis: University of Minnesota Press, 1992), 9–11. C. W. E. Bigsby, "Ten-

nessee Williams: Streetcar to Glory," *Twentieth-Century Interpretations of a Streetcar Named Desire*, edited by Jordan Y. Miller (Englewood Cliffs, N.J.: Prentice Hall, 1971), 103–8. Kazan entered his observations on August 21, 1947, in his "Notebook," which is to be found in the Kazan Papers, Wesleyan University.

17. See Stanley Kaufman's review of the film on the release of a VCR edition in *New Republic* 209 (29 November 1993): 28. Kaufman argues that there had been working-class heroes before this film, but that Brando brought "anger and genitals" and that he was "part infant and part stud." But any heroic qualities were muted by the image that he was also a flawed common man who had no hopes of love, democracy, or uplift in his life. See also Richard Pells, *The Liberal Mind in a Conservative Age: American Intellectuals in the 1940s and 1950s* (New York: Harper and Row, 1985), 374.

18. Joseph Breen to Luigi Luraschi, 27 June 1949; Charles Feldman to Elia Kazan, 3 March 1950; F. McDermind to Charles Feldmam, 29 April 1950; Kazan to Jack Warner, n.d., *A Streetcar Named Desire* file, Warner Brothers Archives. Elia Kazan to Joseph Breen, 14 September 1950; Tennessee Williams to Joseph Breen, 20 October 1950, *A Streetcar Named Desire* file, PCA/AMPAS.

19. Jack Vizzard to Joseph Breen, 12 July 1951, *A Streetcar Named Desire* file, PCA/AMPAS. Gregory D. Black, *The Catholic Crusade Against the Movies, 1940–1975* (Cambridge, UK: Cambridge University Press, 1997). See Kazan's reaction to the Legion of Decency rating in the *New York Times*, 21 October 1951, 28.

20. See Tennessee Williams, "Notes on the Filming of the *Rose Tattoo*," 21 April 1952, and Joseph Breen to Hall Wallis, 5 May 1953, *Rose Tattoo* file, PCA/AMPAS.

21. See Bud Schulberg, *On the Waterfront: The Final Shooting Script* (Carbondale: University of Southern Illinois Press, 1980), 145–50.

22. See William J. Puette, *Through Jaundiced Eyes: How the Media View Organized Labor* (Ithaca, N.Y.: ILR Press, 1992), 21; Christensen, *Reel Politics*, 93; Stead, *Film and the Working-Class*, 174–75; Peter Bisskind, *Seeing Is Believing: How Hollywood Taught Us to Stop Worrying and Love the Fifties* (New York: Pantheon, 1983), 171.

23. Kazan's views on Kowalski and Malloy are noted in his "Notebook," 18 June 1953, Kazan Papers, Wesleyan University. See also Albert Wertheim, "A View from the Bridge," in *The Cambridge Companion to Arthur Miller*, edited by Christopher Bigsby (Cambridge, UK: Cambridge University Press, 1997), 105–8.

24. Eli Kazan, *A Life* (New York: Knopf, 1988), 525–28; see also McCann, *Rebel Males*, 109.

25. See Rocky Graziano (with Rowland Barber), *Somebody Up There Likes Me* (New York: Pocket Books, 1956).

26. Graziano later told investigators that he was offered but did not accept a bribe of $100,000 to lose a fight most people felt he could win prior to his fight with Zale in 1947. See *Time* 49 (3 February 1947): 52; 14 March 1955, 77. *Newsweek* 30 (28 July 1947): 75, reported that Graziano received a welcome home after the fight by a large crowd at Grand Central Station but discovered that his apartment had been robbed while he was away.

27. For another example of a working-class man struggling to succeed on his own, see Elvis Presley in *Jailhouse Rock* (1957). In this story a young construction worker attempts to turn his life around and control his violent behavior by trading prison life for a career as a popular singer. He comes to value money more than loving relationships for a time, but ultimately he learns that money is worthless without relationships.

28. For a discussion of the multiple symbolic uses of the hillbilly in American film and culture, see J. W. Williamson, *Hillbillyland: What the Movies Did to the Mountains and What the Mountains Did to the Movies* (Chapel Hill: University of North Carolina Press, 1955), ix, 2, 53–55, 158–59.

29. See G. M. Shurlock to J. L. Warner, 10 July 1956, and the press book for *A Face in the Crowd*, box 1, *A Face in the Crowd* file, Warner Bros. Archives.

30. G. Hurlock to Frank McCarthy, *No Down Payment* file, 5 February 1957, PCA/AMPAS.

31. See clipping, *Newsweek* 40 (23 December 1957), *Peyton Place* file, PCA/AMPAS.

32. See Emily Toth, *Inside Peyton Place: The Life of Grace Metalious* (Garden City, N.Y.: Doubleday, 1981), 40, 131–38; David Halberstam, *The Fifties* (New York: Fawcett Colombine, 1993), 580–81; Emanuel Levy, *Small Town America in Film: The Decline and Fall of Community* (New York: Continuum, 1991), 122–25. Metalious was somewhat influenced by another novel, *Kings Row*, which explored the dark side of an American town. *Kings Row* appeared as a film in 1942.

33. Thomas Cripps, *Making Movies Black: The Hollywood Message Movie from World War II to the Civil Rights Era* (New York: Oxford University Press, 1993), 284.

34. Ibid., 283–84.

35. See Eileen Shelly to Warner Brothers, 1 November 1951; E. Preston to Warner Brothers, 4 November 1951; H. P. Rubenstein to Warner Brothers, 2 January 1952; Veronica Smith to Warner Brothers, 16 September 1951; J. Jackson to Warner Brothers, 23 October 1951, in *Streetcar Named Desire* file, box 7, Warner Brothers Archives.

36. Philip Hartung, "Weep for Blanche," *Commonweal* 54 (28 September 1951): 596–97; *Variety Film Reviews*, 20 June 1951.

37. *New York Times*, 19 June 1952, 32; 15 June 1956, 32; *Variety Film Reviews*, 14 May 1952; 25 April 1956; *Catholic World* 175 (July 1952): 307.

38. *New York Times*, 13 December 1955, 55; 31 October 1957, 41; 13 December 1957, 35; *Variety Film Reviews*, 17 October 1955; *New Republic* 138 (17 March 1958), 22–23; *Catholic World* 186 (December 1957): 221; *National Parent-Teacher* 53 (February 1958): 39; 52 (December 1957), 34.

39. *Variety Film Reviews*, 14 July 1954; 4 July 1956; *New York Times*, 29 July 1954, 18; 6 July 1956, 16.

40. *National Parent-Teacher* 49 (5 September 1954): 38; *Commonweal* 60 (20 August 1954), 485; *Catholic World* 179 (August 1954): 384; 64 (13 July 1956): 371; New York *Daily Worker*, 13 August 1954, 7.

41. *New York Times*, 15 March 1954, 20; *New Yorker* 27 (20 October 1931): 131; *Variety Film Reviews*, 17 March 1954; 17 April 1957. New York *Daily Worker*, 13 March 1954, 7; 18 March 1954, 7; 24 March 1954, 7.

42. *Time* 69 (14 January 1957): 100; 77 (31 March 1961), 64; *Commonweal* 65 (25 January 1957): 434–35; *Ebony* 16 (April 1961): 53–56; *New Republic* 144 (20 March 1961): 19; *New York Times*, 30 January 1957, 33; 19 October 1961, 39; *Variety Film Reviews*, 2 January 1957; 29 March 1961; 21 September 1961.

43. See *Variety Film Reviews*, 6 January 1954, 66; 5 January 1955, 59; 8 January 1958, 30.


## FIVE. THE PEOPLE IN TURMOIL

1. See Nelson Lichtenstein, "From Corporatism to Collective Bargaining: Organized Labor and the Eclipse of Social Democracy in the Postwar Era," in *The Rise and Fall of the New Deal Order, 1930–1980*, edited by Steve Fraser and Gary Gerstle (Princeton, N.J.: Princeton University Press, 1989), 122–24; Lisa McGirr, *Suburban Warriors: The Origins of the New American Right* (Princeton, N.J.: Princeton University Press, 2001).

2. Christian G. Appy, *Working-Class War: American Combat Soldiers and Vietnam* (Chapel Hill: University of North Carolina Press, 1993), 12; Frank Koscielski, *Divided Loyalties: American Unions and the Vietnam War* (New York: Garland, 1999), 7, 115, 131; Joshua Freeman, "Hardhats: Construction Workers, Manliness and the 1970s Pro-War Demonstrations," *Journal of Social History*, 26 (Summer 1993): 725–37; see also the discussion on the politics of the "hardhats" in Milton Bates, *The Wars We Took to Vietnam: Cultural Conflict and Storytelling* (Berkeley: University of California Press, 1996), 86.

3. Ronald P. Formisano, *Boston Against Busing: Race, Class and Ethnicity in the 1960s and 1970s* (Chapel Hill: University of North Carolina Press, 1991), 3–23; Jonathan Reider, *Canarsie: Jews and Italians Against Liberalism* (Cambridge, Mass.: Harvard University Press, 1985), 57, 141–43. On working-class opposition to the war, see Bates, *Wars We Took to Vietnam*, 88–89.

William Julius Wilson, *The Truly Disadvantaged: The Inner City, the Underclass, and Public Policy* (Chicago: University of Chicago Press, 1987), 6–7.

4. Rhodri Jeffreys-Jones, *Peace Now: American Society and the Ending of the Vietnam War* (New Haven, Conn.: Yale University Press, 1999), 197–221; Dan T. Carter, *The Politics of Rage: George Wallace, the Origins of the New Conservatism and the Transformation of American Politics* (New York: Simon and Schuster, 1995), 352, 368, 379; Godfrey Hodgson, *American in Our Time* (New York: Vintage Books, 1976), 4–11, 65–78, and *The World Turned Right Side Up* (Boston: Houghton-Mifflin, 1996), 147. Catherine A. MacKinnon, *Towards a Feminist Theory of the State* (Cambridge: Harvard University Press, 1989), 157–60.

5. On deindustrialization, see Barry Bluestone and Bennett Harrison, *The Deindustrialization of America: Plant Closings, Community Abandonment, and the Dismantling of Basic Industry* (New York: Basic Books, 1982), 25–37. Rick Fantasia, *Cultures of Solidarity: Consciousness, Action, and Contemporary American Workers* (Berkeley: University of California Press, 1988), 75–108, 241; Staughton Lynd, "The Genesis of the Idea of a Community Right to Industrial Power in Youngstown and Pittsburgh, 1979–1987," *Journal of American History* 74 (December 1987): 926–58. Kathryn Marie Dudley, *The End of the Line: Lost Jobs, New Lives in Postindustrial America* (Chicago: University of Chicago Press, 1994) documents how middle-class professionals in one town proved to be indifferent over the declining economic fortunes of blue-collar people who shared their community.

6. John Lukacs, *The Passing of the Modern Age* (New York: Harper and Row, 1970), 168–70, covers the change of moral outlook from the social to the personal perspective. Peter Clecak, *America's Quest for the Ideal Self: Dissent and Fulfillment in the 60s and 70s* (New York: Oxford University Press, 1983), 9–12, 28, 92–93; Alice Echols, *Daring to Be Bad: Radical Feminism in America, 1967–1975* (Minneapolis: University of Minnesota Press, 1989), 1–16.

7. Donald Lazere, ed., *American Media and Mass Culture: Left Perspectives* (Berkeley: University of California Press, 1987), 206–7; Jack Shadoian, *Dreams and Dead Ends: The American Gangster* (Cambridge: MIT Press, 1977), 328. Barbara Ehrenreich, *The Hearts of Men: American Dreams and the Flight from Commitment* (Garden City, N.Y.: Anchor/Doubleday, 1983), 134–50 discusses cultural efforts to discredit working-class men as "retrograde hard hats."

8. See Peter Lev, *American Films of the 70s: Conflicting Visions* (Austin: University of Texas Press, 2000), 22–38.

9. Columbia Pictures press book, box 18, Martin Scorsese Collection, American Film Institute (AFI). I would like to thank Caroline Cisneros for her assistance in using this collection.

10. "Scorsese's notes and remarks at the Cannes Film Festival, 1976," in

*Taxi Driver*, box 19, Scorsese Collection, AFI. In *The Boston Strangler* (1968), a real-life repairman murders women who live alone. Albert DeSalvo is not interested in creating a virtuous society; his murderous drive is rooted not in social conditions but in a schizophrenic personality disorder. In a sense, this story minimized the connection between lower-class standing and violence that was made in *Taxi Driver*. At the same time, it did tend to reinforce this link because De Salvo is so clearly a blue-collar man living in a crowded apartment with this family.

11. See David Thompson and Ian Christie, *Scorsese on Scorsese* (London: Faber and Faber, 1999), 228–34.

12. Gerald Early, *The Culture of Bruising: Essays on Prizefighting, Literature, and Modern American Culture* (Hopewell, N.J.: Ecco Press, 1994), xiv, 38, 93–100. United Artists expressed confidence that they could sell a film about a man with a "vicious temper;" see press information, *Raging Bull*, box 47, Scorsese Collection, AFI.

13. See *The Last Picture Show* (1971) for another story about dim prospects for young working-class men in a small Texas town set in the 1950s.

14. For another account of miners banding together to fight for their rights in the past, see *Matewan* (1987), which was set in the West Virginia coal fields in the 1920s.

15. For a story of a working-class woman climbing out of poverty, see *Coal Miner's Daughter* (1980).

16. *The River* (1984) told the story of a lower-class farm family struggling to save their farming enterprise from insensitive capitalists who wanted to take over their land.

17. See Robert Rosenstone, "Oliver Stone as Historian," in *Oliver Stone's USA: Film, History, and Controversy*, edited by Robert Brent Toplin (Lawrence: University of Kansas Press, 2000), 26–37; Oliver Stone, "Stone on Stone's Image," ibid., 40–58. Also see Marita Sturken, "Reenactment, Fantasy, and the Paranoia of History: Oliver Stone's Docudramas," *History and Theory* 36 (1997): 64–77.

18. Mark A. Reid, *Redefining Black Film* (Berkeley: University of California Press, 1993), 70. Reid argues that these action heroes represented to some extent the rejection of nonviolent protest by the black community.

19. See belle hooks, *Reel to Reel: Race, Sex, and Class at the Movies* (New York: Routledge, 1996), 3; Wilson, *Truly Disadvantaged*, 6–18.

20. A review by Stanley Kauffmann claimed the "hood" was just one "more old bad neighborhood picture" like those of the thirties. But in the thirties narratives usually made an effort to argue that social disorder could be corrected by the adoption of moral standards. No such solutions were offered in the nineties.

21. The reaction of Tennessee Williams can be found in a clipping from the *Pittsburgh Press*, 6 June 1976, in box 18, Scorsese Collection, AFI. See

also a clipping from the *Miami Herald,* 29 February 1976, ibid; *New Yorker* 51 (9 February 1976), 82–85; *New York Times,* 5 February 1976, 36.

22. Jake LaMotta, *Raging Bull: My Story* (Englewood Cliffs, N.J.: Prentice Hall, 1970); *New York Times,* 14 November 1980, sec. C, p. 11. See clippings from the *Village Voice,* 11 November 1980; *Toronto Sun,* 17 November 1980; and *New York Daily News,* 24 November 1980, in box 49, Scorsese Collection, AFI.

23. *Variety,* 5 October 1983, 20; *New York Times,* 14 October 1973, II:1; *Time* 96 (27 July 1970): 68.

24. *Time,* 24 October 1977, 71; *Los Angeles Times,* 19 December 1974, 19.

25. *New Republic* 178 (20 May 1978): 24; *Newsweek* 91 (1 May 1978): 89; *Time,* 12 March 1979, 76.

26. *Newsweek* 78 (19 July 1971): 80; *Time* 100 (26 July 1971): 51; (11 September 1972), 78; *New York Times,* 30 June 1989, sec. C, p. 16; *Variety Film Reviews,* 20 May 1991; *Christian Science Monitor,* 13 June 1991, 12; 22 July 1991, 11.

27. *Newsweek* 92 (11 December 1978): 114–15; *Time* 112 (18 December 1978): 86; *New York Times,* 15 December 1978; 20 December 1989, Sec. C, 15; *New Statesman,* 3 March 1990, 44.

28. David A. Cook, *Lost Illusions: American Cinema in the Shadow of Watergate and Vietnam, 1970–1979* (New York: Scribners, 2000), 497–503; Stephen Prince, *A New Pot of Gold: Hollywood Under the Electronic Rainbow, 1980–1989* (New York: Scribners, 2000), 447–48.


## LIBERALISM AT THE MOVIES: A CONCLUSION

1. Louis Hartz, *The Liberal Tradition in America: An Interpretation of American Political Thought Since the Revolution* (New York: Harcourt, Brace and World, 1955).

2. Ibid., 7–13. Alan Brinkley, *Liberalism and Its Discontents* (Cambridge, Mass.: Harvard University Press, 1998), 290–95. Gary Gerstle, *American Crucible: Race and Nation in the Twentieth Century* (Princeton, N.J.: Princeton University Press, 2001), 4–6.

3. Reinhold Niebuhr, *The Irony of American History* (New York: Charles Scribner's Sons, 1952), 4, 13, 19.

4. Richard Rorty, *Contingency, Irony, and Solidarity* (Cambridge, UK: Cambridge University Press, 1989), 3. See also Barry Hindess, "Liberalism, Socialism, and Democracy: Variations on a Governmental Theme," in *Foucault and Political Reason: Liberalism, neo-Liberalism, and Rationalities of Government,* edited by Andrew Barry, Thomas Osborne, and Nikolas Rose (Chicago: University of Chicago Press, 1996), 65–80; Merle Curti, *Human Nature in American Thought* (Madison: University of Wisconsin Press, 1980), 120–21.

5. Ruth Feldstein, *Motherhood in Black and White: Race and Sex in American Liberalism, 1930–1965* (Ithaca, N.Y.: Cornell University Press, 2000) shows how liberal politicians could advance democratic and illiberal attitudes at the same time. Robert D. Putnam, *Bowling Alone: The Collapse and Revival of American Community* (New York: Simon and Schuster, 2000), looks at the decline of civic and organizational involvement in modern America without considering the ironic qualities and desires of America's central political idea.

6. See Gary Gerstle, "The Protean Character of American Liberalism," *American Historical Review* 99 (October 1994): 1043–73.

7. Julia Hallam and Margaret Marshment, *Realism and Popular Cinema* (Manchester, UK: Manchester University Press, 2000), 18. Slavoj Zizek, "Introduction: The Spectre of Ideology," in *Mapping Ideology*, edited by Zizek (London: Verso, 1994), 10, cautions against any assumption that widespread discourse can alleviate the need to consider the powerful workings of a dominant ideology. Craig Calhoun, "Introduction: Habermas and the Public Sphere," in *Habermas and the Public Sphere*, edited by Calhoun (Cambridge: MIT Press, 1992), 5–28.

8. Scott Spector, "Was the Third Reich Movie-Made? Interdisciplinarity and the Reframing of Ideology," *American Historical Review* 106 (April 2001): 460–84. For a similar account of the contradictions in films made under Italian fascism, see Ruth Ben-Ghia, "Envisioning Modernity: Desire and Discipline in Italian Fascist Film," *Critical Inquiry* 23 (Autumn 1996): 109–44.

9. Spector, "Third Reich"; Zizek, "Introduction," 9–17. Victoria De Grazia, "Mass Culture and Sovereignty: The American Challenge to European Americans, 1920–1960," *Journal of Modern History* 61 (March 1989): 53–87. Barbara Ehrenreich, *Fear of Falling: The Inner Life of the Middle Class* (New York: HarperCollins, 1990), 97–127.

# SOURCES

## MANUSCRIPT COLLECTIONS

*FCC*  Frank Capra Collection, Cinema Archives, Wesleyan University, Middletown, Connecticut

*EKP*  Elia Kazan Papers, Cinema Archives, Wesleyan University, Middletown, Connecticut

*MPTC*  Motion Picture and Television Collection, Library of Congress, Washington, D.C.

*MCC*  Martin Scorsese Collection, American Film Institute, Los Angeles

*PCAC*  Production Code Authority Collection, Academy of Motion Picture Arts and Sciences, Los Angeles

*WBA*  Warner Brother Archives, University of Southern California, Los Angeles

## FILMS

| | | | |
|---|---|---|---|
| *Adventure* | 1945 | *Baby Face* | 1933 |
| *Air Force* | 1943 | *Bataan* | 1943 |
| *Alamo Bay* | 1985 | *Battle Cry* | 1955 |
| *Alice Adams* | 1935 | *The Best Years of Our Lives* | 1946 |
| *Alice Doesn't Live Here* | | *Black Fury* | 1935 |
| *Anymore* | 1975 | *Black Legion* | 1937 |
| *All My Sons* | 1948 | *The Blackboard Jungle* | 1955 |
| *All the Right Moves* | 1983 | *Blue Collar* | 1978 |
| *America, America* | 1963 | *The Blue Dahlia* | 1946 |
| *American Madness* | 1932 | *Body and Soul* | 1947 |
| *An American Romance* | 1944 | *Bonnie and Clyde* | 1967 |
| *Angels With Dirty Faces* | 1938 | *Born on the Fourth of July* | 1989 |
| *Anna Lucasta* | 1949 | *The Boston Strangler* | 1968 |

| | | | |
|---|---|---|---|
| Boyz N the Hood | 1991 | Gentlemen's Agreement | 1947 |
| Breaking Away | 1997 | The Godfather | 1972 |
| Cabin in the Cotton | 1932 | The Godfather Part II | 1974 |
| Casablanca | 1942 | Going My Way | 1944 |
| The Catered Affair | 1956 | Gold Diggers | 1933 |
| The Champ | 1931 | Golden Boy | 1993 |
| Champion | 1949 | The Grapes of Wrath | 1940 |
| City Across the River | 1949 | Guadalcanal Diary | 1943 |
| City for Conquest | 1940 | Hail the Conquering Hero | 1944 |
| Clash By Night | 1952 | Hangin' with the Homeboys | 1991 |
| Coal Miner's Daughter | 1980 | Happy Land | 1943 |
| Coming Home | 1987 | The Harder They Fall | 1965 |
| Cool Hand Luke | 1967 | Heroes for Sale | 1933 |
| Crooklyn | 1994 | Home of the Brave | 1949 |
| Crossfire | 1947 | Hoosier Schoolboy | 1937 |
| Cry of the City | 1948 | How Green Was My Valley | 1941 |
| Dead End | 1937 | Human Desire | 1954 |
| Dead Reckoning | 1947 | I Am a Fugitive from a | |
| Death of a Salesman | 1951 | Chain Gang | 1932 |
| Death Wish | 1974 | I Married a Communist | 1950 |
| The Deer Hunter | 1978 | I Remember Mama | 1948 |
| Desperate | 1947 | I'm No Angel | 1938 |
| Dirty Harry | 1971 | In the Heat of the Night | 1967 |
| Do the Right Thing | 1988 | Inside Detroit | 1955 |
| Double Indemnity | 1944 | It Happened One Night | 1934 |
| Dr. Strangelove | 1963 | It's a Wonderful Life | 1946 |
| Duck Soup | 1933 | Jailhouse Rock | 1957 |
| Duffy's Tavern | 1954 | The Jazz Singer | 1927 |
| Edge of the City | 1957 | Joe | 1970 |
| F.I.S.T. | 1978 | Joe Smith, American | 1942 |
| A Face in the Crowd | 1957 | Johnny Dark | 1954 |
| Fallen Angel | 1945 | The Jolson Story | 1946 |
| Falling Down | 1993 | Judge Priest | 1934 |
| The Farmer's Daughter | 1947 | Juke Girl | 1942 |
| The Fighting Sullivans | 1944 | Jungle Fever | 1991 |
| Five Easy Pieces | 1970 | Kid Galahad | 1937 |
| Force of Evil | 1948 | The Killers | 1946 |
| From Here to Eternity | 1953 | King's Row | 1942 |
| From This Day Forward | 1946 | Knock on Any Door | 1949 |
| Fury | 1936 | Knute Rockne, All American | 1940 |
| Gabriel Over the White | | The Last American Hero | 1973 |
| House | 1933 | The Last Exit to Brooklyn | 1990 |
| The Garment Jungle | 1957 | The Last Picture Show | 1971 |

| | | | |
|---|---|---|---|
| Lifeboat | 1944 | Pride of the Marines | 1945 |
| Little Caesar | 1931 | The Prowler | 1951 |
| Looking for Mr. Goodbar | 1977 | The Public Enemy | 1931 |
| M*A*S*H | 1970 | Raging Bull | 1980 |
| Mannequin | 1937 | A Raisin in the Sun | 1961 |
| Marked Woman | 1937 | Rambo: First Blood Part Two | 1985 |
| Marty | 1955 | Rebel Without a Cause | 1955 |
| Matewan | 1987 | Riff Raff | 1963 |
| Mean Streets | 1973 | The River | 1984 |
| Meet John Doe | 1941 | Rocky | 1976 |
| The Men | 1950 | The Rose Tattoo | 1955 |
| Metropolis | 1926 | Rosie the Riveter | 1944 |
| Midnight Cowboy | 1969 | Ruggles of Red Gap | 1935 |
| Mildred Pierce | 1945 | Saboteur | 1942 |
| Modern Times | 1936 | Salt of the Earth | 1954 |
| The Molly Maguires | 1970 | The Sands of Iwo Jima | 1949 |
| Mr. Deeds Goes to Town | 1936 | Saturday Night Fever | 1977 |
| Mr. Smith Goes to | | Saturday's Hero | 1951 |
| Washington | 1939 | Scarface | 1932 |
| The Naked City | 1948 | Sergeant York | 1941 |
| Nashville | 1975 | Shaft | 1971 |
| Native Land | 1942 | Silkwood | 1983 |
| The Negro Soldier | 1944 | Since You Went Away | 1944 |
| No Down Payment | 1957 | So Proudly We Hail | 1943 |
| No Way Out | 1950 | Somebody Up There | |
| Norma Rae | 1979 | Likes Me | 1956 |
| On the Waterfront | 1954 | Sounder | 1972 |
| Our Daily Bread | 1934 | The Southerner | 1945 |
| Our Town | 1940 | Stagecoach | 1939 |
| Our Vines Have Tender | | Stanley and Iris | 1989 |
| Grapes | 1945 | The State of the Union | 1948 |
| Paris Blues | 1961 | Steel Against the Sky | 1941 |
| The Pawnbroker | 1965 | Stella Dallas | 1937 |
| Peyton Place | 1957 | Street Scene | 1931 |
| Pin Up Girl | 1944 | A Streetcar Named Desire | 1951 |
| Pinky | 1949 | Sullivan's Travels | 1941 |
| Pittsburgh | 1942 | Sunset Boulevard | 1950 |
| A Place in the Sun | 1951 | Superfly | 1972 |
| Places in the Heart | 1984 | Sweet Sweetback's | |
| Platoon | 1986 | Baadasssss Song | 1971 |
| The Postman Always Rings | | Talk of the Town | 1942 |
| Twice | 1946 | Taxi Driver | 1976 |
| The Power and the Glory | 1933 | Tender Comrade | 1943 |

| | | | |
|---|---|---|---|
| Tender Mercies | 1982 | A View from the Bridge | 1961 |
| They Drive by Night | 1940 | Wake Island | 1942 |
| They Were Expendable | 1945 | West Side Story | 1961 |
| Three on a Match | 1932 | The Whistle at Eaton Falls | 1951 |
| Thunder Road | 1958 | White Heat | 1949 |
| Till the End of Time | 1946 | Who's That Knocking at | |
| The Time of Your Life | 1948 | My Door | 1968 |
| To Hell and Back | 1958 | Wild Boy's on the Road | 1933 |
| To Kill a Mockingbird | 1962 | Wings of the Eagle | 1942 |
| Tobacco Road | 1941 | A Woman Under the | |
| Tortilla Flat | 1942 | Influence | 1974 |
| A Tree Grows in Brooklyn | 1945 | You Can't Take It With You | 1938 |
| Two Seconds | 1932 | Young Mr. Lincoln | 1939 |
| Valley of Decision | 1945 | | |

## BOOKS

Adams, Michael A. A. *The Best War Ever: America and World War II.* Baltimore: Johns Hopkins University Press, 1994.

Adorno, T. W. et. al. *The Authoritarian Personality.* New York: Norton, 1982.

Agee, James, and Walker Evans. *Let Us Now Praise Famous Men.* Boston: Houghton-Mifflin, 1941.

Alexander, William. *Film on the Left: American Documentary Film from 1931 to 1942.* Princeton, N.J.: Princeton University Press, 1995.

Allport, Gordon W. *The Nature of Prejudice.* Cambridge, Mass.: Addison-Wesley, 1954.

Anderson, Sherwood. *Puzzled America.* New York: Scribners, 1935.

Appy, Christian. *Working-Class War: American Combat Soldiers and Vietnam.* Chapel Hill: University of North Carolina Press, 1993.

Balio, Tino. *Grand Designs: Hollywood as a Modern Business Enterprise.* New York: Scribner's, 1993.

Barber, Benjamin A. *A Passion for Democracy.* Princeton, N.J.: Princeton University Press, 1998.

Basinger, Jeanine. *A Woman's View: How Hollywood Spoke to Women, 1930–1960.* New York: Alfred Knopf, 1993.

———. *The World War II Combat Film: Anatomy of a Genre.* New York: Columbia University Press, 1986.

Bates, Milton. *The Wars We Took to Vietnam: Cultural Conflict and Storytelling.* Berkeley: University of California Press, 1996.

Bayles, Martha. *The Loss of Beauty and Meaning in American Popular Music.* Chicago: University of Chicago Press, 1994.

Behlmer, Rudy. *America's Favorite Movies: Behind the Scenes.* New York: Frederick Ungar, 1982.

Bell, Daniel. *The End of Ideology: On the Exhaustion of Political Ideas in the Fifties.* New York: Free Press, 1965.

Bellah, Robert N., et al. *Habits of the Heart: Individualism and Commitment in American Life.* Berkeley: University of California Press, 1985.

Bennett, Tony. *The Birth of the Museum: History, Theory, Politics.* London: Routledge, 1995.

Bennett, Tony, Colin Mercer, and Janet Wollacott, eds. *Popular Culture and Social Relations.* Philadelphia: Open Society Press, 1986.

Bergman, Andrew. *We're In the Money: Depression America and Its Films.* Chicago: New York University Press, 1971.

Bhabha, Homi K. *The Location of Culture.* New York: Routledge, 1994.

Birdwell, Michael E. *Celluloid Soldiers: Warner Bros.'s Campaign Against Nazism.* New York: New York University Press, 1999.

Bisskind, Peter. *Seeing Is Believing: How Hollywood Taught Us to Stop Worrying and Love the Fifties.* New York: Pantheon, 1983.

Black, Gregory. *The Catholic Crusade Against Movies, 1940–1975.* Cambridge, UK: Cambridge University Press, 1997.

Bluestone, Barry, and Bennett Harrison. *The Deindustrialization of America: Plant Closings, Community Abandonment and the Dismantling of Basic Industry.* New York: Basic Books, 1982.

Blum, John Morton. *"V" Was for Victory: Politics and American Culture During World War II.* New York: Harcourt Brace Jovanovich, 1976.

Bodnar, John. *Anthracite People.* Harrisburg: Pennsylvania Historical and Museum Commission, 1983.

Boyer, Paul. *By the Bomb's Early Light: American Thought and Culture at the Dawn of the Atomic Age.* Chapel Hill: University of North Carolina Press, 1994.

Boyle, Kevin. *The UAW and the Heyday of American Liberalism, 1945–1968.* Ithaca, N.Y.: Cornell University Press, 1995.

Brinkley, Alan. *The End of Reform: New Deal Liberalism in Recession and War.* New York: Knopf, 1955.

———. *Liberalism and Its Discontents.* Cambridge, Mass.: Harvard University Press, 1998.

———. *Voices of Protest: Huey Long, Father Coughlin, and the Great Depression.* New York: Vintage Books, 1982.

Bristow, Nancy K. *Making Men Moral: Social Engineering During the Great War.* New York: New York University Press, 1996.

Brock, William. *Welfare, Democracy, and the New Deal.* New York: Cambridge University Press, 1988.

Brownlow, Kevin. *Behind the Mask of Innocence.* New York: Knopf, 1990.

Buhle, Paul, and Dave Wagner. *A Very Dangerous Citizen: Abraham Polonsky and the Hollywood Left.* Berkeley: University of California Press, 2001.

Bunstein, Andrew. *The Language of Democracy: Political Rhetoric in the United States and Britain, 1790–1900.* (Ithaca: Cornell University Press), 1995.

———. *Sentimental Democracy: The Evolution of America's Romantic Self-Image.* (New York: Hill and Wang), 1999.

Caldwell, Erskine. *Tobacco Road.* New York: Scribner, 1932.

Cantor, Norman. *The American Century: Varieties of Culture in Modern Times.* New York: Harper Collins, 1997.

Carney, Raymond. *American Vision: The Films of Frank Capra.* Cambridge, UK: Cambridge University Press, 1986.

Carter, Dan T. *The Politics of Rage: George Wallace, The Origins of the New Conservatism, and the Transformation of America.* New York: Simon and Schuster, 1995.

Capra, Frank. *The Name Above the Title: An Autobiography.* New York: Macmillan, 1971.

Chafe, William. *The American Woman: Her Changing Social, Economic, and Political Roles, 1920–1970.* New York: Oxford University Press, 1972.

Chauncey, George. *Gay New York: Gender, Urban Culture and the Making of a Gay Male World, 1890–1940.* New York: Basic Books, 1994.

Christensen, Terry. *Reel Politics: American Political Movies from Birth of a Nation to Platoon.* New York: Basil Blackwell, 1987.

Clark, Al. *Raymond Chandler in Hollywood.* Los Angeles: Silman-James Press, 1996.

Clecak, Peter. *America's Quest for the Ideal Self: Dissent and Fulfillment in the 60s and 70s.* New York: Oxford University Press, 1983.

Cohen, Lizabeth. *Making a New Deal: Industrial Workers in Chicago, 1919–1939* Cambridge, UK: Cambridge University Press, 1990.

Cook, A. David. *Lost Illusions: American Cinema in the Shadow of Watergate and Vietnam, 1970–1979.* New York: Scribner, 2000.

Corman, Paul R. *Left Intellectuals and Popular Culture in Twentieth-Century America.* Chapel Hill, N.C.: University of North Carolina Press, 1996.

Costello, John. *Virtue Under Fire: How World War II Changed Our Social and Sexual Attitudes.* Boston: Little Brown, 1985.

Courtwright, David T. *Violent Land: Single Men and Social Disorder from the Frontier to the Inner City.* Cambridge, Mass.: Harvard University Press, 1996.

Cripps, Thomas. *Making Movies Black: The Hollywood Message Movie from World War I to the Civil Rights Era.* New York: Oxford University Press, 1993.

Cullen, Jim. *The Art of Democracy: A Concise History of Popular Culture in the United States.* New York: Monthly Review Press, 1996.

Curran, Joseph M. *Hibernian Green on the Silver Screen: The Irish and American Movies*. New York: Greenwood Press, 1989.

Curti, Merle. *Human Nature in American Thought*. Madison: University of Wisconsin Press, 1980.

Custen, George F. *Twentieth Century's Fox: Darryl F. Zanuck and the Culture of Hollywood*. New York: Basic Books, 19977.

Dabakis, Melissa. *Visualizing Labor in American Sculpture: Monuments, Manliness, and the Work Ethic, 1880–1935*. Cambridge, UK: Cambridge University Press, 1999.

Davis, Kenneth. *Two-Bit Culture*. Boston: Houghton-Mifflin, 1984.

Davis, Michael. *City of Quartz: Excavating the Future in Los Angeles*. New York: Vintage Books, 1992.

de Tocqueville, Alexis. *Democracy in America*. 2 vols. New York: Vintage Books, 1990.

Denning, Michael. *The Cultural Front: The Laboring of American Culture in the Twentieth Century*. London: Verso, 1996.

———. *Mechanic Accents: Dime Novels and Working-Class Culture in America*. London: Verso, 1987.

Doherty, Thomas. *Pre-Code Hollywood: Sex, Immorality ,and the Insurrection in American Cinema, 1930–1934*. New York: Columbia University Press, 1999.

———. *Projections of War: Hollywood, American Culture and World War II*. New York: Columbia University Press, 1993.

Doane, Mary Ann. *The Desire to Desire: The Woman's Films of the 1940s*. Bloomington: Indiana University Press, 1987.

Dudley, Kathryn Marie. *The End of the Line: Lost Jobs, New Lives in Postindustrial America*. Chicago: University of Chicago Press, 1994.

Dudziak, Mary L. *Cold War Civil Rights: Race and the Image of American Democracy*. Princeton, N.J.: Princeton University Press, 2000.

Eagleton, Terry. *Ideology*. New York: Longman, 1994.

Early, Gerald. *The Culture of Bruising: Essays on Prizefighting, Literature, and Modern American Culture*. Hopewell, N.J.: Echo Press, 1994.

Echols, Alice. *Daring to Be Bad: Radical Feminism in America, 1967–1975*. Minneapolis: University of Minnesota Press, 1989.

Ehrenreich, Barbara. *Fear of Falling: The Inner Life of the Middle Class*. New York: HarperCollins, 1990.

———. *The Hearts of Men: American Dreams and the Flight from Commitment*. Garden City, N.Y.: Anchor Doubleday, 1983.

Eisler, Lotte H. *Fritz Lang*. New York: Oxford University Press, 1977.

Epp, Charles P. *The Rights Revolution: Lawyers, Activists, and the Supreme Court in Comparative Perspective*. Chicago: University of Chicago Press, 1978.

Fairchild, Louis. *They Called It the War Effort: Oral Histories from World War II in Orange, Texas.* Austin, Tex.: Eakin Press, 1993.

Fantasia, Rick. *Cultures of Solidarity: Consciousness, Action, and Contemporary American Workers.* Berkeley: University of California Press, 1988.

Faue, Elizabeth. *Community of Suffering and Struggle: Women, Men and the Labor Movement in Minneapolis.* Chapel Hill: University of North Carolina Press, 1991.

Feldstein, Ruth. *Motherhood in Black and White: Race and Sex in American Liberalism, 1930–1965.* Ithaca, N.Y.: Cornell University Press, 2000.

Foley, Barbara. *Radical Representations: Politics and Form in U.S. Proletarian Fiction, 1929–1941.* Durham, N.C.: Duke University Press, 1993.

Fones-Wolf, Elizabeth. *Selling Free Enterprise: The Business Assault on Labor and Idealism, 1945–1960.* Chicago: University of Chicago Press, 1994.

Formisano, Ronald. *Boston Against Busing: Race, Class and Ethnicity in the 1960s.* Chapel Hill: University of North Carolina Press, 1991.

Fraser, Steven. *Labor Will Rule: Sidney Hillman and the Rise of American Labor.* New York: Free Press, 1991.

Freeman, Josh. *In Transit: The Transport Workers Union in New York City, 1933–66.* New York: Oxford University Press, 1989.

Fromm, Erich. *The Fear of Freedom.* London: Routledge and Kegan Paul, 1942.

Gerstle, Gary. *American Crucible: Race and Nation in the Twentieth Century.* Princeton, N.J.: Princeton University Press, 2001.

———. *Working-Class Americanism: The Politics of Labor in a Textile City, 1914–1960* Cambridge, UK: Cambridge University Press, 1989.

Giddens, Anthony. *Beyond Left and Right: The Future of Radical Politics.* Stanford: Stanford University Press, 1994.

———. *The Transformation of Intimacy: Sexuality, Love and Eroticism in Modern Society.* Stanford, Calif.: Stanford University Press, 1992.

Glendon, Mary Ann. *Rights Talk: The Impoverishment of Political Discourse.* New York: Free Press, 1991.

Graebner, William. *The Age of Doubt: American Thought in the 1940s.* Boston: Twayne, 1991.

Graziano, Rocky, with Rowland Barber. *Somebody Up There Likes Me.* New York: Pocket Books, 1956.

Greenfield, Leah. *Five Roads to Modernity.* Cambridge, Mass.: Harvard University Press, 1992.

Greenfield, Thomas Allen. *Work and the Work Ethic in American Drama, 1920–1970.* Columbia: University of Missouri Press, 1982.

Greenstone, J. David. *The Lincoln Persuasion: Remaking American Liberalism.* Princeton: Princeton University Press, 1985.

Griswold, Robert. *Fatherhood in America: A History.* New York: Basic Books, 1993.

Halberstam, David. *The Fifties.* New York: Fawcett Colombine, 1993.

Hallam, Julia, with Margaret Marshment. *Realism and Popular Cinema.* Manchester, UK: Manchester University Press, 2000.

Hanson, Russell. *The Democratic Imagination in America: Conversations with Our Past.* Princeton, N.J.: Princeton University Press, 1985.

Hartz, Louis. *The Liberal Tradition in America: An Interpretation of American Political Thought Since the Revolution.* New York: Harcourt, Brace and World, 1955.

Havey, Brett. *The Fifties: A Woman's Oral History.* New York: HarperCollins, 1993.

Henriksen, Margot. *Dr. Stangelove's America: Society and Culture in the Atomic Age.* Berkeley: University of California Press, 1997.

Herman, Ellen. *The Romance of American Psychology: Political Culture in the Age of Experts, 1940–1970.* Berkeley: University of California Press, 1995.

Hodgson, Godfrey. *America in Our Time.* New York: Vintage Books, 1976.

———. *The World Turned Right Side Up.* Boston: Houghton-Mifflin, 1996.

hooks, belle. *Reel to Reel: Race, Sex, and Class at the Movies.* New York: Routledge, 1996.

Jacobs, Lea. *The Wages of Sin: Censorship and the Fallen Women Film, 1928–1942.* Berkeley: University of California Press, 1997.

Jacobs, Lewis. *The Rise of the American Film: A Critical History.* New York: Harcourt, Brace, 1939.

Jameson, Fredric. *Signature of the Visible.* New York: Routledge, 1992.

Jeffreys-Jones, Rhodri. *Peace Now: American Society and the Ending of the Vietnam War.* New Haven, Conn.: Yale University Press, 1999.

Jenkins, Phil. *Using Murder: The Social Construction of Serial Homicide.* New York: Aline de Gruyter, 1994.

Jones, Gerard. *Honey, I'm Home: Sitcoms and the Selling of the American Dream.* New York: St. Martin's Press, 1992.

Jowett, Garth. *Film: The Democratic Art.* Boston: Little-Brown, 1976.

Kaminer, Wendy. *It's All the Rage: Crime and Culture.* Reading, Mass.: Addison-Wesley, 1995.

Kaplan, Amy. *The Social Construction of American Realism.* Chicago: University of Chicago Press, 1988.

Kazan, Elia. *A Life.* New York: Knopf, 1988.

Kazin, Michael. *The Populist Persuasion in American History.* New York: Basic Books, 1995.

Keyser, Les, and Barbara Keyser. *Hollywood and the Catholic Church: The Image of Roman Catholicism in American Movies.* Chicago: University of Chicago Press, 1984.

Kimmel, Michael. *Manhood in America: A Cultural History.* New York: Free Press, 1996.

Koppes, Clayton R., and Gregory D. Black. *Hollywood Goes to War.* Berkeley: University of California Press, 1987.

Komorovsky, Mirra. *The Unemployed Man and His Family.* New York: Dryden Press, 1940.

Koscielski, Frank. *Divided Loyalties: American Unions and the Vietnam War.* New York: Garland, 1999.

LaMotta, Jake. *Raging Bull: My Story.* Englewood Cliffs, N.J.: Prentice Hall, 1970.

Lawson, John Howard. *Film in the Battle of Ideas.* New York: Masses and Mainstream, 1953.

Lazere, Donald, ed. *American Media and Mass Culture: Left Perspectives.* Berkeley: University of California Press, 1987.

Lears, Jackson. *Fables of Abundance.* New York: Basic Books, 1994.

Lev, Peter. *American Films of the 70s: Conflicting Visions.* Austin: University of Texas Press, 2000.

Levine, Lawrence. *Highbrow/Lowbrow: The Emergence of Cultural Hierarchy in America.* Cambridge, Mass.: Harvard University Press, 1989.

———. *The Unpredictable Past: Explorations in American Cultural History.* New York: Oxford University Press, 1993.

Levy, Emanuel. *Small Town America in Film: The Decline and Fall of Community.* New York: Continuum, 1991.

Lhamon, W. T. *Deliberate Speed: The Origins of a Cultural Style in the American 1950s.* Washington, D.C.: Smithsonian Institution Press, 1990.

Lichtenstein, Nelson. *The Most Dangerous Man in Detroit: Walter Reuther and the Fate of American Labor.* New York: Basic Books, 1995.

Lipsitz, George. *Rainbow at Midnight: Labor and Culture in the 1940s.* Urbana: University of Illinois Press, 1994.

Lott, Eric. *Love and Theft: Blackface Minstrelsy and the American Working Class.* New York: Oxford University Press, 1997.

Lourdeaux, Lee. *Italian and Irish Filmmakers in America: Ford, Capra, Coppola and Scorsese.* Philadelphia: Temple University Press, 1990.

Lorence, James J. *The Suppression of Salt of the Earth: How Hollywood, Big Labor and the Politicians Blacklisted a Movie in Cold War America.* Albuquerque: University of New Mexico Press, 1999.

Lukacs, John. *The Passing of the Modern Age.* New York: Harper and Row, 1970.

MacKinnon, Catherine A. *Towards a Feminist Theory of the State.* Cambridge, Mass.: Harvard University Press, 1989.

Mailer, Norman. *The Naked and the Dead.* New York: Henry Holt, 1948.

Maland, Charles J. *Chaplin and American Culture: The Evolution of a Star Image.* Princeton, N.J.: Princeton University Press, 1989.

May, Lary. *The Big Tomorrow: Hollywood and the Politics of the American Way*. Chicago: University of Chicago Press, 2000.

McBride, Joseph. *The Catastrophe of Success*. New York: Simon and Schuster, 1993.

McCann, Graham. *Rebel Males: Clift, Brando, and Dean*. New Brunswick, N.J.: Rutgers University Press, 1993.

McChesney, Robert W. *Rich Media, Poor Democracy: Communication Politics in Dubious Times*. Urbana: University of Illinois Press, 1999.

McGerr, Michael. *The Decline of Popular Politics: The American South, 1865–1928*. New York: Oxford University Press, 1986.

McGilligan, Patrick, and Paul Buhle. *Tender Comrades: A Backstory of the Hollywood Blacklist*. New York: St. Martin's Press, 1997.

McKenney, Ruth. *Industrial Valley*. Boston: Houghton-Mifflin, 1939.

McNamara, Kevin R. *Urban Verbs: Arts and Discourses of American Cities*. Stanford, Calif.: Stanford University Press, 1996.

Melosh, Barbara. *Engendering Culture: Manhood and Womanhood in New Deal Public Art and Theater*. Washington, D.C.: Smithsonian Press, 1991.

Meyerowtiz, Joanne, ed. *Not June Cleaver: Women and Gender in Postwar America, 1945–1960*. Philadelphia: Temple University Press, 1994.

Merton, Robert K. *Mass Persuasion: The Social Psychology of a War Bond Drive*. New York: Harper, 1946.

Musico, Giuliana. *Hollywood's New Deal*. Philadelphia: Temple University Press, 1997.

Nadel, Alan. *Containment Culture: American Narratives, Postmodernism and the Atomic Age*. Durham, N.C.: Duke University Press, 1995.

Naremore, James. *More Than the Night: Film Noir in Its Contexts*. Berkeley: University of California Press, 1998.

Nasaw, David. *Going Out: The Rise and Fall of Public Amusement*. New York: Basic Books, 1993.

Niebuhr, Reinhold. *The Irony of American History*. New York: Scribner, 1952.

Norton, David. *Democracy and Moral Development*. Berkeley: University of California Press, 1991.

Oakley, J. Ronald. *God's Country: America in the Fifties*. New York: W. W. Norton, 1986.

Peeler, David P. *Hope Among Us: Social Criticism and Social Solace in Depression America*. Athens: University of Georgia Press, 1987.

Pells, Richard. *Radical Visions and American Dreams: Culture and Social Thought in the Depression Years* Urbana: University of Illinois Press, 1998.

———. *The Liberal Mind in a Conservative Age: American Intellectuals in the 1940s and 1950s*. New York: Harper and Row, 1985.

Phair, Susan J., and Robert D. Putnam. *Disaffected Democracies: What's*

*Troubling the Trilateral Countries.* Princeton, N.J.: Princeton University Press, 2000.

Pleck, Elizabeth. *Domestic Tyranny: The Making of Social Policy Against Family Violence from Colonial Times to the Present.* New York: Oxford University Press, 1987.

Polan, Dana. *Power and Paranoia: History, Narrative, and the American Cinema, 1940–1950.* New York: Columbia University Press, 1986.

Prince, Stephen. *A New Pot of Gold: Hollywood Under the Electronic Rainbow, 1980–1989.* New York: Scribner, 2000.

Puette, William J. *Through Jaundiced Eyes: How the Media View Organized Labor.* Ithaca, N.Y.: ILR Press, 1992.

Putnam, Robert D. *Bowling Alone: The Collapse and Revival of American Community.* New York: Simon and Schuster, 2000.

Rainwater, Lee, Richard P. Coleman, and Gerald Handel. *Workingman's Wife: Her Personality, World and Life Style.* New York: Oceana Publications, 1959.

Rawles, John. *Political Liberalism.* New York: Columbia University Press, 1993.

Ray, Robert B. *A Certain Tendency of the Hollywood Cinema, 1930–1980.* (Princeton, N.J.: Princeton University Press, 1985.

Reid, Mark A. *Redefining Black Film.* Berkeley: University of California Press, 1993.

Reider, Jonathan. *Canarsie: Jews and Italians Against Liberalism.* Cambridge, Mass.: Cambridge University Press, 1985.

Richards, Jeffrey. *Visions of Yesterday.* London: Routledge and Kegan Paul, 1973.

*Robertson, James C.* The Casablanca Man: The Cinema of Michael Curtiz. *London: Routledge, 1933.*

Roeder, George H. *The Censored War: American Visual Experience During World War Two.* New Haven, Conn.: Yale University Press, 1993.

Roffman, Peter, and Jim Purdy. *The Hollywood Social Problem Film from the Depression to the Fifties.* Bloomington: Indiana University Press, 1981.

Rogin, Michael. *Blackface, White Noise.* Berkeley: University of California Press, 1996.

———. *The Intellectuals and McCarthy.* Cambridge: MIT Press, 1967.

Rorty, Richard. *Contingency, Irony and Solidarity.* Cambridge, UK: Cambridge University Press, 1989.

Ross, Andrew. *No Respect: Intellectuals and Popular Culture.* New York: Routledge, 1988.

Ross, Steve. *Working-Class Hollywood: Silent Film and the Shaping of Class in America.* Princeton, N.J.: Princeton University Press, 1998.

Savran, David. *Communists, Cowboys, and Queers: The Politics of Mascul-*

*inity in the Work of Arthur Miller and Tennessee Williams*. Minneapolis: University of Minnesota Press, 1992.

Sayre, Nora. *Running Time: Films of the Cold War*. New York: Dial Press, 1982.

Schatz, Thomas. *Boom or Bust: The American Cinema in the 1940s*. New York: Scribner, 1993.

Scheuer, Timothy. *Born in the USA: The Myth of America in Popular Music from Colonial Times to the Present*. Jackson: University of Mississippi Press, 1991.

Schlesinger, Arthur. *The Vital Center*. Boston: Houghton-Mifflin, 1949.

Schuker-Haines, Timothy A. "Home Is the Hunter: Representations of World War II Veterans and the Reconstruction of Masculinity, 1944–1951." Ph.D. diss., University of Michigan, 1996.

Schulberg, Bud. *On the Waterfront: The Final Shooting Script*. Carbondale: University of Southern Illinois Press, 1980.

Scott, Joan Wallach. *Gender and the Politics of History*. New York: Columbia University Press, 1988.

Segal, Lynn. *Slow Motion: Changing Masculinities, Changing Men*. New Brunswick, N.J.: Rutgers University Press, 1990.

Shaodian, Jack. *Dreams and Dead Ends: The American Gangster*. Cambridge: MIT Press, 1997.

Shindo, Charles. *Dust Bowl Migrants in the American Imagination*. Lawrence: University of Kansas Press, 1997.

Silverman, Kaja. *Male Subjectivity at the Margins*. London: Routledge, 1992.

Silverton, Deborah. *Salt of the Earth*. New York: Feminist Press, 1978.

Sklar, Robert. *City Boys: Cagney, Bogart, Garfield*. Princeton, N.J.: Princeton University Press, 1992.

———. *Movie Made America: A Cultural History of American Movies*. New York: Vintage Books, 1994.

Slotkin, Richard. *Gunfighter Nation: The Myth of the Frontier in Twentieth Century America*. New York: HarperCollins, 1992.

Smith, Erin A. *Hard-Boiled: Working-Class Readers and Pulp Magazines*. Philadelphia: Temple University Press, 2000.

Smith, Rogers M. *Civic Ideals*. New Haven: Yale University Press, 1997.

Stead, Peter. *Film and the Working-Class: The Feature Film in British and American Society*. New York: Routledge, 1989.

Steinbeck, John. *Grapes of Wrath*. New York: Viking-Penguin, 1939.

Stegner, Wallace. *One Nation*. Boston: Houghton-Mifflin, 1993.

Stern, Fritz. *The Failure of Illiberalism: Essays on the Political Culture of Modern Germany*. New York: Columbia University Press, 1992.

Stouffer, Samuel, et al. *Studies in Social Psychology of World War II*. 4 vols. Princeton, N.J.: Princeton University Press, 1949–52.

Sussman, Warren. *Culture as History: The Transformation of American Society in the Twentieth Century.* New York: Pantheon, 1984.

Thompson, David, and Ian Christie. *Scorsese on Scorsese.* London: Faber and Faber, 1999.

Toplin, Robert Brent. *Oliver Stone's USA: Film, History and Controversy.* Lawrence, Kan.: University of Kansas Press, 2000.

Toth, Emily. *Inside Peyton Place: The Life of Grace Metalious.* Garden City, N.Y.: Doubleday, 1981.

Vaughn, Stephen. *Ronald Reagan in Hollywood: Movies and Politics.* Cambridge, UK: Cambridge University Press, 1994.

Warshow, Robert. *The Immediate Experience.* New York: Doubleday, 1962.

Westbrook, Robert B. *John Dewey and American Democracy.* Ithaca, N.Y.: Cornell University Press, 1991.

Whitfield, Stephen. *The Culture of the Cold War.* Baltimore: Johns Hopkins University Press, 1991.

Wiebe, Robert. *Self-Rule: A Cultural History of American Democracy.* Chicago: University of Chicago Press, 1995.

Williams, Dakin, and Shepherd Mead. *Tennessee Williams: An Intimate Biography.* New York: Arbor House, 1983.

Williams, Raymond. *Modern Tragedy.* Stanford. Calif.: Stanford University Press, 1966.

Williams, Tennessee. *Memoirs.* New York: Doubleday, 1972.

Williamson, J. W. *Hillbillyland: What the Movies Did to the Mountains and What the Mountains Did to the Movies.* Chapel Hill: University of North Carolina Press, 1955.

Wilson, William Julius. *The Truly Disadvantaged: The Inner City, the Underclass, and Public Policy.* Chicago: University of Chicago Press, 1987.

Zaniello, Tom. *Working-Stiffs, Union Maids, Reds, and Riff and Raff: An Organized Guide to Films About Labor.* Ithaca, N.Y.: ILR Press, 1996.

Zizek, Slavoj, ed. *Mapping Ideology.* London: Verso, 1994.

## ARTICLES

Alpers, Benjamin. "This Is the Army: Imagining a Democratic Military." *Journal of American History* 85 (June 1998): 139–63.

Barber, Benjamin A. "Liberal Democracy and the Costs of Consent." In *Liberalism and the Moral Life,* edited by Nancy L. Rosenblum, 54–68. Cambridge, Mass.: Harvard University Press, 1989.

Ben-Ghia, Ruth. "Envisioning Modernity: Desire and Discipline in Italian Fascist Film. *Critical Inquiry* 23 (Autumn 1996): 109–44.

Benjamin, Walter. "The Work of Art in the Age of Mechanical Reproduction," in *Illuminations.* New York: Harcourt, Brace, and World, 1995.

Bieberman, Frank. "Frank Capra's Characters." *New Masses*, 8 July 1941, 26–27.

Bigsby, C. W. E. "Tennessee Williams: Streetcar to Glory." In *Twentieth-Century Interpretations of a Streetcar Named Desire*, edited by Jordan Y. Miller, 103–8. Englewood Cliffs, N.J.: Prentice Hall, 1971.

Boelhower, William. "We the People: Shifting Forms of Sovereignty." *American Literary History* 9 (Summer 1997): 364–79.

Calhoun, Craig. "Introduction: Habermas and the Public Sphere." In *Habermas and the Public Sphere*, edited by Craig Calhoun. Cambridge: MIT Press, 1992.

Chambers, Simone. "Discourse and Democratic Practices." In *The Cambridge Companion to Habermas*, edited by Stephen K. White, 233–59. Cambridge, UK: Cambridge University, 1995.

Charney, Leo, and Vanessa R. Schwartz. "Introduction." In *Cinema and the Invention of Modern Life*, edited by Charney and Schwartz, 1–12. Berkeley: University of California Press, 1995.

Chauncey, George. "The Postwar Sex Crime Panic." In *True Stories from the American Past*, edited by William Graebner, 160–78. New York: McGraw-Hill, 1993.

Cogley, John. "The Mass Hearings." In *The American Film Industry*, edited by Tino Balio, 410–31. Madison: University of Wisconsin Press, 1976.

Cohen, David L. "Do American Men Like Women?" *Atlantic Monthly* 178 August 1946): 71–74.

Corwin, Norman. "Our Heroes." *Saturday Review of Literature* 24 (October 25, 1941).

Cuordileone, K. A. "Politics in an Age of Anxiety: Cold War Political Culture and the Crisis in American Masculinity, 1949–1960." *Journal of American History* 87 (September 2000): 515–45.

De Grazia, Victoria. "Mass Culture and Sovereignty: The American Challenge to European Americans, 1920–1960." *Journal of Modern History* 61 (March 1989): 53–87.

De Hart, Jane Sherron. "Containment at Home: Gender, Sexuality, and National Identity in Cold War America." In *Rethinking Cold War Culture*, edited by Peter J. Kuznick and James Gilbert, 124–55. Washington, D.C.: Smithsonian Institution Press, 2001.

Denning, Michael. "The End of Mass Culture." In *Modernity and Mass Culture*, edited by James Naremore and Patrick Brantlinger, 253–68. Bloomington: Indiana University Press, 1991.

Foley, Barbara. "Renarrating the Thirties in the Forties and Fifties." *Prospects* 20 (1995): 455–66.

Freeman, Joshua. "Hardhats, Construction Workers, Manliness and the 1970s Pro-War Demonstrations." *Journal of Social History* 26 (Summer 1993): 725–44.

Freedman, Estelle. "Uncontrolled Desires: The Response to the Sexual Psychopath, 1920–1960." *Journal of American History* 74 (June 1987): 83–106.

Gerstle, Gary. "The Protean Character of American Liberalism." *American HistoricalReview* 99 (October 1994): 1043–73.

Gitlin, Todd. "Bites and Blips: Chunk News, Savy Talk, and the Bifurcation of American Politics." In *Communications and Citizenship: Journalism and the Public Sphere in the New Media Age,* edited by Peter Dahlgren and Colin Sparks, 119–36. London: Routledge, Chapman and Hall, 1991.

Gledhill, Christine. "Genre and Gender: The Case of Soap Opera." In *Representations: Cultural Representations and Signifying Practices,* edited by Stuart Hall, 357–60. London: Sage, 1997.

———. "The Melodramatic Field: An Investigation." In *Home Is Where the Heart Is: Studies in Melodrama and the Woman's Film,* edited by Christine Gledhill, 5–39. London: British Film Institute, 1987.

Gordon, Linda. "Social Insurance and Public Assistance: The Influence of Gender in Welfare Thought, 1890–1935." *American Historical Review* 97 (February 1992): 19–51.

Graebner, William. "Norman Rockwell and American Mass Culture: The Crisis of Representation in the Great Depression." *Prospects* 22 (1997): 323–56.

Gubar, Susan. "'This is My Rifle, This is My Gun': World War II and the Blitz on Women." In *Behind the Lines: Gender and the Two World Wars,* edited by Margaret Higonnnet et al., 227–59. New Haven, Conn.: Yale University Press, 1987.

Hall, John R. "The Reworking of Class Analysis." In *Reworking Class,* edited by John R. Hall, 1–37. Ithaca, N.Y.: Cornell University Press, 1997.

Hall, Stuart. "Notes on Deconstructing the Popular." In *People's History and Socialist Theory,* edited by Raphel Samuel, 227–40. London: Routledge and Kegan Paul, 1981.

Haralovich, Mary Beth. "The Proletarian Woman's Film of the 1930s: Contending with Censorship and Entertainment." *Screen* 31 (1990): 172–87.

Hartman, Susan. "Prescriptions for Penelope: Literature on Women's Obligations to Returning World War II Veterans." *Women's Studies* 5 (1978): 223–39.

Hindess, Barry. "Liberalism, Socialism, and Democracy: Variations on a Governmental Theme." In *Foucault and Political Reason: Liberalism, Neo-Liberalism, and Rationalities of Government,* edited by Andrew Barry, Thomas Osborne, and Nikolas Rose, 65–80. Chicago: University of Chicago Press, 1996.

Jacobs, Lea. "Censorship and the Fallen Women Cycle." In *Home Is Where the Heart Is: Studies in Melodrama and the Woman's Film,* 100–112. London: British Film Institute, 1987.

Jameson, Frederic. "Reification and Utopia in Mass Culture." *Social Text* 1 (Winter 1979): 130–48.

Koppes, Clayton. "Regulating the Screen: The Office of War Information and the Production Code Administration." In Schatz, *Boom or Bust: The American Cinema in the 1940s*, 261–81. New York: Scribners, 1993.

Kunzel, Regina. "Pulp Fictions and Problem Girls: Reading and Rewriting Single Pregnancy in Postwar United States." *American Historical Review* 100 (December 1995): 1465–87.

Lichtenstein, Nelson. "From Corporatism to Collective Bargaining: Organized Labor and the Eclipse of Social Democracy in the Postwar Era." In *The Rise and Fall of the New Deal Order*, edited by Steve Fraser and Gary Gerstle, 122–52. Princeton, N.J.: Princeton University Press, 1989.

Lynd, Staughton. "The Genesis of the Idea of a Community Right to Industrial Power in Youngstown and Pittsburgh, 1979–1987." *Journal of American History* 74 (December 1987): 926–58.

Malthy, Richard. "'To Prevent the Prevalent Type of Book': Censorship and Adaptation in Hollywood, 1924–1934." In *Movies, Censorship and American Culture*, edited by Francis G. Couvares, 97–128. Washington, D.C.: Smithsonian Institution Press, 1996.

Marchand, Roland. "Visions of Classlessness: Quests for Dominion." In *Reshaping America: Society and Institutions, 1945–1960*, edited by Robert H. Bremner and Gary W. Reichard, 163–90. Columbus: Ohio State University Press, 1982.

May, Lary. "Making the American Consensus: The Narrative of Consensus and Subversion in World War II Film." In *The War in American Culture: Security and Consciousness During World War II*, edited by Lewis A. Erenberg and Susan A. Hirsh, 71–102. Chicago: University of Chicago Press, 1996.

May, Lary, with Stephen Lassonde. "Making the American Way: Modern Theaters, Audience and the Film Industry, 1929–1935." *Prospects* 12 (1987): 89–124.

McDonagh, Edward. "The Discharged Serviceman and His Family." *American Journal of Sociology* 51 March 1946): 408–13.

Pauly, Thomas H. "Black Images and White Culture During the Decades Before the Civil Rights Movement." *American Studies* 31 (Fall 1990): 101–19.

Peters, John Durham. "Democracy and American Mass Communication Theory: Dewey, Lippman, and Lazarsfeld." *Communication* 11 (1989): 199–220.

Pfister, Joel. "On Conceptualizing the Cultural History of Emotional and Psychological Life in America." In *Inventing the Psychological: Toward a Cultural History of Emotional Life in America*, edited by Joel Pfister and Nancy Schnog, 17–59. New Haven: Yale University Press, 1997.

Polonsky Abraham. "The Best Years of Our Lives." *Hollywood Quarterly* 2 (April 1947).

———. "How the Blacklist Worked in Hollywood." *Film Culture* 50–51 (Fall-Winter 1970): 257–60.

Quart, Leonard. "Frank Capra and the Popular Front." In *American Media and Mass Culture: Left Perspectives,* edited by Donald Lazere, 178–83. Berkeley: University of California Press, 1987.

Rosenstone, Robert. "Oliver Stone as Historian." In *Oliver Stone's USA: Film, History, and Controversy,* edited by Robert Brent Toplin, 26–37. Lawrence: University of Kansas Press, 2000.

Roth, Michael S. "*Hiroshima Mon Amour:* You Must Remember This." In *Revisioning History: Film and the Construction of the Past,* edited by Robert A. Rosenstone, 91–101. Princeton: Princeton University Press, 1995.

Smoodin, Eric. "This Business of America: Fan Mail, Film Reception, and *Meet John Doe.*" *Screen* 37 (Summer 1996): 111–28.

———. "Viewing for Every Citizen: Mr. Smith and the Rhetoric of Reception." *Cinema Journal* 35 (Winter 1996): 3–23.

Sobchack, Vivian C. "*The Grapes of Wrath*: Thematic Emphasis Through Visual Style." In *American Film in Cultural Context,* edited by Peter Rollins, 68–77. Lexington: University Press of Kentucky, 1983.

Sommers, Margaret A. "Deconstructing and Reconstructing Class Formation Theory: Narrativity, Relational Analysis and Social Theory." In *Reworking Class,* edited by John R. Hall, 73–105. Ithaca, N.Y.: Cornell University Press, 1997.

Spector, Scott. "Was the Third Reich Movie-Made? Interdisciplinarity and the Reframing of Ideology." *American Historical Review* 106 (April, 2001): 460–84.

Stearns, Peter N., and Carol Z. Stearns. "Emotionology: Clarifying the History of Emotions and Emotional Standards." *American Historical Review* 90 (October 1985): 813–36.

Stone, Oliver. "Stone on Stone's Image." In *Oliver Stone's USA: Film, History, and Controversy,* edited by Robert Brent Toplin, 40–58. Lawrence: University of Kansas Press, 2000.

Sturken, Marita. "Reenactment, Fantasy, and the Paranoia of History: Oliver Stone's Docudramas." *History and Theory* 36 (1997): 64–77.

Thompson, James. "After the Fall: Class and Political Language in Britain, 1780–1900." *Historical Journal* 39 (1996): 785–806.

Vaughn, Stephen. "Morality and Entertainment: The Origins of the Motion Picture Production Code." *Journal of American History* 77 (June 1990): 39–65.

Walsh, Frank. "The Films We Never Saw: American Movies View Organized Labor, 1934–35." *Labor History* 27 (Fall 1986): 564–80.

Wertheim, Albert. "A View from the Bridge." In *The Cambridge Companion to Arthur Miller*, edited by Christopher Bigsby, 105–8. Cambridge, UK: Cambridge University Press, 1997.

Westbrook, Robert. "I Want a Girl Just Like the Girl that Married Harry James: The Problem of Political Obligation in World War II." *American Quarterly* 42 (December 1990): 587–614.

Williams, Linda. "Melodrama Revised." In *Figuring American Film Genres: Theory and History*, edited by Nick Browne, 42–88. Berkeley: University of California Press, 1998.

Zizek, Slavoj. "Introduction: The Spectre of Ideology." In *Mapping Ideology*, edited by Slavoj Zizek. London: Verso, 1994.

## NEWSPAPERS AND JOURNALS

*Catholic World*

*Commonweal*

*Ebony*

*Literary Digest*

*Motion Picture Herald*

*The Nation*

*National Parent-Teacher*

*The New Masses*

*The New Republic*

*Newsweek*

*The New York Daily Worker*

*The New York Times*

*The New Yorker*

*Time*

*Variety*

# INDEX

Waters, Ethel, 125
West, Mae, 27
Westbrook, Robert, 58, 77
*West Side Story*, 169, 174
*Whistle at Eaton Falls, The*, 139–42, 174, 226
*White Heat*, 121–22
Wiebe, Robert, xxix
Williams, Raymond, 2
Williams, Tennessee, 147, 150–51, 213–14
*Wings of the Eagle*, 70–71
*Woman on Pier 13, The*, 138–39
*Woman Under the Influence, A*, 202–3
women: and abortion rights, 182; in film, xxi, xxiii, 2, 26–34, 41, 50–51, 53, 60–61, 75–77, 78–79, 82–83, 95–103, 199–204, 215; status of, 4–5, 58. *See also* gender roles
Worker's Film and Photo League of America, 45
working people: diversity of, 219–27; in fiction, xix; impact of Vietnam war on, 179; as leaders in class struggle, 18–26; mobilization of, 3–4; in monuments, xviii–xix; politics of, 180–81; rights of, 23; transformation of, 153–58; and the Vietnam war, 179; women as, 199–204

Young, Robert, 72

Zale, Tony, 157, 158
Zanuck, Darryl, 13, 29, 42, 125, 154